**FOR MY STUDENTS**

# Contents

# Foreword

When I was approached by Cambridge University Press and asked if I would be interested in writing a revision of my late father's *The Elements of New Testament Greek*, I was grateful for the invitation, but I declined. I am someone who uses Greek in my work, but I have not taught beginners' Greek very much at all. My father's book came out of practical classroom teaching, and any effective revision would have to be done by a teacher.

Dr Jeremy Duff is such a teacher, and a very effective one. When he began teaching Greek at Wycliffe Hall in Oxford, what is often an unpopular subject suddenly started to go down very well. Students actually enjoyed Greek! So it occurred to me that Jeremy would be a worthy reviser of the *Elements*. I was very glad that Cambridge University Press, having been put in touch with Jeremy, agreed that he should be given the task of revising the book.

In fact what has come out is much more than a revision. It is in almost all respects a brand new book, though arising out of Wenham. There is an excellent precedent for such a revision, because my father's work was a similarly radical revision of H.P.V. Nunn's earlier book.

My pleasure in writing this foreword is twofold. First, Jeremy is a friend and a colleague of mine at Wycliffe Hall in Oxford; he is someone who has brought energy and interest to the college, and not just to the teaching of Greek. Secondly, of course, I am glad to write this foreword because of my father. He was amazed at how long and well his version of the *Elements* lasted. It is a tribute to how good his book was that it went on and on while other books came and went. But he firmly expected it to be superseded before too long, and I am sure he would be glad to see it superseded by someone like Jeremy! And maybe it is good anyway to be superseded as the author of a Greek textbook: my father sometimes said that he was probably the best-hated name in the theological college world. That was in the days when most theological students had to study Greek, even if they weren't any good at it and even if they didn't wish to. Maybe the hatred is diminished now, but if Jeremy is willingly taking over the role of best-hated name, then we may be grateful on my father's part!

The other side to that, of course, is that significant numbers of people in many countries are grateful for my father's book. Learning Greek may be a slog, especially for some; but, just as with learning a musical instrument, the rewards for hard work can be very great.

Admittedly, that point is not appreciated by many in the modern world. Studying ancient languages seems completely pointless to them. It isn't, of course. Historical study, including the study of ancient languages, can be most instructive for understanding culture and for understanding human beings and human nature. But for most of those who study New Testament Greek it is not just any old historical language: it is a door into the Christian Scriptures, which makes it significant for anyone who is interested in Christianity. For Christians it makes it very significant indeed, since the Bible is their foundational text, which they believe to have been given by God's inspiration and to contain God's word for the world.

This was my father's interest in it. He wrote numerous books on the Bible, starting with *Christ and the Bible*, in which he showed that Christian reverence for the Bible has its roots in Jesus' own teaching. His interest in Greek was because he believed that the Bible should be studied with great care: the words matter, and so does the original meaning of those words. Translations are often very good, but not always, and going back to the original is very worthwhile, as well as exciting for those who get some facility in the language.

I am personally grateful to my father for the example and inspiration he was as a Christian scholar who cared about the Bible and its words, and who encouraged me and many others to study it with academic integrity and honesty. Those many others include thousands of those who have been helped to get into the Greek New Testament through his book.

One of my favourite stories in the New Testament is the account of the walk to Emmaus in Luke 24: Jesus' two companions comment on how their hearts 'burned within them' as Jesus opened the Scriptures to them. Studying Greek isn't always as exciting as that, but I hope that Jeremy's book, like my father's, will be used by many and prove a door into understanding the New Testament and the remarkable person it portrays.

David Wenham,
*Dean and Tutor in New Testament at Wycliffe Hall, Oxford.*

# Preface

Students are the ones who matter. Students, and more generally all those wishing to learn, are the only reason for teachers and academic books to exist. For ninety years those wishing to learn to read the New Testament in Greek have been ably served by *The Elements of New Testament Greek* published by Cambridge University Press. First, in the book of that name by H.P.V. Nunn published in 1914, and then in its 1965 replacement by J.W. Wenham. So successful was John Wenham's book that for much of its forty-year history it has been the standard first-year Greek course not only in the UK but across large parts of the English-speaking world. For generations of students, 'Wenham' was synonymous with Greek.

Wenham's success was that he cared about students and did everything possible to make learning 'the elements' of New Testament Greek as simple and painless as possible. The most striking example of this was his handling of Greek accents. The scholarly tradition behind the use of accents went back many centuries, though not, as Wenham was keen to point out, back to the time of the New Testament itself. Nevertheless Wenham dispensed with accents. Or at least he dispensed with most of them – keeping only the few cases where they were useful to the student in distinguishing between otherwise identical words. Even today many scholars and teachers find this regrettable, if not even scandalous. I have never met a student, though, who shares that opinion. The student working hard to master the basic structure and vocabulary of New Testament Greek welcomes every help and simplification offered. Wenham wrote his book for them.

Time moves on, however, and by the mid-1990s Wenham's *The Elements of New Testament Greek* was beginning to look dated. Greek might not have changed much, but students had. It was time for Wenham to be replaced, just as Nunn had been forty years earlier. It was a great privilege to be asked to undertake this task.

Wenham explained his relationship to Nunn in these words: 'This started out as a radical revision, it ended as a new book.' The same is true of this book. Having taught Greek using Wenham, I was convinced of the soundness of his approach – step-by-step learning of grammar and vocabulary, clear explanations, lots of practice exercises, and the overriding principle of teaching only 'the elements' of New Testament Greek, not every 'interesting' peculiarity. However, it could be improved and updated. Its handling of participles was often criticised for being too late, and too dense. It did not contain enough New Testament in its examples and exercises. The drip-feed of forty-four chapters wore students down. It seemed to assume a knowledge of grammatical forms. Its opening English grammar was off-putting. Its lack of a proper Greek–English dictionary was infuriating. It seemed old-fashioned.

This book aims to stand in continuity with Wenham. Other approaches to learning Greek are possible and are represented in the multitudinous Greek grammars available. But the aim of this book has been to continue with the basic approach of Wenham, and Nunn before him, but to update, improve and revise as appropriate. As I have worked on this revision, I have been overwhelmed by the amount of good-will towards *The Elements of New Testament Greek* within the Greek-teaching 'community'. Partly, of course, this is because many of them first encountered Greek under Wenham's guidance. But more significantly, it is because they have struggled to find anything better. For one reason or another many have moved on from Wenham, experimenting with more recent books. And yet they remain unsatisfied – what is wanted is a 'twenty-first-century Wenham'. I hope that in some measure this book fulfils that need.

A large number of different people have helped in the writing of this book. Particular mention must be made of Susan Blackburn Griffith, who did much of the labour in producing the vocabulary lists and exercises. Thanks also are due to Jon Connell, Travis Derico, Claerwyn Frost, Jon Hyde, Hannah Rudge, Rachel Thorne and Richard Trethewey. Without their work and support it is unclear if the book would ever have seen the light of day.

Initial drafts have been used across the world by various teachers and their students, whose feedback has contributed in countless ways to the final shape and content of this book. The teachers can be named: Atsuhiro Asano, Stephanie Black, Mark Butchers, Philip Church, Peter Groves, Nicholas King, Jonathan Pennington, Marian Raikes, Daniela Schubert, Margaret Sim, Matthew Sleeman, Henry Wansborough and Paul Woodbridge. Their students, who pointed out both the good and the bad in the early drafts, are unknown to me, but deserve thanks none the less. I have also felt greatly supported in this endeavour by the wide community of Greek teachers. Among these, special thanks are due to John Dobson, who despite being the author of a notable beginners' Greek textbook himself which takes a rather different approach, provided invaluable comments on a draft version. Naturally the mistakes and infelicities that remain are mine; indeed, various of the those mentioned above will soon discover where I failed to take their advice.

More personally, four people deserve credit in different ways for sparking off and nurturing my own interest in Greek: Douglas Cashin, Rodney Lavin, John Roberts and Brenda Wolfe. More than anyone though, thanks for this belong to Tim Duff, the real Greek expert in the Duff family. Many of the trials and tribulations of 'the Wenham project' have been borne by my wife Jill with characteristic love and wisdom. Final credit, though, belongs to my own students in Oxford who for almost ten years have inspired me to keep honing and developing the material, have been gracious to my mistakes and supportive of improvements, and most of all have convinced me of the value of teaching Greek. It is to them, and future students, that this book is dedicated.

Jeremy Duff
*Wycliffe Hall, Oxford*
*May 2004*

# The aim of this book

This book has a single aim:

**To help you learn enough Greek to read the New Testament.**

This might seem obvious for a book entitled *The Elements of New Testament Greek*. However, there are many books designed for those beginning to study New Testament Greek that do not focus exclusively on this aim. The point will become clearer if I highlight certain things that this book does not aim at.

This book does not set out to present my understanding of New Testament Greek. It is a book for you, not for me. If I want to impress my colleagues with my Greek expertise, I will do that elsewhere. You deserve a book written to help you. In the same way it is not a 'Greek Grammar', as if my work was merely to set out Greek grammar, and it is then up to you to understand it and learn it. This is a textbook, written to help you in the process of learning.

This book does not try to teach you Christianity. It assumes that you want to read the New Testament in Greek in order to understand the New Testament better. For many the reason for wanting to understand it better will be a religious motivation, and that is great – I personally share that motivation. But for others it will be different. You may be unsure about Christianity, or indeed negative towards it. Nevertheless if you want to understand the New Testament better by learning Greek, this book is for you. Knowing Greek is a tool. My aim in this book is to help you acquire that tool, not to persuade you to use it in certain ways. The reason for this approach is straightforward: learning Greek takes some effort, and this book has been written to help. And it can help most if it focuses clearly on the task in hand, and does not try to engage in wider issues. In this book you will get help with learning Greek, and nothing else.

This book does not intend to help you feel superior, to initiate you into the ranks of an elite, or to give you ammunition for pointing out the errors of others. Unfortunately, the teaching of Greek often seems to encourage this. Part of this is natural. You are acquiring a valuable new skill that will aid your understanding of the New Testament. You should be proud of this. It should help you see the truth of what the New Testament says more clearly. However, Greek is a language, not a theological weapon. Understanding a language comes slowly. Gradually you will begin to appreciate the difficulties of Bible translators, and see how there are emphases, connections and flavours present in the Greek New Testament that are inevitably lost in translation. There are many riches to be gained from reading the New Testament in Greek. However, if you hope that after four lessons of Greek you will be shown theological secrets undreamt of by those relying on translations, you will be sadly disappointed. Reading the New Testament in Greek rather than in English is like watching a sports game on television rather than hearing it on the radio. Superior in many ways, but the score does not change.

This book does not pretend that you are leaning Greek as a modern language, or that you are 'picking up the language' as children do. If you were learning Greek to speak it and hear it, you would learn it differently. But you are not. Young children are remarkably successful at learning languages by hearing it all around them and gradually making sense of it. But you are an adult, not a child. And adult learners, in general, want to understand and to make sense of things. After all, they are talented, rational people who are used to understanding what goes on around them. Therefore this book aims to help you progress step by step, explaining how Greek works, and as far as possible highlighting patterns and principles to make sense of what you are being asked to learn. You will not be 'thrown in at the deep end' and expected simply to 'pick it up'.

Finally, the driving force of this book is not for you to have fun. I hope that you will, and you will certainly learn far better if you are enjoying it. However, let us be honest. If you wanted to have fun, you could probably think of many better ways than sitting here reading this book! You are reading this because you want to learn Greek. All Greek teachers struggle with the negative reputation that learning Greek has of being boring, complicated or too difficult. This leads to a great temptation – to sacrifice the goal of people learning Greek upon the altar of ensuring that everyone is happy and that Greek is popular. Thus a well-known phenomenon is for people to enjoy their Greek lessons greatly, but a year later to be no closer to being able to read the New Testament in Greek for themselves than they were at the beginning. My commitment to you is different. Working through this book will not always be easy. But you can rely on the fact that there is nothing in it that is not focused on helping you read the New Testament in Greek, and that when you have mastered what is in the book, you will be able to do just that. I sincerely hope that you do enjoy learning Greek, just as a coach might hope that the athlete enjoys the training sessions. But the real enjoyment for the athlete comes from winning the medal.

# How to use this book

As well as having a clear aim, this book has been designed with particular principles in mind that give it a particular shape and structure. You will find the learning process easier if you understand these principles and are aware of the structure.

## KEY PRINCIPLE OF SELECTION

In keeping with the title 'The Elements' and the aim to 'learn enough Greek to read the New Testament', this book does not contain all of the Greek grammar there is to know. Rather it contains all that you need to know to be able to make a good start in reading the New Testament in Greek. There are various irregularities, or rare features of Greek, that are not tackled here: they are best dealt with in context later on when you meet them as you read the New Testament. This book is about equipping you to begin reading the New Testament – you will then improve by practice. The 'Going Further' section at the end of the book (page 237) contains ideas on how to build on what you have learnt. For now we need to focus on what is important.

The order in which material is presented has not been chosen at whim or according to some arcane academic tradition. Rather it is arranged according to what occurs most frequently in the New Testament (with slight alterations according to what forms a logical order for learning). This is most apparent in two areas. First, the order in which grammar is introduced has been based on the relative frequency of the different parts of grammar in the New Testament. Thus many teachers may find the leaving of the Passive until Chapter 15 surprising. However, in practice the Passive is rare in Greek. Similarly rare are many of the uses of the Infinitive (Chapter 18). However, the basic use of participles is common in the New Testament, and therefore it is learnt much earlier here than in many books (Chapter 7). Second, the vocabulary presented in this book is the 600 most common words in the New Testament, organised with the most common ones first (although no word will be introduced before you understand how to use it). Thus as a learner you can be sure that each step you are asked to make has been chosen to be the most useful next step in the development of your understanding of Greek.

## CHAPTERS

There are twenty chapters in this book. Each of these focuses on a particular area of Greek grammar, as you build up your knowledge of the Greek language step by step. Each chapter is designed to be equally challenging. If you can handle the first chapter, you just need to repeat that nineteen more times, and you will be there.

## KEY GRAMMAR, HINTS AND ENGLISH GRAMMAR

The major part of the text in each of the chapters is explanation – helping you to understand a particular element of the Greek language. However, at regular intervals throughout the text you will see four different types of box appear, each with a different function.

**KEY GRAMMAR**

This box contains a brief one-line summary of the point being discussed. Learn and remember these points and you are halfway there.

**Hint**

This box contains a hint or suggestion to help you with the point being discussed. They do not add to the proper explanation, but rather are an aside – something that might help you remember it or recognise it in practice.

These boxes contain a cross-reference to the comparative guide to English grammar on pages 240–9. This is because Greek is often very similar to English and a pause to think about how something works in English might make the corresponding point in Greek easier to understand.

1 Tim. 1.1: Παυλος ἀποστολος Χριστου Ἰησου ...

This marks out quotations from the New Testament, which provide a preview of the grammar point about to be explained in the following section. Many students find that these examples give a useful introduction to what is about to come and provide a 'fixed point' they can look back to as they start to learn the detail.

## EXERCISES AND PRACTICE

You learn by doing, not just by seeing. Therefore throughout the book there are exercises and practices for you to do. These fall into a number of different categories.

**Practice**: After each important grammar point in every chapter there is a practice section containing a number of very brief (often one word) questions. These are focused directly on the piece of grammar that has just been explained. Thus the practice questions are aimed at helping reinforce that particular grammar point.

**Half-way practice**: This occurs at about the mid-point in each chapter, except in the first two. It always consists of twelve short sentences (eight from Greek to English, four from English to Greek) giving an opportunity to consolidate the first half of the chapter before going on to the second part.

**Sentences**: At the end of each chapter, there are two sets of sentences (Chapter 1 is different since by then we have only learnt the alphabet). Each of these consists of twelve sentences for you to translate (again eight Greek to English, four English to Greek). These sentences have been chosen to help you practise what you have learnt in that chapter (grammar and vocabulary), while also integrating it into what you have learnt in previous chapters.

Thus the practice questions have been specifically created to help you focus on the new thing you are learning, while the exercises help you put this new thing in the context of what has gone before (and help you keep practising what you have already learnt). The sentences themselves are not taken directly from the New Testament – unfortunately it was not written in such a way as to provide enough sentences that only used or practised certain words or points of grammar. However, nor were the sentences simply made up. Instead, as far as possible, they are based on phrases and sentences from the New Testament that have been altered to suit the learning need – for example one word of vocabulary replaced with another. This means that from the beginning you are meeting exactly the sort of Greek that you will find in the New Testament, even if it has been altered to fit the needs of the step-by-step approach. It also means that occasionally you will notice that a sentence does not obey the rules that you have learnt. This will be because the New Testament passage it is drawing on did not follow the rules precisely either – Greek is a language, not a mathematical code. One part of learning a language is understanding which rules are a little flexible and which are not.

If you are interested in where the sentences have been drawn from, a list is provided on pages 330–2. It can be useful to see some of the slightly more unusual phrases in their original context. Of course, you can also practise your New Testament knowledge by trying to guess the source for the sentences. How many can you identify?

You might wonder why you need to translate from English into Greek (you want to read the New Testament, not write it!). Some teachers feel that this is not an important exercise, but many believe that it is only when you try writing some Greek yourself that you really understand how it works.

**Passages:** At the end of each chapter (except for the first two) a passage from the New Testament is given, quoted exactly. These have been chosen so that you should be able to translate them. However, there are always odd items that you have not yet met – particularly items of vocabulary. Therefore help is given in brackets [*like this*] throughout these passages. Thus the *sentences* are drawn from the New Testament but have been altered to fit what you know. The *passages* are exact quotations from the New Testament, with some extra help given.

**Answers:** There are many good reasons for giving the answers to the questions in the back of the book. In particular, it helps you take control of your learning. You can try out the question, and then look and see whether you have got it right. If not, you can then try to work out why. After all, the aim of the exercise is to help you learn, not to demonstrate what you do or do not know. However, as a teacher it can be helpful to be able to set questions to which you know answers are not provided, for then you can see how different learners are progressing and what further guidance they might need. Therefore, answers are provided in the back to the practice questions and to half of the sentences (section A sentences). Also, an answer to the passages can be found in any English Bible. However, no answers are provided to the section B sentences, to give your teacher the opportunity of seeing your unaided work.

## VOCABULARY

This book makes use of 600 Greek words. These have been chosen to be the most common words in the New Testament, plus a handful of others that are needed to illustrate important elements of Greek grammar, or that are particularly worth learning. This works out as meaning all of the words that occur at least twenty-three times in the New Testament, plus a handful of others. It may surprise you to learn that these words represent over 90 per cent of all the words in the New Testament. Thus familiarity with these words is an important goal to aim at: learn to recognise these 600 words, and you will recognise 90 per cent of all the words in the New Testament.

Take the following entry in the vocabulary at the end of Chapter 2 as an example:

ἀγγελος (175) – messenger, angel

This means that the Greek word ἀγγελος (pronounced an-gel-os) occurs 175 times in the New Testament and means 'messenger' or 'angel'. The one Greek word overlaps with the meaning of two English words. Which would be the best way to translate it in any given situation would depend on the context. Of course, what is going on underneath is that an angel is a messenger of God, and hence it is not surprising that Greek uses the one word with both meanings – a messenger in general, or a messenger of God. You should be aware that it is rare that a word in one language is exactly equivalent to one word in another language. There are often shades of meanings or 'flavours' that a word has which the 'equivalent' word in the other language does not have. However, you need to walk before you can run. Focus for the moment on learning the 'basic English equivalent(s)' of the Greek words you meet. Over time you will gain an appreciation for the particular 'flavour' of different Greek words.

Learning words is never easy, but it is important: grammar with no words is dead. You should follow your teacher's guidance in what he or she wants you to memorise, but the book is designed on the basis that you do learn the vocabulary step by step. If you try to learn too many words all in one go it becomes very difficult, but broken down into weekly or daily portions it is achievable with a bit of determination, and the fact that you know that the word occurs many times in the New Testament can be an encouragement.

A hint for learning vocabulary – you need to engage your whole body in the process, not just your eyes. Staring at the list of words will get you nowhere. Write them out, say them aloud, test your friends; different approaches suit different people, but *do* something, don't just stare. Also, it is very important to have a system of going back to the words you have previously learnt. As you keep on learning, half forgetting and then revisiting words, they will gradually stick permanently in your mind. Also, after each vocabulary, a number of 'word helps' are given, which are words in English that are derived from the Greek words in the vocabulary. For example, the English word 'agriculture' can help you remember that the Greek word ἀγρος (pronounced ag-ros) means 'field'. Your first step in becoming familiar with the vocab should be working out which Greek word these 'word helps' relate to. Finally, for a particularly troublesome word, it can be helpful to think of a funny illustration involving the word. For example, to remember that δουλος (doo-los) means 'slave', remember that 'slaves do lots', or remember προσωπον (pros-oh-pon) meaning 'face' by the phrase 'pour soap on'. Have a competition with your friends for who can think of the best ways of remembering the words.

## TWO PATHWAYS

As noted above, this book makes use of 600 Greek words. The first chapter contains eight words that you can understand as soon as you know the alphabet. All of the rest of the chapters contain thirty-two words. The last chapter contains the final sixteen words. One pathway to learning the elements of New Testament Greek using this book is to learn these words chapter by chapter as you progress.

Some teachers, however, find that thirty-two words in a chapter is too many, given that you are trying to master the grammar as well. Therefore this book contains an alternative pathway, focused around a more limited vocabulary of 390 words. In each vocab list and in the Greek–English dictionary, certain words are marked with an asterisk (e.g. *βαλλω). These are the words that form this more limited group. The practice questions have been chosen so that they use only this more limited vocabulary. The sentences do use all of the words, not just these marked ones (since those taking the other pathway need practice in all the words). However, in each set of sentences at least half of them are marked with an asterisk to indicate that they use only words from the more restricted group. Thus, there are two pathways:

1. Aim at all 600 words, allowing you to do any practice questions and sentences.
2. Just focus on the 390 asterisked words, allowing you to do any practice questions, and those sentences marked with an asterisk (and the others, of course, if you are willing to look up the odd words unfamiliar to you).

## DICTIONARIES

At the end of this book there are two dictionaries – one 'Greek–English' and one 'English–Greek'. These dictionaries simply gather together all of the words presented in the vocabularies at the end of each chapter. The entries for ἀγγελος (the example used above) read as follows.

> ἀγγελος (175) – messenger, angel 2
> angel (messenger) – ἀγγελος (175) 2
> messenger (angel) – ἀγγελος (175) 2

Notice the number 2 after each of these entries. This tells you that the word is first introduced in Chapter 2. The 175 is the number of times ἀγγελος occurs in the New Testament. Notice also that in the Greek–English dictionary both possible English equivalents are given, and that in the English–Greek dictionary you are reminded of the range of meaning of the Greek word by the mention in brackets of other possible English translations.

## GRAMMAR REFERENCE

Towards the end of this book you will find grammar reference tables. For easy reference these gather together in one place material that has been introduced throughout the book.

# The history of the Greek language

Greek is a remarkable language. We first have examples of it written down in the thirteenth century BC, and it continues to be written and spoken by millions of Greeks across the world today. Throughout this long history it has changed and evolved in many different ways, but it has always remained Greek. Such developments are not degeneration from best to worst, nor progress from simple to complex. They are simply change. As you embark on your study of Greek, it is useful to understand a little of this history, if only so that you understand what is meant by terms such as 'classical' or 'koine' or 'modern' Greek.

Our first glimpse of Greek is around 1300 BC, because we possess tablets dating to that period written in Greek, though using a different script (called Linear B). We then lose sight of it during the so-called 'dark ages' (dark because they have left us no written records) until about the eighth century BC, when we have our first inscriptions using the Greek alphabet. Not long after this the poems of Homer were written down, one of the great glories of the Greek language. By the fifth and fourth centuries BC Athens had grown to be the cultural capital of the Greek world, producing great drama, oratory, history writing and philosophy. Later this was seen as the 'golden age' of Greek literature and language – 'classical' Greek. The next crucial step came with Alexander the Great, who in ten years conquered all the lands between Greece and India. In his wake came 'hellenization' – the spreading of Greek language and culture. While certain aspects of Greek culture caused controversy (for example among some Jews), the language soon became the international language across a huge area. This language was known as 'common Greek' (the Greek word for 'common' is κοινη – *koine* – so you will hear it called 'koine Greek'; modern scholars sometimes also call it 'hellenistic Greek'). This is the language of the New Testament. By the time of Jesus the Romans had become the dominant military and political force, but the Greek language remained the 'common language' of the eastern Mediterranean and beyond, and Greek was still seen as the language of culture. However, many writers at this time thought that the normal spoken language of their day was inelegant and so imitated the 'classical' Greek of hundreds of years before. On the whole, though, the New Testament texts show little sign of this (except, perhaps, Luke, Acts and Hebrews): they are written in common (koine) Greek, the language of normal people at the time.

Greek continued as the language of the Eastern Roman Empire (the Byzantine Empire) through to its destruction in the fifteenth century AD. Around the same time during the Renaissance in Western Europe, Greek began to be studied by scholars in order to gain access to the great Greek literature of the ancient world, including the New Testament. In the process the idea of two types of Greek – classical and New Testament – was formed, though in fact New Testament Greek is just the standard language of its day and not a separate category. Meanwhile, of course, Greeks continued to speak Greek, throughout their domination by the Empire of the Ottoman Turks, and it became the official language of the new Greek state at its independence in 1821.

# The alphabet

## 1.1 THE LETTERS OF THE GREEK ALPHABET

The first task in learning Greek is to learn the alphabet, which consists of twenty-four letters. Many are similar to English ones, and you may already be familiar with some others (for example, pi π and theta θ from mathematics). Learning the alphabet has three parts.

### 1.1.1. Learning how to write each of the Greek letters

In Greek, just as in English, different people will have different styles of handwriting. Also, printed Greek often looks a little different from handwritten Greek. That is fine – the aim is not to win prizes for the artistic quality of your lettering. What matters is for the different letters to be clearly distinguished from each other. In practice, you will probably copy the style of your teacher.

### 1.1.2. Learning which sounds the different Greek letters make

Greek has been spoken for over three thousand years, and in many different dialects. This means that there is no single right way to pronounce Greek. What matters is to make each letter have its own distinctive sound. It is also useful if your pronunciation is similar to that of other biblical scholars (and your teacher and classmates) so you can understand each other.

You may wonder why pronouncing the letters is important at all, since your desire is to read Greek, not speak it. The answer is that is it almost impossible to learn vocabulary (and grammar) by sight alone – it is saying the word to yourself that helps it stick in your mind. This is why Modern Greek pronunciation is not suggested here, for in Modern Greek several vowels are pronounced alike, which makes remembering the correct spelling very difficult.

### 1.1.3. Learning the order of the Greek alphabet

This is important because you need to know Greek 'alphabetical order' in order to look words up in a dictionary. It is very similar to English alphabetical order, and starts alpha, beta, which is where the word 'alpha-bet' comes from.

| Greek Letter Normal | Greek Letter Capital | Called In English | Called In Greek | Written in English | Sound | Note |
|---|---|---|---|---|---|---|
| α | Α | Alpha | ἀλφα | a | a as in 'h<u>a</u>t' | 1 |
| β | Β | Beta | βητα | b | as English b | |
| γ | Γ | Gamma | γαμμα | g | hard g as in 'get' | 2 |
| δ | Δ | Delta | δελτα | d | as English d | |
| ε | Ε | Epsilon | ἐψιλον | e | short e as in 'm<u>e</u>t' | 1 |
| ζ | Ζ | Zeta | ζητα | z | as English z | |
| η | Η | Eta | ἠτα | ē | long e as in 'ob<u>ey</u>' | 1, 3 |
| θ | Θ | Theta | θητα | th | as English th | |
| ι | Ι | Iota | ἰωτα | i | i as in 'h<u>i</u>t' | 1, 4 |
| κ | Κ | Kappa | καππα | k | as English k | 5 |
| λ | Λ | Lambda | λαμβδα | l | as English l | |
| μ | Μ | Mu | μυ | m | as English m | |
| ν | Ν | Nu | νυ | n | as English n | 6 |
| ξ | Ξ | Xi | ξι | x | as English x | |
| ο | Ο | Omicron | ὀμικρον | o | short o as in 'n<u>o</u>t' | 1 |
| π | Π | Pi | πι | p | as English p | |
| ρ | Ρ | Rho | ῥω | r or rh | as English r | 7, 8 |
| σ or ς | Σ | Sigma | σιγμα | s | as English s | 9 |
| τ | Τ | Tau | ταυ | t | as English t | |
| υ | Υ | Upsilon | ὐψιλον | u | as English u | 1, 10 |
| φ | Φ | Phi | φι | ph or f | as English f | |
| χ | Χ | Chi | χι | ch or kh | hard as in 'lo<u>ch</u>' | 5 |
| ψ | Ψ | Psi | ψι | ps | as in 'li<u>ps</u>' | |
| ω | Ω | Omega | ὠμεγα | ō | long o as in 't<u>o</u>ne' | 1 |

## Notes

1 While there are five vowels in English, there are seven in Greek. This is because there are separate letters for the 'long' and 'short' versions of 'e' and 'o'.

| | a | e | i | o | u |
|---|---|---|---|---|---|
| Short | α | ε | ι | ο | υ |
| Long | α | η | ι | ω | υ |

Thus, α, ι and υ can be either short or long (h<u>a</u>t or f<u>a</u>ther, h<u>i</u>t or ant<u>i</u>que, b<u>u</u>t or r<u>u</u>se) but focus on the short pronunciation for now.

2 γγ is pronounced as 'ng'. Thus αγγελος is angelos (angel).
3 There are notable variations in how η is pronounced. While here 'obey' is suggested, others say 'bear' or 'honey'. I suggest that you follow your teacher's way of pronouncing it.
4 ι can sometimes behave as a consonant when it begins a word (i.e. like a y in English). Thus Ιακωβ is Yakōb (Jacob).
5 Ensure that there is a difference in sound between κ and χ, by (over-) emphasising the 'h' sound in χ.
6 Watch ν – it looks like an English v but is an n (there is no v in Greek).
7 Greek ρ should really be pronounced 'aspirated' (i.e. as 'rh' or rolled).
8 Watch ρ – it looks like an English p but is an r (the Greek p is π).
9 The letter σιγμα is written in two different ways, depending on where it is in the word. If it is the last letter of a word it is written ς, otherwise σ. Look at the two occurrences of the letter σιγμα in Χριστος (Christos – Christ).
10 It can often be helpful to know that in English words derived from Greek the υ has become a y (e.g. μυστηριον → mystery).

## Writing the letters

There is no special way in which to write the letters – it is sensible to begin by copying how someone else writes them (i.e. your teacher) and develop your own style from there. A few pointers can be given though:

- Some people write γ with a loop at the bottom – ɣ.
- ι is written without a dot.
- Notice the difference between υ (round bottom) and ν (pointed bottom).
- Many of the letters are written without taking the pen off the page, and with curves rather than straight lines. In particular, β, δ, θ, ρ, σ and ω.

The relative heights of the letters are important. The following chart shows which parts of the letters are written above the line and which below. In general, however, Greek letters are far more uniform in their size than English ones, the majority of every letter being contained within the lines.

αβγδεζηθικλμνξοπρσςτυφχψω

- β, δ, ζ, θ, λ and ξ stretch above the line (and the central stroke of φ and ψ in many people's handwriting). Contrary to English, κ and τ do not.
- β, γ, ζ, η, μ, ξ, ρ, ς, φ, χ, ψ have 'tails' which stretch below the line.

**PRACTICE 1.1**

A. Write out the Greek alphabet (small letters) in order and the English equivalents of each letter.

**Hint**

Use ē to represent η and ō for ω.

B. Write out the English alphabet and give the Greek (small) letter equivalent to each one as far as possible (ignore h, q, v and w).

C. Write the sound of the following Greek words in English letters. Also, since these words have come into English from Greek, have a guess at their meaning.

**Hint**

Greek puts special endings on words, so when thinking which English words may have been derived from a Greek word, ignore the Greek ending. Also remember (note 10 above) that a Greek υ is often equivalent to an English y.

1. βαπτισμα
2. θρονος
3. κοσμος
4. μεγας
5. μικρος
6. μυστηριον
7. παραβολη
8. παραλυτικος
9. σαββατον

D. The following are real Greek words written in English letters. Write them in Greek (small) letters, and have a guess at their meaning.

1. blasphēmē
2. kardia
3. logikos
4. mētēr
5. patēr
6. pneumatikos
7. prophētēs
8. pyr
9. phōnē

## 1.2 BREATHINGS

Breathings are a mark over a vowel to show whether it is spoken normally or at the same time as *breathing* out heavily – which is equivalent in English to placing an 'h' in front of the vowel (think about 'am' and 'ham'). The technical term for this adding of an 'h' to a vowel is called *aspiration.* In fact there are two breathing marks in Greek – the rough breathing marking that the vowel should be aspirated (pronounced with an 'h' before it), and the smooth breathing marking that it shouldn't.

It is only possible to aspirate a vowel if it is the first letter of a word. Therefore vowels that occur elsewhere are left without breathings, since by definition they will be unaspirated. Vowels at the beginning of a word that should be aspirated carry the rough breathing, and those that shouldn't carry a smooth breathing – not to alter the pronunciation, but just to mark the absence of an 'h'.

| | Sound / English | Written | Example |
|---|---|---|---|
| Rough breathing | h | ‛ | ἅγιος (hagios – holy) |
| Smooth breathing | nothing | ’ | ἄγγελος (angelos – angel) |

Notes

- Breathings are written on top of the letter – ἀ, ἁ, ἐ, ἑ, ἠ, ἡ, ἰ, ἱ, ὀ, ὁ, ὐ, ὑ, ὠ, ὡ.
- Smooth breathings are not optional just because they are not pronounced (εκκλησια must be wrong – it should be ἐκκλησια – church)
- In addition, if a ρ is the first letter in a word, it must carry a rough breathing ῥ (because a Greek ρ is always aspirated), e.g. ῥαββι – rabbi.

KEY GRAMMAR

Every Greek vowel (α, ε, η, ι, ο, υ, ω) at the beginning of a word must have a breathing

PRACTICE 1.2

**In which of these Greek words is there an error in the breathing?**

1. αγω 2. ᾿βλεπω 3. ἐχω 4. λἐγω 5. πιστευω

## 1.3 CAPITAL LETTERS

Capital letters are used less frequently in Greek than in English – only for the beginning of speech, paragraphs and names (i.e. not for the start of sentences).

Their form is given on the chart of the alphabet earlier. Most of these are easy to remember. However, H, P, Y and X look like the wrong English letters. Also the capitals Γ, Δ, Μ, Ξ, Σ and Ω are unlike their small equivalents.

If a breathing needs to be put on a capital letter, the breathing is placed just before the letter e.g. Ἰσραηλ (Israel).

## 1.4 DIPHTHONGS AND IOTA SUBSCRIPTS

When two vowels are pronounced together it is called a diphthong. In English, for example, 'bear' is pronounced with the two vowels 'e' and 'a' combined to make a single sound. There are seven common diphthongs in Greek.

αι 'ai' as in Thailand, or the English word 'eye'
ει 'ei' as in veil, or the 'ay' in say
οι 'oi' as in oil
υι 'ui' as in quit

| | |
|---|---|
| αυ | 'au' as in sauerkraut, or the 'ow' in how |
| ου | 'ou' as in soup, or the 'oo' in hoop |
| ευ / ηυ | 'eu' as in feud, or the English word 'you' |

If a diphthong begins a word, the breathing is put over the second of the letters of the diphthong, e.g. αἱμα (haima) – blood.

There are vowel pairs which occur that are not diphthongs. In these cases, the pair is treated as two separate letters – they are pronounced separately, and any breathing comes on the first letter, e.g. ἐαν (e-an) – if; υἱος (hui-os) – son; εὐαγγελιον (eu-angelion) – good news.[1]

The **iota subscript** is a special form of diphthong. It occurs when an iota follows a long vowel (η, ω, or long α), particularly at the end of a word. By convention these iota are written 'subscripted', i.e. under the long letter thus: ᾳ, ῃ, ῳ. These are not pronounced (the ι being swallowed up in the long vowel). This is unfortunate, since they must be written and if they are not pronounced it is easy to overlook them. Thus λογῳ is pronounced as logō, but for the moment think of it in English as logō(i).

## PRACTICE 1.3 AND 1.4

A. Write these names in English letters

| | | | |
|---|---|---|---|
| 1. Παυλος | 3. Ἀβρααμ | 5. Σιμων | 7. Ἰερουσαλημ |
| 2. Μαρια | 4. Ἰωσηφ | 6. Ἡρῳδης | 8. Καισαρ[2] |

B. Write these names in Greek letters

| | | | |
|---|---|---|---|
| 1. Barnabas | 3. Philippos | 5. Timotheos | 7. Satanas |
| 2. Petros | 4. Pilatos | 6. Joudaea[2] | 8. Pharisaios |

C. Here is the first half of the Lord's Prayer from Matthew (6.9-10). Work out how to pronounce it. (To begin with the easiest way of doing this may be to write it out in English letters.)

Πατερ ἡμων ὁ ἐν τοις οὐρανοις
ἁγιασθητω το ὀνομα σου
ἐλθετω ἡ βασιλεια σου
γενηθητω το θελημα σου
ὡς ἐν οὐρανῳ και ἐπι γης

[1] If there is any doubt as to whether the two vowels form a diphthong, then a diaeresis can be used to show that the letters do not form a diphthong, e.g. Μωϋσης is Μω-υ-σης.

[2] Note: When a Greek word containing the dipthong αι is transliterated into English letters (for example in a name) the 'αι' is normally represented by 'ae'.

## 1.5 ACCENTS AND STRESS

Ancient Greek was written without accents. However, naturally when people spoke the language there were accepted ways of pronouncing the words. After the period of the New Testament a system of writing accents (acute ´, grave ` and circumflex ^) gradually emerged until it developed into the system for accentuation now followed by scholars of Greek, and present in printed copies of the New Testament. This system probably reflects the way the words were originally pronounced – with the accents showing what were originally changes of pitch in the pronunciation of words, and then later changes of stress.

However, accents are not taught in this book, for three important reasons.

1. Accents were not present in written Greek in the New Testament period.
2. The rules of accentuation are complicated, and you have enough to learn.
3. Accents don't help you translate or understand Greek.

Point three is not completely true – in a very small number of situations accents can distinguish between two similar or identical-looking words. In these cases, a special note will be given pointing this out, and these are collected together on pages 273–4 in the reference section.[3]

However, as a matter of tradition printed Greek texts still use accents. Therefore, to help you get used to seeing an accented text, when sample passages from the New Testament are printed in this book they will be printed with accents. Otherwise accents will not be used, except when they are useful in distinguishing between identical looking words. You should not try to learn the accents now.[4]

This leaves the question of where you should put the stress when pronouncing Greek words. As with the question of the pronunciation of the letters themselves, this is a matter of some dispute, and not central to your immediate needs, so just concentrate on pronouncing the word clearly (and follow your teacher's suggestion).

KEY GRAMMAR

Breathings – Essential
Accents – Unimportant, so ignore

---

[3] However, remember that the original manuscripts do not have accents. So when an accent distinguishes between two words, in fact it only reveals which the editor of the printed text thinks is the correct one.

[4] In the Going Further section (page 237) information is given for those who wish to learn more about accents.

**PRACTICE 1.5**

### Which of the following words has a smooth breathing?

1. βάλλω 2. ἄγω 3. εὑρίσκω 4. ἅγιος 5. ἰῶτα

## 1.6 PUNCTUATION

Ancient Greek was written with little punctuation. However, there is a standard system now accepted for punctuation, which does make reading the text very much easier (unlike the accents).[5] In Greek there are four punctuation marks.

| Greek | English Equivalent | Used for |
|---|---|---|
| . (on the line) | . | End of sentence |
| , | , | Minor break within a sentence |
| · (above the line) | ; or : | Major break within a sentence |
| ; | ? | Questions |

Also, if a word beginning with a vowel follows a word ending in a vowel *elision* will sometimes take place – the final vowel of the first word is dropped, and this fact is marked by an apostrophe ᾿, e.g. ἀλλ᾿ ἐγω instead of ἀλλα ἐγω.

**PRACTICE 1.6**

### Which are questions?

1. βλεπεις; 2. ἐχω· 3. λυουσιν. 4. βαλλει; 5. λεγετε,

## VOCAB FOR CHAPTER 1

(The numbers in brackets after the Greek word are the number of times the word occurs in the New Testament. The asterisked words are in the more limited group of 390 words – see the discussion of the two pathways presented in this book on page 7.)

[5] As one learns more Greek, it is important to remember that the punctuation has only been added by the editors of your printed text and is not part of the Greek text itself. However, to begin with, assume the editors have been sensible in their judgements!

Seven Hebrew words, written in Greek just as they sound

| | |
|---|---|
| Ἀβρααμ (73) – Abraham | Ἰακωβ (27) – Jacob |
| ἀμην (129) – amen, truly | Ἰσραηλ (68) – Israel |
| Δαυιδ (59) – David | Ἰωσηφ (35) – Joseph |
| ῥαββι (15) – rabbi[6] | |

And the second most common word in Greek: *και (9161) – and

---

## Exercises

It is important to get used to going from Greek letters to the sound they make (i.e. being able to pronounce the Greek words), and from the sound of a word to the Greek letters you would use to represent it. Without this, Greek will remain just a series of marks on a page, and this makes it almost impossible to learn. As mentioned on page 7, the best way to learn vocabulary or grammar is by the sound of the words or testing your friends, both of which require you to be able to write and read Greek letters happily.

1. Work out how to pronounce the following passage from John 1.1-14.
To begin with, the easiest way of doing this may be to write it out in English letters. To distinguish between the long and short versions of 'o' and 'e' you may find it helpful to use 'e' for ε, 'ē' for η, 'o' for ο, and 'ō' for ω. Although they are not pronounced, represent iota subscripts as (i).

[1] ἐν ἀρχῃ ἠν ὁ λογος, και ὁ λογος ἠν προς τον θεον, και θεος ἠν ὁ λογος.
[2] οὑτος ἠν ἐν ἀρχῃ προς τον θεον. [3] παντα δι᾽ αὐτου ἐγενετο, και χωρις
αὐτου ἐγενετο οὐδε ἑν. ὁ γεγονεν [4] ἐν αὐτῳ ζωη ἠν, και ἡ ζωη ἠν το φως
των ἀνθρωπων· [5] και το φως ἐν τῃ σκοτιᾳ φαινει, και ἡ σκοτια αὐτο οὐ
κατελαβεν. [6] ἐγενετο ἀνθρωπος ἀπεσταλμενος παρα θεου, ὀνομα αὐτῳ
Ἰωαννης· [7] οὑτος ἠλθεν εἰς μαρτυριαν, ἱνα μαρτυρησῃ περι του φωτος,
ἱνα παντες πιστευσωσιν δι᾽ αὐτου. [8] οὐκ ἠν ἐκεινος το φως, ἀλλ᾽ ἱνα
μαρτυρησῃ περι του φωτος. [9] ἠν το φως το ἀληθινον, ὁ φωτιζει παντα

---

[6] It is arguable how best to translate ῥαββι. As an Aramaic word it literally means 'my great one', and therefore might be translated 'master' or 'lord'. You can see this in Mark 9.5, where Peter calls Jesus ῥαββι, while in the same sentence in Matthew (17.4) he calls him κυριος (lord), and in Luke (9.33) ἐπιστατα (master). However, in John 1.38 and 20.16 ῥαββι is translated into Greek as διδασκαλος (teacher) (see also Matthew 23.8 and John 3.2). This fits with its usage in Aramaic when it is used for revered teachers. However, to translate it into English merely as 'teacher' loses something – ῥαββι is not the normal Greek word for teacher but is a term coming from a very particular historical and linguistic context. A useful rule is that if a Greek writer uses an Aramaic word (rather than translating it into Greek), then you should keep the Aramaic word (rather than translating it into English). Therefore, I would 'translate' ῥαββι as rabbi.

ἀνθρωπον, ἐρχομενον εἰς τον κοσμον. 10 ἐν τῳ κοσμῳ ἠν, και ὁ κοσμος δι᾽
αὐτου ἐγενετο, και ὁ κοσμος αὐτον οὐκ ἐγνω. 11 εἰς τα ἰδια ἠλθεν, και οἱ
ἰδιοι αὐτον οὐ παρελαβον. 12 ὁσοι δε ἐλαβον αὐτον, ἐδωκεν αὐτοις
ἐξουσιαν τεκνα θεου γενεσθαι, τοις πιστευουσιν εἰς το ὀνομα αὐτου,
13 οἱ οὐκ ἐξ αἱματων οὐδε ἐκ θεληματος σαρκος οὐδε ἐκ θεληματος
ἀνδρος ἀλλ᾽ ἐκ θεου ἐγεννηθησαν. 14 και ὁ λογος σαρξ ἐγενετο και
ἐσκηνωσεν ἐν ἡμιν, και ἐθεασαμεθα την δοξαν αὐτου, δοξαν ὡς
μονογενους παρα πατρος, πληρης χαριτος και ἀληθειας.

2. John 1.15-23 has been written out below in English letters to represent how it would sound when read. Turn these sounds back into the Greek words, that is, write out the passage in Greek letters. Remember smooth breathings and the two different forms of sigma.

15 Iōannēs marturei peri autou kai kekragen legōn, Houtos ēn hon eipon, Ho
opisō mou erchomenos emprosthen mou gegonen, hoti prōtos mou ēn. 16
hoti ek tou plērōmatos autou hēmeis pantes elabomen kai charin anti
charitos; 17 hoti ho nomos dia Mōuseōs edothē, hē charis kai hē alētheia dia
Iēsou Christou egeneto. 18 theon oudeis heōraken pōpote; monogenēs theos
ho ōn eis ton kolpon tou patros ekeinos exēgēsato.

19 Kai hautē estin hē marturia tou Iōannou, hote apesteilan pros auton hoi
Ioudaioi ex Hierosolumōn hiereis kai Leuitas hina erōtēsōsin auton, Su tis
ei? 20 kai hōmologēsen kai ouk ērnēsato, kai hōmologēsen hoti Egō ouk eimi
ho Christos. 21 kai ērōtēsan auton, Ti oun? Su Ēlias ei? kai legei, Ouk eimi.
Ho prophētēs ei su? kai apekrithē, Ou. 22 eipan oun autō(i), Tis ei? hina
apokrisin dōmen tois pempsasin hēmas; ti legeis peri seautou? 23 ephē, Egō
phōnē boōntos en tē(i) erēmō(i), Euthunate tēn hodon kuriou, kathōs eipen
Ēsaias ho prophētēs.

# Basic sentences

## 2.1 THE PRESENT TENSE OF λυω

Mark 11.4: λυουσιν αὐτον – they untie him
Luke 13.15: λυει τον βουν αὐτου – he unties his ox

The Greek word λυω ('I untie') has different endings to show who is doing the untying – λυουσιν = they untie and λυει = he unties. The one Greek word means more than one English word – λυει means 'he' plus 'unties'.

The Present tense of the Greek verb λυω, which means 'I untie', is as follows.[1]

| Grammatical Label | Greek | English *Either* | *Or* |
|---|---|---|---|
| 1st person singular | λυω | I am untying | I untie |
| 2nd person singular | λυεις | You are untying | You untie |
| 3rd person singular | λυει | He, she or it is untying | He, she or it unties |
| 1st person plural | λυομεν | We are untying | We untie |
| 2nd person plural | λυετε | You are untying | You untie |
| 3rd person plural | λυουσιν *or* λυουσι | They are untying | They untie |

### Notes

**Person?**
See it in English
Section 5
Page 246

- **2nd singular and plural**: Notice the distinction between λυεις and λυετε. Greek distinguishes between 'you' meaning one person ('you

[1] Technically, this is the Present Indicative Active of λυω. We will meet other *tenses* than the *Present* in Chapter 6, other *moods* than the *Indicative* in Chapter 7, and other *voices* than the *Active* in Chapter 15. However, don't worry about these distinctions at the moment – you have to walk before you can run!

singular' – λυεις) and more than one person ('you plural' – λυετε) in a way that modern English does not. Keep thinking, 'Is this "you singular" or "you plural"?'

- **3rd singular**: The 3rd singular means 'he', 'she' or 'it'. The context will usually reveal which is appropriate.
- **3rd plural**: Notice the two possibilities – λυουσιν or λυουσι. Either form is acceptable, though the form including the '*optional* ν' is more common and is always used before a vowel and at the end of a sentence.

### 2.1.1 Endings, roots and conjugations

Each of these six forms of λυω can be split into two parts:

*the stem*: λυ
*the ending*: -ω, -εις, -ει, -ομεν, -ετε, -ουσιν.

*The stem* denotes the basic meaning of the word: λυ meaning 'untie'.
*The ending* indicates the person (who is doing the action):

| | | | | | |
|---|---|---|---|---|---|
| -ω | means | I | -ομεν | means | we |
| -εις | means | you singular | -ετε | means | you plural |
| -ει | means | he, she or it | -ουσιν | means | they |

Put *stem* and *ending* together and we have a single Greek word (e.g. λυομεν) which means several English words ('we are untying').

KEY GRAMMAR
One Greek word often means more than one English word

A pattern of the forms of a verb (a particular set of endings on the stem) is called a *conjugation*. We have now learnt the Present (Indicative Active) *conjugation* of λυω. You can now *conjugate* it (i.e. go through the pattern in order).

The good news is that almost all Greek verbs follow the same pattern (*conjugation*) as λυω. Thus if you know that 'I say' is λεγω and 'I see' is βλεπω, then you can work out all six forms of each verb:

| | | | |
|---|---|---|---|
| λεγω | I am saying | βλεπω | I am seeing |
| λεγεις | You (sing.) are saying | βλεπεις | You (sing.) are seeing |
| λεγει | He, she or it is saying | βλεπει | He, she or it is seeing |
| λεγομεν | We are saying | βλεπομεν | We are seeing |
| λεγετε | You (pl.) are saying | βλεπετε | You (pl.) are seeing |
| λεγουσιν | They are saying | βλεπουσιν | They are seeing |

### 2.1.2 Meaning of the Present tense

KEY GRAMMAR
Once you know the Present of λυω, you know the Present of almost every Greek verb[2]

The Present tense in Greek signifies an action:

- taking place in the present
- which is either (a) process or (b) undefined in nature.

Thus λυω can be translated in English as either: (a) I am untying, or (b) I untie. Which is the more appropriate depends on the context.

---

PRACTICE 2.1

**Translate**

1. λαμβανει.
2. διδασκομεν.
3. ἀκουουσιν.
4. ἐχετε.
5. βλεπω.
6. λυεις.
7. She is throwing.
8. They have.
9. We are leading.

---

**Hint**

The vocabulary you need is listed on page 29 at the end of the chapter. Verbs are always given in their most simple form in a vocabulary list or dictionary (e.g. the 1st person singular form of the Present Indicative Active).

---

## 2.2 THE PRESENT TENSE OF -εω VERBS (φιλεω)

1 John 1.10: ψευστην ποιουμεν αὐτον – we make him a liar

ποιεω (I make/do) has very slightly different endings from λυω.
'we make' is ποιουμεν not ποιεομεν.

KEY GRAMMAR
Greek grammar is very regular, but with many minor adjustments when certain letters combine

There are many Greek verbs whose stem ends in ε, such as φιλε-ω 'I love'. They are called -εω *verbs*. These verbs are regular and have exactly the same endings as λυω. However, the weak

---

[2] λυω is chosen as the model word because it is completely regular in all its forms, and it is short – try chanting the forms of θεραπευω and you will see the difference!

exposed ε at the end of the stem combines with the vowel at the beginning of the ending. This combining or contracting of the vowels means these verbs are also known as 'contract verbs'.

The rules for the contractions are: ε + ε → ει
ε + ο → ου
ε + any long vowel or diphthong is absorbed
(i.e. the ε disappears without making any difference)

Thus, the Present Indicative Active of φιλεω is:

| | Actual Form | The process of getting there |
|---|---|---|
| I am loving | φιλω | φιλε+ω → φιλω |
| You are loving | φιλεις | φιλε+εις → φιλεις |
| He, she or it is loving | φιλει | φιλε+ει → φιλει |
| We are loving | φιλουμεν | φιλε+ομεν → φιλουμεν |
| You are loving | φιλειτε | φιλε+ετε → φιλειτε |
| They are loving | φιλουσιν *or* φιλουσι | φιλε+ουσιν → φιλουσιν |

**Hint**

-εω verbs like φιλεω are always listed in vocabularies or dictionaries in their uncontracted form (i.e. φιλεω) although in fact this form will never be found in actual Greek (since it would have contracted into φιλω).

**PRACTICE 2.2**

### Translate

1. φιλουσιν.
2. ποιειτε.
3. καλει.
4. τηρουμεν.
5. ζητω.
6. λαλεις.
7. They are speaking.
8. She is doing.
9. You (pl.) seek.

## 2.3 THE NOMINATIVE AND ACCUSATIVE CASES

John 6.24: εἰδεν ὁ ὀχλος – the crowd saw
Mark 6.34: εἰδεν πολυν ὀχλον – he saw a great crowd

The Greek word for crowd changes depending on how it fits into the sentence – ὀχλος when the crowd is doing the seeing, ὀχλον when it is being seen.

## 2.3.1 The forms of λογος

Nouns, like verbs, are *inflected* in Greek. This means that each noun will have a stem and an ending – *the stem* denoting the basic meaning of the word, and *the ending* communicating more precise information about the function of the word in this particular sentence.

A noun occurs in one of five *cases* (forms used to indicate the word's function in the sentence, such as being the subject), and in either the singular or the plural (whether a noun is singular or plural is called its *number*, which shouldn't be confused with verbs being in the 1st, 2nd or 3rd persons). The pattern of endings for a noun is called a *declension*: going through them is called *declining* it. While most verbs conjugate like λυω, nouns fall into in a number of different declensions. We will first learn the declension of λογος, which means 'word'.

| Case | Number | |
|---|---|---|
| | Singular | Plural |
| Nominative | λογος | λογοι |
| Accusative | λογον | λογους |

Noun?
See it in English
Section 1.1
Page 241

Using λογος as a pattern, you can work out the nominative and accusative forms, both singular and plural, of many other Greek nouns (some are listed in the vocabulary at the end of this chapter).

Examples

- ἀδελφος (brother): ἀδελφος, ἀδελφον, ἀδελφοι, ἀδελφους.
- κυριος (lord): κυριος, κυριον, κυριοι, κυριους.

PRACTICE 2.3.1

### What case and number are the following words in?

1. ἀρτον
2. ἀγγελοι
3. οὐρανους
4. υἱοι
5. ὀχλος
6. θεους
7. δουλοι
8. νομον

## 2.3.2 The meaning of the nominative and accusative cases

KEY GRAMMAR
Nominative – Subject
Accusative – Object

**In English, word order** distinguishes subject from object – the subject comes before the verb, the object after the verb. Thus 'the dog bites the man' means something rather different from 'the man bites the dog'.

**Subject and object?**
See it in English
Section 3
Page 245

**In Greek, cases** distinguish subject from object. Word order does not matter. [3]

## 2.3.3 Forming a sentence

**Sentence?**
See it in English
Section 2
Page 244

We now need to put together a verb and one or more nouns to form a sentence.

- βλεπεις. – You (singular) see.
- βλεπεις ἀγγελον. – You (singular) see an angel.
- βλεπεις ἀγγελους. – You (singular) see angels.

Note: There is no word for 'a' (indefinite article) in Greek. Thus λογος means 'word' or 'a word' – the context will make it clear.

Once we use a noun (in the nominative) as the subject of the sentence, we meet the important concept of *agreement.* The different parts of the sentence have to fit properly together.

KEY GRAMMAR
Verbs agree with their subject in number

So, if the subject is singular, the verb must be singular, and if plural the verb must be plural.

**Hint**

We do this in a limited fashion in English – he sees, they see

Also, if the verb is in the 1st or 2nd persons (I, we or you) there is unlikely to be a separate subject (because the verb itself contains the 'I, we or you' information). However, if there is a separate subject (e.g. 'the king', 'a girl', 'the mountain', 'pigs') then the verb will be in the 3rd person (he, she, it or they).

[3] Or at least word order in Greek only communicates a difference *in emphasis*, not *in meaning*. This is discussed further in Chapter 5, section 5.7.

Examples

- βλεπετε. – You see.
- ἀγγελος βλεπει. – An angel sees.
- βλεπετε ἀγγελον. – You see an angel.
- δουλος βλεπει ἀγγελον. – A slave sees an angel.
- δουλοι βλεπουσιν ἀγγελον. – Slaves see an angel.
- δουλοι βλεπουσιν ἀγγελους. – Slaves see angels.

**Hint**

There are three steps to translation:

1. Work out the cases of the words.
2. Work out why the different words have the cases they do.
3. Translate the sentence accordingly.

- κυριος ἐχει δουλους.

1. κυριος is *nom.* sing. δουλους is *acc.* pl.
2. κυριος is *nom.* because it is the subject δουλους is *acc.* – the object
3. Sentence = 'A lord has slaves.'

δουλους κυριος ἐχει would mean exactly the same, since κυριος is still *nominative* and so the subject, and δουλους *accusative* so the object. The change in word order would not change the sentence's meaning, although the stress would have changed; there is more on word order and stress in Chapter 5 (section 5.7).

**PRACTICE 2.3.3**

## Translate

1. ἀδελφος διδασκει ὀχλους.
2. ζητουμεν ἀρτον.
3. δουλους λυεις.
4. κυριος λεγει λογον.
5. ἀνθρωποι καλουσιν.
6. ἀγγελοι τηρουσιν νομους.
7. A brother sees a house.
8. People are watching.
9. We love a world.
10. God leads.

## 2.4 THE DEFINITE ARTICLE

In Greek the definite article ('the') also has to be declined. It must always *agree* with the noun it is going with in *case* and *number*. It will normally come immediately before the noun. (Note that because there is no indefinite article 'a' in Greek, the definite article is often referred to simply as 'the article'.)

| Case | Number | |
|---|---|---|
| | Singular | Plural |
| Nominative | ὁ | οἱ |
| Accusative | τον | τους |

Examples

- βλεπεις τον ἀγγελον. – You (singular) see the angel.
- οἱ ἀγγελοι βλεπουσιν. – The angels see.
- ἀνθρωπος βλεπει τους ἀγγελους. – A person sees the angels.

In comparison ὁ λογον cannot be right, whatever is meant, since ὁ does not agree with λογον.

## 2.5 SPECIAL USES OF THE DEFINITE ARTICLE

Normally the definite article is used in Greek in the same situations as 'the' in English. However, there are three special uses of the article in Greek.

1. **Names.** Greek often uses the definite article before a name e.g. ὁ Δαυιδ = David (not 'the David').
2. **Abstract Nouns.** Greek normally uses the definite article with abstract nouns or generalisations, e.g. ὁ ἀνθρωπος can mean 'the person', but can also mean 'humanity' in general; similarly ὁ νομος can mean 'law' (as a concept) as well as 'the law'.
3. **God.** Writers from a monotheistic perspective will also normally use the article before θεος (similar to the distinction in English between 'god' and 'God').

**PRACTICE 2.4 and 2.5**

### Translate

1. οἱ υἱοι ἐχουσιν οἰκον.
2. καλειτε τον ἀδελφον.
3. ὁ θεος ποιει τους οὐρανους.
4. ἀγει ἀγγελος ὀχλους.
5. ὁ κυριος ἀκουει.
6. We are seeking the Messiah.
7. The sons are speaking words.
8. The people love God.

## VOCAB FOR CHAPTER 2

Nine verbs like λυω

*ἀγω (67) – I lead, bring
*ἀκουω (428) – I hear, listen to
*βαλλω (122) – I throw
*βλεπω (133) – I see, watch
*διδασκω (97) – I teach
*ἐχω (708) – I have, hold
*λαμβανω (258) – I take, receive
*λεγω (2354) – I say, speak, tell
*λυω (42) – I untie

And six that are like φιλεω

*ζητεω (117) – I seek
*καλεω (148) – I call
*λαλεω (296) – I speak, say
*ποιεω (568) – I do, make
*τηρεω (70) – I keep
*φιλεω (25) – I love, like

Fourteen nouns declining like λογος

*ἀγγελος (175) – messenger, angel
*ἀδελφος (343) – brother
*ἀρτος (97) – bread
*δουλος (124) – slave
*θεος (1317) – god, God
*κοσμος (186) – world
*κυριος (717) – lord, master, sir
*λογος (330) – word, message
*νομος (194) – law
*οἰκος (114) – household, house
*οὐρανος (273) – heaven
*ὀχλος (175) – crowd
*υἱος (377) – son
*Χριστος (529) – Christ, Messiah

The most common word in Greek
*ὁ, ἡ, το (19867) – the

Plus two more that decline like λογος with similar but distinct meanings

*ἀνθρωπος (550) – human being, person
*λαος (142) – people (as in 'a people' or 'a nation')

(The plural of λαος means peoples or nations; for 'people' meaning 'a number of persons' Greek would use the plural of ἀνθρωπος.)

### Word helps

acoustics, ballistics/ball, didactic, call, glossolalia, philosophy, Philadelphia, angel, theology, cosmology, dialogue/prologue, antinomian/astronomy/Deuteronomy, Uranus, anthropology, laity.

## Exercises

### Section A

*1. ἐχω υἱον.
*2. ὁ ἀνθρωπος καλει δουλον.
*3. τον νομον φιλεις.
*4. ἀμην ἀμην λεγω ...
*5. διδασκει ὁ Χριστος τον ὀχλον.
*6. ὁ θεος ποιει τον κοσμον και τον οὐρανον.
*7. ὁ Ἰωσηφ[4] λαμβανει τους ἀδελφους.
*8. ἀκουομεν και φιλουμεν τον λογον.
*9. Christ says the words.
*10. The crowd listens to the law.
*11. You (s.) are setting free [*use* λυω] the slaves.
*12. (Some) People are making bread.

### Section B

*1. οἱ υἱοι λαλουσιν.
*2. οἱ ἀγγελοι βλεπουσι τον θεον.
*3. ὁ ὀχλος τον θεον ζητει.
*4. βαλλετε τον ἀρτον.
*5. ὁ Ἰακωβ ἀγει τον ἀδελφον.
*6. τον νομον τηρει ὁ λαος Ἰσραηλ.[4]
*7. τον Δαυιδ[4] ὁ κυριος ζητει.
*8. ὁ κυριος Χριστος τους ἀνθρωπους λυει.
*9. God has messengers.
*10. I teach the sons.
*11. We are seeking the lord.
*12. You (pl.) are calling the brother.

---

[4] Often when foreign words are used in Greek they are indeclinable. This is true of all seven Hebrew words in the vocab for Chapter 1. A word being indeclinable means that its form does not change, regardless of the case it is in. Thus, for example, Ἀβρααμ could be nominative or accusative (though normally, being a name, it will appear with the definite article, thus: ὁ Ἀβρααμ, τον Ἀβρααμ).

# Cases and gender

## 3.1 THE GENITIVE AND DATIVE CASES

Rev. 19.1: ἠκουσα ... φωνην ... ὀχλου – I heard the sound of a crowd
Matt. 23.1: ὁ Ἰησους ἐλαλησαν τοις ὀχλοις – Jesus spoke to the crowds
Changing the endings on ὀχλος can express the idea of 'of' or speaking 'to'.

There are two more cases in which nouns can occur:

| Case | ὁ – the Singular | ὁ – the Plural | λογος – word Singular | λογος – word Plural |
|---|---|---|---|---|
| Genitive | του | των | λογου | λογων |
| Dative[1] | τῳ | τοις | λογῳ | λογοις |

The *genitive* case equates to the use of *of* in English (or adding 's); the *dative* is used to denote the person or thing *to* or *for* which anything is done, which is technically known as the *indirect object.*[2]

**Indirect object?**
See it in English
Section 3
Page 245

KEY GRAMMAR

| | | |
|---|---|---|
| Genitive | – | Possessor (≈ 'of') |
| Dative | – | Indirect object (≈ 'to' or 'for') |

Examples

- ὁ ἀγγελος του θεου λεγει τον λογον.

1. ὁ ἀγγελος = the angel – *nominative*    του θεου = God – *genitive*
   τον λογον = the word – *accusative*
2. Angel is *nom.* because it is the subject    God is *gen.* – the possessor
   Word is *acc.* – the object

[1] Notice the iota subscripts in τῳ and λογῳ (see Chapter 1, section 1.4).

[2] There are other, less common, uses of the genitive and dative which we shall meet later.

3. Sentence = 'The angel of God speaks the word.'

- ὁ ἀγγελος λεγει τῳ δουλῳ.

1. ὁ ἀγγελος = the angel – *nom.* τῳ δουλῳ = the slave – *dat.*
2. Angel is *nom.* because it is the subject Slave is *dat.* – the indirect object
3. Sentence = 'The angel speaks to the slave.'

- ὁ ἀγγελος λεγει τον λογον του θεου τῳ δουλῳ.

1. ὁ ἀγγελος = the angel – *nom.* τον λογον = the word – *acc.*
   του θεου = God – *gen.* τῳ δουλῳ = the slave – *dat.*
2. Angel is *nom.* because it is the subject Word is *acc.* – the object
   God is *gen.* – the possessor Slave is *dat.* – the indirect object
3. Sentence = 'The angel speaks the word of God to the slave.'

---

**PRACTICE 3.1**

### If these sentences were in Greek, which case would the underlined word be in?

1. I like <u>lectures</u>.
2. The <u>teacher's</u> voice is boring.
3. I am cooking for my <u>wife</u>.
4. The <u>students</u> eat many cakes.
5. I have the books of a <u>friend</u>.
6. We are making a hat for the <u>tutor</u>.
7. I hate <u>essays</u>.
8. <u>Classes</u> end too quickly.

### Give the case and number of the following

9. ἀδελφου
10. κυριοις
11. τους
12. δουλῳ
13. των
14. κοσμου
15. νομοι
16. θεον

---

## 3.2 SPECIAL USES OF THE GENITIVE AND DATIVE

Earlier, in Chapter 2, section 2.3, we learnt that the accusative is used for the object of a verb. In grammatical language, most verbs '*govern*' a noun in the accusative. Thus, 'he sees an angel' is βλεπει ἀγγελον – βλεπω governs a noun in the accusative (its object); or as it is often put – 'βλεπω takes the accusative'.

In Chapter 3, section 3.1 we learnt the general meaning of the dative cases. In fact certain verbs are always likely to govern a noun in the dative, because they naturally have an indirect object. For example, after λεγω (I say) you often get a noun in the dative expressing to whom you are speaking: λεγω τῳ κυριῳ – 'I am speaking to the master'. However, λεγω can have a normal object (in the accusative) – the thing which is said: λεγω <u>λογον</u> τῳ κυριῳ – 'I am speaking <u>a word</u> to the master'. This can be summarised as:

λεγω means 'I speak', + accusative of thing said, + dative of person spoken to.

For λεγω this matches English, since in English we use the word 'to' in front of the person spoken to. However, English and Greek do not always match in this way. Therefore, if a word habitually governs a noun in a case other than the accusative this will be stated in the vocabulary lists and dictionary.

For example, in the vocab for this chapter, you will see the word πιστευω which means 'I believe (in), trust, have faith in'. This is listed as πιστευω + dat. because the person or thing you believe/trust/have faith in is put in the dative (e.g. πιστευω τῳ λογῳ – I believe the word).

We can now also add a further detail to one of the items of vocabulary learnt in Chapter 2:

ἀκουω – I hear, listen to + acc. of *thing* heard, + gen. of *person* heard

Examples

- ἀκουομεν του κυριου – We hear the Lord
- ἀκουομεν τον λογον – We hear the message
- πιστευουσιν τῳ θεῳ – They believe in God

**PRACTICE 3.2**

## Translate

1. ἀκουω του κυριου.
2. βλεπει τον ἀγγελον του θεου.
3. πιστευομεν τῳ Χριστῳ.
4. ἀκουετε τους λογους.
5. They hear God.
6. I believe the lord.

**HALF-WAY PRACTICE**

1. ἐχομεν τον νομον του θεου.
2. οἱ δουλοι λαλουσιν τῳ κυριῳ.
3. ζητω τον οἰκον του Χριστου.
4. ποιειτε ἀρτον τοις ἀδελφοις.
5. ὁ ὀχλος ἀκουει τον λογον του κυριου.
6. βλεπει τον ἀγγελον και ἀκουει του ἀγγελου.
7. πιστευει τῳ υἱῳ του θεου.
8. ὁ ἀδελφος λυει δουλον τῳ κυριῳ.

9. I teach the word of God.
10. They hear the son.
11. We keep the law of heaven.
12. You speak to the crowd.

## 3.3 FEMININE AND NEUTER NOUNS

Mark 13.31: ὁ <u>οὐρανος</u> και ἡ <u>γη</u> παρελευσονται
– (The) <u>heaven</u> and (the) <u>earth</u> will pass away

οὐρανος and γη are both subjects and therefore nominative, but they have different endings because they come from different patterns of words – οὐρανος is masculine and γη is feminine.

### 3.3.1 The idea of gender

So far we have met one type of noun – those which decline like λογος. Almost all of these words are masculine. We now need to learn how to decline the main family of feminine nouns, and the main family of neuter nouns.

When we talk of masculine, feminine and neuter, this refers to a *grammatical gender*, which is a way of classifying nouns. Sometimes it will match what English speakers might think the gender of the nouns should be, but sometimes it will not. In effect, rather than talking of masculine, feminine and neuter nouns, we could just as well talk about class 1, class 2 and class 3 nouns, or even blue, green and yellow nouns. 'Gender' is just a way of grouping together nouns that behave in similar ways.

**Gender?**
See it in English
Section 10
Page 249

Chapter 8 contains more about the gender of nouns. For now, though, things are simple:

- nouns ending in -ος are masculine and decline like λογος
- nouns ending in -η or -α are feminine and decline like ἀρχη, ἡμερα or δοξα
- nouns ending in -ον are neuter and decline like ἐργον

So, for example, because ἀγαπη ends in -η you know that it is feminine.

## 3.3.2 The feminine and neuter declensions

| | Case | Feminine words | Neuter words |
|---|---|---|---|
| | | (beginning) | (work) |
| Sing. | Nom. | ἀρχη | ἐργον |
| | Acc. | ἀρχην | ἐργον |
| | Gen. | ἀρχης | ἐργου |
| | Dat. | ἀρχῃ | ἐργῳ |
| Plural | Nom. | ἀρχαι | ἐργα |
| | Acc. | ἀρχας | ἐργα |
| | Gen. | ἀρχων | ἐργων |
| | Dat. | ἀρχαις | ἐργοις |

Notes

- The nom. and acc. of ἐργον are identical. This is always true for neuter words.
- There is a special rule for neuter plural nouns. They normally take a singular verb. Thus 'the children keep the law' is 'τα τεκνα <u>τηρει</u> τον νομον' **not** 'τα τεκνα <u>τηρουσιν</u> τον νομον'.

KEY GRAMMAR
Neuter plural nouns take a singular verb

PRACTICE 3.3.2

### What case and number are the following words in?

1. ἀγαπην
2. εὐαγγελιῳ
3. τεκνα
4. γης
5. ἀδελφαις
6. βιβλιων
7. ψυχη
8. δαιμονιου

## 3.3.3 The feminine and neuter of the definite article. agreement

The definite article ('the') also comes in a feminine and neuter form, supplementing the masculine forms we have already seen.

| | | Masculine | Feminine | Neuter |
|---|---|---|---|---|
| Sing. | Nom. | ὁ | ἡ | το |
| | Acc. | τον | την | το |
| | Gen. | του | της | του |
| | Dat. | τῳ | τῃ | τῳ |
| Plural | Nom. | οἱ | αἱ | τα |
| | Acc. | τους | τας | τα |
| | Gen. | των | των | των |
| | Dat. | τοις | ταις | τοις |

We have already learnt that the definite article must agree with the noun it is going with in case and number. It also must agree in gender.

KEY GRAMMAR
Article and noun agree in gender, case and number

PRACTICE 3.3.3

**Which part of the definite article agrees with these nouns?**

1. θεον
2. ἀγαπῃ
3. ἐργων
4. ἀρχη
5. τεκνα
6. λογοις
7. ζωην
8. ἱερα

## 3.3.4 Overview of nouns and the article

This chart, putting the definite article ('the') in all its forms alongside the masculine, feminine and neuter nouns, highlights the patterns and similarities.

| | | Masculine | | Feminine | | Neuter | |
|---|---|---|---|---|---|---|---|
| | | Article | Noun | Article | Noun | Article | Noun |
| Sing. | Nom. | ὁ | λογος | ἡ | ἀρχη | το | ἐργον |
| | Acc. | τον | λογον | την | ἀρχην | το | ἐργον |
| | Gen. | του | λογου | της | ἀρχης | του | ἐργου |
| | Dat. | τῳ | λογῳ | τῃ | ἀρχῃ | τῳ | ἐργῳ |
| Plural | Nom. | οἱ | λογοι | αἱ | ἀρχαι | τα | ἐργα |
| | Acc. | τους | λογους | τας | ἀρχας | τα | ἐργα |
| | Gen. | των | λογων | των | ἀρχων | των | ἐργων |
| | Dat. | τοις | λογοις | ταις | ἀρχαις | τοις | ἐργοις |

**Note:** The endings of the article are the same as the endings of the nouns of the corresponding gender, except in the masculine nominative singular and the neuter nominative and accusative singular.

### 3.3.5 Variant feminine forms

Most feminine nouns follow the pattern of ἀρχη outlined above. However, in some nouns in the singular only, there are slight variations on this pattern.

| | | (day) | (glory) | (beginning) |
|---|---|---|---|---|
| Sing. | Nom. | ἡμερα | δοξα | ἀρχη |
| | Acc. | ἡμεραν | δοξαν | ἀρχην |
| | Gen. | ἡμερας | δοξης | ἀρχης |
| | Dat. | ἡμερᾳ | δοξῃ | ἀρχῃ |
| Plural | Nom. | ἡμεραι | δοξαι | ἀρχαι |
| | Acc. | ἡμερας | δοξας | ἀρχας |
| | Gen. | ἡμερων | δοξων | ἀρχων |
| | Dat. | ἡμεραις | δοξαις | ἀρχαις |

Notes

- The pattern is that in the singular ἀρχη has an η, ἡμερα an α, and δοξα starts with an α but then changes to an η (they all have an α in the plural).
- The rule is that if the letter before the ending is
  - a vowel or ρ, it goes like ἡμερα
  - σ, ξ, ζ (i.e. any 's' sound), it goes like δοξα
  - anything else, it goes like ἀρχη

  (except note ζωη follows the pattern of ἀρχη)
- Despite these variations, the feminine of the definite article always follows the same pattern (given in 3.3.3). Thus, for example, ἡ δοξα, την ἡμεραν.

**PRACTICE 3.3.4 AND 3.3.5**

### Parse[3] the following

1. βιβλια
2. οἰκιων
3. κυριου
4. τῳ
5. ἀρτοις
6. την
7. ζωῃ
8. φωναις
9. Πετρον

[3] *Parse* means explain the form of the word. Thus for nouns you need to give the case and number, and for the definite article the case, number and gender. For example, λογον – accusative singular; της – feminine genitive singular.

### Do the article and noun in the following agree?

| | | | | | |
|---|---|---|---|---|---|
| 10. | ὁ Χριστον | 13. | το ἐργον | 16. | τους σημεια |
| 11. | τον λαον | 14. | τῳ εὐαγγελια | 17. | ὁ Παυλος |
| 12. | την ὡραν | 15. | την νομον | 18. | τας ἁμαρτιαν |

## 3.4 THE VOCATIVE

There is a fifth case in Greek, the vocative, though it is rare and simple.

The vocative is used when addressing people. In form it is almost always identical to the nominative, except in the singular of words that follow the λογος pattern. Sometimes a word in the vocative is preceded by ὠ – O!

| Vocatives: | Singular | | Plural | |
|---|---|---|---|---|
| | Most words | As nominative | All words | As nominative |
| | λογος | λογε | | |

Examples

- Μαρια, φιλεις τον κυριον; – Mary! Do you love the lord?

John 4.11: λεγει αὐτῳ· Κυριε, οὐτε ἀντλημα ἐχεις.
– She says to him, 'Sir, you have no bucket.'

Rom. 12.1: παρακαλω οὐν ὑμας, ἀδελφοι ... – Therefore, brothers, I urge you . . .

**Hint**

An ancient piece of Christian liturgy is the Kyrie Eleison (κυριε ἐλεησον), which means 'Lord, have mercy'. If you can remember this, it will remind you that the vocative of κυριος is κυριε. (Matt. 17.15: κυριε ἐλεησον μου [my] τον υἱον).

**PRACTICE 3.4**

### Which of these could be vocatives?

1. θεον    2. ἀδελφη    3. ἀδελφος    4. κυριοι    5. υἱε

## 3.5 Ἰησους

Jesus is unique, at least in grammatical form! The name Ἰησους – Jesus or Joshua – declines in a way similar to, but not quite the same as, λογος (the variations are the result of the strong ου sound dominating the normal endings).

| | | |
|---|---|---|
| Nom. | Ἰησους | |
| Acc. | Ἰησουν | (Vocative is Ἰησου) |
| Gen. | Ἰησου | |
| Dat. | Ἰησου | |

E.g. οἱ ὀχλοι ζητουσιν τον Ἰησουν. – The crowds are seeking Jesus.
ὁ δουλος του Ἰησου λεγει. – The slave of Jesus is speaking.

**Hint**

Because Ἰησους usually has the definite article, spotting which case it is in is easy – τῳ Ἰησου must be dative because τῳ is dative and the article and nouns have to agree in case (and number and gender).

## 3.6 αὐτος

**Pronoun?**
See it in English
Section 1.3
Page 242

αὐτος is an extremely important *pronoun* in Greek. It is the 3rd person pronoun. Therefore in the singular it means 'he', 'she' or 'it' depending on its gender, and 'they' in the plural. The English translation of each part of it is given below for ease.

| | | Masculine | | Feminine | | Neuter | |
|---|---|---|---|---|---|---|---|
| Sing. | Nom. | αὐτος | he | αὐτη | she | αὐτο | it |
| | Acc. | αὐτον | him | αὐτην | her | αὐτο | it |
| | Gen. | αὐτου | his[4] | αὐτης | her[4] | αὐτου | its[4] |
| | Dat. | αὐτῳ | to him | αὐτῃ | to her | αὐτῳ | to it |
| Plural | Nom. | αὐτοι | they | αὐται | they | αὐτα | they |
| | Acc. | αὐτους | them | αὐτας | them | αὐτα | them |
| | Gen. | αὐτων | their[4] | αὐτων | their[4] | αὐτων | their[4] |
| | Dat. | αὐτοις | to them | αὐταις | to them | αὐτοις | to them |

Notes

- The endings of αὐτος are identical to those of the nouns of the appropriate gender (λογος, ἀρχη or ἐργον), **except** in the neuter nominative and accusative singular where the ending is -ο not -ον, though this is the same variation as is found in the article (which is το, not τον).
- αὐτος does not normally occur in the nominative, because λυει itself means 'he, she or it unties': there is no need for a word for 'he, she or it'. It can be

[4] Or, 'of him', 'of her', 'of it', and 'of them'.

used in this way for emphasis, but that is discussed in Chapter 9. When translating English to Greek, you should not use αὐτος in the nominative unless you intend a particular emphasis on the subject.
- When the genitive of αὐτος is used to express possession (his, her, its, their) the definite article is used with the noun as well the genitive of αὐτος. Thus 'his word' is not λογος αὐτου but ὁ λογος αὐτου (think of 'his word' as 'the word of him').

Examples

- λαλουμεν αὐτῃ. – We are speaking to her.
- ὁ κυριος αὐτου φιλει αὐτον. – His master loves him.
- βλεπεις αὐτο; – Do you see it?

**PRACTICE 3.6**

## Translate

1. φιλω αὐτον.
2. τους λογους αὐτου διδασκει.
3. ἐχουσιν αὐτο.
4. ἀκουω την φωνην αὐτης.
5. ὁ Παυλος καλει αὐτους.
6. They see the slave.
7. She keeps his child.
8. Jesus loves their children.

## VOCAB FOR CHAPTER 3

(For the meaning of the asterisks marking certain words and exercises, see the explanation of the two pathways on page 7.)

Seventeen feminine nouns:

Seven with η endings like ἀρχη
*ἀγαπη (116) – love[5]
*ἀδελφη (26) – sister
ἀρχη (55) – beginning
*γη (250) – earth, soil, land
*ζωη (135) – life
*φωνη (139) – sound, voice
ψυχη (103) – soul, self

Eight with α endings like ἡμερα
*ἁμαρτια (173) – sin
*βασιλεια (162) – reign, kingship, kingdom
*ἐκκλησια (114) – assembly (later 'church')
*ἡμερα (389) – day

[5] Remember the use of the article with abstract nouns (Chapter 2, section 2.5). Thus ἡ ἀγαπη can mean 'love' (as a concept).

*καρδια (156) – heart
Μαρια (27) – Mary
Also the Hebrew form Μαριαμ – Mary[6]
*οἰκια (93) – house, household[7]
ὡρα (106) – hour, occasion

Plus, with the mixed endings
*δοξα (166) – splendour, glory
*θαλασσα (91) – sea, lake

Ten neuter nouns like ἐργον
βιβλιον (34) – book, scroll
*δαιμονιον (63) – demon
*ἐργον (169) – work, deed
*εὐαγγελιον (76) – good news, gospel
*ἱερον (71) – temple
*πλοιον (68) – boat
*προσωπον (76) – face
σαββατον (68) – Sabbath
*σημειον (77) – sign, miracle
*τεκνον (99) – child

One very important word:
*αὐτος αὐτη αὐτο (5597) – he, she, it, they

And three names
*Ἰησους (917) – Jesus
*Παυλος (158) – Paul
*Πετρος (156) – Peter

One more verb
*πιστευω + dat. (241) – I believe (in), trust, have faith in

## Word helps

<u>agape</u>, <u>arch</u>aic, <u>ge</u>ology/<u>ge</u>ography, <u>zoo</u>logy, <u>phone</u>tics/tele<u>phone</u>, <u>psych</u>ology, <u>basil</u>ica, <u>eccles</u>iastic/<u>eccles</u>iology, ep<u>hemera</u>l, <u>cardia</u>c, <u>hor</u>oscope, <u>dox</u>ology, <u>bible</u>/<u>bibli</u>ophile, <u>demon</u>, <u>erg</u>onomics, <u>evangelise</u>, <u>hiero</u>glyphics, <u>sem</u>aphore/<u>sem</u>antics.

## Exercises

### Section A

*1. ἡ ἀδελφη λεγει τῳ Ἰησου· Κυριε,[8] πιστευω.
*2. ποιω τα ἐργα του θεου.
*3. ὁ θεος φιλει τον υἱον και λαλει αὐτῳ.
*4. λαμβανομεν και τηρουμεν τα βιβλια αὐτου.
*5. ὁ ὀχλος λεγει τῳ Ἰησου· Δαιμονιον[8] ἐχεις.
*6. Πετρε, διδασκεις την βασιλειαν του θεου.

---

[6] Μαριαμ is indeclinable (see page 30, note 4).
[7] οἰκια and οἰκος (previous chapter) are used interchangeably.
[8] The capital letter marks the beginning of speech.

7. αἱ ἀδελφαι και οἱ ἀδελφοι τηρουσι τους νομους και το σαββατον.
8. το σαββατον τηρει ὁ υἱος του ἀνθρωπου;
*9. Their church is seeking the glory of God.
*10. Paul teaches the household of the Lord.
*11. Brothers and sisters, you (pl.) are receiving the love of God.
*12. The children are throwing soil.

## Section B

*1. λεγει αὐτοις τον λογον ὁ Ἰησους.
*2. τα τεκνα λυει το πλοιον.
3. ἡ Μαρια ἀκουει την φωνην της θαλασσης.
*4. βλεπομεν τα σημεια του εὐαγγελιου του κυριου.
*5. αὐτων ἐστιν [*is*] ἡ βασιλεια των οὐρανων.
6. ἡ ἀγαπη του θεου καλει τας ψυχας αὐτων.
7. ὁ θεος ποιει τας ἡμερας και τας ὡρας της ζωης.
*8. ζητειτε την δοξαν του προσωπου του θεου;
*9. Jesus receives the children.
*10. Paul, do you believe the angel of the Lord?
*11. We are making the bread of the temple.
*12. Do you see the sins of the heart?

## Section C

From now on after each chapter a piece of the New Testament will be given for you to translate. These passages will be printed exactly as they appear in the New Testament. Thus (a) the text will be accented (look back at page 17 to understand why accents are ignored in this book but are present in printed copies of the New Testament); (b) there may be words that you have not yet met – their meaning will be given in square brackets.

**Mark 1.1** Ἀρχὴ τοῦ εὐαγγελίου Ἰησοῦ Χριστοῦ υἱοῦ θεοῦ.

# Prepositions

## 4.1 BASIC PREPOSITIONS

Mark 12.41: ὁ ὀχλος βαλλει χαλκον <u>εἰς</u> το γαζοφυλακιον.
– the crowd throws money <u>into</u> the treasury.
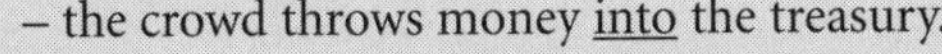
John 18.28: ἀγουσιν ... τον Ἰησουν <u>ἀπο</u> του Καϊαφα <u>εἰς</u> το πραιτωριον.
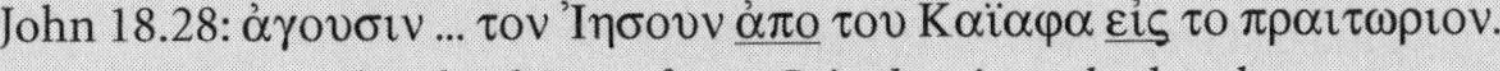
– they lead Jesus <u>from</u> Caiaphas <u>into</u> the headquarters.

A *preposition* is a word (or phrase) in front of a noun (or pronoun) to indicate how it fits into the rest of the sentence:

**Preposition?**
See it in English
Section 1.5
Page 243

e.g. (i) God sent the messenger *into* the village
(ii) The women came *out from* the city.

The key to prepositions in Greek is that they determine the case of the noun that comes after them (the word that they *govern*). Thus in (i) above, the case of 'village' (and therefore of 'the' which agrees with village) is determined by the 'into', and in (ii) the case of 'city' is determined by 'out from'.

KEY GRAMMAR
Prepositions determine the case of the noun they precede

For each preposition you must learn which case it 'goes with' (i.e. which case the noun it governs will be found in). Here are five of the most common prepositions.

| Preposition | Case |
|---|---|
| εἰς – to, into<br>προς – to, towards | Accusative |
| ἀπο – (away) from<br>ἐκ – (out) from | Genitive |
| ἐν – in | Dative |

## Notes

- εἰς signifies *motion to*, while the dative is used on its own to translate 'to' without motion (when it signifies personal interest or involvement). Thus, I go to the town (εἰς plus accusative) and I speak to God (just the dative).
- This chart illustrates the differences between εἰς and προς, and ἐκ and ἀπο.

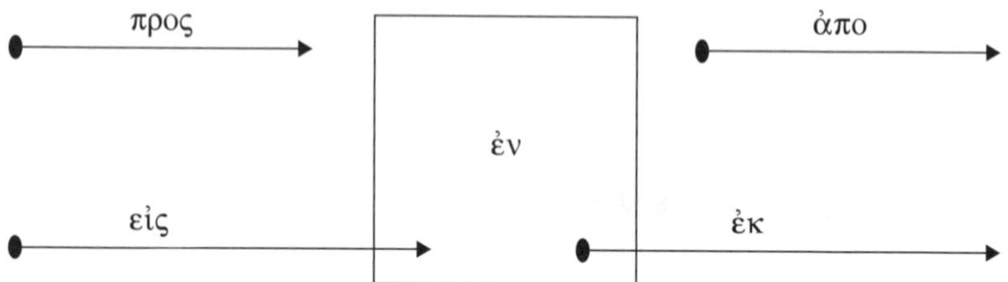


## Examples

- ὁ κυριος ἀγει τον δουλον εἰς την οἰκιαν.

1. ὁ κυριος = the master – *nom.* τον δουλον = the slave – *acc.* την οἰκιαν = the house – *acc.*
2. Master is *nom.* because it is the subject Slave is *acc.* – the object House is *acc.* because it is governed by εἰς which takes the *accusative*
3. Sentence = 'The master is leading the slave into the house.'

- ὁ κυριος ἀγει τον δουλον ἐκ της οἰκιας.

1. ὁ κυριος = the master – *nom.* τον δουλον = the slave – *acc.* της οἰκιας = the house – *gen.*
2. Master is *nom.* because it is the subject Slave is *acc.* – the object House is *gen.* because it is governed by ἐκ which takes the *genitive*
3. Sentence = 'The master leads the slave out of the house.'

**PRACTICE 4.1**

## Translate

1. ἐν τῳ κοσμῳ
2. εἰς τους οὐρανους
3. προς τα πλοια
4. ἐκ της οἰκιας
5. ἀπο του ἱερου
6. ἐν τῃ ἐκκλησιᾳ
7. from the heart
8. into the crowds
9. away from him

**Hint**

We have now met two different factors that determine which case a noun will be in – because of its function in the sentence (subject, object, possessor etc.), and because it is governed by a preposition.[1] Fortunately, these two never clash.

## 4.2 MORE PREPOSITIONS

Matt. 10.24: οὐκ ἐστιν ... δουλος ὑπερ τον κυριον αὐτου.
– A slave is not above the master of him (his master).
1 Cor. 15.3: Χριστος ἀπεθανεν ὑπερ των ἁμαρτιων ἡμων.
– Christ died on behalf of the sins of us (our sins).
The same preposition ὑπερ has a different meaning when followed by an accusative ('above the master') compared to a genitive ('on behalf of the sins').

### 4.2.1 The principle of prepositions with more than one case

The five prepositions we have already met (εἰς, προς, ἐκ, ἀπο and ἐν) can only be used with a single case.[2] Thus each of these will always be followed by a noun in that particular case, and each always conveys the same basic meaning. However, many Greek prepositions can be used with two or even three different cases, and they convey a different meaning depending on which case they are governing. Thus μετα + *acc.* has a different meaning from μετα + *gen.*

KEY GRAMMAR

The **same preposition** has a **different meaning** when it is used with a **different case**

The case that a preposition governs when conveying a particular meaning needs to be learnt (i.e. it is no good learning that μετα means 'with' – it doesn't; μετα + *acc.* means 'after' and μετα + *gen.* means 'with').[3]

---

[1] At a deeper level it can be argued that the case of a noun after a preposition is determined by the meaning conveyed by the different cases, not by the preposition. However, in practice it is easier to think of the prepositions governing certain cases.

[2] In fact on rare occasion προς can be used with the genitive or dative.

[3] There are some general principles underlying the connection between the meaning of a preposition and the case used with it. However, while helpful to understand, these principles cannot be relied upon – the preposition and its case still needs to be learnt.

- The *accusative* is connected with ideas of *extension* (whether in time or space). Thus 'movement to' takes the *acc.* (as εἰς and προς do).
- The *genitive* has two senses. (i) The idea of *separation* (whether in time or space). Thus 'movement from' takes the *gen.* (as ἀπο and ἐκ do). (ii) The idea of *kind* (i.e. describing the nature of something, often corresponding to the English 'of').
- The *dative* is connected to ideas of *location* (whether in time or space). Thus ἐν takes the *dat.*

### 4.2.2 Prepositions with three cases

| | |
|---|---|
| παρα + | |
| *accusative* | motion *beside* – περιπατει παρα την θαλασσαν – she walks beside the sea |
| *genitive* | *from beside* (a person) – ἀνθρωπος παρα του θεου – a man from God |
| *dative* | location *beside* – διδασκει παρα τῃ θαλασσῃ – he teaches besides the sea |
| ἐπι + | |
| *accusative* | *onto* – βαλλει τον ἀρτον ἐπι το βιβλιον – she throws the bread onto the book |
| *genitive*[4] | location *on* – ἐπι της γης – on the land/earth<br>*in the time of* – περιπατει ἐπι του Ἰησου – he lives in the time of Jesus |
| *dative*[4] | location *on/in* – ἐπι τοις οὐρανοις – in the heavens<br>*on the basis of* – οὐ περιπατει ἐπι ἀρτῳ – she does not live by bread |

### 4.2.3 Prepositions with two cases[5]

| | |
|---|---|
| δια + | |
| *accusative* | because of – δια τον ὀχλον – because of the crowd |
| *genitive* | through – δια του ἀγγελου – through the messenger |
| κατα + | |
| *accusative* | according to – κατα νομον – according to law |
| *genitive* | against – κατα του Ἰησου – against Jesus |
| μετα + | |
| *accusative* | after – μετα το σαββατον – after the Sabbath |
| *genitive* | with – μετα αὐτου – with him (written μετ᾽ αὐτου, see section 4.2.5) |

[4] In practice there is often little difference between the meaning of ἐπι when it occurs with the genitive and with the dative.

[5] Notice that for each of these prepositions (except for ὑπο) the English meaning with the accusative comes earlier in the alphabet than the English meaning when it comes with the genitive. This *might* help you distinguish the meanings!

| περι + | |
|---|---|
| *accusative* | approximately, around – περι τον Παυλον – around Paul |
| *genitive* | concerning, about – περι ἁμαρτιας – concerning sin |
| ὑπερ + | |
| *accusative* | above – ὑπερ την γην – above the earth |
| *genitive* | on behalf of – ὑπερ τεκνου – on behalf of a child |
| ὑπο + | |
| *accusative* | under – ὑπο νομον – under law |
| *genitive* | by – ὑπο του Πετρου – by Peter (as in 'it was done by Peter') |

Note

- The English words 'by' and 'with' are sometimes represented in Greek by a preposition (ὑπο and μετα), sometimes just by the use of the dative. This is explained further in Chapter 4, section 4.3.

### 4.2.4 Prepositions with one case

There are five more prepositions that occur with a single case to add to those from section 4.1 to give ten.

| | | |
|---|---|---|
| εἰς | + *accusative* | to, into |
| προς | | to, towards |
| ἀπο | + *genitive* | (away) from |
| ἐκ | | (out) from |
| ἐνωπιον | | before (place) – ἐνωπιον του θεου – before God |
| ἐξω | | outside – ἐξω της οἰκιας – outside the house |
| ἑως | | until – ἑως του σαββατου – until the Sabbath |
| προ | | before (time) – προ σαββατου – before Sabbath |
| ἐν | + *dative* | in |
| συν | | with – συν αὐτοις – with them |

**Note:** Naturally there is not a perfect overlap between the range of meanings of a Greek preposition and those of any one English preposition. The meanings given above are the basic meanings, which will point you in the right direction when translating. However, as you become more practised at reading Greek, you will get used to being more flexible. For example, εἰς means 'into' but in Mark 1.4 John proclaims a baptism 'εἰς ἀφεσιν *(forgiveness)* ἁμαρτιων'. 'Baptism into forgiveness of sins' does not sound quite right in English, although it makes the meaning clear. We might say 'baptism resulting in forgiveness of sins', 'aiming at forgiveness of sins' or 'for forgiveness of sins'.

### 4.2.5 Elision in prepositions

Many prepositions that end in a vowel drop the vowel when the following word begins with a vowel (this is called *elision*). ἐκ also has its own peculiarities. The rules are as follows.

In front of a word beginning with a vowel:

| | |
|---|---|
| ἀπο, δια, ἐπι, κατα, μετα, παρα, ὑπο | drop their final vowel[6] |
| ἐξω, περι and προ | remain unchanged |
| ἐκ | becomes ἐξ |

Examples

- δι᾽ αὐτου – through him.
- περι ἁμαρτιας – concerning sin.
- ἐξ οἰκιας – from a house.

**PRACTICE 4.2**

#### Translate

1. μετ᾽ αὐτων
2. δια τον νομον
3. κατα του θεου
4. ὑπερ του κυριου
5. παρα του θεου
6. δια του Χριστου
7. about love
8. out of the sea
9. under the earth

**HALF-WAY PRACTICE**

1. δια τον λογον του κυριου πιστευω.
2. ὁ Ἰησους ἀγει τους ἀδελφους προς τα πλοια.
3. λαλουσιν αὐτῳ περι του ἱερου.
4. λεγει ὁ κυριος της οἰκιας ὑπερ του τεκνου.
5. ὁ υἱος λαμβανει τον ἀρτον μετ᾽ αὐτου.
6. ὁ θεος φιλει τα ἐργα κατα τον νομον.

---

[6] In addition, if the vowel has a rough breathing, a final τ will become a θ and a π will become a φ. Thus: 'under sin' = ὑφ᾽ ἁμαρτιαν (ὑπο ἁμαρτιαν → ὑπ᾽ ἁμαρτιαν → ὑφ᾽ ἁμαρτιαν). Similarly ἀπο → ἀφ᾽, ἐπι → ἐφ᾽, κατα → καθ᾽, μετα → μεθ᾽.

7. ὁ Παυλος λεγει τῳ λαῳ κατα του Χριστου του θεου.
8. ἀγουσιν τα τεκνα εἰς τον οἰκον.
9. I see it in her heart.
10. Jesus is teaching the crowd outside the temple.
11. God loves the peoples under heaven.
12. God speaks the law through angels.

## 4.3 INSTRUMENTS AND AGENTS

In English we use the words 'with' or 'by' to indicate the means by which something happens, or the instrument or agent used:

I was helped by her. I was walking with a stick. I was hit by a stone.

However, we also use the word 'with' in a different sense, not meaning 'by means of' but rather 'along with':

I went with him.

Greek has a clear way of expressing instruments and agents that removes some of the ambiguity of English words such as 'with' and 'by'.

### Instrument

An instrument is an inanimate object by means of which the action of the verb happens. In Greek this is normally expressed by the instrument just occurring in the dative, without a preposition.

- God makes the heavens with a word – ὁ θεος ποιει τους οὐρανους λογῳ.

However, sometimes an instrument is expressed by the preposition ἐν + dat.[7]

### Agent

An agent is a living being by means of which the action of the verb happens. In Greek this is expressed by the preposition ὑπο + gen.

- The gospel was proclaimed by Peter – . . . ὑπο του Πετρου.[8]

---

[7] This use of ἐν + dat. for instrument is unusual in the normal Greek of the period, but relatively common in the New Testament because of the influence of Hebrew and Aramaic in which the preposition ב is used to express both 'in' and 'by means of'.

[8] Agents normally only occur in 'Passive' sentences, which are quite rare in Greek (left until Chapter 15), but it makes sense to learn ὑπο now alongside the other prepositions.

### Along with

'With' meaning 'along with' rather than 'by means of' is expressed in Greek by the preposition μετα + gen (or more rarely συν + dat.).

- I depart with Peter – ὑπαγω μετα του Πετρου.

Example

ὁ θεος λεγει μετα τεκνων και ποιει τον κοσμον λογῳ.
God speaks with children and makes the world with a word.

**PRACTICE 4.3**

### Which of the following would use an instrumental dative in Greek?

1. I went with him.
2. I was hit by a stone.
3. I was helped by her.
4. I was walking with a stick.

## 4.4 COMPOUND VERBS

In Greek many words are constructed by combining a basic word with a preposition. For example, ἐκ means 'out of' and βαλλω means 'I throw', so ἐκβαλλω means 'I throw out'. Later on (Chapter 6) identifying compound verbs becomes important. For now, though, thinking about compound verbs helps build up your vocabulary. You will find 11 compound verbs in this chapter's vocabulary.

Notes

- In English you cannot deduce the meaning of 'understand' by thinking of its two constituent parts 'under' and 'stand'. Similarly in Greek you cannot always deduce the meaning of a word from its parts.
  - In some verbs, the force of both the verb and the preposition is preserved e.g. ἐκβαλλω – I throw out
  - In some verbs, the preposition intensifies or completes the meaning, though without the force of the preposition being clearly preserved. e.g. ἀπολυω – I release (λυω itself means 'I untie')
  - In some verbs, the preposition seems to give the verb a new meaning, which is not easily connected to the force of the preposition. e.g. ἀναγινωσκω – I read (γινωσκω itself means 'I know' and ἀνα means 'upwards' or 'again').

- When forming compounds, the rules for the *elision* of prepositions (section 4.2.5) are particularly important. Thus ἀπο + ἀγω = ἀπαγω (I lead away).
- Even though a compound verb may 'contain' a preposition, the correct preposition will still be found in the sentence used in the normal way e.g. ἐκβαλλω αὐτον ἐκ της οἰκιας.

## 4.5 QUESTIONS

Asking questions is simple in Greek:[9]

*Either* **1. Use a question word**

There are question words in Greek such as πως; – how? or που; – where?

e.g. πως βλεπεις τον θεον; – How do you see God?

*Or* **2. Rely on tone of voice**

Of course, you can't see the tone of voice when it is written down! Therefore all that marks out the question is the question mark:

e.g. βλεπεις τον θεον. – You see God.
βλεπεις τον θεον; – Do you see God?

## 4.6 NEGATIVES

A verb in the *Indicative* (which means all the verbs we have met so far) is made negative by the addition of the word οὐ (= 'not').

Before a vowel with a *smooth* breathing this becomes οὐκ.
Before a vowel with a *rough* breathing this becomes οὐχ.

Examples

- οὐ βλεπω. – I do not see.
- οὐκ ἀκουουσιν. – They do not hear.
- οὐχ εὑρισκει το τεκνον. – She does not find the child.

[9] Remember (page 18) the question mark in Greek is ; Like all punctuation, question marks are not actually part of the text but have been added by editors.

PRACTICE 4.5 and 4.6

## Translate

1. ὁ θεος ἀκουει;
2. ὁ θεος οὐκ ἀκουει.
3. πως ὁ θεος λεγει;
4. οὐ πιστευω αὐτῳ.
5. που ἀγεις τον ὀχλον;
6. τον νομον τηρειτε;

## VOCAB FOR CHAPTER 4

Eighteen common prepositions – remember they have different meanings with different cases (a fuller list of prepositions is given in the reference section, page 271).

*ἀπο (646) + gen. – (away) from
*δια (667) + acc. – because of
+ gen. – through
*εἰς (1767) + acc. – into
*ἐκ (914) + gen. – (out of) from
*ἐν (2752) + dat. – in[10]
ἐνωπιον (94) + gen. – in front of, in the presence of
ἐξω (63) + gen. – outside
*ἐπι (890) + acc. – onto
+ gen. – on, in the time of
+ dat. – on, in, on the basis of
ἑως (146) + gen. – until
*κατα (473) + acc. – according to
+ gen. – against
*μετα (469) + acc. after
+ gen. with
*παρα (194) + acc. – alongside
+ gen. – from beside
+ dat. – beside
*περι (333) + acc. – around, approximately
+ gen. – concerning, about
προ (47) + gen. – before
*προς (700) + acc. – to, towards
συν (128) + dat. – together with
*ὑπερ (150) + acc. – above
+ gen. – on behalf of
*ὑπο (220) + acc. – under
+ gen. – by, at the hands of

And eleven compound verbs
ἀναβλεπω (25) – I look up, receive sight[11]
*ἀπολυω (66) – I set free, divorce, dismiss
*ἐκβαλλω (81) – I drive out, cast out, throw out
ἐπικαλεω (30) – I call upon, name
κατοικεω (44) – I dwell, inhabit, live
*παρακαλεω (109) – I exhort, request, comfort, encourage
παραλαμβανω (49) – I take, receive
*περιπατεω (95) – I walk about, live
*προσκυνεω (60) + dat. – I worship
*συναγω (59) – I gather, bring together
*ὑπαγω (79) – I depart

[10] ἐν + dat. can also more rarely mean 'by' or 'with'; see note 7 page 49.
[11] ἀνα is a rare preposition meaning 'upwards' or 'again'.

Plus, two question words and the negative

*πως (103) – how?

που (48) – where?

*οὐ, οὐκ, οὐχ (1606) – not

## Word helps

apostasy, diameter, eisegesis, exodus/exit/exegesis, epitaph, catacomb/cataclysm, metamorphosis/metaphysics, parallel/paramedic, perimeter, prologue, sympathy/symphony/synthesis, hyperactive/hyperbole, hypodermic, paraclete, peripatetic, synagogue.

## Exercises[12]

### Section A

*1. δοξαν παρα ἀνθρωπων οὐ λαμβανω.
*2. πιστευεις εἰς τον υἱον του ἀνθρωπου;
3. ὁ κυριος λεγει αὐτοις· Που αὐτους ἀγετε;
*4. ὁ Πετρος διδασκει αὐτους περι της βασιλειας παρα τοις πλοιοις.
5. ἀναβλεπομεν εἰς τον οὐρανον ἐνωπιον του ἱερου.
*6. ὁ Ἰησους ἐκβαλλει τα δαιμονια ἐκ του ἀνθρωπου λογῳ.
*7. περιπατω ὑπο ἁμαρτιαν και κατα του νομου του θεου.
*8. ὁ Πετρος συναγει την ἐκκλησιαν εἰς τον οἰκον της ἀδελφης του Ἰακωβ.
*9. We are departing towards the sea.
*10. You (pl.) are exhorting the brothers in the Lord.
11. Do you (s.) keep the Sabbath because of the law?
*12. The people in the boat are worshipping the Lord.

### Section B

*1. ἐν τῃ ἡμερᾳ του κυριου βλεπομεν τον θεον προσωπον προς προσωπον.
*2. κυριε, οὐ πιστευω εἰς αὐτον.
3. προσκυνουμεν τῳ θεῳ ἐν τῳ ἱερῳ.
4. δια την ὡραν ὁ κυριος ἀπολυει τον ὀχλον.
*5. περιπατειτε ἐν τῃ ἀγαπῃ του θεου κατα τον λογον αὐτου;

---

12 From now on increasing numbers of the sentences in the exercises will be based on sentences from the New Testament. This means that occasionally they will not quite follow the 'rules' you have learnt – Greek is a language, not a mathematical code. So, for example, in A1 you would expect to see παρ᾽ ἀνθρωπων not παρα ἀνθρωπων, the final vowel of παρα eliding (as explained in section 4.2.5). However, while normally you would find παρ᾽ this sentence is taken directly from John 5.41, where παρα is found. See page 5 for further discussion of the rationale behind the sentences, and what difference it makes.

6. ὁ ἀγγελος λυει τον Πετρον και παραλαμβανει αὐτον προς τους ἀδελφους.
7. μετα την ἀρχην του σαββατου ὁ ῥαββι και οἱ υἱοι αὐτου οὐ ποιουσιν ἐργον.
8. που ὁ κυριος διδασκει περι του εὐαγγελιου της βασιλειας του θεου;
9. Mary gathers the sisters and they seek the Lord with the brothers.
*10. The child dwells in the house of the Lord, and does not depart from it.
*11. The voice of God is [ἐστιν] above the heavens and in their hearts.
*12. The people do works on behalf of the children because of the love of Christ.

## Section C[13]

**John 1.1-4** Ἐν ἀρχῇ ἦν [*was*] ὁ λόγος, καὶ ὁ λόγος ἦν πρὸς[14] τὸν θεόν, καὶ θεὸς ἦν ὁ λόγος.[15] οὗτος [*this one*] ἦν ἐν ἀρχῇ πρὸς[14] τὸν θεόν. . . . ἐν αὐτῷ ζωὴ ἦν, καὶ ἡ ζωὴ ἦν τὸ φῶς [*light*] τῶν ἀνθρώπων.

---

[13] Remember, the biblical text in section C is given exactly as it appears in printed texts of the New Testament. This means that the words have accents on them, and there will be some words that you have not met yet whose meaning is given in brackets. See the explanation on page 6.

[14] We have learnt προς + acc. means 'to' or 'towards'. It is also sometimes used metaphorically in situations when there is a direction or orientation, but no actual movement ('with a view to', 'aiming at'). What do you think it means here?

[15] λογος is the subject here, not θεος. The reason for this is explained in Chapter 5, section 5.8.

# Adjectives

## 5.1 FORMATION OF ADJECTIVES

Rev. 21.1-2: εἶδον οὐρανον καινον και γην καινην. ὁ ... πρωτος οὐρανος και ἡ πρωτη γη ἀπηλθαν – I saw a new heaven and a new earth. The first heaven and the first earth departed.

καινος (new) and πρωτος (first) are adjectives. They add further description to a noun. In Greek they have to *agree* with the noun they are describing. Thus οὐρανον καινον but γην καινην. Both οὐρανον and γην are accusative singular, but οὐρανος is masculine and γη feminine.

καινος does not have a gender itself; instead it uses a masculine form when describing a masculine noun, and a feminine form when describing a feminine noun. Similarly πρωτος and πρωτη are both nominative singular, but one is 'in the masculine' (agreeing with οὐρανος) and the other 'in the feminine' (agreeing with γη).

Most adjectives *decline* like ἀγαθος (good):

| | | Masculine | Feminine | Neuter |
|---|---|---|---|---|
| Sing. | Nom. | ἀγαθος | ἀγαθη | ἀγαθον |
| | Acc. | ἀγαθον | ἀγαθην | ἀγαθον |
| | Gen. | ἀγαθου | ἀγαθης | ἀγαθου |
| | Dat. | ἀγαθῳ | ἀγαθῃ | ἀγαθῳ |
| Plural | Nom. | ἀγαθοι | ἀγαθαι | ἀγαθα |
| | Acc. | ἀγαθους | ἀγαθας | ἀγαθα |
| | Gen. | ἀγαθων | ἀγαθων | ἀγαθων |
| | Dat. | ἀγαθοις | ἀγαθαις | ἀγαθοις |

Notes

- We have already learnt these endings. They are the same as those for nouns of the corresponding gender (and hence similar to αὐτος and the article).

- In the *feminine singular* adjectives whose stems end in a vowel or a ρ have endings in α rather than η. (This is the same variation in the endings as we saw between ἡμερα and ἀρχη). Thus the feminine singular of ἁγιος (holy) is ἁγια, ἁγιαν, ἁγιας, ἁγιᾳ. (No adjectives go like δοξα.)

**Adjective?**
See it in English
Section 1.4
Page 242

PRACTICE 5.1

### Parse

| | | | |
|---|---|---|---|
| 1. ἁγιοι | 3. νεκρον | 5. πισταις | 7. ἰδια |
| 2. μονων | 4. τυφλη | 6. δικαιαν | 8. πονηροις |

## 5.2 USE OF ADJECTIVES (1) – ATTRIBUTIVE

The most common use of an adjective is called the *attributive* use. This is where the adjective defines more precisely an *attribute* of one of the nouns or pronouns in a sentence.

KEY GRAMMAR
Adjectives must agree with the noun they qualify in gender, case and number

Example

- They see the beautiful land.

Here we have a basic sentence 'they see the land', but then the 'land' has been further qualified or described by the addition of the adjective 'beautiful'. This is the normal (*attributive*) use of the adjective.

Furthermore, because 'beautiful' is qualifying 'land', it will have to agree with 'land' in gender, case and number.

### Word order

When a noun is qualified by both the article and an (attributive) adjective, there are two possible word orders in Greek. The first is the same as in English.

| | | |
|---|---|---|
| They see the beautiful land. | *either* | βλεπουσιν την καλην γην. |
| | *or* | βλεπουσιν την γην την καλην. |

Thus, if the adjective comes after the noun, the article is repeated.

When there is no definite article, things are simpler and the adjective can come either before or after the noun it qualifies:

| They see a new earth. | *either* | βλεπουσιν καινην γην. |
|---|---|---|
| | *or* | βλεπουσιν γην καινην. |

PRACTICE 5.2

**Translate**

1. τηρουμεν τον ἀγαθον νομον.
2. ὁ ἀδελφος ὁ ἁγιος ἀκουει.
3. τυφλον δουλον ἐχει.
4. ἁγιος λαος φιλει τον θεον.
5. ὁ κυριος οὐκ ἐχει καλον υἱον.
6. ἐκβαλλει τα δαιμονια τα πονηρα.
7. καλειτε τας ἀγαθας ἀδελφας.
8. I seek a wicked life.
9. She believes her own heart.
10. The crowd seeks the only god.

## 5.3 εἰμι – I AM

As in most languages, the verb 'to be' has its own distinctive pattern:

| | | |
|---|---|---|
| 1st sing. | I am | εἰμι |
| 2nd sing. | You are | εἶ |
| 3rd sing. | He, she or it is | ἐστι(ν) |
| 1st plural | We are | ἐσμεν |
| 2nd plural | You are | ἐστε |
| 3rd plural | They are | εἰσι(ν) |

- Note the first and second plural have similarities with λυω
  ἐσ-μεν compared to λυ-ο-μεν
  ἐσ-τε compared to λυ-ε-τε

**Hint**

Normally, accents do not convey any useful information. However, there are two different words written as εἰ which can be distinguished by their accents:

εἶ – with the circumflex – you are (2nd singular of εἰμι)
εἰ – no accent – if
Thus: Matt. 4.3: εἰ υἱος εἶ του θεου → If you are the son of God.

Noticing this may help you.

PRACTICE 5.3

## Translate

1. ἐστε 2. εἰμι 3. εἰσιν 4. εἶ 5. ἐστιν

## 5.4 USE OF ADJECTIVES (2) – PREDICATIVE

Rom. 7.12: ὁ νομος [ἐστιν] ἁγιος – 'The law is holy.'

This sentence is in the form 'x (noun) is y (adjective).' Many sentences using the verb 'to be' are similar. The adjective is still describing the noun (ask 'what is holy?' and the answer is 'the law') but it is being used differently from the way it is used in a sentence such as ζητω ἁγιον νομον – I seek a holy law.

In these sentences it is important to understand that the adjective is **not** an object, but rather is an adjective qualifying the noun: 'holy' is telling us something further about 'the law'. Thus it needs to agree with the noun in gender, case and number. However, such use of an adjective is different from the attributive use, because the adjective is not merely qualifying one of the nouns in the sentence – the whole point of the sentence is to make this description. The adjective itself completes the sentence (hence the adjective is called a *complement*). This use of the adjective is called the *predicative* use.

**Complement?**
See it in English
Section 4
Page 245

Hint

To tell the difference between the attributive and predicative use, try deleting the adjective from the sentence. If it still makes sense, the adjective was attributive. If it doesn't, it was predicative.

### Word order

Predicative adjectives follow a different word order from the attributive. Again, there are two options, one being the same as in English.[1]

KEY GRAMMAR
Predicative adjectives are never immediately preceded by the article.

The law is holy. *either* ὁ νομος ἐστιν ἁγιος.
*or* ἁγιος ἐστιν ὁ νομος.

[1] It is quite unusual to have a predicative use when there is no definite article, but when this does happen the options are predictably νομος ἐστιν ἁγιος or ἁγιος ἐστιν νομος.

### Omission of the verb 'to be'

However, Rom. 7.12 does not in fact say ὁ νομος ἐστιν ἁγιος but ὁ νομος ἁγιος. This is because the Greeks often let the verb 'to be' drop out of sentences. In these cases you need to put it back in (*supply* it). It is normally easy to spot when this is necessary: (a) if the sentence does not appear to have a verb in it, one must have dropped out; (b) the adjective will be in the *predicative* position.

Example

- Rom. 7.12: ὁ νομος ἁγιος και ἡ ἐντολη ἁγια και δικαια και ἀγαθη.
  = The law (is) holy and the commandment (is) holy and just and good.

---

**PRACTICE 5.4**

### Translate

1. ἐστε ἀγαθοι;
2. ἁγιος ἐστιν ὁ νομος του θεου.
3. Ἰουδαια τα τεκνα.
4. ἡ τυφλη ἀδελφη ἐστιν νεκρα;
5. αἰωνια τα Ἱεροσολυμα τα ἁγια;
6. Is the gospel good or evil?
7. The only God is in heaven.
8. We are in the synagogue.

---

**HALF-WAY PRACTICE**

1. ὁ Πετρος φιλει το νεκρον τεκνον.
2. ὁ υἱος ὁ τυφλος βλεπει τον Χριστον.
3. ἁγιον καλουσιν τον κυριον.
4. βαλλει αὐτο εἰς την καλην γην.
5. ἑτερῳ εὐαγγελιῳ οὐ πιστευομεν.
6. ὁ δουλος του θεου μακαριος.
7. ἁγια ἡ βασιλεια του Ἰησου;
8. ὁ ἀγαθος ἀδελφος οὐκ ἐστιν μονος.
9. A wicked crowd seeks signs.
10. Is God dead?
11. We are departing to our own houses.
12. The Jewish sister is good.

---

## 5.5 USE OF ADJECTIVES (3) – AS NOUNS

Greek has a way of making nouns from adjectives, which is very common. The adjective is just put with the article. The case of the adjective is then determined by its function in the sentence (subject, object etc.). Its gender reveals whether it is a person or a man (masc.), a woman (fem.) or a thing (neuter). Note that Greek uses the masculine as the default when referring to people in general. This is called the *substantive* use of an adjective.

### Examples

- ὁ ἀγαθος - the good person/man
- ἡ καλη – the beautiful woman
- τα ἁγια - the holy things
- οἱ νεκροι – the dead (ones)

Matt. 5.8: μακαριοι οἱ καθαροι ... – blessed are the pure ...

**PRACTICE 5.5**

### Translate

1. ὁ θεος φιλει τους Ἰουδαιους.
2. οἱ ἀγαθοι διδασκουσιν.
3. ὁ Παυλος λεγει τοις ἁγιοις.
4. ὁ τυφλος ὑπαγει.

## 5.6 πολυς AND μεγας

These two important adjectives, πολυς meaning 'much/many' and μεγας meaning 'large/great', decline in the same way as ἀγαθος but with a slight irregularity.

| | *Masc.* | *Fem.* | *Neuter* | *Masc.* | *Fem.* | *Neuter* |
|---|---|---|---|---|---|---|
| Singular | | | | | | |
| Nom. | πολυς | πολλη | πολυ | μεγας | μεγαλη | μεγα |
| Acc. | πολυν | πολλην | πολυ | μεγαν | μεγαλην | μεγα |
| Gen. | πολλου | πολλης | πολλου | μεγαλου | μεγαλης | μεγαλου |
| Dat. | πολλῳ | πολλῃ | πολλῳ | μεγαλῳ | μεγαλῃ | μεγαλῳ |
| Plural | | | | | | |
| Nom. | πολλοι | πολλαι | πολλα | μεγαλοι | μεγαλαι | μεγαλα |
| Acc. | πολλους | πολλας | πολλα | μεγαλους | μεγαλας | μεγαλα |
| Gen. | πολλων | πολλων | πολλων | μεγαλων | μεγαλων | μεγαλων |
| Dat. | πολλοις | πολλαις | πολλοις | μεγαλοις | μεγαλαις | μεγαλοις |

If you look closely at this you will see that:

- πολυς is πολλος with a shortened *nom.* and *acc., masc.* and *neuter* sing.
- μεγας is μεγαλος with a shortened *nom.* and *acc., masc.* and *neuter* sing.

Examples

(Mark 1.34, Col. 4.13, and Mark 1. 26 slightly simplified.)

- δαιμονια πολλα ἐκβαλλει = He throws out many demons.
- ἐχει πολυν πονον [toil] ὑπερ των ἐν Λαοδικειᾳ = He has much labour on behalf of those in Laodiceia (i.e. 'he has worked very hard ...').
- λεγει φωνῃ μεγαλῃ = He says in loud (great) voice.

**PRACTICE 5.6**

**Which part of πολυς would agree with the following?**

1. ἁμαρτιαι 2. σημεια 3. βιβλιων 4. δοξαν 5. σαββατοις

**Which part of μεγας would agree with the following?**

6. ὀχλον 7. ἐργων 8. βασιλειαν 9. καρδιᾳ 10. ἱερον

## 5.7 WORD ORDER IN GREEK SENTENCES

### In general

As we have already seen, because the case of a noun communicates its function in a sentence and agreement shows which adjectives go with which nouns, word order can be more flexible in Greek than it is in English.

Thus, the basic meaning of these two sentences is the same:

(i) ὁ θεος διδασκει τους Ἰουδαιους.
(ii) τους Ἰουδαιους ὁ θεος διδασκει.

However, the word order can communicate emphasis. The word that comes first carries more stress – thus (i) seems to be emphasising that it is God who is teaching the Jews, while (ii) emphasises that it is the Jews whom God is teaching. In longer sentences, the final word also carries quite a lot of stress.

### 'Sandwich' constructions

We have now learnt three different ways of qualifying a noun (i.e. adding further description to it):

| | | | |
|---|---|---|---|
| Adjectives: | *Either* | (i) | βλεπω το ἱερον το καλον. |
| | *Or* | (ii) | βλεπω το καλον ἱερον. |
| Genitives: | βλεπω το ἱερον του κυριου. | | |
| Prepositions: | βλεπω το ἱερον ἐν τῃ γῃ. | | |

If you look carefully you will see that the word order in the examples above using genitives and prepositions is very similar to example (i) using adjectives – the descriptive word or phrase comes after the noun.[2]

There is an alternative word order for genitives and prepositions which is similar to order (ii) for adjectives. This is called the 'sandwich' construction because the του κυριου or the ἐν τῃ γῃ is put between the το and the ἱερον, just as the καλον was between the το and the ἱερον.

βλεπω το του κυριου ἱερον.
βλεπω το ἐν τῃ γῃ ἱερον.

The occurrence of two articles on the run (το του) or the article followed by a preposition (το ἐν) can be confusing initially. However, the advantage of this construction is that it is clear which noun the descriptive phrase is going with.

## 5.8 SPECIAL USES OF εἰμι

### Preparatory use

While ἐστι(ν) and εἰσι(ν) normally mean 'he, she or it is' and 'they are', if they are put first in the sentence they mean 'there is' or 'there are':

e.g. ὁ τυφλος ἐστιν ἐν τῃ συναγωγῃ. – The blind man is in the synagogue.
ἐστιν τυφλος ἐν τῃ συναγωγῃ. – There is a blind man in the synagogue.

### Nouns as complements

We met earlier the idea of an adjective as a *complement*, noting that the adjective is not an object, but agrees with the noun it is describing and will therefore be in the nominative. Thus 'the son is good' is:

ὁ υἱος ἐστιν ἀγαθος *or* ἀγαθος ἐστιν ὁ υἱος

Unsurprisingly, the complement can be a noun, instead of an adjective, e.g. 'the son is the lord'

ὁ υἱος ἐστιν ὁ κυριος

Note that ὁ κυριος here is in the nominative. It is not an object, but a complement which is further describing ὁ υἱος and therefore in the same case as it.

---

[2] Indeed, sometimes the article is repeated before the genitive or preposition, just as it is before the καλον, e.g. το ἱερον το του κυριου and το ἱερον το ἐν τῃ γῃ.

In this situation it is easy to imagine that ἐστιν simply functions as an 'equals sign': ὁ υἱος = ὁ κυριος. However, it is a little more complicated because 'the king is the judge' is not quite the same as 'the judge is the king'.

Thus it is necessary to distinguish between the subject and any noun that is a complement, although both will be in the nominative. Greek does this in the following way:

*Either* the subject comes before the complement
*or* the article is dropped from the complement.

E.g. The son is the lord is *either* ὁ υἱος ἐστιν ὁ κυριος *or* κυριος ἐστιν ὁ υἱος

## Examples (subjects underlined)

KEY GRAMMAR

If the complement precedes the subject it cannot have the definite article

Mark 2.28: κυριος ἐστιν <u>ὁ υἱος</u> του ἀνθρωπου ... – <u>the son</u> of man is lord . . .
John 1.1: θεος ἠν (=was) <u>ὁ λογος</u> – <u>the word</u> was (the) god.[3]

PRACTICE 5.7 and 5.8

## Translate

1. ἐστιν θεος ἐν οὐρανῳ;
2. σημειον το του Ἀβρααμ τεκνον.
3. εἰσιν πολλοι ἁγιοι Ἰουδαιοι.
4. ὁ του Ἰησου λογος εὐαγγελιον.

## VOCAB FOR CHAPTER 5

Eighteen standard adjectives
*ἀγαθος (102) – good
ἀγαπητος (61) – beloved
*ἁγιος (233) – holy
δικαιος (79) – upright, just
ἑκαστος (82) – each
*ἑτερος (98) – another, different
*ἰδιος (114) – one's own
*Ἰουδαιος (195) – Jewish, a Jew
κακος (50) – bad
*καλος (100) – beautiful, good
καινος (42) – new
*μακαριος (50) – blessed, happy
*μονος (114) – only, alone
*νεκρος (128) – dead
*ὁσος (110) – as/how great, as/how much
πιστος (67) – faithful, believing
*πονηρος (78) – evil, wicked
*τυφλος (50) – blind

[3] Because θεος is a complement preceding the subject it can't have the article (the rule we have just learnt), thus grammatically we can't tell if the author meant that the word was θεος or ὁ θεος, but we do know the sentence means 'the word was (the) god', not 'god was the word'.

Two slightly irregular adjectives
*μεγας μεγαλη μεγα (243) – large, great
*πολυς πολλη πολυ (416) – much, many

Four more feminine nouns
Γαλιλαια (61) – Galilee
*εἰρηνη (92) – peace
*κεφαλη (75) – head
*συναγωγη (56) – synagogue

Four important conjunctions
*ἀλλα (638) – but
εἰ (502) – if
ἠ (343) – or
*ὡς (504) – as, like

Plus
καιρος (85) – time, season
*εἰμι (2462) – I am

Two special words:
(i) There are two alternatives for 'Jerusalem': either *Ἱεροσολυμα (77) – a neuter plural word with a rough breathing, or *Ἰερουσαλημ (63) a feminine singular indeclinable word with a smooth breathing. (For the meaning of indeclinable see note 4 on page 30.)
(ii) *αἰωνιος (71) an adjective meaning 'eternal'. αἰωνιος never uses the feminine forms. It uses the masculine endings when agreeing with a feminine noun, e.g. ἡ αἰωνιος ζωη.

## Word helps

hagiography, heterosexual, idiot/idiosyncratic, cacophony, calligraphy, monologue/monotheism, necropolis/necromancer, megaphone/megalomania, polytheism, irenic, encephalitis/cap.

## Exercises

### Section A

*1. ὁ Ἰησους λεγει αὐτῃ· Εἰμι ἡ ζωη και ἡ εἰρηνη.
*2. και Πετρος λεγει αὐτῳ· Εἶ ὁ Χριστος ὁ υἱος του θεου.
*3. λαμβανω την του θεου βασιλειαν ὡς τεκνον.
*4. οὐκ ἐστιν θεος νεκρων.
*5. το δαιμονιον λεγει· Ἰησου, εἶ ὁ ἁγιος του θεου.
6. βλεπει θεου τον καινον οὐρανον και την καινην γην.
7. Ἀγαπητοι, νομον ἑτερον οὐ διδασκω ἀλλα τον ἀπ᾽ ἀρχης.
8. ἡ μεγαλη φωνη ἐκ των οὐρανων λεγει· Εἶ ὁ υἱος μου [*my*] ὁ ἀγαπητος.
9. The days are evil and evil people do evil things.
10. The law is just, but it is the Gospel's moment (time).

*11. Each one has his own house.
*12. Christ is head of the church.

## Section B

*1. λεγει Ἰησους ἐν τῃ συναγωγῃ· Ἡ βασιλεια των οὐρανων οὐκ ἐστιν ἐκ του κοσμου.
2. εἰσιν ψυχαι πολλαι των ἀγαθων και των δικαιων ἐν τῃ οἰκιᾳ του αἰωνιου θεου.
*3. ἡ ἀγαπη του θεου ἐστιν ἐν ταις καρδιαις αὐτων δια του Χριστου.
4. ἐστιν αἰωνιος εἰρηνη τοις πιστοις.
*5. ὁ θεος ἀγαπη ἐστιν· ἀνθρωποι της ἀγαπης ἐν τῳ θεῳ εἰσιν και ὁ θεος ἐν αὐτοις ἐστιν.
*6. τοις Ἰουδαιοις τοις ἐν Ἱεροσολυμοις λεγει ὁ Ἰησους.
7. εἰ τα του κοσμου ἐργα πονηρα ἐστιν, πως οἱ πιστοι ποιουσι τα δικαια και τα καλα;
8. ἀγουσιν τον τυφλον προς τους Ἰουδαιους ἐν τῳ ἱερῳ τῳ μεγαλῳ.
*9. We are sons of men.
*10. You (pl.) are alone in Galilee.
11. The faithful Jews are teaching the law of peace.
*12. Does God have a new holy people?

## Section C

**Matthew 12.35** ὁ ἀγαθὸς ἄνθρωπος ἐκ τοῦ ἀγαθοῦ θησαυροῦ [*treasure box/storeroom*] ἐκβάλλει ἀγαθά, καὶ ὁ πονηρὸς ἄνθρωπος ἐκ τοῦ πονηροῦ θησαυροῦ ἐκβάλλει πονηρά.

**2 Corinthians 13.13** Ἡ χάρις [*grace*] τοῦ κυρίου Ἰησοῦ Χριστοῦ καὶ ἡ ἀγάπη τοῦ θεοῦ καὶ ἡ κοινωνία [*fellowship*] τοῦ ἁγίου πνεύματος [*spirit*] μετὰ πάντων [*all*] ὑμῶν [*you (pl.)*].

# The tenses

## 6.1 IDEA OF TENSES

John 14.1: πιστευετε εἰς τον θεον – you believe in God.
John 11.48: παντες πιστευσουσιν εἰς αὐτον
– everyone will believe in him.
John 7.5: οἱ ἀδελφοι αὐτου ἐπιστευον εἰς αὐτον
– his brothers were believing in him.
John 4.50: ἐπιστευσεν ὁ ἀνθρωπος τῳ λογῳ
– the man believed the word.

Alterations in a verb change its tense: πιστευετε – believe; πιστευσουσιν – will believe; ἐπιστευον – were believing; ἐπιστευσεν – believed.

- The Future, Imperfect and Aorist are *tenses*, to put alongside the Present.
- Greek indicates tense by altering the form of the verb, while in English we add extra words. Thus, λυσομεν (note the added σ) means 'we will untie'.
- The different tenses communicate both the *time* when the action is taking place (Present, Future, Past etc.) and the *aspect* (the nature of the action – whether it was a process, or completed etc.).
- The Present, Future, Imperfect and Aorist are the four common tenses – the final two will be added much later (Chapter 16).

## 6.2 DISTINGUISHING THE TENSES

The different tenses are formed by

(i) adding **prefixes** and **suffixes** to the stem
(ii) by having a **different set of endings**.

The **prefixes** and **suffixes** are the easiest thing to spot:

| | | | Stem | | Ending |
|---|---|---|---|---|---|
| *Tense:* | Present | | λυ | | ω |
| | Future | | λυ | σ | ω |
| | Imperfect | ἐ | λυ | | ον |
| | Aorist | ἐ | λυ | σ | α |

- The two Past tenses (Aorist and Imperfect) have an ἐ prefix (called an *augment*).
- The Future and the Aorist both have a σ suffix.

Thus:

KEY GRAMMAR

| | | | | |
|---|---|---|---|---|
| **no** prefix | | **no** suffix | | Present |
| **no** prefix | plus | σ suffix | = | Future |
| ἐ prefix | | **no** suffix | | Imperfect |
| ἐ prefix | | σ suffix | | Aorist |

PRACTICE 6.2

## Which tense are the following in?

Hint

Ignore the endings – look for the prefixes and suffixes

1. ἀκουσ-ομεν
2. ἐβλεπ-ον
3. ἐπιστευσ-ατε
4. ἐδιδασκ-εν
5. λυσ-ουσιν
6. ἀγ-ω

## 6.3 THE MEANING OF THE TENSES

| Greek tense | Time | Aspect | English equivalent |
|---|---|---|---|
| Present | Present | Process<br>*or* Undefined | I am untying<br>*or* I untie |
| Future | Future | Undefined | I will untie |
| Imperfect | Past | Process | I was untying |
| Aorist | Past | Undefined | I untied |

The meaning of the tenses is built up from the combination of *time* and *aspect.* Time is just as in English – Past, Present or Future. Aspect needs more attention.

- *Process* Aspect means that the action is being viewed as part of an ongoing process – either continuous or repeated
- *Undefined* Aspect can be used for two different reasons:
  - (i) It is truly undefined – or default – nothing is being implied at all about the manner in which the action occurred.
  - (ii) It is deliberately being used as opposed to using the *process* aspect, thus a punctilliar ('one-time') sense is meant.

## Present

If you want to express present time, there is no choice in Greek. You just use the Present tense, even though this can have two different aspects – undefined or process. This is why we learnt earlier (Chapter 2, section 2.1) that the Greek Present tense can mean *either* 'I am untying' (process) *or* 'I untie' (undefined).

## Future

If you want to express future time, there is no choice. You use the Future.

## Past: The Difference between the Imperfect and the Aorist

If you want past time, there is a choice – the Imperfect carries the *process* aspect, and the Aorist the *undefined* aspect.

The **Aorist** describes a past action without reference to continuance, repetition or completion, often but not always implying a single past action.

– I untied, you untied etc.

The **Imperfect** describes an action in the past that is viewed as a process. This itself gives rise to three different possibilities:

- Continuous process gives the English translations using 'was' or 'were'
  - I was untying, you were untying, etc.
- Repeated (or habitual) process gives the English translations using 'used to'
  - I used to untie, you used to untie, etc.
- Plus, the Imperfect can also be used for a process in the past that is viewed as just beginning.
  - I began to untie, you began to untie, etc. For example:

Matt. 5.2: He opened his mouth (Aorist) and began to teach (Imperfect).

### 6.3.1 Basic English equivalents

Although you should try to understand the meaning and 'flavour' of the different Greek tenses, many students do find it easier *to begin with* to identify English equivalents.

| | Present | Future | Imperfect | Aorist |
|---|---|---|---|---|
| 1st sing. | I am untying | I will untie | I was untying | I untied |
| 2nd sing. | You are untying | You will untie | You were untying | You untied |
| 3rd sing. | He is untying | He will untie | He was untying | He untied |
| 1st pl. | We are untying | We will untie | We were untying | We untied |
| 2nd pl. | You are untying | You will untie | You were untying | You untied |
| 3rd pl. | They are untying | They will untie | They were untying | They untied |

**Remember:** 3rd person singular is 'he', 'she' or 'it'; Present can be 'I untie', 'you untie', etc.; Imperfect can be 'I used to untie', etc.

**PRACTICE 6.3**

#### Which Greek tenses are correct for the following?

1. I will see.
2. They were hearing.
3. She used to eat.
4. You are throwing.
5. He sent.
6. I see.

#### Translate

**Hint**

Don't worry about the endings – they are all in the first person singular.

7. ἀκουσω.
8. λαμβανω.
9. ἐπεμπον.
10. ἐβαπτιζον.
11. ἐπιστευσα.
12. ἐχω.

## 6.4 THE ENDINGS

| | Present | Future | Imperfect | Aorist |
|---|---|---|---|---|
| I<br>You (sing.)<br>He, she, it | λυ-ω<br>λυ-εις<br>λυ-ει | λυσ-ω<br>λυσ-εις<br>λυσ-ει | ἐλυ-ον<br>ἐλυ-ες<br>ἐλυ-ε(ν) | ἐλυσ-α<br>ἐλυσ-ας<br>ἐλυσ-ε(ν) |
| We<br>You (pl.)<br>They | λυ-ομεν<br>λυ-ετε<br>λυ-ουσι(ν) | λυσ-ομεν<br>λυσ-ετε<br>λυσ-ουσι(ν) | ἐλυ-ομεν<br>ἐλυ-ετε<br>ἐλυ-ον | ἐλυσ-αμεν<br>ἐλυσ-ατε<br>ἐλυσ-αν |

Notes

- The endings of the Future are the same as the Present (but there is the σ suffix to distinguish them).
- The Present, Future and Imperfect have an 'o' or 'e' sound at the beginning of the ending; the Aorist tends to have an 'a' sound.
- The endings in the 1st and 2nd person plural are very similar in all the tenses.
- There is an *optional* ν in the Imperfect and Aorist 3rd person singular, just as there is in the Present (and so Future) 3rd person plural.

**PRACTICE 6.4**

### Translate

1. ἐβαλλομεν.
2. ἐλυσαμεν.
3. ἀκουσετε.
4. ἐκβαλλεις.
5. ἐπιστευσαν.
6. ἀπολυσουσιν.
7. We are writing.
8. They will believe.
9. You (pl.) were taking.

### 6.4.1 Examples of the tenses

- ὁ Ἰησους ἐδιδασκεν ἐν τῃ συναγωγῃ και πολλοι ἐπιστευσαν.

ἐδιδασκεν is Imperfect, therefore describing a past process – 'Jesus was in the process of teaching in the synagogue'. ἐπιστευσαν is Aorist, therefore describing a past undefined (not a process) action – 'many believed' or 'many came to believe' = Jesus was teaching in the synagogue and many believed.

- ὁ θεος ἐπεμπεν τους ἀγγελους, ἀλλα νυν ἐσμεν μονοι.

ἐπεμπεν is Imperfect, therefore describing a past process – 'God used to send messengers.' ἐσμεν is Present, therefore describing the current situation – 'we are alone.' = God used to send messengers, but now we are alone.

**HALF-WAY PRACTICE**

1. ἐδιδασκεν τον ὀχλον.
2. ὁ θεος ἀκουσει αὐτου.
3. οἱ ἁγιοι ἐχουσιν τον νομον.
4. λυσομεν το πλοιον.
5. δια τον λογον ἐπιστευσατε;
6. ἐλεγον περι της βασιλειας.
7. πως ἀπολυσεις αὐτην;
8. οἱ ἀδελφοι οὐκ ἐπιστευσαν.
9. We used to take the boat.
10. They believed God.
11. The good master will set free the slaves.
12. I used to speak but now I will listen.

## 6.5 POINTS TO NOTE ABOUT ἐ PREFIXES

### 6.5.1 Words beginning with a vowel

Look at what happens when the ἐ prefix is added to a word beginning with a vowel:

ἀκουω – I hear (Present)
ἠκουον – I was hearing (Imperfect)

In order to indicate that a verb is in the Imperfect or Aorist, an ἐ (*augment*) needs to be added to the beginning of the stem. This is fine if the stem begins with a consonant but not if it begins with a vowel – you can't say ἐἀκουον!

KEY GRAMMAR
Watch out when an ἐ (*augment*) is added to a word beginning with a vowel

What happens is that the normal rule for adding the ἐ *augment* is followed, but contractions then take place (ἐ + ἀ → ἠ etc.).[1]

KEY GRAMMAR

| | | | |
|---|---|---|---|
| ἐ plus | α | becomes | η |
| | ε | becomes | η |
| | ο | becomes | ω |
| | η, ι, υ and ω | remain | η, ι, υ and ω |

[1] Some people prefer to understand this as the vowel being lengthened instead of the ἐ being added. The result is the same, but this seems to be an extra rule to remember.

Diphthongs follow the logic of the above chart. For example,

| | | | | | | | | |
|---|---|---|---|---|---|---|---|---|
| αι | → | η | ει | → | η | οι | → | ῳ |
| αυ | → | ηυ | ευ | → | ηυ[2] | | | |

Thus, since the Imperfect of λυω is ἐλυον

- the Imperfect of ἀκουω is ἠκουον.
- the Imperfect of οἰκοδομεω is ᾠκοδομουν.[3]
- the Imperfect of εὐλογεω is ηὐλογουν.[3]

The ἐ behaves in the same way in the Aorist, so

- the Aorist of ἀκουω is ἠκουσα.

### 6.5.2 Compound verbs

Look at what happens when the ἐ prefix is added to a compound verb (Chapter 4, section 4.4):

ἀπολυω – I set free (Present)
ἀπ<u>ε</u>λυον – I was setting free (Imperfect)

In compound verbs the ἐ (*augment*) comes **between** the preposition and the verb's stem. You can understand this by thinking of the following four steps.

KEY GRAMMAR
Watch out when an ἐ (*augment*) is added to a compound verb

1. Take off the preposition
2. Add the ἐ to the verb as normal (take care if the verb begins with a vowel)
3. Replace the preposition
4. Watch out for *elision*, since the preposition now precedes a vowel (look back at the rules in Chapter 4, section 4.2.5)

Examples

| Present | Imperfect | | | |
|---|---|---|---|---|
| | Actual form | Meaning | Process of getting there | |
| ἀπολυω | ἀπελυον | I was setting free | ἀπο-ελυον | |
| ἐκβαλλω | ἐξεβαλλον | I was throwing out | ἐκ-εβαλλον | |
| ὑπαγω | ὑπηγον | I was departing | ὑπο-εαγον | ὑπο-ηγον |
| συναγω | συνηγον | I was gathering | συν-εαγον | συν-ηγον |

[2] In fact it is more common for ευ to be left unchanged, despite ηυ being more logical.

[3] The endings used by the -εω verbs in the Imperfect are explained in Chapter 6, section 6.8.

The augment behaves in the exactly the same fashion in the Aorist.
e.g. The Aorist of ἀπολυω is ἀπελυσα

**Hint**

Observe carefully the difference between the *contractions* that occur when an augment is added to a verb that begins with a vowel and the *elision* that happens when a preposition is followed by a vowel. A vowel at the beginning of a verb combines with the augment, while a vowel at the end of a preposition is normally destroyed by the augment.

ἐ + ἀγον → ἠγον   ἐ + ἀναβλεπον → ἀνεβλεπον   ἐ + ἀναγον → ἀνηγον

**PRACTICE 6.5**

### Put these verbs into the Imperfect (1st singular)

| | | | |
|---|---|---|---|
| 1. ἀγω | 3. βλεπω | 5. παραλαμβανω | 7. ἀνοιγω |
| 2. ὑπαγω | 4. ἀναβλεπω | 6. ἀποκαλυπτω | 8. διδασκω |

## 6.6 POINTS TO NOTE ABOUT THE σ SUFFIX

Look at what happens when the σ suffix is added to verbs which end in particular consonants:

βλεπω – I see (Present)
βλεψω – I will see (Future)

**KEY GRAMMAR**
Watch out when an σ is added to stem of a verb ending in a consonant

A σ suffix (for the Future or Aorist) will often combine with the final consonant of the verb's stem. This should not be seen as a special rule about the Future and Aorist of verbs; it is more a matter of pronunciation. We will meet the same changes later on in certain nouns (Chapter 12).[4]

[4] The groupings of letters here is not random. The sounds π, β, φ are all made with the lips (and are called 'labials'), τ, δ, θ, ζ are made by the tongue touching the teeth (called 'dentals') and κ, γ and χ are made further back in the throat (called 'gutturals').

KEY GRAMMAR

| | | | | |
|---|---|---|---|---|
| π, β, φ | + | σ | → | ψ |
| τ, δ, θ, ζ | + | σ | → | σ[5] |
| κ, γ, χ, σσ | + | σ | → | ξ |

Examples

| Present | Future | | |
|---|---|---|---|
| | Actual form | Meaning | Process |
| βλεπω | βλεψω | I will see | βλεπ-σω |
| βαπτιζω | βαπτισω | I will baptise | βαπτιζ-σω |
| ἀνοιγω | ἀνοιξω | I will open | ἀνοιγ-σω |

The σ behaves in the same fashion in the Aorist (Aorist of βλεπω is ἐβλεψα).

**Hint**

Because the Aorist involves the addition of the ε prefix and the σ suffix, both sets of complications can occur. Thus the Aorist of ἀνοιγω is ἠνοιξα (εανοιγσα).

**PRACTICE 6.6**

### Put these verbs into the Aorist (1st singular)

| | | | |
|---|---|---|---|
| 1. βαπτιζω | 3. ἀκουω | 5. κηρυσσω | 7. ἀποκαλυπτω |
| 2. πεμπω | 4. ἀπολυω | 6. ἀναβλεπω | 8. δοξαζω |

## 6.7 DEALING WITH THE PREFIXES AND SUFFIXES

You need to think carefully about the way in which these prefixes and suffixes behave (as described in sections 6.5 and 6.6) because they make it harder to spot which tense verbs are in. You need to get used to realising that

ἠγον is really ἐ-ἀγον and thus is an Imperfect
ἀνοιξω is really ἀνοιγ-σω and thus a Future

[5] Except for κραζω which behaves as if it were κρασσω. Thus since σσ + σ → ξ its Future is κραξω and its Aorist is ἐκραξα.

**Hint**

Very few verbs begin with η or ω in their basic form[6] – if you see a verb beginning in this way, it is very likely to have been something else initially (α, ε, or ο) to which an ἐ has been added – it will therefore be in the Imperfect or the Aorist.

Almost no verbs end in ψ, ξ, or a single σ (they do end in σσ) naturally[7] – if you see a stem ending in this way it must have been something else initially to which an σ has been added – it will therefore be in the Future or the Aorist.

**Note:** ἐχω (I have) is unusual.

| | |
|---|---|
| Imperfect | εἰχον (ἐ being augmented to εἰ not ἡ) |
| Future | ἑξω (χ+σ → ξ as expected, but ἑ not ἐ) |

The Aorist of ἐχω is actually ἐσχον which is arrived at by following a different pattern (see Chapter 11, Section 11.1.3) but is quite rare, since 'having' in the past normally implies 'over a period' and hence the Imperfect.

**PRACTICE 6.7**

## What tense are the following in?

| | | | |
|---|---|---|---|
| 1. ἐκραζεν | 3. βλεψετε | 5. εἰχομεν | 7. πεισομεν |
| 2. ἐδιωξα | 4. ἐγραψαν | 6. ἀνεβλεπετε | 8. ἐκηρυξεν |

## 6.8 TENSES IN THE -εω VERBS

In Chapter 2, section 2.2 we learnt that there was a family of verbs with a weak ε at the end of their stems. This combined with the endings in the Present, giving forms such as φιλ<u>ου</u>μεν (φιλε-ομεν).

- In the *Imperfect* the same pattern of contractions occurs.
- In the *Future* and *Aorist* the addition of the σ suffix causes two changes:
  - (i) The ε lengthens to a η (except καλεω keeps the ε: καλεσω, ἐκαλεσα)
  - (ii) The endings are now next to the σ, not the weak ε, so there are no contractions (i.e. the Future and Aorist of -εω verbs are identical to λυω).

---

[6] In the NT only ἡγεομαι, ἡκω and ὠφελεω (which occur 28, 26 and 15 times respectively) and the very rare words ἡσυχαζω, ἡτταομαι, ὠδινω, ὠνεομαι, ὠρυομαι.

[7] In the NT only ὑψοω (20 times) and αὐξω and θαρσεω, both of which are uncommon.

Thus the full pattern for φιλεω (I love) is as follows:

| | Present | Future | Imperfect | Aorist |
|---|---|---|---|---|
| I<br>You (sing.)<br>He, she, it | φιλω<br>φιλεις<br>φιλει | φιλησω<br>φιλησεις<br>φιλησει | ἐφιλουν<br>ἐφιλεις<br>ἐφιλει | ἐφιλησα<br>ἐφιλησας<br>ἐφιλησεν |
| We<br>You (pl.)<br>They | φιλουμεν<br>φιλειτε<br>φιλουσιν<br>*or* φιλουσι | φιλησομεν<br>φιλησετε<br>φιλησουσιν | ἐφιλουμεν<br>ἐφιλειτε<br>ἐφιλουν | ἐφιλησαμεν<br>ἐφιλησατε<br>ἐφιλησαν |

**PRACTICE 6.8**

### Translate

1. ἐποιησαν
2. φιλησει
3. προσεκυνουμεν
4. αἰτησουσιν
5. ἐτηρησεν
6. ἐζητουν
7. εὐχαριστησατε
8. ᾠκοδομησαν

## VOCAB FOR CHAPTER 6

Thirteen more verbs like λυω

*ἀνοιγω (77) – I open
*βαπτιζω (77) – I baptise, dip
*γραφω (191) – I write
διωκω (45) – I persecute, pursue
*δοξαζω (61) – I praise, glorify
*κηρυσσω (61) – I proclaim, preach
*κραζω (56) – I cry out
*πεμπω (79) – I send
πειθω (52) – I convince, persuade
*σωζω (106) – I save, rescue, heal (sometimes written σῴζω)

Three of which are compounds

ἀποκαλυπτω (26) – I reveal, uncover
*προσεχω (24) + dat. – I take heed of, pay attention to
ὑπαρχω (60) – I exist, I am

Four more verbs like φιλεω
One which is clearly not a compound
*αἰτεω (70) – I ask (for)[8]

Three that look like compounds but do not behave as compounds (e.g. augments are added to the beginning)

*εὐλογεω (42) – I speak well of, bless, praise
*εὐχαριστεω (38) – I give thanks
*οἰκοδομεω (40) – I build (up)

[8] αἰτεω is followed by a double accusative – both <u>the person asked</u> and <u>what is asked for</u> occur in the accusative. E.g. 'I ask God for life' is αἰτω τον θεον ζωην.

Twelve words all about time.

ἀρτι (36) – now, just now
*ἐτι (93) – still, yet
*ἠδη (61) – already
*νυν (147) – now
*ὁτε (103) – when
οὐκετι (47) – no longer
οὐπω (26) – not yet

*παλιν (141) – back, again
παντοτε (41) – always
*ποτε (29) – once (at some time)[9]
σημερον (41) – today
*τοτε (160) – then

Plus *δυο (135) – two

A couple of extra nouns: *Τιμοθεος (24) – Timothy *τοπος (94) – place

## Word helps

apocalypse, baptize, graph/bibliography, doxology, kerygma, soteriology, etiology, eulogy, eucharist, palindrome, dual/duel/duet, topology/topic.

## Exercises

### Section A

*1. ἐβαπτισα ποτε, ἀλλα νυν αὐτος βαπτισει.
*2. φωνη ἐκ του οὐρανου ἐκηρυξεν· Και ἐδοξασα αὐτο και παλιν δοξασω.
3. και δαιμονια πολλα ἐξεβαλλεν ἐν ἑκαστῳ τοπῳ.
*4. ἐκαλεσεν και ἐσωσεν αὐτους· τοτε προσεκυνησαν αὐτῳ.
5. ὁ Ἰησους παρελαμβανεν τα τεκνα και τα τεκνα ἠκουσεν του Ἰησου.
*6. ὁ ἁγιος ἀγγελος ἠνοιγεν τους οὐρανους.
*7. και καλεσεις το τεκνον Ἰησουν· σωσει τον λαον αὐτου ἀπο των ἁμαρτιων αὐτων.
8. και ἐλαλησαν τον λογον του κυριου τοις πιστοις ἀδελφοις ἐν τῃ οἰκιᾳ αὐτου.
*9. Now we will bless the Lord.
*10. I have already written (=I already wrote) to them, but now I will write again.
11. He revealed his love when he wrote to her.
*12. They asked for signs and cried out with a loud voice to Jesus.

### Section B

*1. ὁ Παυλος και ὁ Πετρος ἐγραψαν περι των ἐργων του κυριου.
2. οὐκ ἐδιωξαν τους ἀδελφους ἐν τῃ συναγωγῃ ἐν τῳ σαββατῳ.
3. τυφλοι ἀνεβλεψαν, χωλοι (lame) περιεπατησαν και κωφοι (deaf) ἠκουσαν.

[9] ποτε is an ‘timid word’ (technically a ‘*postpositive*’) which means that it cannot come first in a sentence (we will meet more of these in Chapter 9, section 9.4.1).

4. ὁ Παυλος ποτε ἐδιωκεν την ἐκκλησιαν ἀλλα οὐκετι· ὁ θεος ἐσωσεν αὐτον.
*5. ἐσωζεν τον λαον αὐτου ἀπο του πονηρου.
*6. περιεπατησατε ποτε κατα τον κοσμον και τον πονηρον, ἀλλα νυν προσεχετε τῳ κυριῳ της δοξης και οἰκοδομησετε τους ἀδελφους.
7. πεμψομεν ἀγγελους ἀρτι προς αὐτους, ἀλλ᾽ οὐκετι πεισουσιν αὐτους.
8. ὁ Τιμοθεος ἐκηρυξεν παντοτε το εὐαγγελιον ἀλλ᾽ οὐπω ἐπιστευετε τοις λογοις αὐτου.
*9. We built a house beside the sea.
10. The faithful ones worshipped Christ, and the evil ones were persecuting them.
11. Will the great temple exist again?
*12. He was preaching the good news and was baptizing the saints (holy ones).

## Section C

**John 9.13-21** 13 Ἄγουσιν[10] αὐτὸν πρὸς τοὺς Φαρισαίους τόν ποτε τυφλόν.
14 ἦν [*it was*] δὲ [*and/but*] σάββατον ἐν ᾗ [*which*] ἡμέρᾳ τὸν πηλὸν [*mud, clay*]
ἐποίησεν ὁ Ἰησοῦς καὶ ἀνέῳξεν [=ἤνοιξεν] αὐτοῦ τοὺς ὀφθαλμούς [*eyes*] ...
16 ἔλεγον οὖν [therefore] ἐκ τῶν Φαρισαίων τινές [*some – nom.*] Οὐκ ἔστιν
οὗτος [*this one*] παρὰ θεοῦ ὁ ἄνθρωπος, ὅτι [because] τὸ σάββατον οὐ τηρεῖ.
ἄλλοι [*others*] δὲ ἔλεγον, Πῶς δύναται [*he is able*] ἄνθρωπος ἁμαρτωλὸς
[*sinful*] τοιαῦτα [*such*] σημεῖα ποιεῖν [*to do*]; ... 17 λέγουσιν οὖν τῷ τυφλῷ
πάλιν, Τί [*what?*] σὺ [*you – nom.*] λέγεις περὶ αὐτοῦ, ὅτι ἠνέῳξέν [=ἤνοιξεν]
σου [*you, gen.*] τοὺς ὀφθαλμούς; ὁ δὲ εἶπεν ὅτι [*but he said* "] Προφήτης
[*prophet*] ἐστίν. 18 Οὐκ ἐπίστευσαν οὖν οἱ Ἰουδαῖοι περὶ αὐτοῦ ὅτι ἦν τυφλὸς
καὶ ἀνέβλεψεν ἕως ὅτου [*until*] ἐφώνησαν [φωνεω – I call] τοὺς γονεῖς
[*parents*] αὐτοῦ ... 21 πῶς δὲ νῦν βλέπει οὐκ οἴδαμεν [*we know*], ἢ τίς [*who?*]
ἤνοιξεν αὐτοῦ τοὺς ὀφθαλμοὺς ἡμεῖς [*we*] οὐκ οἴδαμεν.

---

[10] Note the Present tense here. Greek sometimes uses a Present tense when relating a story in the past. This is called a 'historic present' and can make the account more vivid. It is very common in the gospels.

# Moods

## 7.1 IDEA OF MOODS

The Mood of a verb indicates the manner in which the action is to be regarded – is it a statement, a command, hypothetical etc.? There are five moods in Greek – we have already met one (Indicative). This chapter introduces three others (Imperative, Infinitive, Participle) and one is left until Chapter 17 (Subjunctive).

| Mood | Used to express | Example in English |
|---|---|---|
| **Indicative** | Statements and questions | I am listening |
| **Imperative** | Commands | Listen! |
| **Infinitive** | The idea of the verb in general | To listen |
| **Participle** | Verbal adjective | Listening, he understood |
| **Subjunctive** | Uncertainty | I may listen |

- Often the Indicative behaves in one way and all four other moods behave in a different way – therefore they are known as the *other moods.*
- In the *other moods,* there is no Future tense or Imperfect.
- In the *Indicative,* tense communicates both *time* and *aspect.* In the *other moods,* the *time* part falls away – thus the difference between the Present and the Aorist becomes solely one of *aspect* – process or undefined.
- In the *Indicative,* verbs are made negative by the addition of οὐ (or οὐκ/οὐχ) – see Chapter 4, section 4.6. In the *other moods,* a different word is used – μη. This also affects any compounds of οὐ. Thus, οὐκετι means 'no longer', but this becomes μηκετι with a verb in one of the *other moods.*

**Mood?**
See it in English
Section 9
Page 248

KEY GRAMMAR

| | |
|---|---|
| Negation – Indicative | οὐ |
| Other moods | μη |

## 7.2 THE IMPERATIVE

Acts 16.31: πιστευσον ἐπι τον κυριον Ἰησουν – Believe on the Lord Jesus!

πιστευσον is communicating a command (or exhortation). πιστευω is now in a different *mood* – the *Imperative.*

### 7.2.1 The formation of the Imperative[1]

| | Present | Aorist |
|---|---|---|
| 2nd person singular | λυε | λυσον |
| 2nd person plural | λυετε | λυσατε |

Notes

- Imperatives are either singular (to one person) or plural (to more than one).
- Imperatives are either in the Present tense or in the Aorist.
- These imperatives are known as 2nd person imperatives – this is because they are commands to 'you' to do something.[2]
- Note that the Aorist Imperatives do not have the augment. This is because the augment marks past time, but in the Imperative the difference between the tenses is only one of aspect, not of time.
- The Aorist Imperative has a σ suffix, just as it does in the Indicative.
- The 2nd plural Present Imperative looks identical to the 2nd plural Present Indicative (λυετε could be 'you untie' or 'keep on untying!' but the context normally makes it clear which it is).
- The εω verbs follow the normal rules for the contractions (pages 24 and 71) which gives the imperatives: φιλει, φιλειτε, φιλησον, φιλησατε.

**Hint**

It's easy to mix up the Future Indicative and the Aorist Imperative (both have a σ suffix and no prefix). The endings are the key – if it looks like a Future but doesn't seem to have the right endings, think 'Aorist in another mood'.

- Acts 16.31: πιστευσον ἐπι τον κυριον Ἰησουν
  – Believe in the Lord Jesus! (Aorist Imperative)

---

[1] Throughout this section, 'command' needs to be understood quite broadly, covering the whole range of more or less forceful/polite expressions – thus a request, exhortation, plea etc.

[2] There are 3rd person imperatives ('let him/them listen'). Since these are rare, they are left until Chapter 18.

- Matt. 27.42: πιστευσομεν ἐπ' αὐτον
  – We will believe in him. (Future Indicative)

## 7.2.2 The difference between the Present and Aorist Imperatives

English only has one Imperative. However, Greek has the flexibility of putting a command in either the Present or Aorist tense, to communicate aspect.

KEY GRAMMAR
Present – Process
Aorist – Undefined

The **Present Imperative** expresses a 'process'– that is, a command for something to be done either repeatedly or continuously – 'keep on doing it'.

The **Aorist Imperative** is undefined. Sometimes this will be truly undefined (or default) – the simplest form of the Imperative. Sometimes it is deliberately used as opposed to using the Present for process, to stress a 'one-time' sense.

It is hard to put into an English translation the difference between the Present and Aorist Imperative – that's why you need to read the Bible in Greek!

**Hint**

Most students wrongly think of the Present Imperative as the normal one, and then either forget the Aorist or think of it as stressing a 'one-time' action. In fact, the Aorist is the normal or default – if you see a Present Imperative being used you should ask yourself, 'Why is the process command being used here?'

Examples

- κηρυσσετε το εὐαγγελιον. – Preach (pl.) the good-news! (continually: 'go on preaching')
- βλεψατε τα προβατα. – Watch (pl.) the sheep! (default)
- κυριε, σωσον τον λαον. – Lord, save the people! (default)

PRACTICE 7.2

### Translate

1. ἐκβαλλε.
2. μετανοησον.
3. τηρειτε τον νομον.
4. γραψον αὐτῃ.
5. ἀκουετε την φωνην.
6. ζητησατε τον θεον.
7. ζητησετε τον θεον.
8. Open (s.) the heavens!
9. Teach (pl.) her! (continually)
10. Untie (pl.) the children!

## 7.3 THE INFINITIVE

John 16.12: πολλα ἐχω ὑμιν λεγειν. – I have many things to say to you.

λεγειν is the equivalent of 'to say' in English. This is clearly closely related to λεγω meaning 'I say' – it is the same verb but now in the *Infinitive mood.*

Infinitives come in just one form in each of the Present and Aorist tenses.

| | Present | Aorist |
|---|---|---|
| Infinitive | λυειν | λυσαι |

Notes

- The Infinitive can be translated in English as 'to . . . '. Both λυειν and λυσαι mean 'to untie'.
- As in the Imperative, the Aorist Infinitive has a σ suffix, but no augment.
- The εω verbs follow the normal rules: φιλειν, φιλησαι.

The **difference between the Present and Aorist Infinitive** is the same as between the Present and Aorist Imperative – the Aorist is the default, undefined, aspect; the Present is process (either continuous or repeated).

Later (in Chapter 18) we will learn some special uses of the Infinitive in Greek.

However, it is often used just as it is in English. In particular, it is used to convey purpose, and tends to follow certain verbs, such as:

θελω – I wish / want to . . .
μελλω – I intend to . . ., I am about to . . .
δει – It is necessary to . . .
ἐξεστι – It is permitted to . . .

Examples

Mark 3.14-15: ἐποιησεν δωδεκα ... ἐχειν ἐξουσιαν ἐκβαλλειν τα δαιμονια.
And he made twelve . . . to have authority to throw out the demons.
These infinitives are Present, because the twelve will continuously have authority and will repeatedly throw out demons.

ὁ Ἰησους θελει σωσαι αὐτην. – Jesus is willing to save her.
This Infinitive is Aorist because it does not point to a continual action.

PRACTICE 7.3

## Translate

1. θελεις βλεψαι;
2. ἐζητουμεν ἀκουειν.
3. δει περιπατειν.
4. ἐμελλετε γραφειν.
5. Do you (pl.) want to repent?
6. It is necessary to love God.

HALF-WAY PRACTICE

1. βαπτιζετε τους ἀδελφους.
2. ἀκουσον αὐτου.
3. ἐξεστι λαλησαι;
4. δει λεγειν τῳ Τιμοθεῳ.
5. προσκυνειτε τῳ ἁγιῳ θεῳ.
6. ἀκουσατε αὐτου.
7. θελω πεμψαι ἀγγελον.
8. μη ζητει ἀπολυσαι.
9. Do you (pl.) want to give thanks?
10. Seek (pl.; continually) the good news!
11. Do not walk (s.; in general) in the temple!
12. They are about to cry out, 'Amen'.

## 7.4 PARTICIPLES

Philem. 4-5: εὐχαριστω τῳ θεῳ ... ἀκουων σου την ἀγαπην.

– I give thanks to God . . . hearing of your love.

Acts 18.8: πολλοι των Κορινθιων ἀκουοντες ἐπιστευον.

– many of the Corinthians hearing were believing.

ἀκουων and ἀκουοντες are from ἀκουω (I hear) but are in the *Participle mood* meaning 'hearing' (one is singular, one is plural). A participle works alongside a main verb adding a further layer of meaning: not just 'I give thanks' but 'hearing of your love', not just 'they were believing' but 'hearing'.

The frequent use of participles is one of the most characteristic features of Greek. The full scheme for participles is quite complicated, and so is left until Chapter 14. However, we will learn one particular usage now that is particularly common in the New Testament.

Participles are **verbal adjectives** – part of the verb behaving like an adjective.

**Like adjectives:**

KEY GRAMMAR
Participles must agree with the noun they qualify in gender, case and number

For now, we will learn only the masculine nominative of the participle, because often in the New Testament participles are qualifying (further describing) masculine nouns in the nominative. You will need to ensure they agree in number – singular or plural.

**Like verbs:**

KEY GRAMMAR
Participles have tense (Present or Aorist), and may have an object

### 7.4.1 The form of the participle

| | (Masculine nominative) Present | Aorist |
|---|---|---|
| Singular | λυων | λυσας |
| Plural | λυοντες | λυσαντες |

Notes

- As in the Infinitive and Imperative, the Aorist does not have an augment (time is not expressed outside of the Indicative), but it does have a σ.
- The plural participles both have endings in -ντες.
- The Aorist participles have an 'a' sound, the Present an 'o' sound.
- The εω verbs follow the normal rules, thus the participles are:

| | (Masculine nominative) Present | Aorist |
|---|---|---|
| Singular | φιλων | φιλησας |
| Plural | φιλουντες | φιλησαντες |

PRACTICE 7.4.1

### Parse the following (giving tense, gender, case and number)

| | | | |
|---|---|---|---|
| 1. βαλλοντες | 3. διωξαντες | 5. γραφων | 7. ὑπαγοντες |
| 2. πεμψας | 4. ποιησας | 6. παρακαλων | 8. ἀκουσας |

## 7.4.2 The meaning of the participle

Greek participles do not easily translate word for word into English. The technique is to start with the 'wooden translation' given below and rephrase it into good English, guided by the underlying 'idea' of the participle.

| **Wooden translations** | Present participle | untying |
|---|---|---|
| | Aorist participle | having untied |

**Idea** The heart of understanding participles is that the participle is dependent upon a main verb (Indicative, or possibly Imperative) in the sentence. It expresses meaning **in relation to that main verb**, not absolutely.

| | |
|---|---|
| Present Participle | *Simultaneous* process – the action in the participle is a process going on at the same time as the action in the main verb. |
| Aorist Participle | *Sequence* – the action in the participle occurred before the action in the main verb.[3] |

KEY GRAMMAR

| | |
|---|---|
| Present Participle | Simultaneous |
| Aorist Participle | Sequence |

## Good English

Rephrasing into appropriate, good English is really a matter of practice.

For a **Present** participle, this often involves '**while**' or '**as**'. Thus from ἐσθιοντες ἠκουσαν you get 'eating they heard' and so 'while they were eating, they heard'.

For an **Aorist** participle, this often involves '**after**' or '**when**'. Thus βλεψαντες ἐπιστευσαν is rephrased from 'having seen they believed' to 'after they had seen they believed' or 'when they had seen they believed'.

[3] The connection between this and ideas of aspect will be discussed more in Chapter 18, section 18.5.

Examples

Matt. 4.18: περιπατων παρα την θαλασσαν της Γαλιλαιας εἰδεν (he saw) δυο ἀδελφους.
– While he was walking alongside the Sea of Galilee, he saw two brothers.

Mark 6.16: ἀκουσας δε (but) ὁ Ἡρῳδης ἐλεγεν ...
– But when Herod heard (this) he said (was saying) . . .

PRACTICE 7.4.2

**Translate**

1. βλεποντες ὑπηγον.
2. ἐκραξεν λεγων.
3. βλεψας λεγει αὐτῳ.
4. περιεπατουν τηρουντες τον νομον.
5. ἀκουσας τον λογον ἐδοξασα τον θεον.
6. πιστευσαντες μετενοησαν.

### 7.4.3 Participles with objects

Because the participle is a verb, it can have its own object (in the accusative). This is not complicated once you get the hang of it:

- βλεψας τον ὀχλον ὁ Ἰησους ἐκηρυξεν τον λογον.

The main sentence is underlined above: Jesus (subject) proclaimed (main i.e. Indicative verb) the word (object). The participle introduces a subordinate clause. It agrees with the subject of the sentence (Jesus) and is telling us something extra involving its own object: 'having seen the crowd'.

= When he saw the crowd, Jesus proclaimed the word.

Hint

If the simple subject-verb-object sentence is the trunk of the tree, the participle starts off a new branch:

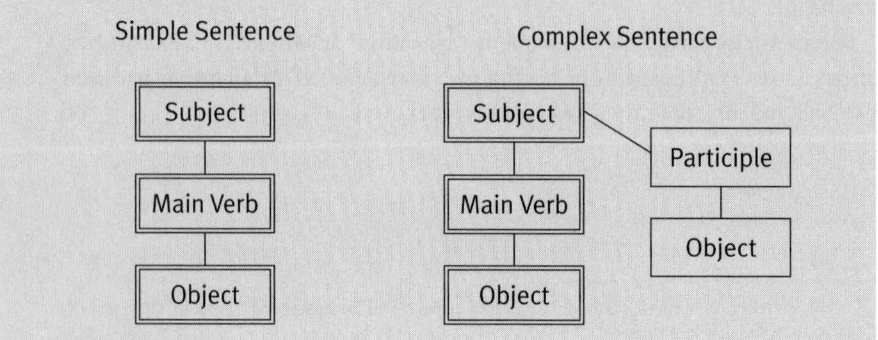

PRACTICE 7.4.3

## Translate

1. ἀνοιξαντες τους ὀφθαλμους αὐτων ἐβλεψαν την θαλασσαν.
2. λεγων τῳ ὀχλῳ ὁ ἀποστολος ἐθεωρει τον οὐρανον.
3. γραψας το βιβλιον ὁ Πετρος ἐπεμψεν αὐτο τῃ ἐκκλησιᾳ.
4. After proclaiming the word, they worshipped God.

## 7.5 PARTICIPLES AS NOUNS

We learnt in Chapter 5, section 5.5 that adjectives can be 'turned into' nouns by the addition of the article. Thus ὁ ἀγαθος means 'the good man'. Since participles are verbal adjectives, unsurprisingly the same can be done with participles.

- Mark 4.14: <u>ὁ σπειρων</u> τον λογον σπειρει.

σπειρων = sowing (Present masculine nom. sing. participle of σπειρω – I sow)
ὁ σπειρων = the sowing person = the sower
Sentence = The sower is sowing the word.

- Mark 4.18: οὗτοι (these) εἰσιν <u>οἱ</u> τον λογον <u>ἀκουσαντες</u>.

ἀκουσαντες = having heard (Aorist masculine nom. pl. participle of ἀκουω)
οἱ ἀκουσαντες = the having heard ones = those who heard
Sentence = These are the people who heard the word.

**Hint**

Don't be afraid to introduce words like 'who' in your translation of participles that are acting as nouns. The aim is to convey the meaning in good English.

PRACTICE 7.5

## Translate

1. ὁ πεμψας αὐτον σωζει.
2. μακαριος ἐστιν ὁ βλεπων τον θεον.
3. οἱ μαρτυρουντες κηρυξουσιν.
4. ὁ πιστευων λεγει την εἰρηνην.

## VOCAB FOR CHAPTER 7

Fourteen more important nouns

Some feminine
*δικαιοσυνη (92) – righteousness
*ἐντολη (67) – commandment
*ἐξουσια (102) – authority
*παραβολη (50) – parable
παρρησια (31) – outspokenness, boldness
χαρα (59) – joy

Some masculine
*ἀποστολος (80) – apostle
*θανατος (120) – death
*ὀφθαλμος (100) – eye
*Φαρισαιος (98) – Pharisee

And some neuter
*θηριον (46) – animal, beast
*ἱματιον (60) – garment
μνημειον (40) – tomb, monument
*προβατον (39) – sheep

Four negatives, used in the 'other moods'
*μη (1042) – not
*μηδε (56) – and not, but not
μηκετι (22) – no longer
μητε (34) – and not, nor

Eleven more verbs
*ἀκολουθεω (90) + dat. – I follow
ἀναγω (23) – I lead up, restore
δεω (43) – I bind, tie up
*δοκεω (62) – I think, seem
ἐλεεω (29) – I have mercy on, pity
*θελω[4] (208) – I wish, want
*θεωρεω (58) – I look at
καταργεω (27) – I make ineffective, abolish
*μαρτυρεω (76) – I bear witness, testify
*μελλω (109) – I intend, am about (to)
*μετανοεω (34) – I repent, change my mind

Plus two verbs which only occur in the 3rd singular (called 'impersonal verbs')
*δει (101) – it is necessary
ἐξεστι (31) – it is permitted

One more preposition
*ὀπισω (35) + gen. – behind

### Word helps

parable, apostle, euthanasia, ophthalmologist, mnemonic, acolyte, diadem, docetic, theory, martyr.

[4] θελω is slightly irregular: Imperfect ἠθελον, Future θελησω, Aorist ἠθελησα.

## Exercises

### Section A

1. και λεγει τοις Φαρισαιοις· Ἐξεστιν ἐν τοις σαββασιν[5] ἀγαθον ποιησαι ἠ κακοποιησαι [*do evil*], ψυχην σωσαι ἠ μη σωσαι;
*2. ἀμην ἀμην λεγω, ὁ πιστευων ἐχει ζωην αἰωνιον.
*3. ἡ ἐντολη αὐτου ἐστιν ζωη αἰωνιος.
*4. και τα προβατα την φωνην αὐτου ἀκουει και τα ἰδια προβατα ἀκολουθει ὀπισω αὐτου.
5. ἡ ἀδελφη ἡ πιστη ἐκραζεν τῳ Ἰησου· Ἐλεησον, κυριε υἱε Δαυιδ.
*6. και ἐκηρυξεν ὁ Ἰησους λεγων· Μετανοειτε και πιστευετε ἐν τῳ εὐαγγελιῳ.
7. λεγει τῳ ὀχλῳ συν τοις ἀποστολοις αὐτου· Εἰ θελεις ὀπισω του κυριου ἀκολουθειν, δει παρρησιαν ἐχειν.
*8. ἀνθρωπος εἰμι ὑπο ἐξουσιαν, και λεγω δουλῳ· Ποιησον αὐτο, και ποιει.
9. He was telling a parable concerning joy.
10. Do not lead blind animals up into the temple.
11. Are you (pl.) looking at the tomb?
*12. Jesus was speaking in parables but with [*use* κατα + *acc.*] authority.

### Section B

*1. μη δοκειτε λεγειν· Ἐσμεν υἱοι του Ἀβρααμ.
2. οἱ Φαρισαιοι καταργουσιν την ἐντολην της ἀγαπης.
3. πολλοι συνηγον θεωρειν το μνημειον.
*4. λεγει αὐτῳ· Ἀκολουθει[6] τῳ Ἰησου και μαρτυρει[6].
*5. δει προσκυνειν τῳ θεῳ δια την δοξαν αὐτου.
6. ἐλεγεν ὁ ἀγγελος αὐτοις· Ἀκολουθειτε ὀπισω της φωνης αὐτου και μαρτυρειτε παρρησιᾳ και χαρᾳ.
*7. οἱ ἀποστολοι ἐκηρυσσον το εὐαγγελιον λεγοντες· Μετανοειτε.
8. το δαιμονιον ἐδησεν αὐτην ἀλλ᾽ οἱ Φαρισαιοι λεγουσιν· Οὐ δει και οὐκ ἐξεστιν λυσαι αὐτην ἀπο του πονηρου ἐν τῳ σαββατῳ.
*9. People do not seek death.
10. A man bound Paul, but an angel released him.

---

[5] Normally in the New Testament we find σαββασιν when we would expect σαββατοις (this is presumably because the plural of σαββατον looks like the 3rd declension pattern for neuter nouns, in which the dative plural ending is -σιν; see Chapter 12, section 12.3).

[6] Because of the way -εω verbs work there are two different possible ways of parsing these verbs. Can you work out what they are? In your translation use the imperative.

*11. Lord, open the eyes of the blind.
*12. They are about to bear witness concerning the righteousness of Christ.

## Section C

**1 John 3.4-10** Πᾶς [*everyone*] ὁ ποιῶν τὴν ἁμαρτίαν καὶ [*also*] τὴν ἀνομίαν [ἀνομία- *lawlessness*] ποιεῖ, καὶ ἡ ἁμαρτία ἐστὶν ἡ ἀνομία. [5] καὶ οἴδατε [*you know*] ὅτι [*that*] ἐκεῖνος [*that one*] ἐφανερώθη [*was revealed*], ἵνα [*so that*] τὰς ἁμαρτίας ἄρῃ [*he might take*], καὶ ἁμαρτία ἐν αὐτῷ οὐκ ἔστιν. [6] πᾶς ὁ ἐν αὐτῷ μένων [μένω – *I remain*] οὐχ ἁμαρτάνει [ἁμαρτανω – *I sin*]. πᾶς ὁ ἁμαρτάνων οὐχ ἑώρακεν [*he has known*] αὐτὸν οὐδὲ ἔγνωκεν [*irreg. Aorist of* γινωσκω] αὐτόν. [7] Τεκνία [=τεκνα], μηδεὶς [*nobody*] πλανάτω [*let him deceive*] ὑμᾶς [*you*]· ὁ ποιῶν τὴν δικαιοσύνην δίκαιός ἐστιν, καθὼς [*just as*] ἐκεῖνος δίκαιός ἐστιν· [8] ὁ ποιῶν τὴν ἁμαρτίαν ἐκ τοῦ διαβόλου [διάβολος – *devil*] ἐστίν, ὅτι ἀπ᾽ ἀρχῆς ὁ διάβολος ἁμαρτάνει. εἰς τοῦτο [*for this reason*] ἐφανερώθη ὁ υἱὸς τοῦ θεοῦ, ἵνα λύσῃ [*so that he might release/destroy*] τὰ ἔργα τοῦ διαβόλου. [9] Πᾶς ὁ γεγεννημένος [*having been born*] ἐκ τοῦ θεοῦ ἁμαρτίαν οὐ ποιεῖ, ὅτι σπέρμα [*seed*] αὐτοῦ ἐν αὐτῷ μένει, καὶ οὐ δύναται [*he is able*] ἁμαρτάνειν, ὅτι ἐκ τοῦ θεοῦ γεγέννηται [*he has been born*]. [10] ἐν τούτῳ [*in this way*] φανερά [*revealed*] ἐστιν τὰ τέκνα τοῦ θεοῦ καὶ τὰ τέκνα τοῦ διαβόλου· πᾶς ὁ μὴ ποιῶν δικαιοσύνην οὐκ ἔστιν ἐκ τοῦ θεοῦ, καὶ ὁ μὴ ἀγαπῶν [*loving*] τὸν ἀδελφὸν αὐτοῦ.

# Other patterns of nouns and verbs

## 8.1 DEPONENT VERBS

John 21.13: ἐρχεται Ἰησους και λαμβανει τον ἀρτον.
– Jesus comes and takes the bread.

Both ἐρχεται and λαμβανει are 3rd person Present Indicative verbs. However, they have different endings. This is because ἐρχεται is from a different family of verbs called the deponent verbs, with their own set of endings.

The majority of Greek verbs conjugate like λυω. However, there are two other groups. One, the μι verbs, only contains a handful of words and will be left until Chapter 19. The other group, the deponent verbs, needs to be learnt now.

The deponent verbs behave just as other verbs do, including sharing the same pattern of ε and σ in the different tenses, but simply have different endings.

### 8.1.1 The deponent endings

**Indicative of** ῥυομαι – I rescue

| | Present | Future | Imperfect | Aorist |
|---|---|---|---|---|
| I | ῥυ-ομαι | ῥυσ-ομαι | ἐρυ-ομην | ἐρυσ-αμην |
| You (sing.) | ῥυ-ῃ | ῥυσ-ῃ | ἐρυ-ου | ἐρυσ-ω |
| He, she, it | ῥυ-εται | ῥυσ-εται | ἐρυ-ετο | ἐρυσ-ατο |
| We | ῥυ-ομεθα | ῥυσ-ομεθα | ἐρυ-ομεθα | ἐρυσ-αμεθα |
| You (pl.) | ῥυ-εσθε | ῥυσ-εσθε | ἐρυ-εσθε | ἐρυσ-ασθε |
| They | ῥυ-ονται | ῥυσ-ονται | ἐρυ-οντο | ἐρυσ-αντο |

Notes

- The endings are completely different from those of λυω.
- As in λυω the Aorist endings have 'a' sounds, the other tenses 'o' or 'e'.
- As in λυω the endings in the Future are the same as the Present.
- The endings are very similar in the different tenses, except for the 2nd sing.
- The addition of the ε and the σ have the same features as in λυω. Thus from ἀρχομαι (I begin), the Future is ἀρξομαι, the Imperfect ἠρχομην and the Aorist ἠρξαμην.

**Other moods of** ῥυομαι

| | | Present | Aorist |
|---|---|---|---|
| **Imperative** | 2nd Sing. | ῥυου | ῥυσαι |
| | 2nd Pl. | ῥυεσθε | ῥυσασθε |
| **Infinitive** | | ῥυεσθαι | ῥυσασθαι |
| **Participle** | Sing. | ῥυομενος | ῥυσαμενος |
| (masc. nom.) | Pl. | ῥυομενοι | ῥυσαμενοι |

Notes

- As in λυω the 2nd plural Present Imperatives are the same as the 2nd plural Present Indicatives.
- As in λυω the Aorists in the other moods lack the ε but still have the σ and the 'a' sound in the endings.
- The Present endings are very similar to those of the Aorist.
- The participles have a distinctive -μεν-.

PRACTICE 8.1.1

## Parse

1. ἐρχονται
2. ἐλογιζετο
3. συνηρχομην
4. ἀρνησαμενος
5. δεξεται
6. ἁπτου
7. εἰσερχομενοι
8. ἐργαζομενος
9. ἀσπαζεσθε

## 8.1.2 Using deponent verbs

KEY GRAMMAR
Deponent Verbs mean exactly the same as Normal Verbs

It is crucial to understand that deponent verbs are simply a second group of verbs.

For example, the Future of a deponent verb means just the same as the Future of a normal verb (like λυω). Some verbs are deponent verbs and use the deponent endings, most are normal and use the normal endings – that is just the way it is – and it makes no difference to the meaning.

### 8.1.3 Which verbs are deponent?

It is very difficult to produce a rule for why certain verbs are deponent when most are normal. Many of the deponent verbs are *intransitive verbs*, that is they cannot have objects (e.g. I go), but there are so many exceptions that this is not a useful guide.

The form of a verb in a vocabulary list or dictionary reveals whether the verb is deponent, since verbs are always quoted in their 1st person singular Present Indicative. If the verb is listed as ending in -ω, it is therefore like λυω (normal); if it is listed as ending in -ομαι, it will be deponent, like ῥυομαι.

For example, πιστευω (I believe) and βαπτιζω (I baptize) are normal like λυω, while ἐρχομαι (I come) and ἀρχομαι (I begin) are deponent like ῥυομαι.

---

**PRACTICE 8.1.3**

### Put the verb in the form indicated

1. βλεπω, 3rd plural Present Indicative
2. ἐρχομαι, 3rd singular Present Indicative
3. δεχομαι, 2nd plural Imperfect Indicative
4. ἀρχομαι, Masculine nominative plural Aorist participle
5. γραφω, 1st plural Future Indicative
6. ἐξερχομαι, Present Imperative (plural)
7. λογιζομαι, 3rd plural Aorist Indicative
8. πειθω, Masculine nominative singular Present participle
9. προσευχομαι, Present Infinitive
10. ἀρνεομαι, 3rd plural Imperfect Indicative

---

### 8.1.4 Terminology

Grammatically, the deponent verbs are said to be in the *Middle Voice*, and the normal verbs in the *Active Voice*. This is potentially confusing because it could imply that it is possible for a deponent verb to be put into the Active Voice rather than the Middle Voice, which is not true.

Later (in Chapter 15) we will need to use the terminology of *Middle* and *Active* Voices. For now, it is easier to think of two types of verbs – normal and deponent – each with their own family of endings. Indeed, the details in Chapter 15 will be easier to understand if you have got used to the ideas of two different types of verb, and have learnt the different endings appropriate to each.

When parsing (e.g. ἐρχομαι) you can say either Middle or deponent (1st sing. Present) – the former is technically better, though the second more helpful.

### HALF-WAY PRACTICE

1. ἐρχονται εἰς το ἱερον.
2. θελω ῥυσασθαι αὐτον.
3. δεχεσθε τον λογον.
4. ἀκουσαντες ἠρξαντο ἐρχεσθαι.
5. ἀπερχομενος ἐδοξαζεν τον θεον.
6. μελλω προσευχεσθαι λεγων·
7. οἱ Ἰουδαιοι ἐξερχονται ἐκ της συναγωγης.
8. μη εὐαγγελιζεσθε.
9. The Pharisees began to work.
10. They were greeting the wicked.
11. I will refuse to keep the law.
12. It is necessary to go into the temple.

## 8.2 IMPERFECT, FUTURE AND OTHER MOODS OF εἰμι

We have already learnt the Present of εἰμι (I am). Unfortunately, most of its forms are irregular, and so also need to be learnt specially.

| | | Present | Future | Imperfect |
|---|---|---|---|---|
| **Indicative** | I | εἰμι | ἐσομαι | ἠμην |
| | You (sing.) | εἰ | ἐσῃ | ἠς (or ἠσθα) |
| | He, she, it | ἐστι (ν) | ἐσται | ἠν |
| | We | ἐσμεν | ἐσομεθα | ἠμεν (or ἠμεθα) |
| | You (pl.) | ἐστε | ἐσεσθε | ἠτε |
| | They | εἰσι (ν) | ἐσονται | ἠσαν |
| **Present Infinitive** | | εἰναι | | |
| **Present participle** (masc. nom.) | | Sing. ὠν | Plural ὀντες | |

### Notes

- The Imperfect begins with an η, the Present and Future an ε. This makes sense – if you add the augment for the Imperfect to an ε, you get an η.

- The Future is almost exactly ἐ plus σ (for the Future) plus deponent endings (except the 3rd singular is ἐσται rather than ἐσεται).
- There can be no Aorist of εἰμι – since if you are talking of 'being' in the past, it is naturally Imperfect, describing a 'process' or 'continued state'.

**PRACTICE 8.2**

## Translate

1. ἁγιαι ἠσαν αἱ ἐντολαι.
2. ὁ Δαυιδ ἠν μεγας.
3. θελω εἰναι μετ᾽ αὐτων.
4. ὁ φιλων θεον ἐσται μακαριος.
5. προσηυχετο ὠν ἁγιος.
6. The children were alone.
7. The slaves will be dead.
8. Being Jewish, we wish to enter the synagogue.

## 8.3 NOUNS OF CONFUSING GENDER

John 20.3: ὁ Πετρος και ὁ ἀλλος μαθητης ... ἠρχοντο εἰς το μνημειον.
– Peter and the other disciple were coming to the tomb.

The words ὁ, Πετρος, ἀλλος and μαθητης are nominative masculine singular since 'Peter' and 'disciple' are both the subjects of the sentence, and ὁ and ἀλλος are agreeing with them. However, μαθητης does not look like a masculine nominative singular – this is because it is from a new pattern of nouns.

So far we have learnt that masculine nouns decline like λογος and feminine nouns like ἀρχη (or ἡμερα/δοξα). However, there is a family of masculine nouns that decline similarly to ἀρχη, and a couple of feminine nouns that decline like λογος.

### 8.3.1 Masculine nouns *similar* to ἀρχη – προφητης and Ἰουδας

There is a group of masculine nouns that are either proper names or are the names of types of people. Their endings are identical to those of ἀρχη / ἡμερα except in the nominative and genitive singular.

| | | (prophet) | (Judas/Judah) |
|---|---|---|---|
| Sing. | Nom. | προφητης | Ἰουδας |
| | Acc. | προφητην | Ἰουδαν |
| | Gen. | προφητου | Ἰουδα |
| | Dat. | προφητῃ | Ἰουδᾳ |

| | | | |
|---|---|---|---|
| Plural | Nom.<br>Acc.<br>Gen.<br>Dat. | προφηται<br>προφητας<br>προφητων<br>προφηταις | (the few words in -ας for which a plural is logical have the same endings as in προφητης) |

Notes

- These nouns are unusual for not having vocatives identical to their nominatives – the vocatives are προφητα and ʼΙουδα.
- Nouns in -ας whose stems end in ε, ι or ρ (e.g. ʼΗλιας) have a genitive in -ου (ʼΗλιου), copying προφητης.

### 8.3.2 Feminine nouns *identical* to λογος

Here are three words that decline exactly the same as λογος but are feminine.

ὁδος – way  ἐρημος – wilderness  Αἰγυπτος – Egypt

### 8.3.3 Agreements

For both of these types of noun you need to watch agreements carefully, for these nouns are the gender they are (e.g. προφητην is masculine, ὁδου is feminine) despite what the endings might suggest.

When these nouns have the article, adjective or anything else that has to agree with them, the agreement is with the actual gender of the noun, rather than simply 'the endings matching'.

e.g. τον προφητην, της ὁδου, τῳ πιστῳ Βαρναβᾳ.

### 8.3.4 Terminology

Traditionally the different declensions we have learnt are labelled as follows:

| | Masculine | Feminine | Neuter |
|---|---|---|---|
| 1st declension | (Limited number of words like προφητης) | ἀρχη | (none) |
| 2nd declension | λογος | (Few words like ὁδος declining like λογος) | ἐργον |

However, since the adjectives, pronouns and the article all take endings like λογος in the masculine, like ἀρχη in the feminine and like ἐργον in the neuter, it is more helpful to think of all these words belonging to a single pattern, with the minor variations noted in this section.

| | Masculine | Feminine | Neuter |
|---|---|---|---|
| Normal Pattern | λογος | ἀρχη | ἐργον |
| Exceptions | (Limited number of nouns like προφητης which have feminine-looking endings) | (Few nouns like ὁδος which decline like the masculine λογος) | (none) |

However, occasionally it might be necessary for you to understand the traditional terminology of 1st declension and 2nd declension.

PRACTICE 8.3

## Translate

1. οἱ μαθηται αὐτου ἐρχονται.
2. ἐλεγεν τῳ Ἰουδᾳ.
3. ὁ ἀδελφος δεξεται τον Ἰωαννην.
4. πολλοι στρατιωται προσηρχοντο.
5. Jesus was proclaiming the way.
6. The prophets were not holy.

## VOCAB FOR CHAPTER 8

Nineteen deponent verbs
*ἐρχομαι (634) – I come, go
*ἀπερχομαι (117) – I depart, go away
διερχομαι (43) – I cross over
*εἰσερχομαι (194) – I go into, enter
*ἐξερχομαι (218) – I go out, go away
παρερχομαι (29) – I go by, pass by
*προσερχομαι (86) – I come to, go to, approach
συνερχομαι (30) – I come together

ἁπτομαι (39) + gen. – I touch
*ἀρνεομαι (33) – I refuse, deny
*ἀρχομαι (86) – I begin
*ἀσπαζομαι (59) – I greet
*δεχομαι (56) – I receive
*ἐργαζομαι (41) – I work
*εὐαγγελιζομαι (54) – I proclaim good news (a compound εὐ-ἀγγελιζομαι)
λογιζομαι (40) – I calculate, consider
*προσευχομαι (85) – I pray
προσκαλεομαι (29) – I summon
*ῥυομαι (17) – I rescue

Six masculine nouns like προφητης
Ἡρῳδης, ὁ (43) – Herod
*Ἰωαννης or Ἰωανης, ὁ (135) – John
*μαθητης, ὁ (261) – disciple
*προφητης, ὁ (144) – prophet
*στρατιωτης, ὁ (26) – soldier
ὑπηρετης, ὁ (20) – servant

And three like Ἰουδας
Βαρναβας, ὁ (28) – Barnabas
*Ἰουδας, ὁ (44) – Judah, Judas

Σατανας, ὁ (36) – Satan

Plus one like Ἰουδας but with a genitive in -ου
*Ἠλιας, ὁ (29) – Elijah

Three feminine words declining like λογος
Αἰγυπτος, ἡ (25) – Egypt
*ἐρημος, ἡ (48) – wilderness, desolate land
*ὁδος, ἡ (101) – way, road

**Hint**

It is easy to confuse ἀρχομαι and ἐρχομαι particularly since they look identical in the Imperfect – ἠρχομην.

Don't try to use ἐρχομαι (or its compounds) yet in the Future or Aorist – these are irregular (we will meet them in Chapter 11, section 11.1 and Chapter 18, section 18.4).

## Word helps

archaic, deck/dock, energy, evangelise, logic, mathematics, strategy, exodus, hermit.

## Exercises

Section A

*1. ἐρχεται ὁ Ἰησους και λαμβανει τον ἀρτον.
*2. και ὁ ὀχλος ἠρχετο παλιν παρα την θαλασσαν προς αὐτον, και ἐδιδασκεν αὐτους.
*3. ἀπο τοτε ἠρξατο ὁ Ἰησους κηρυσσειν και λεγειν· Μετανοειτε· προσερχεται ἡ βασιλεια των οὐρανων.
4. ἐλεγεν ἐν παραβολῃ αὐτοις· Δει παντοτε προσευχεσθαι.
5. και ὁ ὀχλος ἐζητουν[1] ἁπτεσθαι αὐτου· σημεια ἐξουσιας παρ᾽ αὐτου ἐξηρχετο.
6. ὁ Ἰωαννης ἐσται μεγας ἐνωπιον του κυριου ὡς ὁ Ἠλιας· ἀλλ᾽ ὁ Ἡρῳδης πονηρος.
7. μελλει ὁ υἱος του ἀνθρωπου ἐρχεσθαι ἐν τῃ δοξῃ του θεου μετα των ἀγγελων αὐτου, και τοτε δεξεται ἑκαστος κατα την ζωην αὐτου.
*8. ἐλεγεν προς τους μαθητας· Εἰ θελετε ὀπισω του υἱου του ἀνθρωπου ἐρχεσθαι, ἀρνησασθε τον Σαταναν και ἀκολουθειτε τῳ κυριῳ καθ᾽ ἡμεραν.[2]

---

[1] Here (following Luke 6.19) a plural verb is used with ὀχλος. While technically incorrect, this is perfectly understandable since in a sense an ὀχλος is plural.
[2] καθ᾽ ἡμεραν is a Greek idiom for 'each day' or 'daily'.

9. The house of Judah prayed, 'Lord, rescue Israel from Egypt!'
*10. Elijah was a great prophet.
*11. They were going away from the synagogue when we were going in.
*12. Barnabas and Paul were proclaiming good news on the road from Jerusalem with the faithful disciples.

## Section B

*1. οἱ προφηται ἐκηρυξαν· Ἐκ της καρδιας ἐξερχεται πονηρα και ἀγαθα.
2. δει διερχεσθαι δια της ἐρημου συν τοις στρατιωταις.
3. ἡ ἀγαπη κακον οὐκ ἐργαζεται· ἡ μεγαλη ἐντολη ἐστιν ἀγαπη.
*4. Ἀσπαζονται ἐν κυριῳ Βαρναβας και Ἰουδας οἱ μαθηται τας ἐκκλησιας της Ἰερουσαλημ.
*5. λεγει προς τον ἀγγελον· Πως ἐσται;
6. ὁτε ἠμην τεκνον, ἐλαλουν ὡς τεκνον, ἐλογιζομην ὡς τεκνον.
7. ἀλλα ἐρχεται ὡρα και νυν ἐστιν, ὁτε οἱ μαθηται χαρᾳ προσκυνησουσιν τῳ κυριῳ, ὡς αὐτους ζητει και προσκαλειται ὁ θεος.
*8. ῥυσῃ ἀνθρωπον ἁμαρτιας ἐκ του θανατου του αἰωνιου;
*9. John was a brother and disciple.
10. The soldiers of Herod are passing on the road.
*11. Do you (pl.) wish to go into church or to be alone?
12. Because of Herod, Joseph and Mary were going along the sea on the road to Egypt with the child Jesus.

## Section C

**Mark 4.1-2** Καὶ πάλιν ἤρξατο διδάσκειν παρὰ τὴν θάλασσαν· καὶ συνάγεται [*it was gathered*] πρὸς αὐτὸν ὄχλος πλεῖστος [*very large*], ὥστε [*with the result that*] αὐτὸν εἰς πλοῖον ἐμβάντα [*getting in*] καθῆσθαι [*sat*] ἐν τῇ θαλάσσῃ, καὶ πᾶς [*all*] ὁ ὄχλος πρὸς τὴν θάλασσαν ἐπὶ τῆς γῆς ἦσαν.[3]
2 καὶ ἐδίδασκεν αὐτοὺς ἐν παραβολαῖς πολλὰ καὶ ἔλεγεν αὐτοῖς ἐν τῇ διδαχῇ [*teaching, instruction*] αὐτοῦ, . . .

---

[3] See note 1 on page 98.

# Pronouns and conjunctions

## 9.1 ἐκεινος AND οὑτος (THAT AND THIS)

Matt. 21.11: ἐλεγον· Οὑτος ἐστιν ὁ προφητης Ἰησους ...
– They were saying: 'This is the prophet Jesus . . .'
Matt. 14.1: ἐν ἐκεινῳ τῳ καιρῳ ἠκουσεν Ἡρῳδης ...
– At that time Herod heard . . .

### 9.1.1 Formation

ἐκεινος ('that', plural 'those') declines just like αὐτος (Chapter 3, section 3.6) – i.e. like ἀγαθος except in the nominative and accusative neuter singular, where the ending is -ο rather than -ον.

| | | Masculine | Feminine | Neuter |
|---|---|---|---|---|
| Sing. | Nom. | ἐκεινος | ἐκεινη | ἐκεινο |
| | Acc. | ἐκεινον | ἐκεινην | ἐκεινο |
| | Gen. | ἐκεινου | ἐκεινης | ἐκεινου |
| | Dat. | ἐκεινῳ | ἐκεινῃ | ἐκεινῳ |
| Plural | Nom. | ἐκεινοι | ἐκειναι | ἐκεινα |
| | Acc. | ἐκεινους | ἐκεινας | ἐκεινα |
| | Gen. | ἐκεινων | ἐκεινων | ἐκεινων |
| | Dat. | ἐκεινοις | ἐκειναις | ἐκεινοις |

οὗτος ('this', plural 'these') is a little more awkward:

| | | Masculine | Feminine | Neuter |
|---|---|---|---|---|
| Sing. | Nom. | οὗτος | αὕτη[1] | τουτο |
| | Acc. | τουτον | ταυτην | τουτο |
| | Gen. | τουτου | ταυτης | τουτου |
| | Dat. | τουτῳ | ταυτῃ | τουτῳ |
| Plural | Nom. | οὗτοι | αὗται | ταυτα |
| | Acc. | τουτους | ταυτας | ταυτα |
| | Gen. | τουτων | τουτων | τουτων |
| | Dat. | τουτοις | ταυταις | τουτοις |

Notes

- The *endings* of οὗτος are the same as for ἐκεινος (and therefore the same as αὐτος and similar to ἀγαθος).
- οὗτος begins with a τ in most of its forms. However, there is a rough breathing instead in the nominative, masculine and feminine, singular and plural. This is the same as in the article (which begins with a τ except for ὁ, ἡ, οἱ and αἱ).
- The first vowel fluctuates between ου and αυ. The rule is that it matches the second vowel (the one in the ending). If the second vowel has an ο sound, the first vowel is ου, but if it has an η or α sound, it is αυ.

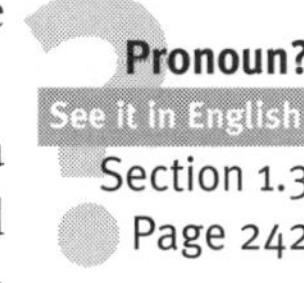


Hint

Initially, what is important is simply to be able to recognise the forms of οὗτος in Greek. This is relatively easy, but watch for the forms without the τ.

PRACTICE 9.1.1

## Parse

| | | | |
|---|---|---|---|
| 1. ἐκειναι | 3. ταυτα | 5. αὐτοι | 7. ἐκεινο |
| 2. τουτου | 4. ἐκεινα | 6. οὗτοι | 8. αὕτη |

## 9.1.2 Use

οὗτος and ἐκεινος can both be used either as a pronoun or as an adjective. Although this sounds complicated, it is exactly the same as English (pronoun – this is boring; adjective – this book is boring).

[1] αὕτη (from οὗτος, with a rough breathing) is easily confused with αὐτη (from αὐτος).

Their **use as pronouns** is straightforward (if it is not clear what noun they are standing in place of, try supplying in English 'person' or 'man' if they are masculine, 'woman' [feminine] or 'thing' [neuter]).

> ἐβλεψα ἐκεινους. – I saw those people.
> ἀρξεται ταυτα. – He will begin these things.

Their **use as adjectives** is almost as simple, but two points need to be learnt.

(i) The article must always be used in addition.
(ii) They are placed in the predicative word order (i.e. before the article or immediately after the noun, but never immediately after the article) despite the fact that their use is really attributive.[2]

| | |
|---|---|
| In English: | This brother |
| In Greek: | οὗτος ὁ ἀδελφος (This the brother) |

- ὁλος ('whole') declines like ἀγαθος but it is used like οὗτος (i.e. it comes before the article), e.g. the whole crowd = ὁλος ὁ ὀχλος not ὁ ὁλος ὀχλος

PRACTICE 9.1.2

### Translate

1. οὗτος ἠν ὁ τοπος.
2. νεκρα τα προβατα τουτων.
3. ὁλος ὁ ὀχλος ἠκουεν.
4. λεγει ἐκειναις ταις παραβολαις.
5. οἱ προφηται αὐτου ἐρχονται.
6. τυφλοι εἰσιν οὗτοι οἱ μαθηται.

## 9.2 THIRD PERSON PRONOUNS

### 9.2.1 Further use of αὐτος

We have already met the common 3rd person pronoun αὐτος (he, she, it, they – Chapter 3, section 3.6). As well as its use as a pronoun, αὐτος can be used as an adjective, in which case it has two different meanings, depending on its position:

- Adjective meaning 'same'
  Normal attributive position (between article and noun)
- Emphatic adjective (himself, herself, itself, themselves)
  Coming before the article (predicative position) 'for emphasis'

[2] You can rationalise this by thinking that 'this' and 'that' are by nature emphatic words, and so come first for emphasis.

Examples

- λεγω <u>αὐτῃ</u>. – I am speaking <u>to her</u>.
- οἱ μαθηται <u>αὐτου</u> ἐλεγον. – <u>His</u> disciples were speaking.
- ὁ <u>αὐτος</u> κυριος σωζει τον λαον. – The <u>same</u> Lord saves the people.
- <u>αὐτος</u> ὁ κυριος σωζει τον λαον. – The Lord <u>himself</u> saves the people.

### 9.2.2 ἑαυτος

ἑαυτος is the 3rd person reflexive pronoun (himself, herself, itself, themselves). This is confusing, because English uses the same words (e.g. himself) to cover two different meanings – an emphatic adjective and a reflexive pronoun. In Greek the emphatic adjective is αὐτος, the reflexive pronoun ἑαυτος.

ἑαυτος declines exactly as αὐτος does, but because of its meaning will never occur in the nominative.

Examples

- ὁ κυριος σωζει <u>ἑαυτον</u>. – The Lord saves <u>himself</u>.
- <u>αὐτος</u> ὁ κυριος σωζει τον λαον. – The Lord <u>himself</u> saves the people.

**Hint**

You can tell whether 'himself' etc. is *reflexive* or *emphatic* by deleting it. If the sentence's basic meaning is unaltered, it was *emphatic*; if not, it was *reflexive*.

### 9.2.3 ἀλλος and ἀλληλος

ἀλλος (other) and ἀλληλος (one another) both decline like ἐκεινος.

ἀλλος is an adjective meaning 'other'. It is used in the same way as a normal adjective, i.e. in the attributive position (not like ἐκεινος and οὑτος).

ἀλληλος is a pronoun meaning 'one another'. It is used exactly as one would expect (note: because of its meaning, it can never appear in the nominative).

Examples

Mark 4.36: και <u>ἄλλα</u> πλοια ἠν μετ᾽ αὐτου. – And <u>other</u> boats were with him.[3]
Mark 4.41: ἐλεγον προς <u>ἀλληλους</u>. – They were saying <u>to one another</u>.

---

**HALF-WAY PRACTICE**

1. ἀρνουνται ἑαυτους.
2. φιλω ἐκεινον τον μαθητην.

---

[3] The neuter plural nom. or acc. of ἀλλος looks the same as the word for 'but'. Here accents can help us – ἀλλὰ means 'but' while ἄλλα is from ἀλλος.

3. συναγει ταυτα τα προβατα.
4. ἐδιδασκεν ἀλλαις παραβολαις.
5. ἐν τῃ αὐτῃ ἡμερᾳ ἡ Μαρια ἐβλεψεν τον κυριον.
6. δια ταυτα ὁ ὀχλος ἐλαλει ἀλληλοις.
7. αὐτος ὁ Ἰησους προσηυχετο.
8. ὑπηρετης ἠν τουτου του ἱερου.
9. We are praying to the same God.
10. Peter himself denied Jesus.
11. They began to listen after this.
12. Those demons were evil.

## 9.3 FIRST AND SECOND PERSON PRONOUNS AND ADJECTIVES

### 9.3.1 Pronouns

| | 1st Person | | | | 2nd Person | | |
|---|---|---|---|---|---|---|---|
| | Sing. | | Plural | | Sing. | | Plural |
| Nom. | ἐγω | *I* | ἡμεις | *we* | συ | *you* | ὑμεις |
| Acc. | ἐμε *or* με | *me* | ἡμας | *us* | σε | *you* | ὑμας |
| Gen. | ἐμου *or* μου | *of me, mine* | ἡμων | *of us, our* | σου | *of you, your* | ὑμων |
| Dat. | ἐμοι *or* μοι | *to/for me* | ἡμιν | *to/for us* | σοι | *to/for you* | ὑμιν |

#### Note

- λυομεν itself means 'we untie'. There is no need for a word for 'we'. Indeed, these pronouns should be used in the nominative (ἐγω, ἡμεις, συ, ὑμεις) *only* when particular emphasis or contrast is intended.

#### Examples

Gal. 5.2: <u>ἐγω</u> Παυλος λεγω <u>ὑμιν</u> ... – <u>I</u> Paul tell <u>you</u> . . .
John 12.27: σωσον <u>με</u> ἐκ της ὡρας ταυτης. – Save <u>me</u> from this hour.
John 21.17: λεγει αὐτῳ ... Φιλεις <u>με</u>; ... και λεγει αὐτῳ· Κυριε ... <u>συ</u> γινωσκεις ὁτι φιλω <u>σε</u>. – he said to him . . . 'Do you love <u>me</u>?' . . . and he said to him, 'Lord . . . <u>you</u> know that I love <u>you</u>'.

### 9.3.2 Reflexive pronouns

| | |
|---|---|
| Myself | ἐμαυτος (declines like αὐτος) |
| Yourself (sing.) | σεαυτος (declines like αὐτος) |
| Ourselves | just use plural of ἑαυτος |
| Yourselves (pl.) | just use plural of ἑαυτος |

### 9.3.3 Possessive adjectives

The most common way of expressing possession is by using the genitive of the personal pronouns – μου, σου, ἡμων, ὑμων (of me, of you, of us, of you).

However, there are also adjectives (which decline like ἀγαθος) for 'my' and 'you' (singular).

| | | | |
|---|---|---|---|
| My | ἐμος | Your (sing.) | σος |

**Hint**

'My words' is οἱ λογοι μου not λογοι μου. (Compare: 'his words', οἱ λογοι αὐτου.) ἐμος, σος, μου, ἡμων, σου and ὑμων all need the article.

Examples

John 10.26: οὐκ ἐστε ἐκ των προβατων των ἐμων. – You are not of my sheep.
John 20.28: Ὁ κυριος μου και ὁ θεος μου. – My Lord and my God!

**PRACTICE 9.3**

### Translate

1. ὁ νομος σου σωζει.
2. ὁ θεος σωζει σε.
3. ἡμεις ἐπιστευσαμεν ἀλλα συ οὐκ ἠκουσας.
4. συ σωσεις σεαυτον ἀλλ᾽ ἐγω ἀλλους.
5. Save yourself!
6. I will proclaim your (pl.) deeds.

## 9.4 CONJUNCTIONS

Conjunctions are words that join together two sentences – words such as 'therefore', 'thus', 'when' etc. There are equivalent words in Greek and so translation is quite straightforward. However, there are four points to note.

### 9.4.1 Timid words

There are a number of conjunctions that are 'timid', in that they cannot stand first in their sentence or clause (the technical name for them is *postpositives*).

KEY GRAMMAR

| | |
|---|---|
| ἀρα – so | μεν – on the one hand |
| γαρ – because / for | οὐν – therefore |
| δε – but | τε – and |

cannot come as the first word[4]

When translating you need mentally to move the *postpositive* one word earlier in the sentence.[5]

Examples

Mark 3.10: πολλους γαρ ἐθεραπευσεν
– because he healed many

1 Thes. 2.20: ὑμεις γαρ ἐστε ἡ δοξα ἡμων και ἡ χαρα.
– because you are our glory and joy.

### 9.4.2 μεν and δε

μεν is normally used preceding a δε. In these cases, a contrast between two things is being stressed. You can think of μεν meaning 'on the one hand' and then δε as meaning 'on the other hand' (although this can sound excessive in English).

λογιζεσθε ἑαυτους εἰναι νεκρους μεν τῃ ἁμαρτιᾳ ζωντας δε τῳ θεῳ (Rom. 6.11) – consider yourselves to be (on the one hand) dead to sin but (on the other hand) alive to God.

1 Cor. 1.12: ἑκαστος ὑμων λεγει· Ἐγω μεν εἰμι Παυλου, ἐγω δε Ἀπολλω, ἐγω δε Κηφα, ἐγω δε Χριστου. – Each of you says, 'I am Paul's, I am Apollos', I am Cephas', I am Christ's' (or 'I belong to Paul, I belong to Apollos . . .').

If μεν and δε are used just with the article, they mean 'some . . . but others . . .'.

Acts 14.4: ... και οἱ μεν ἠσαν συν τοις Ἰουδαιοις, οἱ δε συν τοις ἀποστολοις.
– and some were with the Jews but others were with the apostles.

### 9.4.3 Use of δε

Normally every Greek sentence needs to be connected to the previous one by a conjunction in a way that is not necessary in English. Greek will tend to use the word δε to do this. Therefore, a Greek δε will often be untranslated in English.

---

4 Plus ποτε (once, at some time) learnt in Chapter 6.

5 Notice that in English we sometimes do put conjunctions later in the sentence – for example, saying 'I find, however, that Greek is enjoyable' in place of 'However, I find that Greek is enjoyable.' In Greek, though, there is less flexibility: most conjunctions will occur at the beginning of the sentence; the *postpositives* never do.

Thus δε is a weak 'but'. Another conjunction, ἀλλα (which is not *postpositive*), expresses 'but' more strongly.

δε is also used just with the article (e.g. ὁ δε) to point out that the subject has changed (e.g. Mark 6.37-38: λεγουσιν αὐτῳ ... ὁ δε λεγει αὐτοις, Ποσους ἀρτους ἐχετε; – They said to him . . . he said to them, 'How many loaves of bread do you have?')

### 9.4.4 Use of και

και normally means 'and'.[6] However, it can also be used to give emphasis, equivalent to 'also' or 'even' in English. The rule for translating it is that if 'and' is necessary (i.e. there is no other conjunction), then it is 'and'. If 'and' is not necessary (i.e. the και seems redundant), then it is there for emphasis and should be translated 'also' or 'even'.

τε is often followed by και giving the meaning 'both . . . and'.

Examples

Mark 2.28: κυριος ἐστιν ὁ υἱος του ἀνθρωπου και του σαββατου.
– The son of man is lord even over the Sabbath.

Acts 1.1: (ὡν) ἠρξατο ὁ Ἰησους ποιειν τε και διδασκειν.
– (which) Jesus began both to do and to teach.

---

PRACTICE 9.4

### Translate

1. πολλοι ἐπιστευσαν, οἱ γαρ μαθηται εὐηγγελιζοντο.
2. ὁ μεν θεος ἐπεμψεν τους προφητας, τυφλος δε ὁ λαος.
3. ὁ θεος φιλει και τους πονηρους;
4. ὁ Ἰωσηφ λεγει αὐτῳ. ὁ δε οὐκ ἀκουσει.
5. οἱ μεν προσερχονται, οἱ δε ὑπαγουσιν εἰς τους οἰκους αὐτων.
6. Therefore we will seek the lord.

---

## VOCAB FOR CHAPTER 9

Sixteen pronouns or personal adjectives

*ἀλληλος (100) – each other, one another

*ἀλλος (155) – other

*ἑαυτος (319) – himself, herself, itself (reflexive)

*ἐγω, ἡμεις (2666) – I, we

---

[6] Like δε it is sometimes used merely as the necessary conjunction between two sentences, and so is unnecessary in English.

*ἐκεινος (265) – that (pl. those)
ἐμαυτος (37) – myself
ἐμος (76) – my, mine
*κἀγω (84) – and I (= και + ἐγω).[7]
*ὁλος (109) – whole, entire
*οὑτος αὑτη τουτο (1387) – this (pl. these)
ποιος (33) – of what kind?
ποσος (27) – how great, how much?
*σεαυτος (43) – yourself
σος (27) – your, yours (sing.)
*συ, ὑμεις (2907) – you (sing.), you (pl.)
τοιουτος (57) – of such a kind, such

Twelve conjunctions
ἀρα (49) – so
*γαρ (1041) – because, for
γε (25) – indeed
*δε (2792) – but
*διο (53) – therefore
διοτι (23) – because
*εἰτε (65) – if
(εἰτε ... εἰτε – if ... if, whether ... or)
ἐπει (26) – since
*μεν (179) – on the one hand
μηποτε (25) – never
*οὐν (499) – therefore, consequently
*τε (215) – and
(τε ... και – both ... and)

Four more neuter nouns
*ἀρνιον (30) – lamb, sheep
δενδρον (25) – tree
μυστηριον (28) – mystery, secret
*ποτηριον (31) – cup

## Word helps

parallel, allotropic, autobiography/autograph, egotist, holistic/catholic, rhododendron, mystery, pottery.

## Exercises

### Section A

*1. αὐτος δε Ἰησους οὐκ ἐπιστευεν[8] ἑαυτον αὐτοις.
*2. και ἐλεγεν αὐτοις· Ὑμεις ἐκ τουτου του κοσμου ἐστε, ἐγω οὐκ εἰμι ἐκ του κοσμου τουτου.
*3. και τοιαυταις παραβολαις πολλαις ἐλαλει αὐτοις τον λογον.
*4. και ἐρχονται παλιν εἰς Ἱεροσολυμα. και ἐν τῳ ἱερῳ περιπατει ὁ Ἰησους και ἐρχονται προς αὐτον οἱ Ἰουδαιοι.
5. ἐλεγον οὐν οἱ Ἰουδαιοι προς ἑαυτους· Που οὑτος μελλει ἐρχεσθαι;

[7] This combining of και and ἐγω to give κἀγω is technically called *crasis* and can occur with other words, e.g. κἀκεινον for και εκεινον, though is relatively rare. The breathing on the vowel in the middle of the word highlights that *crasis* has taken place.
[8] Here πιστευω has the relatively unusual meaning of ' I entrust'.

*6. ἐκ του θεου ἐσμεν και ὁ κοσμος ὁλος ἐν τῳ πονηρῳ ἐστιν.
7. και ἐλεγεν αὐτοις· Ὑμιν το μυστηριον διδασκω της βασιλειας του θεου· ἐκεινοις δε τοις ἐξω ἐν παραβολαις ταυτα λεγω.
8. ἐλεγεν γαρ ὁ Ἰωαννης τῳ Ἡρῳδῃ· Οὐκ ἐξεστιν σοι ἐχειν την γυναικα [*wife*] του ἀδελφου σου.
*9. This is my commandment: Have love for one another, because you are my disciples.
*10. I am the bread of life.
*11. Jesus says to them, 'I do not tell you (pl.) by (use ἐν) what authority I am doing these things.'
12. Having received his sight, he was saying, 'I see people, but they are walking about like trees.'

## Section B

*1. ἐζητουν οὐν τον Ἰησουν και ἐλεγον μετ' ἀλληλων ἐν τῳ ἱερῳ· Πως ποιει ταυτα;
2. ἐστιν χαρα ἐν ὑμιν δια την ἀγαπην ὑμων τε και ἐμου.
3. Σαδδουκαιοι [*Sadducees*] μεν γαρ λεγουσιν μη εἰναι ζωην μετα θανατον μητε ἀγγελον, Φαρισαιοι δε διδασκουσιν ταυτα.
*4. κἀγω δε σοι λεγω ὁτι [*that*] συ εἶ Πετρος, και ἐπι ταυτῃ τῃ πετρᾳ [*rock*] οἰκοδομησω μου την ἐκκλησιαν.
*5. ἐκραζον φωνῃ μεγαλῃ λεγοντες· Ἁγιον ἐστιν το ἀρνιον.
*6. και ἐλεγεν· Οὐ θελω το ποτηριον τουτο· ἀλλα τουτο θελεις, διο ἐγω δεξομαι αὐτο.
7. και εἰ γαρ εἰσιν ἀλλοι θεοι εἰτε ἐν οὐρανῳ εἰτε ἐπι γης, ἡμιν ἐστιν εἱς [*one*] θεος· και γε οὑτος ἐστιν ὁ κυριος του οὐρανου και της γης· αὐτῳ ἀρα προσκυνησομεν.
8. τοτε προσκαλεσαμενος αὐτον ὁ κυριος αὐτου λεγει αὐτῳ, Δουλε πονηρε, ποιησω ἐκεινο σοι, ἐπει παρεκαλεσας με.
*9. The Pharisees therefore were saying to him, 'You are bearing witness about yourself.'
*10. The whole earth exists for his glory, so we bless him and give thanks.
*11. If I cast out demons by the authority of God, the reign of God is upon you (pl.).
12. On the one hand, you come together with one another, on the other hand, you persecute one another.

## Section C

**Matthew 16.13-18** Ἐλθὼν [*Aorist participle* of ἐρχομαι] δὲ ὁ Ἰησοῦς εἰς τὰ μέρη [*the region*] Καισαρείας τῆς Φιλίππου ἠρώτα [*he began to ask*] τοὺς μαθητὰς

αὐτοῦ λέγων [*saying*], Τίνα [*whom*] λέγουσιν οἱ ἄνθρωποι εἶναι τὸν υἱὸν
τοῦ ἀνθρώπου; 14 οἱ δὲ εἶπαν [*they said*], Οἱ μὲν Ἰωάννην τὸν βαπτιστήν, ἄλλοι
δὲ Ἠλίαν, ἕτεροι [*others*] δὲ Ἰερεμίαν ἢ ἕνα [*one*] τῶν προφητῶν.
15 λέγει αὐτοῖς, Ὑμεῖς δὲ τίνα με λέγετε εἶναι; 16 ἀποκριθεὶς [*in reply*] δὲ
Σίμων Πέτρος εἶπεν [*said*], Σὺ εἶ ὁ Χριστὸς ὁ υἱὸς τοῦ θεοῦ τοῦ ζῶντος [*living*].
17 ἀποκριθεὶς δὲ ὁ Ἰησοῦς εἶπεν αὐτῷ, Μακάριος εἶ, Σίμων Βαριωνᾶ, ὅτι σὰρξ
[*flesh*] καὶ αἷμα [*blood*] οὐκ ἀπεκάλυψέν σοι ἀλλ᾽ ὁ πατήρ [*father*] μου ὁ ἐν
τοῖς οὐρανοῖς. 18 κἀγὼ δέ σοι λέγω ὅτι σὺ εἶ Πέτρος, καὶ ἐπὶ ταύτῃ τῇ πέτρᾳ
[*rock*] οἰκοδομήσω μου τὴν ἐκκλησίαν καὶ πύλαι [*gates*] ᾅδου [*of Hades*] οὐ
κατισχύσουσιν [*they will overcome + gen.*] αὐτῆς.

# Complex sentences

## 10.1 RELATIVE PRONOUN

Rom. 16.5: ἀσπασασθε Ἐπαινετον τον ἀγαπητον μου, ὅς ἐστιν ἀπαρχη της Ἀσιας εἰς Χριστον.
– Greet my beloved Epaenetos, who is a beginning of Asia for Christ.

Luke 7.27: οὑτος ἐστιν περι οὑ γεγραπται ...
– this is (the one) concerning whom it is written . . .

Luke 6.46: τί δε με καλειτε· κυριε κυριε, και οὐ ποιειτε ἅ λεγω;
– why do you call me, 'Lord, Lord', and do not do what I say?

The Greek word ὅς (which declines giving forms such as οὑ and ἅ) is equivalent to the English 'who' (which itself produces whom, whose, what and which). These words join together two sentences/clauses: they come in the second, but point back to a noun in the first, exactly as they do in English.

### 10.1.1 Understanding relatives

The relative pronoun is not difficult in Greek – it functions in basically the same way as in English. However, because the function of the relative is to join together into one sentence what could be two sentences, you do need to have a firm grasp of the basics of Greek sentences (from Chapters 2, 3 and 4). In particular:

**Pronoun?**
See it in English
Section 1.3
Page 242

- There will be two main verbs in a complex sentence – one from each of the two constituent sentences. You need to be clear which verb is going with which subject.
- The relative pronoun functions as the join between the two constituent sentences – both of these sentences have a role in determining its gender, case and number.

- In formal English the relative pronoun changes in different cases ('who' is different from 'whom'), but most English speakers do not now use this distinction, and so find it frustrating that there is not a single word for 'who' in Greek.[1]

KEY GRAMMAR
The relative pronoun links together two basic sentences

Examples

*Two basic sentences*: 1. The lord sent the messenger.
2. The messenger saw the sea.

Since 'the messenger' occurs in both sentences, he can be replaced in the second by the relative pronoun.

*One complex sentence*: The lord sent the messenger who saw the sea.

When this is written in Greek, it is vital to be aware that:

- there are still two basic sentences here (e.g. there are two main verbs – 'sent' and 'saw')
- 'who' is standing in for 'the messenger'. Grammatically 'the messenger' is called the *antecedent* of 'who' – the word in the previous sentence that the 'who' is looking back to.

*One complex sentence*: They are keeping the law which he teaches.

*Two basic sentences*: 1. They are keeping the law.
2. He teaches the law.

Thus, in the complex sentence, 'the law' is the antecedent of 'which'.

Hint

- The antecedent will come in the first sentence.
- The relative will be in the second sentence (replacing the antecedent).
- In English the antecedent normally immediately precedes the relative.

PRACTICE 10.1.1

**Break down these complex sentences into two basic sentences. Which word is the antecedent of the relative in these sentences?**

1. Jesus threw out the demon which was in the man.
2. I am the man whom you are seeking.

---

[1] However, 'whose' as the genitive of 'who' is still generally used in English.

3. She ate the meal which the king sent.
4. The prophet offered the sacrifice, because of which the rain came.
5. Is this the Messiah for whom we are waiting?
6. The governor sent the soldiers who arrested Jesus.

### 10.1.2 Formation of the relative in Greek

The relative pronoun ὅς (English: who, whom, whose, what, which) declines very similarly to the definite article. To highlight this in the table below, the article is declined in the white columns next to the corresponding part of the relative.

| | | Masculine | | Feminine | | Neuter | |
|---|---|---|---|---|---|---|---|
| Sing. | Nom. | ὅς | ὁ | ἣ[2] | ἡ | ὃ[2] | το |
| | Acc. | ὅν | τον | ἥν | την | ὃ[2] | το |
| | Gen. | οὗ | του | ἧς | της | οὗ | του |
| | Dat. | ᾧ | τῳ | ᾗ | τῃ | ᾧ | τῳ |
| Plural | Nom. | οἳ[2] | οἱ | αἳ[2] | αἱ | ἅ | τα |
| | Acc. | οὕς | τους | ἅς | τας | ἅ | τα |
| | Gen. | ὧν | των | ὧν | των | ὧν | των |
| | Dat. | οἷς | τοις | αἷς | ταις | οἷς | τοις |

Key: ὅν Relative pronoun τον Definite article for comparison

**Hint**

A very short word with a rough breathing is almost certain to be part of the relative pronoun. Replace the rough breathing with a τ and you will have the corresponding part of the article which, hopefully, you will be able to recognise.

[2] The forms ἡ, ὁ, οἱ and αἱ occur in both the relative and the article. Context will normally make clear which is meant. However, accents can help here, since the relative always has an accent (normally grave), while the article almost never does. These forms will be accented in this book to help you; you may find it helpful to write them yourself.

PRACTICE 10.1.2

## Parse

| | | | | |
|---|---|---|---|---|
| 1. ὅ | 3. οὗ | 5. αἳ | 7. οὓς | 9. ὧν |
| 2. ὅν | 4. ἥ | 6. αἵ | 8. την | 10. οἵς |

### 10.1.3 Using the relative in Greek

To get the relative correct in Greek, it is useful first to identify the two basic sentences, and the relative's antecedent.

KEY GRAMMAR

In the relative:
**Number** and **Gender** agree with the antecedent
**Case** is determined within its own sentence, by the normal rules (e.g. whether it is the object, governed by a preposition etc.)

Examples

- The lord sent the messenger <u>who</u> saw the sea.
  Antecedent: the messenger
  2nd sentence: who (the messenger) saw the sea

  The antecedent is masculine singular; 'who' is the subject of its sentence. Relative should be masculine, singular, nominative = ὅς

= ὁ κυριος ἐπεμψεν τον ἀγγελον <u>ὅς</u> ἐβλεψεν την θαλασσαν.

- They are keeping the law <u>which</u> he teaches.
  Antecedent: the law
  2nd sentence: he teaches which (the law)

  The antecedent is masculine singular; 'which' is the object of its sentence. Relative should be masculine singular, accusative = ὅν

= τηρουσιν τον νομον <u>ὅν</u> διδασκει.

- That is the synagogue <u>into which</u> they are coming.
  Antecedent: the synagogue
  2nd sentence: they are coming into which (the synagogue)

  The antecedent is feminine singular; 'who' is governed by εἰς and therefore must be accusative. Relative should be feminine, singular, accusative = ἥν.

= ἐκεινη ἐστιν ἡ συναγωγη <u>εἰς ἥν</u> ἐρχονται.

## Further points[3]

- Often the relative clause will come in the middle of the complex sentence, not neatly at the end. English also does this, but not as often as in Greek.
  e.g. τα τεκνα ἁ ἐδιδασκον κραζει.
  – The children whom I was teaching are crying out.

- If the antecedent should be part of αὐτος, οὑτος or ἐκεινος it will often be omitted.
  e.g. ὁ υἱος οὑς θελει ζῳοποιει. = ὁ υἱος ζῳοποιει <u>αὐτους</u> οὑς θελει.
  – The son makes alive those whom he wishes (John 5.21)

- Also Greek will often put the relative clause first.
  e.g. ἁ βλεπω φιλω = φιλω <u>αὐτα</u> ἁ βλεπω.
  – I like the things which I see = I like what I see.

Examples

John 6.2: ἐθεωρουν τα σημεια ἁ ἐποιει.
– They were seeing the signs which he was doing.
Rom. 9.18: ἀρα οὐν ὁν θελει ἐλεει.
– So then, he has mercy on whom he wishes.

---

**HALF-WAY PRACTICE**

1. βλεπω τον δουλον ὁν ἐκαλεσεν.
2. ὑπαγε ἐκ του οἰκου ἐν ᾡ εἶ.
3. που ἐστιν τα ποτηρια ἁ φιλουμεν;
4. ἐπιστευσαν γαρ τῳ εὐαγγελιῳ ὁ οἱ ἀποστολοι ἐκηρυσσον.
5. ἀσπαζεσθε οἳ ἐρχονται προς ὑμας.
6. οὑτος ἐστιν ὁ κυριος δι᾽ οὑ προσευξομεθα.
7. ἁ ἠκουσα ταυτα λεγω ὑμιν.
8. ἀσπαζεσθε τον Τιμοθεον ὑπερ οὑ ἡ ἐκκλησια προσευχεται.
9. He keeps the bread which he made.
10. It is necessary to love the God who saves us.
11. Do you (s.) believe the gospel which you heard?
12. Did the disciple who denied Jesus repent?

---

[3] The relative is also occasionally *attracted* into the case of its antecedent, rather than being in the case appropriate for its own sentence. Thus 1 Cor 7.1 περι ὡν ἐγραψατε, should really be περι αὐτων ἁ ἐγραψατε (concerning the things which you wrote), but the ἁ has been attracted into the case of the αὐτων, which has then dropped out!

## 10.2 SLANTED QUESTIONS

In Chapter 4, section 4.5 we learnt how to ask questions in Greek (using either a question word or just the question mark).

However, in Greek just as in English it is possible to ask questions in such a way as to imply that you are expecting the answer 'yes' or 'no'. Greek does this in a very compact and straightforward way.

KEY GRAMMAR

A question expecting the answer: 'no' – μη ... ; 'yes' – οὐ ... ;

In English we have various different ways of expressing these kinds of question, often involving tone of voice. What is important is the we understand the meaning conveyed by the question, and then find some suitable way of putting it in English.

### Examples

John 6.67: Μη και ὑμεις θελετε ὑπαγειν;
– You don't also wish to go away, do you?
– Surely you don't also want to go away?

John 7.25: Οὐχ οὑτος ἐστιν ὁν ζητουσιν;
– This is whom they are seeking, isn't it?
– Surely this is the one they are after?

### Notes

- It is difficult to find any logical reason behind the use in slanted questions of these two forms of 'not'.
- Word order can help distinguish this special use of οὐ and μη from their use as negatives. As question words they will normally come first in the sentence, but this is very unusual when they are simple negatives. (When they are question words there will also be a question mark, of course.)
- μητι is also sometimes used instead of μη, and οὐχι instead of οὐ.[4]

Luke 4.22: και ἐλεγον, Οὐχι υἱος ἐστιν Ἰωσηφ οὑτος;
– And they were saying, 'Isn't this Joseph's son?'
John 8.22: ἐλεγον οὐν οἱ Ἰουδαιοι, Μητι ἀποκτενει [to kill] ἑαυτον;
– So the Jews were saying, 'He isn't going to kill himself, is he?'

[4] μητι can also be used for a hesitant question wondering whether something could be the case. For example John 4.29: μητι οὑτος ἐστιν ὁ Χριστος; – Could he be the Messiah? or He cannot be the Messiah, can he?

PRACTICE 10.2

## Translate

1. μη βλεπετε; 2. οὐ φιλεις με; 3. ἐγω οὐ φιλω σε. 4. μη ἐγω;

## 10.3 DIRECT AND INDIRECT STATEMENTS

In English a verb of saying can be followed either by the words that were said enclosed in quotation marks or by the word 'that' followed by a report of what was said. The former is said to be direct speech or a *direct statement*, the latter indirect speech or an *indirect statement.*

He said, 'I am the Christ.' – Direct statement
He said that he was the Christ. – Indirect statement

Indirect statements also occur after other '*verbs of saying or thinking*' (such as feeling, believing, knowing, learning, fearing etc.).

I thought that he was the Christ.

### Direct statements

Direct statements are expressed in four different ways in Greek:

1. The word ὁτι is used to introduce the direct statement (thus the ὁτι is equivalent to the opening inverted commas or speech marks in English).
2. The participle of λεγω is added immediately before the direct statement (again, the participle is then equivalent to the opening inverted commas in English).
   e.g. και ἐκηρυσσεν λεγων· Ἐρχεται... (Mark 1.7)
   and he used to preach (saying), 'He is coming . . .'
3. Both ὁτι and the participle of λεγω (i.e. 1 and 2 combined).
4. Nothing marks out the beginning of the direct statement.

In most printed texts the beginning of a direct statement is also marked out with a capital letter. However, early manuscripts were written completely in capitals, and so this marking out of direct statements merely expresses the opinion of the editors of your printed text and is not part of the text itself (but to begin with, it is sensible to assume they are right!).

- Nothing marks out the end of a direct statement in Greek. Thus it is hard to be certain where direct speech finishes (e.g. in John 3 it is not clear where between verses 10 and 21 the speech begun in verse 10 ends).

## Indirect statements

Indirect statements are expressed in Greek by the word ὁτι (meaning 'that'), and so are quite straightforward.

> e.g. θεωρω ὁτι προφητης εἶ συ. (John 4.19)
> – I see that you are a prophet.

However, when the words or thoughts were in the past, Greek uses a tense for the words / thoughts that is different from the tense used in English.

**KEY GRAMMAR**
Greek uses the tense of the original words or thoughts

For example, take the English sentence, 'She heard that Jesus was coming.' This is an indirect statement and so will be translated into Greek using ὁτι. However, the actual report that she heard was 'Jesus is coming.' Hence it will be translated into Greek using the Present tense of coming (*is coming*), whereas in English we use a past tense (*was coming*).

> She heard that Jesus was coming.
> ἠκουσεν ὁτι Ἰησους ἐρχεται. (John 11.20)

Similarly, to translate into Greek the sentence 'The Jews did not believe that he had been blind', you need to identify that the original words/thoughts were '. . . he was blind'; thus, this would be an Imperfect in Greek:

> The Jews did not believe about him that he had been blind.
> οὐκ ἐπιστευσαν οἱ Ἰουδαιοι περι αὐτου ὁτι ἠν τυφλος. (John 9.18)

**Hint**

Do not be confused by the *three* different meanings of ὁτι:

1. To introduce direct statements (= open speech marks)
2. To introduce indirect statements (= 'that')
3. As a word meaning 'because'

**PRACTICE 10.3**

### Do these sentences include direct or indirect statements? If indirect, which Greek tense would be used in the indirect statement?

1. The centurion says that he is going.
2. I said to him, 'Worship me.'
3. The women said that he had been blind.
4. The soldiers thought that they saw him.

5. The blind people said, 'We want to see.'
6. Then they cried out that he was coming.

## 10.4 TIME EXPRESSIONS

Greek expresses time in a rather clever but compact way. No preposition is used – the word referring to the period of time is simply put in the appropriate case.

KEY GRAMMAR
Time 'how long' – *accusative*
Time 'during' – *genitive*
Time 'at which' – *dative*

Examples

- δυο ἡμερας ἀκουουσιν του κυριου.
1. ἡμερας is *acc. plural*[5]
2. In a time expression *acc.* means time 'how long', expressed in English by 'for'
3. Sentence = 'For two days they listen to the Lord.'

- της ἡμερας ἀκουουσιν του κυριου.
1. ἡμερας is *gen. sing.*[6]
2. In a time expression *gen.* means time 'during', expressed in English by 'during' or 'by'
3. Sentence = 'During the day they listen to the Lord.' or 'By day they listen to the Lord.'

- τῃ ἡμερᾳ ἀκουουσιν του κυριου.
1. ἡμερᾳ is *dat.*
2. In a time expression *dat.* means time 'at which', expressed in English by 'on'.
3. Sentence = 'On the day they listen to the Lord.'

**Note:** Sometimes, although no preposition is needed, ἐν is used as well as the dative (ἐν τῃ ἡμερᾳ βλεπουσιν). This makes no difference to the meaning.

[5] In form it could be *gen. sing.* but δυο meaning 'two' shows it must be a plural.
[6] In form it could be *acc. pl.* but της in front of it shows it must be *gen. sing.*

PRACTICE 10.4

**In Greek, what case would be used for these time expressions?**

1. They came on the Sabbath.
2. He fasted for forty days.
3. Nicodemus came by night.
4. Three days he was in the tomb.
5. At dawn the stone moved.
6. He was arrested during Passover.

## VOCAB FOR CHAPTER 10

A host of important words
*ἀληθεια (109) – truth
ἀληθινος (28) – true, genuine, real
ἐγγυς (31) – near
*ἐκει (105) – there (in that place)
ἐκειθεν (37) – from there
*εὐθυς (51) – immediately
*καθως (182) – just as
καλως (37) – appropriately, well
ναι (33) – yes, of course
ὁμοιος (45) – similar, like
  *ὁμοιως (30) – likewise
*ὁπου (82) – where
*ὁς ἡ ὅ (1398) – who, which, what
*ὁτι (1296) – that, because, or "(marking beginning of speech)
οὑ (24) – where
*οὐδε (143) – and not
*οὐτε (87) – neither
  οὐτε ... οὐτε – neither . . . nor
*οὑτως (208) – in this manner, thus
*οὐχι (54) – not, no
πλην (31) – however, yet
ποθεν; (29) – from where? (or how?)
*ὡδε (61) – here

Four more prepositions
*ἐμπροσθεν + gen. (48) – in front of
ἑνεκα + gen. (26) – for the sake of
περαν + gen. (23) – on the other side of
*χωρις + gen. (41) – separate, apart from

*Πιλατος (55) – Pilate

And five more verbs
*ἐγγιζω + dat. (42) – I approach, come near
ἡγεομαι (28) – I lead
*θαυμαζω (43) – I am amazed
*θεραπευω (43) – I heal
*καθευδω (22) – I sleep

### Word helps

homoiousios, hegemony, thaumaturge, therapeutic/therapy.

### Exercises

Section A

*1. οὐκ εἰμι ἀποστολος; οὐχι Ἰησουν τον κυριον ἡμων ἐβλεψα; ἀκουσατε ἁ λεγω ὑμιν.

*2. οἱ δ᾽ ἐκ των Φαρισαιων ἠκουσαν ταυτα και ἐθαυμαζον λεγοντες αὐτῳ· Μη και ἡμεις τυφλοι ἐσμεν;
*3. οὐ μονον δε, ἀλλ᾽ ἐγγιζομεν τῳ θεῳ δια του κυριου ἡμων Ἰησου Χριστου δι᾽ οὑ νυν την εἰρηνην μετα του θεου λαμβανομεν.
*4. ἀλλοι ἐλεγον· Οὑτος ἐστιν ὁ Χριστος, οἱ δε ἐλεγον· Μη ἐκ της Γαλιλαιας ὁ Χριστος ἐρχεται;
5. και Δαυιδ λεγει ὁτι Μακαριος ἐστιν ὁ ἀνθρωπος ᾡ ὁ θεος λογιζεται δικαιοσυνην χωρις ἐργων.
*6. πολλας ἡμερας ὁ λαος ἠν ἐν Αἰγυπτῳ καθως ἐλαλησεν ὁ θεος τῳ Ἀβρααμ.
7. ἠρνησατο ὁ στρατιωτης λεγων· Μητι ἐγω Ἰουδαιος εἰμι;
8. και ἐσμεν ἐν τῳ ἀληθινῳ, ἐν τῳ υἱῳ αὐτου Ἰησου Χριστῳ. οὑτος ἐστιν ὁ ἀληθινος θεος και ζωη αἰωνιος.
*9. Jesus says to him, 'I am the way, the truth, and the life.'
10. Pilate was sleeping on the other side of the sea of Galilee.
11. But what I wrote to you, I bear witness in the presence of God.
12. Do not be amazed because of this, because an hour is coming in which the dead will hear his voice.

## Section B

1. ἐλεγεν δε ὁ Ἰησους· Ἀμην λεγω ὑμιν, πολλοι οὐκετι ἐχουσιν οἰκιαν ἠ ἀδελφους ἠ ἀδελφας ἠ τεκνα ἑνεκα ἐμου και ἑνεκα του εὐαγγελιου.
2. πλην οὐτ᾽ ἀδελφη χωρις ἀδελφου οὐτ᾽ ἀδελφος χωρις ἀδελφης ἐν κυριῳ.
*3. ἐδιδασκεν αὐτους λεγων ὁτι Αὐτος Δαυιδ λεγει αὐτον κυριον, και ποθεν αὐτου ἐστιν υἱος; και ὁ πολυς ὀχλος ἠκουεν αὐτου.
4. και ὁ Ἰησους ἐλεγεν αὐτῳ· Ὑπαγε. και εὐθυς ἀνεβλεψεν και ἠκολουθει αὐτῳ ἐν τῃ ὁδῳ.
*5. ἐρχομενοι δε κηρυσσετε λεγοντες ὁτι Ἐγγιζει ἡ βασιλεια των οὐρανων.
*6. καθως θελετε λαμβανειν ἀπο των ἀνθρωπων, ποιειτε αὐτοις ὁμοιως.
7. εἰ βλεπετε ταυτα, θαυμαζετε· ἐγγυς ἐστιν ἡ βασιλεια του θεου.
8. ἀλλοι ἐλεγον ὁτι Οὑτος ἐστιν, ἀλλοι ἐλεγον, Οὐχι, ἀλλα ὁμοιος αὐτῳ ἐστιν. ἐκεινος ἐλεγεν ὁτι Ἐγω εἰμι.
9. During the Sabbath the brothers were sleeping but the sisters were giving thanks to God.
*10. Likewise neither life nor death is outside of (use χωρις) God's authority.
*11. You have done these things well; go in peace.
*12. Pilate was amazed because that man did nothing evil but healed many.

## Section C

**Mark 6.3-6** οὐχ οὗτός ἐστιν ὁ τέκτων [*builder, carpenter, stonemason*], ὁ υἱὸς
τῆς Μαρίας καὶ ἀδελφὸς Ἰακώβου καὶ Ἰωσῆτος [*Joses (gen.)*] καὶ Ἰούδα καὶ
Σίμωνος [*Simon (gen.)*]; καὶ οὐκ εἰσὶν αἱ ἀδελφαὶ αὐτοῦ ὧδε πρὸς ἡμᾶς; καὶ
ἐσκανδαλίζοντο [*they were scandalized*] ἐν αὐτῷ. 4 καὶ ἔλεγεν αὐτοῖς ὁ
Ἰησοῦς ὅτι Οὐκ ἔστιν προφήτης ἄτιμος [*unhonoured*] εἰ μὴ [*except*] ἐν τῇ
πατρίδι [*homeland*] αὐτοῦ καὶ ἐν τοῖς συγγενεῦσιν [*kinsmen*] αὐτοῦ καὶ ἐν
τῇ οἰκίᾳ αὐτοῦ. 5 καὶ οὐκ ἐδύνατο [*he was able*] ἐκεῖ ποιῆσαι οὐδεμίαν
[*no, none, no one*] δύναμιν [*act of power, miracle*], εἰ μὴ ὀλίγοις [*a few*]
ἀρρώστοις [*sick, ill*] ἐπιθεὶς [*laying on*] τὰς χεῖρας [*hands*] ἐθεράπευσεν.
6 καὶ ἐθαύμαζεν διὰ τὴν ἀπιστίαν [*unbelief*] αὐτῶν. Καὶ περιῆγεν [*go about*]
τὰς κώμας [*villages*] κύκλῳ [*in a circle, round about*] διδάσκων.

# Special verbs

John 1.11: εἰς τα ἰδια ἠλθεν, και οἱ ἰδιοι αὐτον οὐ παρελαβον.

– he came to his own, and his own received him not.

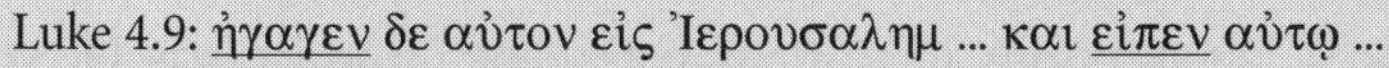
Luke 4.9: ἠγαγεν δε αὐτον εἰς Ἰερουσαλημ ... και εἰπεν αὐτῳ ...

– he led him to Jerusalem . . . and said to him . . .

The four verbs here – ἠλθεν, παρελαβον, ἠγαγεν and εἰπεν – are all in the Aorist tense, as is reflected in their translations. However, the Aorist has not been formed in accordance with the pattern we learnt in Chapter 6 (in particular, while there is an ε augment, there is no added σ). This is because these four verbs belong to the group of verbs that form their Aorist in a different way, called the 'Second ($2^{nd}$) Aorist'.

In the $2^{nd}$ Aorist, verbs use different stems. Sometimes these are similar to the normal stem – παρελαβον from παραλαμβανω and ἠγαγεν from ἀγω – at other times they are completely different – ἠλθεν from ἐρχομαι and εἰπεν from λεγω.

## 11.1 SECOND AORISTS

### 11.1.1 The principle

There is a group of Greek verbs that do not form their Aorist in the normal way. They are said to use a *$2^{nd}$* (form of the) *Aorist* rather than the more common *$1^{st}$* (form of the) *Aorist*, which is the one we have already met. It is crucial to realise that the *$1^{st}$ Aorist* and the *$2^{nd}$ Aorist* are simply different ways of forming the Aorist – they are not two different tenses.[1]

**KEY GRAMMAR**

The $2^{nd}$ Aorist has the same meaning as the $1^{st}$ Aorist
A verb will have *either* a $1^{st}$ Aorist *or* a $2^{nd}$ Aorist but *not* both

[1] Some grammars call the *$1^{st}$ Aorist* the *weak Aorist* and the *$2^{nd}$ Aorist* the *strong Aorist*. This is confusing because neither is stronger nor weaker than the other.

Thus, in this chapter you need to learn which verbs have a 2nd Aorist and how to form the 2nd Aorist, but there will be no discussion of its meaning or use, because its meaning and use are the same as those of the 1st Aorist in Chapter 6.

### 11.1.2 Compare in English

Most English verbs form their Past tense by adding –ed.

e.g. walk → walked; row → rowed; attack → attacked

Some verbs form their Past tense by changing their stem instead of adding -ed.

e.g. sing → sung; see → saw; throw → threw

Only very rare words can do both.

e.g. hang → hung *or* hanged.

There is no 'different quality of pastness' depending on which way the verb forms its Past tense. The form is different, but the meaning is the same.

There is no rule for determining which pattern a given word follows. When learning English you simply have to learn which verbs form their Past tense by changing their stem, and learn what their stem changes to. You know that all the other verbs will form their Past tense by adding –ed. Those learning English may sometimes get this wrong and create forms such as 'sayed'. This is wrong, but understandable, and not too serious a mistake, because 'sayed' is simply wrong rather than meaning anything different from 'said'.

All of the points are also true of the Greek 1st and 2nd Aorists.

| English | Greek |
|---|---|
| There is a standard form of the Past tense | Most verbs have a 1st Aorist |
| Certain words follow a different pattern | Some verbs have a 2nd Aorist |
| Very few words can follow both patterns | No verb has a 1st and a 2nd Aorist |
| The normal pattern forms the Past tense by adding –ed to the stem | 1st Aorists are formed by adding σ to the stem |
| The other group forms the Past tense by changing the stem | 2nd Aorists are formed by changing their stem |

### 11.1.3 The formation of the 2nd Aorist

The distinguishing feature of the 2nd Aorist is the changed stem. This changed stem is always present in the 2nd Aorist and is only present in the 2nd Aorist.

KEY GRAMMAR
2nd Aorist = Changed Stem

## Stems

Unfortunately, there is no way of *working out* what the changed stem will be. You have to learn the changed stems of the verbs which have a 2nd Aorist. There are 21 such verbs which occur with any frequency in the New Testament. These are listed here and in the grammar reference pages on page 270.

**KEY GRAMMAR**

It is impossible to spot a 2nd Aorist unless you recognise the 2nd Aorist stem Learn them!

Some 2nd Aorist stems are shortened versions of the Present stem:

| | **Present** | **2nd Aorist** |
|---|---|---|
| I sin | ἁμαρταν-ω | ἡμαρτ-ον |
| I die | ἀποθνῃσκ-ω | ἀπεθαν-ον |
| I throw | βαλλ-ω | ἐβαλ-ον |
| I find | εὑρισκ-ω | εὑρ-ον |
| I leave | καταλειπ-ω | κατελιπ-ον |
| I take | λαμβαν-ω | ἐλαβ-ον |
| I learn | μανθαν-ω | ἐμαθ-ον |
| I suffer | πασχ-ω | ἐπαθ-ον |
| I drink | πιν-ω | ἐπι-ον |
| I flee | φευγ-ω | ἐφυγ-ον |

These include two whose endings are a little different:

| | | |
|---|---|---|
| I go[2] | βαιν-ω | ἐβ-ην |
| I know | γινωσκ-ω | ἐγν-ων |

Others make other minor adjustments to the stem:

| | | |
|---|---|---|
| I lead | ἀγ-ω | ἠγαγ-ον |
| I have | ἐχ-ω | ἐσχ-ον |
| I fall | πιπτ-ω | ἐπεσ-ον |

One is deponent (and therefore has deponent endings):

| | | |
|---|---|---|
| I become | γιν-ομαι | ἐγεν-ομην |

Five have 2nd Aorists that bear no resemblance to their forms in the Present.[3]

| | | |
|---|---|---|
| I come | ἐρχ-ομαι | ἠλθ-ον |
| I say | λεγ-ω | εἰπ-ον |

---

[2] βαινω is only ever used in compounds such as καταβαινω and ἀναβαινω.

[3] What is happening here is that there are two different verbs with the same meaning, one of which is used in the Present and the other in the (2nd) Aorist (as in English 'go' and 'went').

| | | |
|---|---|---|
| I eat | ἐσθι-ω | ἐφαγ-ον |
| I see | ὁρα-ω[4] | εἰδ-ον |
| I carry | φερ-ω | ἠνεγκ-ον |

## Endings

The 2nd Aorist does not use the (1st) Aorist endings. Instead it uses the endings more normally associated with other tenses – the Imperfect in the Indicative, and the Present in the other moods (where there is no Imperfect).

KEY GRAMMAR

2nd Aorist Indicative – Imperfect Endings
2nd Aorist Other Moods – Present Endings

Thus for βαλλω (I throw), the 2nd Aorist forms are:

| | | | | | |
|---|---|---|---|---|---|
| **Indicative** | I | ἐβαλον | **Imperative** | 2nd Sing. | βαλε |
| | You (sing.) | ἐβαλες | | 2nd Pl. | βαλετε |
| | He, she, it | ἐβαλεν | **Infinitive** | | βαλειν |
| | We | ἐβαλομεν | **Participle** | Sing. | βαλων |
| | You (pl.) | ἐβαλετε | (masc. nom.) | Plural | βαλοντες |
| | They | ἐβαλον | | | |

### 11.1.4 Indicative 2nd Aorists

Notice that in the Indicative the 2nd Aorist looks very similar to the Imperfect – having the augment, no σ and the Imperfect endings, just as the Imperfect does. In fact, the only difference between, for example, the 2nd Aorist and Imperfect of βαλλω is that the 2nd Aorist uses the changed stem, hence ἐβαλον, ἐβαλες, ἐβαλεν etc. rather than the Imperfect ἐβαλλον, ἐβαλλες, ἐβαλλεν etc.

### Examples

| | | |
|---|---|---|
| ἐφευγον | 3rd Plural Imperfect Indicative | They were fleeing |
| ἐφυγον | 3rd Plural Aorist Indicative | They fled |
| ἐγινετο | 3rd Singular Imperfect Indicative | It was happening |
| ἐγενετο | 3rd Singular Aorist Indicative | It happened |
| ἐλεγετε | 2nd Plural Imperfect Indicative | You were saying |
| εἰπετε | 2nd Plural Aorist Indicative | You said |

[4] ὁραω belongs to the -αω groups of verbs. These verbs are quite rare and so will not be dealt with until Chapter 19. However, εἰδον, the 2nd aorist of ὁραω, is much more common and regular (for a 2nd Aorist!) and so is dealt with here.

PRACTICE 11.1.4

## Translate

| | | | |
|---|---|---|---|
| 1. ἐπεσομεν | 3. ἐβαλλετε | 5. ἐγενετο | 7. ἐφευγεν |
| 2. ἐλαβον | 4. εἰπεν | 6. ἠλθον | 8. εἰδες |

### 11.1.5 Other moods 2nd Aorists

#### Augments

The 2nd Aorist Indicative has an augment. However, as in the 1st Aorist, the augment is removed in the *other moods*. You need to be aware that the forms listed above included the augments. This is obvious in the case of, say, ἐλαβον, but less so in the case of ἠλθον (whose unaugmented form is ἐλθ-). A list of the more confusing unaugmented forms is given on page 270.

εἰπον and εἰδον are confusing, in as much as while the augment can be removed from εἰδον to give ἰδ-, even in the other moods εἰπον remains εἰπ-.

#### Endings

In the other moods, the 2nd Aorist can look like a Present (just as, in the Indicative, it can look like the Imperfect). For example, the -ων in βαλων tricks many students into thinking that it is a Present participle like λυων. However, in fact, the Present (simultaneous) participle of βαλλω is βαλλων while the Aorist (sequence) participle is βαλων.

#### Examples

| | | |
|---|---|---|
| λαμβανων | Masc. Nom. Sing. Present participle | Taking |
| λαβων | Masc. Nom. Sing. Aorist participle | Having taken |
| ἐλθειν | Aorist Infinitive | To come (undefined) |
| ἰδοντες | Masc. Nom. Pl. Aorist participle | Having seen |
| μανθανε | 2nd Singular Present Imperative | Learn! (process/ongoing) |

PRACTICE 11.1.5

## Parse

| | | | |
|---|---|---|---|
| 1. μαθειν | 3. μανθανειν | 5. ἐνεγκοντες | 7. λαβετε |
| 2. εὑρων | 4. εἰπε | 6. ἐλθων | 8. ἰδειν |

### 11.1.6 Unusual endings

**(i) γινωσκω and καταβαινω**

γινωσκω (I know) and βαινω (I go) have unusual endings in the 2nd Aorist. In Greek of the New Testament period, βαινω only exists in compounds such as καταβαινω and ἀναβαινω. Therefore we will use καταβαινω as a model.

| | | | |
|---|---|---|---|
| Indicative | ἐγνων, ἐγνως, ἐγνω, ἐγνωμεν, ἐγνωτε, ἐγνωσαν | | |
| Imperative | γνω, γνωτε | Infinitive | γνωναι |
| Participle | γνους, γνοντες | | |
| Indicative | κατεβην, κατεβης, κατεβη, κατεβημεν, κατεβητε, κατεβησαν | | |
| Imperative | καταβηθι, καταβητε | Infinitive | καταβηναι |
| Participle | καταβας, καταβαντες | | |

These can best be understood as the result of the form being dominated by the strong long vowel with which their stems end (ω or η). These verbs also have irregularities in the other tenses (see Chapter 18, section 18.4 and the lists on pages 253–4).

**(ii) 2nd Aorists with 1st Aorist endings**

ἠλθον, εἰπον, εἰδον and ἠνεγκον are sometimes found with 1st Aorist endings (i.e. what we learnt in Chapter 6 as the Aorist endings) rather than with the Imperfect/Present endings you would expect for the 2nd Aorist. This makes no difference to the meaning.

e.g. εἰπαν rather than εἰπον (Acts 16.31)
ἠλθατε rather than ἠλθετε (Matt. 25.36)

**PRACTICE 11.1.6**

**Translate**

1. καταβας 2. ἀνεβη 3. ἠλθαν 4. ἐγνωτε 5. γνους

**HALF-WAY PRACTICE**

1. πολλοι ἀπεθανον.
2. ἠγον αὐτο.
3. ἐφαγον τον ἀρτον.
4. ἐλθοντες εἰδον αὐτον.
5. ἰδε την ὁδον.
6. δει ἐλθειν εἰς τα Ἱεροσολυμα.
7. εἰπων ταυτα ὁ Ἰησους ἐξηλθεν.

8. ἀναβας εἰς το ἱερον ἀπεθανεν.
9. The prophets spoke.
10. I loved the son.
11. I want to see the sea.
12. When I found it, I took it.

## 11.2 THE FUTURE AND AORIST OF LIQUID VERBS

1 Cor. 1.17: οὐ γαρ ἀπεστειλεν με Χριστος βαπτιζειν ...
– because Christ did not send me to baptize . . .

Luke 11.49: ἀποστελῶ εἰς αὐτους προφητας και ἀποστολους ...
– I will send to them prophets and apostles . . .

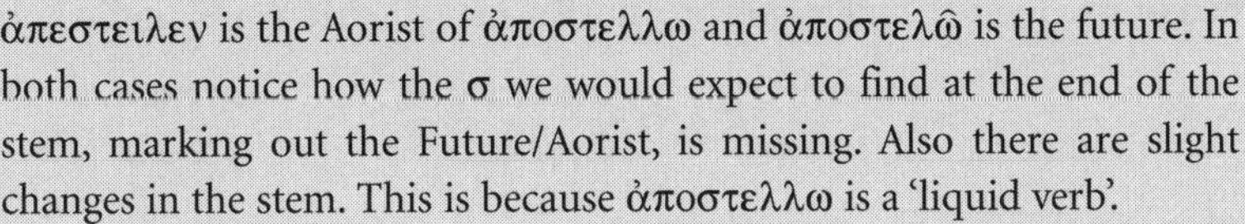

ἀπεστειλεν is the Aorist of ἀποστελλω and ἀποστελῶ is the future. In both cases notice how the σ we would expect to find at the end of the stem, marking out the Future/Aorist, is missing. Also there are slight changes in the stem. This is because ἀποστελλω is a 'liquid verb'.

Verbs whose stems end in λ, μ, ν or ρ (called *liquid verbs*)[5] have peculiar Aorists and Futures. However, this is not because they form a new class of verbs. What is happening is that for both the Aorist and the Future a σ is added to the stem. However, *for reasons of pronunciation* a σ cannot follow a λ, μ, ν or ρ – thus the expected σ disappears, and there are various compensatory changes.

### The Future

- A different stem is used.
- No σ is added (which you would expect for the Future).
- The endings from the Present of φιλεω are used (-ω, -εις, -ει, -ουμεν, -ειτε, -ουσιν).

### The Aorist

- A different stem is used.
- No σ is added (which you would expect for the Aorist).
- The augment and endings of the (1st) Aorist are used as normal.

Fortunately, the stem changes involved are normally minimal – just the shifting between a double and single consonant, or between long and short vowels.

**KEY GRAMMAR**
In liquid verbs there is no σ in the Future or Aorist

[5] Some students find it helpful to think of these liquid verbs as the 'mineral water' verbs – since the consonants in mineral are the consonants in question – μ, ν, ρ, λ.

### 11.2.1 Common liquid verbs[6]

Many use the same stem in the Aorist as the Present. In the Future this stem is altered by the final vowel of the stem being shortened:

| | **Present** | **Future**[7] | **Aorist** |
|---|---|---|---|
| I sow | σπειρω | σπερεω | ἐσπειρα |
| I raise | ἐγειρω | ἐγερεω | ἠγειρα |
| I kill | ἀποκτεινω | ἀποκτενεω | ἀπεκτεινα |

Similar is:

| | | | |
|---|---|---|---|
| I lift up | αἱρω | ἀρεω | ἠρα |

Others move from a final double consonant in the Present to a single consonant in the Future, and to a single consonant with a lengthened vowel in the Aorist:

| | | | |
|---|---|---|---|
| I send | ἀποστελλω | ἀποστελεω | ἀπεστειλα |
| I announce | ἀγγελλω | ἀγγελεω | ἠγγειλα |

Some are similar but show no change in the Future, since in the Present their final vowel is already short, and their final consonant is not doubled:

| | | | |
|---|---|---|---|
| I remain | μενω | μενεω | ἐμεινα |
| I judge | κρινω | κρινεω | ἐκρινα |

Some follow the same general principles but have 2nd Aorists:

| | | | |
|---|---|---|---|
| I die | ἀποθνῃσκω | ἀποθανεομαι | ἀπεθανον |
| I throw | βαλλω | βαλεω | ἐβαλον |

Examples

John 15.10: μενειτε ἐν τῃ ἀγαπῃ μου.
– You will remain in my love.

Matt. 21.1: τοτε Ἰησους ἀπεστειλεν δυο μαθητας.
– Then Jesus sent two disciples.

### 11.2.2 Accents in the Future

Because some liquid verbs such as μενω and κρινω use the same stem for the Present as for the Future, the only difference in form between the Present and the Future is that the Future uses the -εω endings. However, once the contraction has happened, often the -εω endings are no different from the normal -ω endings

[6] Because the changes affect *all* verbs whose stems end in λ, μ, ν or ρ, a complete list cannot be given. However, these are the common ones, and the rest behave similarly.

[7] Written uncontracted for clarity.

(e.g. μενω, μενεις, μενει, μενουσιν). Thus the Present does not differ from the Future. In these cases the accent can be helpful.

KEY GRAMMAR
A liquid verb has a circumflex if (and only if) it is Future

e.g. μένεις is Present (you remain), μενεῖς is Future (you will remain).

PRACTICE 11.2.2

## Translate

1. ἐμειναν.
2. ἀπαγγελοῦμεν.
3. ἠγειρεν.
4. ἀπεκτειναν.
5. κρινεῖ τον κοσμον.
6. ἀποστειλας ἐξηλθεν.
7. θελω σπειραι.
8. ἀραντες, ἠνεγκον.
9. They will announce.
10. You (pl.) will throw.
11. Raise (s.) the dead man!
12. He killed her.

## VOCAB FOR CHAPTER 11

Verbs with 2nd Aorists
ἁμαρτανω (43) – I do wrong, sin
*ἀποθνῃσκω (111) – I die
*γινομαι (669) – I become, happen
  παραγινομαι (37) – I arrive, stand by
*ἐσθιω (158) – I eat
*εὑρισκω (176) – I find
καταλειπω (24) – I leave (behind)
μανθανω (25) – I learn
*ὁραω (454) – I see[8]
πασχω (42) – I suffer
*πινω (73) – I drink
*πιπτω (90) – I fall (down)
*φερω (66) – I bear, carry
  προσφερω (47) – I bring to, offer
*φευγω (29) – I flee

Liquid verbs
ἀπαγγελλω (45) – I report, announce[9]
παραγγελλω (32) + dat. – I order[9]

*αἱρω (101) – I take (away), lift up
ἀποκτεινω (74) – I kill
*ἀποστελλω (132) – I send (out)
*ἐγειρω (144) – I raise up, wake
*κρινω (114) – I judge, decide
*μενω (118) – I remain
ὀφειλω (35) – I owe
σπειρω (52) – I sow
*χαιρω (74) – I rejoice[10]

[8] ὁραω has the 2nd Aorist εἰδον.
[9] Both of these are compounds of the very rare word ἀγγελλω (1) – I announce.
[10] χαιρω is very rarely found in a tense other than the Present, and normally found in the imperatives χαιρε and χαιρετε to mean 'Greetings!'

Verbs with 2nd Aorists with unusual endings

*ἀναβαινω (82) – I go up
*καταβαινω (81) – I go down

*γινωσκω (222) – I know
ἀναγινωσκω (32) – I read
ἐπιγινωσκω (44) – I recognise

Plus, *ἰδου (200) – Look! Behold! [11]

## Word helps

comestibles, heuristic/eureka, horror/panorama, passion/sympathy/ pathology, proffer, Christopher, fugitive, angel, apostle, critic, permanent/remain, diaspora, gnostic.

## Exercises

### Section A

1. προσηλθον αὐτῳ οἱ μαθηται λεγοντες· Ἐρημος ἐστιν ὁ τοπος και ἡ ὡρα ἠδη παρηλθεν· ἀπολυσον τους ὀχλους.
2. και φωνη ἐγενετο ἐκ των οὐρανων· Συ εἶ ὁ υἱος μου ὁ ἀγαπητος.

*3. και ὁτε εἰσηλθεν εἰς οἰκον ἀπο του ὀχλου, εὑρον αὐτον οἱ μαθηται αὐτου και εἰπον αὐτῳ περι της παραβολης.

4. ἐκηρυξα γαρ ὑμιν ὁ και παρελαβον, ὁτι Χριστος ἀπεθανεν ὑπερ των ἁμαρτιων ἡμων κατα το εὐαγγελιον.

*5. ἐγω γαρ δια νομου ἀπεθανον νομῳ.

6. λεγει οὐν τῳ ἀποστολῳ· Μη γινου παντοτε τυφλος ἐν τῃ καρδιᾳ σου ἀλλα πιστος.

*7. ἐν τῳ κοσμῳ ἠν, και ὁ κοσμος δι᾽ αὐτου ἐγενετο, και ὁ κοσμος αὐτον οὐκ ἐγνω.

*8. κυριε δικαιε, και ὁ κοσμος σε οὐκ ἐγνω, ἐγω δε σε ἐγνων, και οὑτοι ἐγνωσαν ὁτι συ με ἀπεστειλας.

9. And he went up into the boat with them and they fled.
10. After this he went down to Galilee, and Mary and his brothers and his disciples, and they remained there for not many days.

*11. Behold, the son of man will send his angels.

*12. That word which I spoke will judge him on the day of the Lord.

### Section B

1. αὑτη δε ἐστιν ἡ αἰωνιος ζωη, γινωσκειν σε τον μονον ἀληθινον θεον και ὁν ἀπεστειλας Ἰησουν Χριστον.

[11] ἰδου is related to, but not actually part of, εἰδον – I saw.

2. και ἀλλον ἀπεστειλεν· κἀκεινον[12] ἀπεκτειναν, και πολλους ἀλλους, οὓς μεν διωκοντες, οὓς δε ἀποκτεινοντες.
*3. και λεγει αὐτοις· Οὐκ γινωσκετε την παραβολην ταυτην, και πως ἀλλας τας παραβολας γνωσεσθε;[13]
*4. και παλιν ἠνεγκαν το τεκνον μετα του δαιμονιου προς αὐτον. και εὐθυς πεσων ἐπι της γης ἐκραζεν.
5. ἰδου ὁ σπειρων σπειρει ἐπι την γην· και ἐγενετο ὃ μεν ἐπεσεν παρα την ὁδον, και ἀλλο ἐπεσεν εἰς την γην την καλην, και εὐθυς ἀνεβη καλως.
6. τουτο οὖν το βιβλιον πολλοι ἀνεγνωσαν ὁτι ἐπεγνωσαν την ἀληθειαν.
*7. ὁ δε Ἰησους εἰπεν αὐτῳ ὁτι Σοι λεγω, ἐγειρε ἀρον αὐτο και ὑπαγε εἰς τον οἰκον σου.
8. και οἱ ὑπηρεται καταλιποντες τα προβατα ἐφυγον ἀπαγγελλοντες ἁ εἰδον και ἀλλοι ἀνεβησαν ἰδειν.
*9. And the disciples of John came and took away the dead man.
10. Having received (him) they killed him and cast him outside.
*11. And coming into the house, he said, 'Rejoice! We will eat with one another now.'
*12. It happened that a sheep fled. Therefore the son left the others and found it.

## Section C

**Revelation 1.1-19** Ἀποκάλυψις [*revelation*] Ἰησοῦ Χριστοῦ ἣν ἔδωκεν [*he gave*] αὐτῷ ὁ θεὸς δεῖξαι [*to show*] τοῖς δούλοις αὐτοῦ ἃ δεῖ γενέσθαι ἐν τάχει [*speed*], καὶ ἐσήμανεν [*he showed*] ἀποστείλας διὰ τοῦ ἀγγέλου αὐτοῦ τῷ δούλῳ αὐτοῦ Ἰωάννῃ, 2 ὃς ἐμαρτύρησεν τὸν λόγον τοῦ θεοῦ καὶ τὴν μαρτυρίαν Ἰησοῦ Χριστοῦ ὅσα εἶδεν. 3 μακάριος ὁ ἀναγινώσκων καὶ οἱ ἀκούοντες τοὺς λόγους τῆς προφητείας [*prophecy*] καὶ τηροῦντες τὰ ἐν αὐτῇ γεγραμμένα [*having been written*], ὁ γὰρ καιρὸς ἐγγύς. ... 9 Ἐγὼ Ἰωάννης, ὁ ἀδελφὸς ὑμῶν ... 10 ἐγενόμην ἐν πνεύματι [*spirit in the dat. sing.*] ἐν τῇ κυριακῇ [*lord's*] ἡμέρᾳ καὶ ἤκουσα ὀπίσω μου φωνὴν μεγάλην ὡς σάλπιγγος [*trumpet in the gen. sing.*] 11 λεγούσης [*saying*], Ὃ βλέπεις γράψον εἰς βιβλίον καὶ πέμψον ταῖς ἑπτὰ ἐκκλησίαις, ... 12 Καὶ ἐπέστρεψα [ἐπιστρεφω – *I turn*] βλέπειν τὴν φωνὴν ἥτις [=ἥ] ἐλάλει μετ' ἐμοῦ, καὶ ἐπιστρέψας εἶδον ἑπτὰ [*seven*] λυχνίας [*lampstand*] χρυσᾶς [*gold*] ... 17 Καὶ ὅτε εἶδον αὐτόν, ἔπεσα πρὸς τοὺς πόδας [*feet*] αὐτοῦ ὡς νεκρός, καὶ ἔθηκεν [*he placed*] τὴν δεξιὰν [*right*] αὐτοῦ ἐπ' ἐμὲ λέγων, ... 19 γράψον οὖν ἃ εἶδες καὶ ἃ εἰσὶν καὶ ἃ μέλλει γενέσθαι μετὰ ταῦτα.

---

[12] κἀκεινον = και ἐκεινον. See note 7 page 108.

[13] γνωσομαι is the irregular future of γινωσκω. This is explained in Chapter 18, section 18.4.

# The third declension – Part 1

Rom. 8.9: ὑμεις δε οὐκ ἐστε ἐν σαρκι ἀλλα ἐν πνευματι.
– you are not in flesh but in spirit.

Matt. 16.17: ὁ Ἰησους εἰπεν αὐτῳ· Μακαριος εἶ, Σιμων Βαριωνα, ὁτι σαρξ και αἱμα οὐκ ἀπεκαλυψεν σοι ἀλλ᾽ ὁ πατηρ μου.
– Jesus said to him, 'You are blessed, Simon Bariona, because flesh and blood did not reveal (this) to you, but my father.'

Acts 2.17: λεγει ὁ θεος· Ἐκχεῶ ἀπο του πνευματος μου ἐπι πασαν σαρκα, και προφητευσουσιν οἱ υἱοι ὑμων και αἱ θυγατερες ὑμων.
– God says, 'I will pour out from my spirit on all flesh, and your sons and your daughters will prophesy.'

None of the nouns underlined in these passages have the endings that we would expect. σαρκι and πνευματι must be dative (after ἐν); σαρξ, αἱμα and πατηρ are nominatives (subjects); the του in front of πνευματος shows it is genitive; similarly θυγατερες must be nominative plural (with αἱ). All of this highlights that there is another family of nouns, adjectives and pronouns with a different set of endings.

## 12.1 THE ESSENCE OF THE 3RD DECLENSION

All the nouns, adjectives and pronouns that we have learnt so far form one large family, having endings either identical or very similar to those of ἀγαθος. The traditional terminology divides this group into 1st and 2nd declension nouns (see Chapter 8, section 8.3.4), but they basically form one family.

In this family you can work out the stem from the nominative, and then add the endings to it. Thus, θεος has the stem θε- to which we can add endings, giving θε-ος, θε-ον, θε-ου, θε-ῳ etc.

We now need to learn the other family of nouns, adjectives and pronouns known as the 3rd declension.

There are a few characteristic features of the 3rd declension:

- The masculine and feminine are identical; the neuter is similar.[1]
- The nominative singular form is irregular – it is not formed from the stem plus an ending, although all the other forms are.[2]
- Because the nominative is irregular:
  - for a 3rd declension word you need to learn both the nominative and another form from which the stem can be deduced (the genitive is best)[3]
  - no ending indicates that a word is 3rd declension, in the way that up to now words ending in -ος have always declined like λογος. Indeed, the beauty of the 3rd declension is its ability to cope with words whatever their nominative.

These features are true of all the 3rd declension family. In this chapter we shall learn the standard 3rd declension words (those with consonants at the end of their stems). Chapter 13 covers those with stems ending in vowels.

## 12.2 MASCULINE AND FEMININE NOUNS WITH CONSONANT STEMS

The *endings* are as follows:

| | Singular | Plural |
|---|---|---|
| Nom.[4] | Various | -ες |
| Acc. | -α | -ας |
| Gen. | -ος | -ων |
| Dat. | -ι | -σιν[5] |

### Notes

- On the whole there is no connection between these endings and those of the 1st and 2nd declension, although the *genitive plural* ending -ων is the same.
- Watch out for the endings that are used differently in the 3rd declension from the way they are in the 1st and 2nd (see overleaf):

[1] Indeed, there is no way of identifying the gender of a 3rd declension noun from its form. Therefore, in a vocabulary, a 3rd declension word is always quoted with the appropriate form of the nom. sing. of the article (ὁ, ἡ, or το) to show its gender. Thus: σωμα, σωματος, το is neuter (as revealed by the το); νυξ, νυκτος, ἡ is feminine; and πους, ποδος, ὁ is masculine.

[2] Unsurprisingly, at a deep level there is an underlying pattern behind the 'irregular' forms. However, most students find it far more trouble to go into than it is worth.

[3] The genitive is used because in neuter forms the accusative is always identical to the nominative, thus a neuter accusative will be just as 'irregular' as the nominative, and not based on the stem.

[4] As one would expect, the vocative is the same as the nominative.

[5] Or -σι (the ν is optional), although the form with the ν is far more common.

| | 3rd declension | 1st/2nd declension |
|---|---|---|
| -ος | gen. sing. | masc. nom. sing. |
| -α | acc. sing. (masc. or fem.) | neut. nom. or acc. pl. (or nom. sing. of ἡμερα) |
| -ας | acc. pl. (masc. or fem.) | fem. acc. pl. (or gen. sing. of ἡμερα) |

The *stem* to which these endings are added is found by removing the -ος from the genitive singular of the word (which needs to have been learnt or can be found in the vocabulary).

For example, 'star' is ἀστηρ, ἀστερος and therefore its stem is ἀστερ-.

Hence it declines as follows:

| | Singular | Plural |
|---|---|---|
| Nom. | ἀστηρ | ἀστερες |
| Acc. | ἀστερα | ἀστερας |
| Gen. | ἀστερος | ἀστερων |
| Dat. | ἀστερι | ἀστερσιν |

### 12.2.1 Note on the dative plural

Since the ending for the dative plural is -σιν, the σ will end up next to the consonant with which the stem of the word ends. Then, as happens with verbs (Chapter 6, section 6.6), the σ and the final consonant will combine. Because this is about pronunciation, rather than anything special about the 3rd declension, the combinations are the same as in the Future and Aorist of verbs.

KEY GRAMMAR

| | | | | |
|---|---|---|---|---|
| π, β, φ | + | σιν | → | ψιν |
| τ, δ, θ, ν | + | σιν | → | σιν |
| κ, γ, χ | + | σιν | → | ξιν |

e.g. 'flesh' is σαρξ, σαρκος and so the dative plural is σαρξιν.
'child' is παις, παιδος and so the dative plural is παισιν.

In addition, there can be slight changes to the vowel sounds within the word. This happens according to a standard pattern for those with stems ending in -εντ and -οντ, and then occasionally for other words.[6]

εντ + σιν → εισιν      οντ + σιν → ουσιν

e.g. 'ruler' is ἀρχων, ἀρχοντος and so the dative plural is ἀρχουσιν.

---

[6] The most common being that ἀνηρ, ἀνδρος (man) has a dative plural in ἀνδρασιν and χειρ, χειρος (hand) has a dative plural in χερσιν.

### 12.2.2 The family group

| | | |
|---|---|---|
| father | πατηρ, πατρος | |
| mother | μητηρ, μητρος | all follow the same slightly irregular pattern |
| daughter | θυγατηρ, θυγατρος | |

| | Singular | Plural |
|---|---|---|
| Nom. | πατηρ | πατερες |
| Acc. | πατερα | πατερας |
| Gen. | πατρος | πατερων |
| Dat. | πατρι | πατρασιν |

Note the ε which is sometimes part of the stem and sometimes not. Also the α in the dative plural. πατηρ (alone) also has an irregular vocative πατερ.

---

**PRACTICE 12.2**

#### Parse

1. σωτηρος
2. ἀρχοντες
3. ἐλπιδι
4. μητερων
5. νυκτα
6. σαρκος
7. χερσιν
8. Σιμωνα

#### Put in the form indicated

(You will need to look at the vocab list on pages 142 to find the genitives)

9. ἀνηρ, genitive plural
10. γυνη, dative plural
11. πους, accusative singular
12. χειρ, accusative plural
13. σαρξ, dative singular
14. χαρις, genitive singular
15. θυγατηρ, nominative plural
16. αἰων, dative plural

---

## 12.3 NEUTER NOUNS WITH CONSONANT STEMS

These follow a very similar pattern to the masculine and feminine nouns:

| | Singular | Plural |
|---|---|---|
| Nom. | Various | -α |
| Acc. | Identical to nom. | Identical to nom. |
| Gen. | -ος | -ων |
| Dat. | -ι | -σιν (or -σι) |

The only difference is that, as in all neuters, the acc. is the same as the nom., and the nom. and acc. plural is -α (as in the 1st and 2nd declensions). The dative plural follows the same rules as in the masculine and feminine.

For example, 'body' is σωμα, σωματος. Therefore, it declines as follows:

| | Singular | Plural |
|---|---|---|
| Nom. | σωμα | σωματα |
| Acc. | σωμα | σωματα |
| Gen. | σωματος | σωματων |
| Dat. | σωματι | σωμασιν |

In fact, although there are 3rd declension neuter nouns with a wide variety of stem endings, many 3rd declension neuter words are very similar to σωμα, ending in -μα in the nominative and having a stem ending in -ματ.

**PRACTICE 12.3**

## Parse

1. πνευματι 2. θεληματος 3. ῥηματα 4. ὀνοματων

## Put in the form indicated

5. αἱμα, accusative singular
6. πνευμα, genitive plural
7. σωμα, dative plural
8. ὀνομα, accusative plural

**HALF-WAY PRACTICE**

1. σωτηρ ἐστιν ὁ Ἰησους;
2. ὁ υἱος του πατρος ἐφυγεν.
3. ἐχω ἀγαθην μητερα.
4. εἰδον τους πατερας αὐτων.
5. βαπτιζει ὑδατι.
6. οἱ ἀνδρες ἐξηλθον.
7. ὁ Χριστος ἀπεθανεν ὑπερ ἀνδρων και γυναικων.
8. ποιειτε το θελημα του θεου.
9. He loves two women.
10. The spirit does not like the flesh.
11. I have big feet.
12. They saw the light.

## 12.4 ADJECTIVES WITH CONSONANT STEMS

The few adjectives that follow the 3rd declension have the endings of the masculine/ feminine nouns in their masculine/feminine parts, and of the neuter nouns in their neuter parts. They have a <u>single stem</u>, but <u>both</u> of their nom. sing. forms need to be learnt (i.e. the masculine/feminine and the neuter nom. sing.).

The most common adjectives of this form are the comparatives e.g. 'more': πλειων, πλειον, πλειονος.[7]

| | Singular | | Plural | |
|---|---|---|---|---|
| | Masculine Feminine | Neuter | Masculine Feminine | Neuter |
| Nom. | πλειων | πλειον | πλειονες | πλειονα |
| Acc. | πλειονα | πλειον | πλειονας | πλειονα |
| Gen. | πλειονος | πλειονος | πλειονων | πλειονων |
| Dat. | πλειονι | πλειονι | πλειοσιν | πλειοσιν |

**Hint**

If a noun and an adjective qualifying it are from different families, their endings will differ even when they are agreeing in gender, case and number.

e.g. ὁ ἀγαθος ἐχει πλειον<u>ας</u> φιλ<u>ους</u> – The good man has more friends.

**PRACTICE 12.4**

1. πλειονες στρατιωται ἐρχονται.
2. ἐχεις μειζονα κεφαλην μου.
3. ὁ Ἰησους εἰχεν πλειονας μαθητας ἡ Ἰωαννης;
4. προφητης εἰμι μειζονος ἱερου.

[7] While learning the form of the comparatives, it makes sense to learn how to use them. The normal way of expressing comparison is by putting the second noun in the genitive (ἐγω ἐχω πλειον <u>σου</u> - I have more <u>than you</u>). Another alternative is to use the word ἡ, with the two words being compared put into the same case (<u>ἐγω</u> ἐχω πλειον ἡ <u>συ</u>).

## 12.5 τις AND τίς

There are two pronouns that decline like πλειων. What is a little more confusing, however, is that although the pronouns are different, they look identical – in all their forms – except for the accents they carry.

KEY GRAMMAR

τις is the indefinite pronoun – someone, anyone
τίς is the interrogative pronoun – who? what?[8]

### Formation

Since their neuter sing. is τι and their genitive τινος, they decline as follows:

| | Singular | | Plural | |
|---|---|---|---|---|
| | Masculine Feminine | Neuter | Masculine Feminine | Neuter |
| Nom. | τις | τι | τινες | τινα |
| Acc. | τινα | τι | τινας | τινα |
| Gen. | τινος | τινος | τινων | τινων |
| Dat. | τινι | τινι | τισι | τισι |

### Use

Their use as **pronouns** is quite straightforward, although when using τίς meaning 'who' you need to think about which case is appropriate (since in English the distinction between 'who' and 'whom' is now being lost).

e.g. τίνα θεωρεις; Whom do you see? ἐβλεψα τινα. I saw someone.
τίς ἐρχεται; Who is coming? ἀκουει τις. Someone is listening.
περι τίνων λεγεις; What/Who are you speaking about?

Both can also be used as **adjectives**, when they must agree with their nouns.

e.g. τίνα μισθον ἐχετε; What reward do you have?
στρατιωται τινες ἐρχονται. Some soldiers are coming.

τί can also mean '**why**?'

e.g. τί λεγεις; Why are you speaking? (*or* 'What are you saying?')

---

[8] τίς is always a question word and hence is different from ὅς which is the relative (linking together two sentences), despite the fact that English translates both as 'who'.

## Examples

Mark 2.24: τί ποιουσιν τοις σαββασιν ὃ οὐκ ἐξεστιν;
– Why are they doing on the Sabbath what is not permitted?
Mark 8.29: ὑμεις δε τίνα με λεγετε εἰναι; – But who do you say that I am?
Mark 11.25: εἰ τι ἐχετε κατα τινος – If you have something against someone.

## Distinguishing between τις and τίς

There are three ways of distinguishing between τις (someone) and τίς (who?).

- The context normally makes it very clear (and indeed there will be a question mark if τίς is meant). You just need to start with an open mind.
- τις (someone) cannot be the first word in a sentence, while τίς (who) frequently is.
- You can learn some relatively simple rules about the accents.

## Accents

The full rules of accentation are complicated. But the following test is simple and 99 per cent accurate:

Accent on the first syllable → τίς (who?, what?)
No accent or an accent on the second syllable → τις (someone)

PRACTICE 12.5

## Translate

1. τίς ἐρχεται;
2. θελω ἀρτον τινα.
3. τί φιλειτε τον Χριστον;
4. περι τίνων εἰπεν;
5. πατερες τινες εἰσιν πονηροι.
6. τίνα ζητειτε;
7. Why are you (s.) praying?
8. To whom did you (pl.) speak?
9. Some prophets are calling.
10. What law do you (pl.) keep?

## VOCAB FOR CHAPTER 12

Third declension words, grouped into their rough patterns

*ἀνηρ, ἀνδρος, ὁ (216) – man (male), husband
ἀστηρ, ἀστερος, ὁ (24) – star
*σωτηρ, σωτηρος, ὁ (24) – saviour
*αἰων, αἰωνος, ὁ (122) – age (long time)[9]
ἀρχων, ἀρχοντος, ὁ (37) – ruler, leader
Σιμων, Σιμωνος, ὁ (75) – Simon
*γυνη, γυναικος, ἡ (215) – woman, wife
*ἐλπις, ἐλπιδος, ἡ (53) – hope
νυξ, νυκτος, ἡ (61) – night
*πους, ποδος, ὁ (93) – foot
*σαρξ, σαρκος, ἡ (147) – flesh
*χαρις, χαριτος, ἡ (155) – grace
*χειρ, χειρος, ἡ (177) – hand
θυγατηρ, θυγατρος, ἡ (28) – daughter
*μητηρ, μητρος, ἡ (83) – mother
*πατηρ, πατρος, ὁ (413) – father, ancestor
πυρ, πυρος, το (71) – fire
*ὑδωρ, ὑδατος, το (76) – water
*φως, φωτος, το (73) – light
*αἱμα, αἱματος, το (97) – blood
*θελημα, θεληματος, το (62) – will
*ὀνομα, ὀνοματος, το (231) – name
*πνευμα, πνευματος, το (379) – spirit, wind
ῥημα, ῥηματος, το (68) – word, saying
στομα, στοματος, το (78) – mouth
*σωμα, σωματος, το (142) – body

Two adjectives
μειζων (48) – larger, greater
*πλειων (55) – more

Plus
*τις τι (525) – someone, something
*τίς τί (556) – who? which? what? (τί can also mean why)
ὁστις (153) – who
ὡσπερ (36) – just as

### Word helps

android/polyandry, androgynous, astronomy/asteroid, soteriology, aeon, monarchy, gynaecology, eucharist/charismatic, nocturnal, sarcastic/sarcophagus, chiropodist/tripod, metropolis, patriarch/patristics, pyre/pyrotechnics, hydrant/hydro-electric, photography/phosphorous, haematology/haemorrhage, onomatopoeia/pseudonym, pneumatology/pneumatic, rhetoric, stomach, psychosomatic.

[9] Note the expression, εἰς τον αἰωνα – into the age, forever.

## Exercises

### Section A

*1. πατερ, δοξασον σου το ὀνομα.

*2. ἐγω ἐβαπτισα ὑμας ὑδατι, αὐτος δε βαπτισει ὑμας ἐν πνευματι ἁγιῳ.

3. ὁ δε εἰπεν αὐτῃ· Θυγατηρ, ἡ πιστις σου ἐσωσε σε· ὑπαγε εἰς εἰρηνην.

*4. ἐν αὐτῳ ζωη ἠν, και ἡ ζωη ἠν το φως των ἀνθρωπων.

*5. και ὁ λογος σαρξ ἐγενετο.

6. ἡ γυνη εἰπεν αὐτῳ· Οὐκ ἐχω ἀνδρα. λεγει αὐτῃ ὁ Ἰησους, Καλως εἰπας ὁτι Ἀνδρα οὐκ ἐχω.

*7. εἰπεν αὐτοις ὁ Ἰησους· Εἰπον ὑμιν και οὐ πιστευετε· τα ἐργα ἁ ἐγω ποιω ἐν τῳ ὀνοματι του πατρος μου ταυτα μαρτυρει περι ἐμου.

8. εἰπεν αὐτῳ Σιμων Πετρος· Κυριε, τίνι ἀκολουθησομεν; ῥηματα ζωης αἰωνιου ἐχεις.

9. The Pharisees said to him, 'Why do your disciples not eat appropriately with their hands?'

*10. But in the Lord neither is a wife separate from a husband nor a husband separate from a wife.

*11. Grace to you (pl.) and peace from God our father and the Lord Jesus Christ our saviour.

12. Just as he spoke through the mouth of his holy prophets, he will do this.

### Section B

1. και Σιμων εἰπεν· Κυριε, δι᾽ ὁλης νυκτος ἠργαζομεθα και οὐκ ἐλαβομεν· ἐπι δε τῳ ῥηματι σου ἐργασομεθα παλιν.

2. και ἰδου ἠλθεν ἀνηρ ᾧ ὀνομα Ἰαιρος και οὑτος ἀρχων της συναγωγης ὑπηρχεν, και πεσων παρα τους ποδας Ἰησου παρεκαλει αὐτον εἰσελθειν εἰς τον οἰκον αὐτου.

*3. ὁτι ἀνηρ ἐστιν κεφαλη της γυναικος ὡς και ὁ Χριστος κεφαλη της ἐκκλησιας, αὐτος σωτηρ του σωματος.

*4. Παυλος ἀποστολος Χριστου Ἰησου κατ᾽ ἐξουσιαν θεου σωτηρος ἡμων και Χριστου Ἰησου της ἐλπιδος ἡμων.

*5. τα τεκνα του θεου εἰσιν οὑτοι οἱ οὐκ ἐξ αἱματων οὐδε ἐκ θεληματος σαρκος οὐδ᾽ ἐκ θεληματος ἀνδρος ἀλλ᾽ ἐκ θεου γινονται.

6. το δαιμονιον αὐτον ἐβαλλεν εἰς πυρ και εἰς ὑδατα.

7. οἱ ἀρχοντες εἰσηλθον λεγοντες· Που ἐστιν ὁ ἀρχων των Ἰουδαιων; εἰδομεν γαρ αὐτου τον ἀστερα και ἠλθομεν προσκυνησαι αὐτῳ.

*8. ἐγνω ὁ Ἰησους ὁτι ἠκουσαν οἱ Φαρισαιοι ὁτι Ἰησους πλειονας μαθητας ποιει και βαπτιζει ἡ Ἰωαννης.

*9. For in love we will receive [*use* δεχομαι] the hope of righteousness by the Spirit.

*10. Now hope and love remain, and we wish to have more.

*11. The wife does not have authority over [*of*] her own body, but likewise the husband also does not have authority over his own body but the wife [*does*].

12. In that hour the disciples came to Jesus, saying, 'Who therefore is greater in the kingdom of heaven?'

## Section C

**Mark 3.32-35** καὶ ἐκάθητο [*was sitting*] περὶ αὐτὸν ὄχλος, καὶ λέγουσιν
αὐτῷ, Ἰδοὺ ἡ μήτηρ σου καὶ οἱ ἀδελφοί σου καὶ αἱ ἀδελφαί σου ἔξω
ζητοῦσίν σε. 33 καὶ ἀποκριθεὶς [*answering*] αὐτοῖς λέγει, Τίς ἐστιν ἡ μήτηρ
μου καὶ οἱ ἀδελφοί μου; 34 καὶ περιβλεψάμενος [= περι + βλεπω] τοὺς περὶ
αὐτὸν κύκλῳ [*in a circle*] καθημένους [*the people sitting (acc.)*] λέγει, Ἴδε ἡ
μήτηρ μου καὶ οἱ ἀδελφοί μου. 35 ὃς ἂν [*whoever*] ποιήσῃ [*translate as if* ποιει]
τὸ θέλημα τοῦ θεοῦ, οὗτος ἀδελφός μου καὶ ἀδελφὴ καὶ μήτηρ ἐστίν.

# The third declension – Part 2

In Chapter 12 we learnt the 3rd declension. In this chapter we look at several groups of words that exhibit some variations from the standard pattern.

## 13.1 NOUNS WITH VOWEL STEMS

There are quite a number of nouns with -ι stems. These are all feminine and frequently describe abstract nouns (e.g. γνωσις – knowledge, πιστις – faith). They have a nominative in -ις and a genitive in -εως.

Similarly, there are several nouns with -ευ stems. These are masculine, and frequently describe 'occupations' (e.g. βασιλευς – king, ἱερευς – priest). They have a nominative in -ευς and a genitive in -εως.

e.g. 'city' or 'town' is πολις, πολεως, ἡ and 'king' is βασιλευς, βασιλεως, ὁ

| Singular | Plural |
|---|---|
| πολις | πολεις |
| πολιν | πολεις |
| πολεως | πολεων |
| πολει | πολεσιν |

| Singular | Plural |
|---|---|
| βασιλευς | βασιλεις |
| βασιλεα | βασιλεις |
| βασιλεως | βασιλεων |
| βασιλει | βασιλευσιν |

Notes

- These two patterns are very similar – in particular having the distinctive gen. singular in -εως and nom. and acc. plurals in -εις. The main difference between them is in the acc. singular (-ιν or -εα).
- If you think of -εως as -εος then the -ος ending is what you would expect in the 3rd declension.
- There is another pattern of words that have stems ending in -υ. However, there is only one word in this family that is at all common, ἰχθυς (fish), and even that occurs only 20 times in the New Testament. Its endings are the same

as ἀστηρ except for the accusative singular: ἰχθυς, ἰχθυν, ἰχθυος, ἰχθυι; ἰχθυες, ἰχθυας, ἰχθυων, ἰχθυσιν.

**Hint**

Don't worry too much about these nouns. They are not particularly common, and most of their forms are close enough to either the 1st and 2nd or the 3rd declension endings in the appropriate case and number for you to be able normally to guess them correctly!

**PRACTICE 13.1**

### Parse

1. δυναμεις
2. κρισιν
3. ἀρχιερεων
4. βασιλεα
5. πολεσιν
6. γνωσις

### Put in the form indicated

7. ἱερευς, accusative plural
8. ἀναστασις, genitive singular
9. γραμματευς, dative plural
10. πιστις, accusative singular

## 13.2 CONTRACTING NOUNS AND ADJECTIVES

There is a family of 3rd declension adjectives and neuter nouns that have stems ending in -ε. Unsurprisingly, this weak ε combines with the endings, giving rise to slightly altered forms. However, these are not new endings, but the normal 3rd declension endings hidden by rather predictable contractions.

### 13.2.1 Nouns

These are all neuter. Remember their stem ends in -ε even though this is normally not displayed. E.g. 'nation' is ἐθνος, ἐθνους, το (with a stem ἐθνε).

| | | Form | Process of getting there | |
|---|---|---|---|---|
| Singular | Nom. | ἐθνος | | |
| | Acc. | ἐθνος | Neuter, therefore as nominative | |
| | Gen. | ἐθνους | ἐθνε + ος | ε + ο → ου |
| | Dat. | ἐθνει | ἐθνε + ι | |
| Plural | Nom. | ἐθνη | ἐθνε + α | ε + α → η |
| | Acc. | ἐθνη | Neuter, therefore as nominative | |
| | Gen. | ἐθνων | ἐθνε + ων | ε + ω → ω |
| | Dat. | ἐθνεσιν | ἐθνε + σιν | |

### 13.2.2 Adjectives

These have the standard 3rd declension endings (as in ἀστηρ and σωμα) and the same pattern of contractions as ἐθνος, and E.g. 'true' is ἀληθης, ἀληθες, ἀληθους.

| | | Masculine / Feminine | | Neuter | |
|---|---|---|---|---|---|
| Sing. | Nom. | ἀληθης | | ἀληθες | |
| | Acc. | ἀληθη | ε + α → η | ἀληθες | |
| | Gen. | ἀληθους | ε + ο → ου | ἀληθους | ε + ο → ου |
| | Dat. | ἀληθει | | ἀληθει | |
| Pl. | Nom. | ἀληθεις | ε + ε → ει | ἀληθη | ε + α → η |
| | Acc. | ἀληθεις | copying nom. | ἀληθη | ε + α → η |
| | Gen. | ἀληθων | ε + ω → ω | ἀληθων | ε + ω → ω |
| | Dat. | ἀληθεσιν | | ἀληθεσιν | |

**Note:** It is only the acc. plural masculine/feminine which is slightly peculiar in copying the nom., when you might expect some contraction of -εας.

PRACTICE 13.2

### Parse

1. τελει
2. μελη
3. σκοτους
4. ἀσθενεις
5. ὀρων
6. ἐτος

### Put in the form indicated

7. πληθος, accusative plural
8. ἀσθενης, fem. dative singular
9. σκευος, genitive plural
10. ἐθνος, dative plural

HALF-WAY PRACTICE

1. ὑπαγαγε εἰς τα ἐθνη.
2. ἐκεινῳ τῳ ἐτει ὁ βασιλευς ἀπεθανεν.
3. οἱ γραμματεις εἰπον κατα του Ἰησου.
4. ὁ Πετρος οὐ προσεχει τῳ ἀρχιερει.
5. οἱ ἀληθεις μαθηται εἰσιν ἐν τῃ πολει.
6. δια πιστεως ἐχομεν ἐλπιδα δοξης.
7. ἐχω μερος της βασιλειας.
8. ὁ ζητων την ἀληθειαν και δυναμιν λαμβανει.
9. The king's father spoke to the high priest.

10. Because of his mercy God rescues us.
11. Once we lived under judgement.
12. Faith found its true goal.

## 13.3 πας (ALL/EVERY)

πας defines a hybrid declension called the 3-1-3, because in the masculine and neuter it follows the 3rd declension but in the feminine the 1st declension. Think of πας as a 3rd declension word that wants to have distinct feminine endings. But in the 3rd declension there are no separate feminine endings, so it borrows the only ones available – those of the 1st declension.

To decline a word such as πας, you needs to know four pieces of information:

1. the masculine nominative singular
2. the neuter nominative singular
3. the genitive (or stem) for the masculine and neuter
4. the feminine nominative singular

Points 1–3 are the same as you need to know for any 3rd declension adjective (since there is no rule for deducing the nominative singulars from the stem).

Point 4 is sufficient to generate the whole of the feminine, since in the 1st and 2nd declensions the endings follow on directly from the nominative.

Thus, for πας, once we know the nominative singulars: πας, πασα, παν, and the 3rd declension stem: παντ-, we can deduce the rest of the declension.

| | | Masculine 3rd decl. | Feminine 1st decl.[1] | Neuter 3rd decl. |
|---|---|---|---|---|
| Sing. | Nom. | πας | πασα | παν |
| | Acc. | παντα | πασαν | παν |
| | Gen. | παντος | πασης | παντος |
| | Dat. | παντι | παση | παντι |
| Pl. | Nom. | παντες | πασαι | παντα |
| | Acc. | παντας | πασας | παντα |
| | Gen. | παντων | πασων | παντων |
| | Dat. | πασιν | πασαις | πασιν |

πας is the only common adjective that follows this pattern. However, the pattern is important because half of the participles in Greek also follow it. Up to now we

[1] Because the final letter of the stem of πασα is a σ, it follows the pattern of δοξα.

have only used participles in the nom. masculine (Chapter 7, section 7.4), but in the next chapter we shall need to use them in any case, gender or number.[2]

## Using πας

πας means 'all', but in English this is normally best translated as 'every' or 'whole' when in the singular. It is used in the same manner as other adjectives:

- On its own, in which case its gender reveals what is implied: masculine = person/man; feminine = woman; neuter = thing.

  e.g. John 1.3: παντα δι' αὐτου ἐγενετο. – All things came to be through him.
  Mark 6.50: παντες γαρ αὐτον εἰδον. – For everyone saw him.

- It can occur with a noun without the article.

  e.g. Matt. 7.17: παν δενδρον ἀγαθον καρπους καλους ποιει.
  – Every good tree produces good fruit.

- It can occur with a noun with the article, in which case it normally stands in the *predicative* positive (i.e. before the 'the').

  e.g. Mark 14.53: συνερχονται παντες οἱ ἀρχιερεις.
  – All the chief priests gather.

- It can occur with the article and participle.

  e.g. 1 John 5.1 πας ὁ πιστευων ὁτι Ἰησους ἐστιν ὁ Χριστος.
  – Everyone who believes that the Messiah is Jesus.

---

**PRACTICE 13.3**

### Parse

| | | |
|---|---|---|
| 1. παντες | 3. παντος | 5. παν |
| 2. πασαις | 4. πασαν | 6. παντι |

### Translate

7. παντες οἱ πατερες ἀπεθανον.
8. κηρυξω το εὐαγγελιον ἐν πασιν τοις ἐθνεσιν.
9. πας ἐθαυμασεν δια παντα ἁ ἐποιει.
10. ὁ σωτηρ παντων προσευχεται.

---

[2] Notice that the sing. participles (λυων, λυσας) do not precisely match πας, but that the plural forms (λυοντες, λυσαντες) do share the masculine nom. plural ending -ες. This is to be expected: in the 3rd declension the nom. sing. (alone of the forms) is not fixed.

## 13.4 εἱς – ONE

The word 'one' declines in a manner similar to πας, in as much as its masculine and neuter follow the 3rd declension, and its feminine (using a completely different stem) the 1st declension. Obviously there is no plural of 'one'.

| | Masculine | Feminine | Neuter |
|---|---|---|---|
| Nom. | εἱς | μια | ἑν |
| Acc. | ἑνα | μιαν | ἑν |
| Gen. | ἑνος | μιας | ἑνος |
| Dat. | ἑνι | μιᾳ | ἑνι |

**Hint**

Watch the breathings – ἑν (one) and ἐν (in); εἱς (one) and εἰς (into).

### οὐδεις and μηδεις

Both οὐδεις and μηδεις mean 'no one, nothing'. οὐδεις is used when οὐ would be used (i.e. clauses in the Indicative), and μηδεις is used when μη would be used (i.e. in other moods). They are declined as εἱς plus a prefix:

| | Masculine | Feminine | Neuter |
|---|---|---|---|
| Nom. | οὐδεις | οὐδεμια | οὐδεν |
| Acc. | οὐδενα | οὐδεμιαν | οὐδεν |
| Gen. | οὐδενος | οὐδεμιας | οὐδενος |
| Dat. | οὐδενι | οὐδεμιᾳ | οὐδενι |

| | Masculine | Feminine | Neuter |
|---|---|---|---|
| Nom. | μηδεις | μηδεμια | μηδεν |
| Acc. | μηδενα | μηδεμιαν | μηδεν |
| Gen. | μηδενος | μηδεμιας | μηδενος |
| Dat. | μηδενι | μηδεμιᾳ | μηδενι |

**Note:** In Greek, a sentence is either negative or not. If it is negative (i.e. it contains οὐ or μη), then other suitable forms in the sentence will also be in the negative. That is, in Greek two negatives make a negative, not as in English where two negatives make a positive (e.g. οὐ βλεπω οὐδεν means 'I do not see anything' not 'I do not see nothing', which in English implies that you did see something!).

Examples

Mark 13.32: περι δε της ἡμερας ἐκεινης ἢ της ὡρας <u>οὐδεις</u> οἰδεν [he knows] <u>οὐδε</u> οἱ ἀγγελοι ἐν οὐρανῳ <u>οὐδε</u> ὁ υἱος, εἰ μη ὁ πατηρ.
– But about that day or hour <u>no one</u> knows, <u>neither</u> the angels in heaven, <u>nor</u> the Son, but only the Father.

Mark 14.60: <u>Οὐκ</u> ἀποκρινῃ <u>οὐδεν</u>;
– Do you reply <u>nothing</u>? (<u>Don't</u> you have <u>any</u> answer?)

PRACTICE 13.4

## Translate

1. οὐδεις ἐστιν ἀγαθος;
2. εἰδον μιαν πολιν.
3. οὐχ εὑρες οὐδεν;
4. εἰπετε μηδεν μηδενι.
5. εἰπεν ὁτι ἐστιν εἱς κυριος και μια ἐκκλησια.
6. ἐχω ἑν προβατον.

## VOCAB FOR CHAPTER 13

3rd declension neuter nouns with genitives in -ους (declining like ἐθνος)
*ἐθνος (162) – nation (pl. Gentiles)
*ἐλεος (27) – mercy
*ἐτος (49) – year
μελος (34) – member, part, limb
*μερος (42) – part, share
*ὀρος (63) – mountain, hill
πληθος (31) – multitude, large amount
σκευος (23) – object (pl. property)
σκοτος (31) – darkness
*τελος (40) – end, goal

3rd declension masculine nouns with genitives in -εως (like βασιλευς)
*ἀρχιερευς (122) – high priest, chief priest
*βασιλευς (115) – king
*γραμματευς (63) – scribe, clerk
ἱερευς (31) – priest

3rd declension feminine nouns with genitives in -εως (like πολις)
ἀναστασις (42) – resurrection
γνωσις (29) – knowledge
*δυναμις (119) – power, miracle
*θλιψις (45) – suffering, oppression
*κρισις (47) – judgement
παρακλησις (29) – encouragement
*πιστις (243) – faith
*πολις (162) – city, town
συνειδησις (30) – conscience

3rd declension adjectives with genitives in -ους (like ἀληθης)
*ἀληθης (26) – true, truthful, genuine
*ἀσθενης (26) – weak, sick

*πας (1243) – all, every, whole
ἁπας (34) – all, every
*εἱς μια ἑν (345) – one, a single
*οὐδεις (234) – no one, nothing
μηδεις (90) – no one, nothing

Two 3rd declension masculine words with irregular endings:
*Μωϋσης (80) – Moses (Μωϋσης, Μωϋσην, Μωϋσεως, Μωϋσει or Μωϋση)
νους (24) – mind (νους, νουν, νοος, νοι)

## Word helps

ethnic, melee, merger/polymer, plethora, teleology, basilica, grammatical, hieroglyph/hierarchy, gnostic, dynamite, crisis, paraclete, politics, pantheism.

## Exercises

Section A

*1. ἐλεγον οὐν τῳ Πιλατῳ οἱ ἀρχιερεις των Ἰουδαιων· Μη γραφε· Ὁ βασιλευς των Ἰουδαιων, ἀλλ᾽ ὁτι ἐκεινος εἰπεν, Βασιλευς εἰμι των Ἰουδαιων.

*2. ὁ δε Ἰησους εἰπεν αὐτῳ· Τί με λεγεις ἀγαθον; οὐδεις ἀγαθος εἰ μη εἱς ὁ θεος.

*3. ἡ χαρις του κυριου Ἰησου Χριστου και ἡ ἀγαπη του θεου και ἡ κοινωνια [*fellowship*] του ἁγιου πνευματος μετα παντων ὑμων.

*4. μη καλειτε τινα Ῥαββι· εἱς γαρ ἐστιν ὑμων ὁ διδασκαλος [*teacher*], παντες δε ὑμεις ἀδελφοι ἐστε.

*5. και ὁ Πετρος λεγει[3] τῳ Ἰησου· Ῥαββι, καλον ἐστιν ἡμας ὡδε εἰναι, και οἰκοδομησομεν τρεις σκηνας (three tents) ὑμιν, σοι μιαν και Μωϋσει μιαν και Ἠλιᾳ μιαν.

*6. και ἐσονται οἱ δυο εἰς σαρκα μιαν· οὑτως οὐκετι εἰσιν δυο ἀλλα μια σαρξ.

7. και πας ὁ ὀχλος ἐζητουν ἁπτεσθαι αὐτου, ὁτι δυναμις παρ᾽ αὐτου ἐξηρχετο και ἐθεραπευεν παντας.

8. και ἐξηλθον οἱ μαθηται και ἠλθον εἰς την πολιν και εὑρον καθως εἰπεν αὐτοις.

*9. And one of the scribes, having approached, said to him, 'Rabbi, I will follow you.'

*10. And he will be king over[4] the house of Jacob forever[5], and of his kingdom there will not be an end.

---

[3] Note the Present tense here. Greek sometimes uses a Present tense when relating a story in the past. This is called a 'historic present' and can make the account more vivid. It is very common in the gospels.

[4] For 'over' use ἐπι + acc.

[5] For 'forever' use 'into the ages' (This is a common Jewish way of expressing 'forever', found here in Luke 1.33. The singular 'into the age' is as common.)

*11. In this world you have suffering, but you have peace in me.
12. Some go out into resurrection of life, but others to a resurrection of judgement.

## Section B

1. και ἐρχεται εἱς των ἀρχισυναγωγων[6], ὀνοματι Ἰαϊρος, και ἰδων αὐτον πιπτει προς τους ποδας αὐτου.
2. ὁ νους ἐν τῳ σκοτει ἐργαζεται πονηρα τῃ συνειδησει τῃ κακῃ.
3. το δε πληθος ἐπι τῳ ὀρει αἰτησει την παρακλησιν ἀπο του κυριου.
*4. ἑν ἐτος ὁ ἀρχιερευς ἠν ἀσθενης.
*5. τίς δεξεται το ἐλεος του βασιλεως; οὐδεις ἠ παντες;
6. ἁπασιν μεν ἡ γνωσις της ἀναστασεως, πολλων δε ὁ νους ἐν σκοτει.
*7. ὁ νομος του Μωϋσεως λεγει περι του ἐλεους του ἀληθους θεου.
*8. και ἀπεστειλεν αὐτους κηρυσσειν την βασιλειαν του θεου και θεραπευειν παντας τους ἀσθενεις.
9. Our nation has knowledge about the blind and the weak.
10. He received from his father his part of their property.
11. You are all members of the body of Christ.
12. There will be suffering for everybody, good and bad.

## Section C

**Matthew 28.18-20** καὶ προσελθὼν ὁ Ἰησοῦς ἐλάλησεν αὐτοῖς λέγων, Ἐδόθη [*has been given*] μοι πᾶσα ἐξουσία ἐν οὐρανῷ καὶ ἐπὶ τῆς γῆς. 19 πορευθέντες [*going*] οὖν μαθητεύσατε [μαθητευω = μαθητης ποιω] πάντα τὰ ἔθνη, βαπτίζοντες αὐτοὺς εἰς τὸ ὄνομα τοῦ πατρὸς καὶ τοῦ υἱοῦ καὶ τοῦ ἁγίου πνεύματος, 20 διδάσκοντες αὐτοὺς τηρεῖν πάντα ὅσα ἐνετειλάμην [ἐντελλομαι = *I command*] ὑμῖν· καὶ ἰδοὺ ἐγὼ μεθ᾽ ὑμῶν εἰμι πάσας τὰς ἡμέρας ἕως τῆς συντελείας [*completion*] τοῦ αἰῶνος.

---

[6] ἀρχι-συναγωγος = ἀρχων της συναγωγης (compare ἀρχ-ιερευς).

# Participles

Example 1

In Chapter 7, section 7.4 we learnt the basics of participles:

Luke 18.22: ἀκουσας δε ὁ Ἰησους εἰπεν αὐτῳ· Ἐτι ἑν σοι λειπει·
– having heard Jesus said to him, 'One thing still remains for you . . .'
– when Jesus heard (this) he said to him, 'You still lack one thing . . .'

ἀκουσας is a participle from ἀκουω. It agrees with ὁ Ἰησους (nom. masc. sing.), which tells us that it is Jesus who is doing the hearing. It is in the Aorist to convey the 'sequence' meaning (present would be 'simultaneous'), i.e the action in the participle is happening before that in the main verb: first Jesus hears, then he speaks.

Example 2

Luke 7.9: ἀκουσας δε ταυτα ὁ Ἰησους ἐθαυμασεν αὐτον.
– when he heard these things Jesus was amazed at him.

Once again, ἀκουσας is a participle, but this time it has its own object ταυτα – these things.

Thus the participle has some of the features of a verb, and some of an adjective (grammarians call it a 'verbal adjective').

**Like adjectives:**

KEY GRAMMAR
Participles must agree with the noun they qualify in gender, case and number

**Like verbs:**

KEY GRAMMAR
Participles have a tense (Present or Aorist) and may have an object

Up to now, we have only dealt with participles that are in the nominative – qualifying the subject. However, participles can qualify any noun.

Example 3

Rev. 7.2: και εἰδον ἀλλον ἀγγελον <u>ἀναβαινοντα</u> ἀπο ἀνατολης ἡλιου <u>ἐχοντα</u> σφραγιδα θεου ... – and I saw another angel <u>ascending</u> from the rising of the sun <u>having</u> a seal from God . . .

The basic sentence here is clear:
εἰδον is the main verb, containing in it the subject – 'I saw'.
ἀγγελον is the object – an angel.
ἀλλον is an adjective ('other') in the acc. masc. sing. agreeing with ἀγγελον, thus it is further describing (qualifying) ἀγγελον – not 'an angel', but 'an other angel'.
– 'I saw another angel', but then the sentence is enriched by two participles:

<u>ἀναβαινοντα</u> is a participle – it behaves partly as an adjective and partly as a verb.
As an adjective, it is similar to ἀλλον. It is also in the acc. masc. sing. because it is further describing ἀγγελον.
As a verb, it is in the Present tense – the ascending is going on at the same time as the seeing – and it leads into ἀπο ἀνατολης ἡλιου – from the rising sun.
<u>ἐχοντα</u> is also a participle. Again it is masc. acc. sing. agreeing with ἀγγελον.
It is in the Present tense – having – and has its own object – σφραγιδα – a seal.

Thus we have two participles in the accusative, further describing the object of the main verb. He did not just see an angel, but an angel ascending . . . and having . . .

Example 4

Mark 1.16: <u>παραγων</u> παρα την θαλασσαν . . . εἰδεν Σιμωνα και Ἀνδρεαν . . . <u>ἀμφιβαλλοντας</u> ἐν τῃ θαλασσῃ.
– <u>While he was passing</u> alongside the sea, he saw Simon and Andrew <u>casting</u> (nets) in the sea.

The basic sentence is again clear:
εἰδεν Σιμωνα και Ἀνδρεαν – he saw Simon and Andrew

There are two participles παραγων and ἀμφιβαλλοντας but these agree with different words in the sentence.

<u>παραγων</u> is nominative singular, so it is agreeing with the subject 'he'. The person seeing is the same person as the one going alongside the sea.

<u>ἀμφιβαλλοντας</u> is accusative plural, so it is agreeing with the object 'Simon and Andrew'. Simon and Andrew are the ones casting in the sea.

It is only by identifying the case (and gender and number) of the participle that we can identify which noun in the sentence it is qualifying. Otherwise we might wrongly translate Mark 1.16 as ‘he saw Simon and Andrew passing along the sea casting in the sea’, or ‘while he was casting in the sea he saw Simon and Andrew passing alongside the sea’ or ‘while he was passing along the sea casting in the sea he saw Simon and Andrew’.

## 14.1 FORMATION

We have already met the Present and Aorist participles of the normal (*Active*) verbs like λυω and the deponent (*Middle*) verbs like ῥυομαι.

Thus we have four basic participles:

| | Active | | Deponent (Middle) | |
|---|---|---|---|---|
| Present | λυ-ων | (untying) | ῥυ-ομενος | (rescuing) |
| 1st Aorist | λυ-σας | (having untied) | ῥυ-σαμενος | (having rescued) |

Notes

- In the Aorist there is no augment (there are never augments in the other moods).
- In the Aorist there is a σ and an α sound.
- The 2nd Aorist participle uses the Present participle endings (e.g. βαλων), as does the (Present) participle of εἰμι (ὢν – ‘being’).

What we now need to do is to learn how to decline each of these basic participles, so that we can form, for example, the accusative neuter singular of the Present participle of λυω. Before we do that you should revise the formation of the participles we have already covered (pages 83–7 and 126).

**PRACTICE 14.1 – REVISION**

### Put the verb in the participle form indicated (all nom. masc.)

1. γραφω, Aorist singular
2. ποιεω, Present plural
3. ἐρχομαι, Present singular
4. φιλεω, Aorist plural
5. λογιζομαι, Aorist singular
6. προσευχομαι, Present plural

## 14.2 DECLENSION

The participles follow two different declensions.

**KEY GRAMMAR**
Participles ending in -ος decline like ἀγαθος
Participles ending otherwise decline like πας

**Note:** πας is from the 3rd declension, so its nominative is 'irregular', not following the pattern of stem plus endings. Thus both λυων and λυσας can decline like πας.

### 14.2.1 ῥυομενος and ῥυσαμενος

These decline exactly as ἀγαθος does. Thus:

ῥυομενους – Accusative masculine plural of the Present participle of ῥυομαι
ἀρξαμεναις – Dative feminine plural of the Aorist participle of ἀρχομαι
ἐρχομενα – Nom./acc. neuter plural of the Present participle of ἐρχομαι

### 14.2.2 λυων and λυσας

These follow the 3-1-3 pattern like πας (Chapter 13, section 13.3). Therefore, to decline them, we need their three nominative singulars, and the 3rd declension stem:

| λυων | *nom. sing.* – λυων, λυουσα, λυον | *3rd decl. stem* – λυοντ- |
|---|---|---|
| λυσας | *nom. sing.* – λυσας, λυσασα, λυσαν | *3rd decl. stem* – λυσαντ- |

| | **Present (Active) participle – λυων** | | | **Aorist (Active) participle – λυσας** | | |
|---|---|---|---|---|---|---|
| | Masculine | Feminine | Neuter | Masculine | Feminine | Neuter |
| **Sing.** | | | | | | |
| Nom. | λυων | λυουσα | λυον | λυσας | λυσασα | λυσαν |
| Acc. | λυοντα | λυουσαν | λυον | λυσαντα | λυσασαν | λυσαν |
| Gen. | λυοντος | λυουσης | λυοντος | λυσαντος | λυσασης | λυσαντος |
| Dat. | λυοντι | λυουσῃ | λυοντι | λυσαντι | λυσασῃ | λυσαντι |
| **Pl.** | | | | | | |
| Nom. | λυοντες | λυουσαι | λυοντα | λυσαντες | λυσασαι | λυσαντα |
| Acc. | λυοντας | λυουσας | λυοντα | λυσαντας | λυσασας | λυσαντα |
| Gen. | λυοντων | λυουσων | λυοντων | λυσαντων | λυσασων | λυσαντων |
| Dat.[1] | λυουσιν | λυουσαις | λυουσιν | λυσασιν | λυσασαις | λυσασιν |

Thus:
λυσαν – Nom./acc. neuter singular of the Aorist participle of λυω
γραφοντι – Dative masc./neuter singular of the Present participle of γραφω
ἐλθοντες – Nom. masculine plural of the (2nd) Aorist participle of ἐρχομαι
οὖσιν – Dative masc./neuter plural of the Present participle of εἰμι.

**Hint**

There are two steps in forming a participle. The chart opposite may help you understand the sequence:

Participle → basic forms (essentially a verbal matter – about tense)
→ particular instance of that form (essentially an adjectival matter – about gender, case and number).

When faced with a Greek participle, think about this sequence:

1. Which of the basic forms is it from?
2. Which particular instance of that form is it?

**PRACTICE 14.2**

## Parse

1. βαλλοντες
2. φωνησας
3. ἐρχομεναις
4. πεμψαν
5. διωξαντι
6. ἰδοντων
7. ἐλπιζουσαν
8. ἐγειραντας
9. δεχομενοι

## Put in the form indicated

10. ἀνοιγω, Present Fem. Acc. Pl.
11. ποιεω, Aorist Masc. Nom. Sing.
12. κηρυσσω, Aorist Neut. Gen. Pl.
13. ἁπτομαι, Present Masc. Dat. Sing.
14. ἐρχομαι, Aorist Neut. Nom. Pl.
15. πιστευω, Aorist Fem. Acc. Pl.

[1] Remember, the σιν ending affects the final consonants of the stem (Chapter 12, section 12.2.1).

## The formation of participles

**Verb** (basic meaning) → ① **Basic Form of the Participle** (precise meaning) → ② **Precise Form Wanted** (matter of agreement)

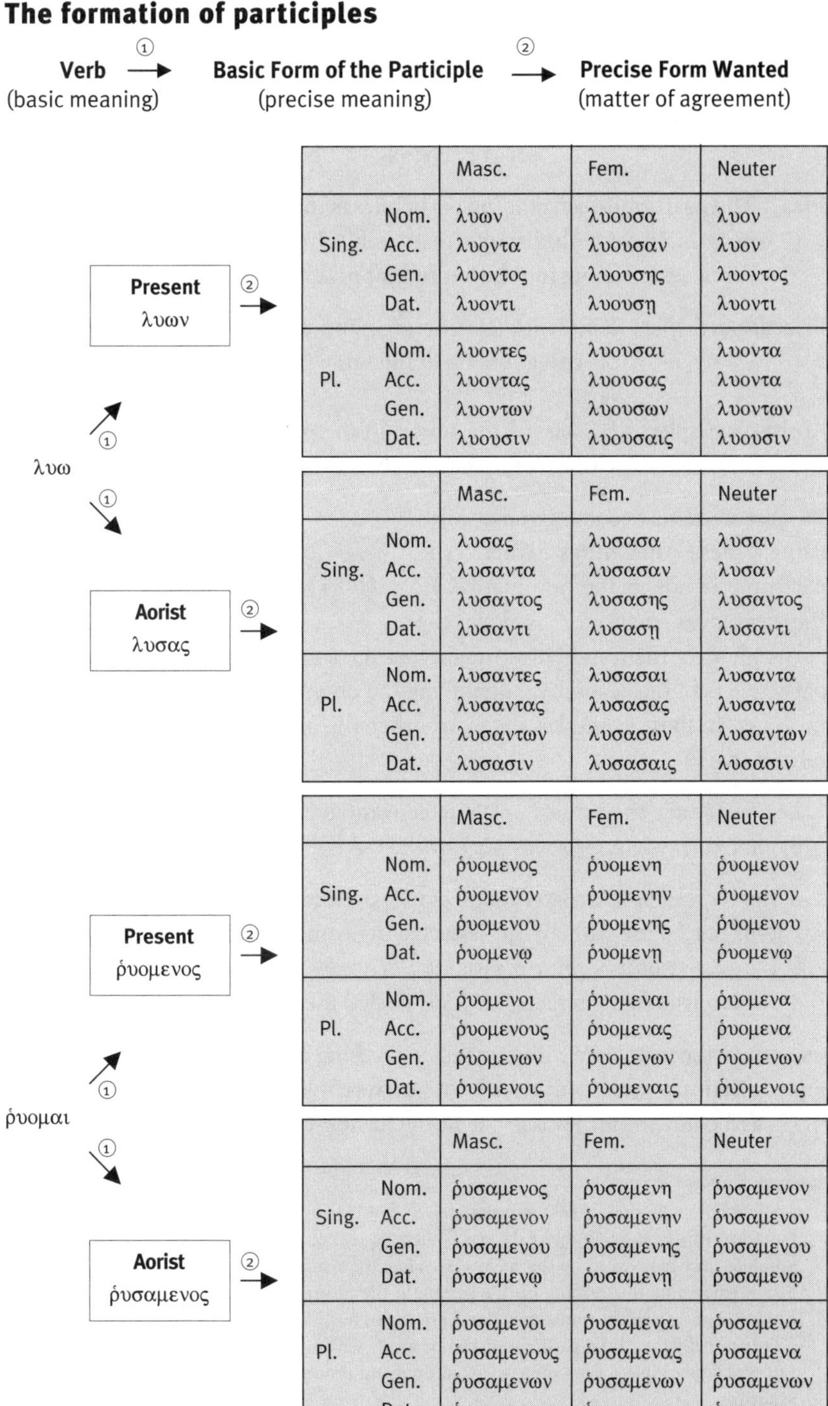


| | | Masc. | Fem. | Neuter |
|---|---|---|---|---|
| Sing. | Nom. | λυων | λυουσα | λυον |
| | Acc. | λυοντα | λυουσαν | λυον |
| | Gen. | λυοντος | λυουσης | λυοντος |
| | Dat. | λυοντι | λυουσῃ | λυοντι |
| Pl. | Nom. | λυοντες | λυουσαι | λυοντα |
| | Acc. | λυοντας | λυουσας | λυοντα |
| | Gen. | λυοντων | λυουσων | λυοντων |
| | Dat. | λυουσιν | λυουσαις | λυουσιν |

| | | Masc. | Fem. | Neuter |
|---|---|---|---|---|
| Sing. | Nom. | λυσας | λυσασα | λυσαν |
| | Acc. | λυσαντα | λυσασαν | λυσαν |
| | Gen. | λυσαντος | λυσασης | λυσαντος |
| | Dat. | λυσαντι | λυσασῃ | λυσαντι |
| Pl. | Nom. | λυσαντες | λυσασαι | λυσαντα |
| | Acc. | λυσαντας | λυσασας | λυσαντα |
| | Gen. | λυσαντων | λυσασων | λυσαντων |
| | Dat. | λυσασιν | λυσασαις | λυσασιν |

| | | Masc. | Fem. | Neuter |
|---|---|---|---|---|
| Sing. | Nom. | ῥυομενος | ῥυομενη | ῥυομενον |
| | Acc. | ῥυομενον | ῥυομενην | ῥυομενον |
| | Gen. | ῥυομενου | ῥυομενης | ῥυομενου |
| | Dat. | ῥυομενῳ | ῥυομενῃ | ῥυομενῳ |
| Pl. | Nom. | ῥυομενοι | ῥυομεναι | ῥυομενα |
| | Acc. | ῥυομενους | ῥυομενας | ῥυομενα |
| | Gen. | ῥυομενων | ῥυομενων | ῥυομενων |
| | Dat. | ῥυομενοις | ῥυομεναις | ῥυομενοις |

| | | Masc. | Fem. | Neuter |
|---|---|---|---|---|
| Sing. | Nom. | ῥυσαμενος | ῥυσαμενη | ῥυσαμενον |
| | Acc. | ῥυσαμενον | ῥυσαμενην | ῥυσαμενον |
| | Gen. | ῥυσαμενου | ῥυσαμενης | ῥυσαμενου |
| | Dat. | ῥυσαμενῳ | ῥυσαμενῃ | ῥυσαμενῳ |
| Pl. | Nom. | ῥυσαμενοι | ῥυσαμεναι | ῥυσαμενα |
| | Acc. | ῥυσαμενους | ῥυσαμενας | ῥυσαμενα |
| | Gen. | ῥυσαμενων | ῥυσαμενων | ῥυσαμενων |
| | Dat. | ῥυσαμενοις | ῥυσαμεναις | ῥυσαμενοις |

## 14.3 MEANING

We have already learnt the meaning of the participles (Chapter 7, section 7.4.2).

| **Wooden translations** | Present participle | untying |
|---|---|---|
| | Aorist participle | having untied |

**Idea** The heart of understanding participles is that the participle is dependent on a main verb (Indicative, or possibly Imperative) in the sentence. It expresses meaning **in relation to that main verb**, not absolutely.[2]

| | |
|---|---|
| Present participle | *Simultaneous* process – the action in the participle is a process going on at the same time as the action in the main verb. |
| Aorist participle | *Sequence* – the action in the participle occurred before the action in the main verb.[3] |

KEY GRAMMAR

| | |
|---|---|
| Present participle | Simultaneous |
| Aorist participle | Sequence |

We just need to become familiar with using these meanings when the participle is not in the nominative. In the sentences marked 1 below, the participle is in the nominative (qualifying the subject). In those marked 2, the participle is in the accusative (qualifying the object), producing a very different meaning. In these examples, the word order will also help, but you can't always rely on that.

1. <u>λεγων</u> βλεπει το δενδρον. – While he was talking, he saw the tree.
2. βλεπει το δενδρον <u>λεγον</u>. – He saw the talking tree.

1. ὁ Ἰησους εἰσελθων ἐθεραπευσεν την γυναικα. – When he came in, Jesus healed the woman (lit: Jesus having come in healed the woman).
2. ὁ Ἰησους ἐθεραπευσεν την εἰσελθουσαν γυναικα. – Jesus healed the woman who had come in (lit: Jesus healed the having-come-in woman).

Of course, the participle could qualify something other than an object:
E.g. ὁ Ἰησους εἰπεν τῃ εἰσελθουσῃ γυναικι. – Jesus spoke to the women who had come in (lit: Jesus spoke to the having-come-in woman).

---

[2] E.g. Matt. 8.7: ἐγω ἐλθων θεραπευσω αὐτον. The participle 'having come' gives time (sequence) <u>in relation to the main verb</u> – first he will come, then he will heal. However, the absolute time is revealed by the main verb. Here the main verb is future, therefore the whole action (including the 'coming') is happening in the future, but the 'coming' occurs before the healing. Thus we might translate it, 'I will come and heal'.

[3] Occasionally the Aorist participle does not imply sequence, but rather is used as a default, or undefined participle – used more to avoid implying process (Present participle) than to imply sequence.

**Hint**

Successive Aorist participles are often best translated by a number of main verbs in English e.g. Mark 5.27 – ἀκουσασα περι του Ἰησου, ἐλθουσα ἐν τῳ ὀχλῳ ὀπισθεν ἡψατο του ἱματιου αὐτου. – When she heard about Jesus, she came up behind in the crowd and touched his cloak.

---

**HALF-WAY PRACTICE**

## Translate

1. ἐλθων ἐθεραπευσεν αὐτον.
2. ἀναβαινων εἰδεν το πνευμα.
3. φυγοντες ἠλθον εἰς ἱερον.
4. ἐβαπτιζεν τους πονηρους μετανοησαντας.
5. εἰπομεν τοις ἐρχομενοις τεκνοις.
6. ἐβλεψατε τους γραμματεις εἰσελθοντας εἰς το ἱερον;
7. ζητω την μελλουσαν βασιλειαν.
8. ὑπαγαγουσα εἰδεν τον πατερα αὐτης λαλουντα.
9. Jesus greeted the approaching crowd.
10. When she saw she believed.
11. The Pharisee taught the Jews who were listening.
12. When the king heard this he sent his soldiers to find the child.

---

## 14.4 OTHER USES OF PARTICIPLES

### 14.4.1 As nouns[4]

This was discussed in Chapter 7, section 7.5.

e.g. John 15.23: ὁ ἐμε μισων και τον πατερα μου μισει.
– The one who hates me (or whoever hates me) also hates my father.[5]

Now we can simply use this construction with a participle in other cases.

e.g. John 12.45: και ὁ θεωρων ἐμε θεωρει τον πεμψαντα με.
– The one who sees me is seeing the one who sent me.

---

[4] Grammatically this is called an adjectival participle, because in being used to form a noun, the participle is behaving as the adjectives do.

[5] Note the difficulty of translating into English without incorporating gender bias. Greek, like Old English, used the masculine forms generically for a person. However, the translation '*he* who hates me' would suggest to many modern English speakers that it is actually males in view, which is very unlikely to have been the intention of the Greek.

Acts 10.44: ἐπεπεσεν το πνευμα το ἁγιον ἐπι παντας τους ἀκουοντας τον λογον. – The holy spirit fell on all those who were listening to the word.

### 14.4.2 Causal, concessive and instrumental uses

Participles can be used to imply a causal, concessive or instrumental sense, although these are relatively rare and still flow out of the 'wooden translations'.

**Causal:** Matt. 1.19: Ἰωσηφ δε ὁ ἀνηρ αὐτης, δικαιος ὢν . . .
But Joseph her husband, because he was (lit: being) righteous . . .

**Concessive:** Rom. 1.21: γνοντες τον θεον οὐχ ὡς θεον ἐδοξασαν.
Although they knew (lit: knowing) God, they did not glorify him as God.

**Instrumental:** 1 Tim. 4.16: τουτο γαρ ποιων και σεαυτον σωσεις και τους ἀκουοντας σου. – For by doing this (lit: doing this) you will save both yourself and your hearers.

### 14.4.3 With Imperatives and Infinitives

Just as Greek will tend to avoid having one main verb immediately followed by a second, replacing one by a participle ('having entered he spoke', rather than 'he entered and he spoke'), Greek also often avoids a sequence of two Imperatives or Infinitives, again replacing the first with a participle.

E.g. οὐκ εἰμι ἱκανος κυψας λυσαι τον ἱμαντα των ὑποδηματων αὐτου. (Mark 1.7) – I am not worthy to stoop down and untie the strap of his sandals (lit: having stooped down, to untie).

**PRACTICE 14.4**

### Translate

1. φιλειτε τους μισουντας ὑμας.
2. ὁ Μωϋσης ἁγιος ὢν ἐλεγεν τῳ θεῳ.
3. θελω εἰσελθων εἰς την συναγωγην ἀκουσαι του ῥαββι.
4. ἐλεγον ἀλληλοις περι των γενομενων.
5. I saw the ones carrying the sick man.
6. Depart and preach the gospel.

## VOCAB FOR CHAPTER 14

Some more nouns

Six 2nd declension like λογος
*ἁμαρτωλος (47) – sinner
*διδασκαλος (59) – teacher
*θρονος (62) – throne
Ἰακωβος (42) – James
*λιθος (59) – stone
*πρεσβυτερος (66) – old person, elder

Eight 3rd declension
*ἀμπελων, ἀμπελωνος, ὁ (23) – vineyard
εἰκων, εἰκονος, ἡ (23) – image
Ἑλλην, Ἑλληνος, ὁ (25) – Greek
*Καισαρ, Καισαρος, ὁ (29) – Caesar
*κριμα, ατος, το (27) – judgement
*οὐς, ὠτος, το (36) – ear
*παις, παιδος, ὁ (24) – child, servant (plus the related noun *παιδιον (52) – child or infant, which declines like ἐργον)
*σπερμα, ατος, το (43) – seed

One indeclinable
*πασχα, το (29) – Passover

And some more verbs
ἀγοραζω (30) – I buy
βλασφημεω (34) – I blaspheme
*διακονεω (37) + dat. – I serve
διαλογιζομαι (16) – I consider, argue, discuss
ἐλπιζω (31) – I hope
*ἑτοιμαζω (40) – I prepare, make ready
*κρατεω (47) – I grasp, arrest
*μισεω (40) – I hate
*πειραζω (38) – I test, tempt
*πρασσω (39) – I do
προφητευω (28) – I prophesy
σκανδαλιζω (29) – I cause to fall/sin
*ὑποτασσω (38) – I subject
φυλασσω (31) – I guard
*φωνεω (43) – I call (out)
χαριζομαι (23) – I give freely

### Word helps

didactic, throne, Jacobite, monolith/paleolithic, presbyter, icon, Hellenistic, crimatology, pedagogy/encyclopaedia, sperm, Paschal, agora, deacon, dialogue, autocratic/democracy, misogynist/misanthropic, practice, scandalize/scandal, prophylactic, telephone/symphony, Eucharist/charity.

## Exercises

### Section A

1. ὁ φιλων την ψυχην αὐτου οὐ σωσει αὐτην, και ὁ μισων την ψυχην αὐτου ἐν τῳ κοσμῳ τουτῳ εἰς ζωην αἰωνιον φυλαξει αὐτην.
2. και ἐξελθων εἰδεν πολυν ὀχλον και ἠλεησεν ἐπ᾽ αὐτους, ὁτι ἠσαν ὡς προβατα μη ἐχοντα ποιμενα [*shepherd*], και ἠρξατο διδασκειν αὐτους πολλα.

*3. Ἀμην ἀμην λεγω ὑμιν ὁτι ὁ τον λογον μου ἀκουων και πιστευων τῳ πεμψαντι με ἐχει ζωην αἰωνιον και εἰς κρισιν οὐκ ἐρχεται.

*4. πας ὁ θεωρων τον υἱον και πιστευων εἰς αὐτον ἐχει ζωην αἰωνιον.

*5. οἱ οὐν Ἰουδαιοι περι αὐτου ἐλαλουν μετ᾽ ἀλληλων ὁτι εἰπεν· Ἐγω εἰμι ὁ ἀρτος ὁ καταβας ἐκ του οὐρανου.

*6. οὑτος γαρ ἐστιν ὁ λογος δια Ἠσαΐου του προφητου λεγοντος· Φωνη κραζοντος ἐν τῃ ἐρημῳ· Ἑτοιμασατε την ὁδον κυριου.

*7. εἰπεν τε προς αὐτους· Ἀνδρες Ἰσραηλ, προσεχετε ἑαυτοις ἐπι τοις ἀνθρωποις τουτοις τί μελλετε πρασσειν.

*8. και ὁ Σατανας ἠν ἐν τῃ ἐρημῳ πολλας ἡμερας πειραζων αὐτον, και ὁ Ἰησους ἠν μετα των θηριων, και οἱ ἀγγελοι διηκονουν αὐτῳ.

*9. For the Father has subjected all things under the feet of the Son.

10. Beloved children, guard yourselves against [ἀπο] those who hate your soul.
11. That stone has the image of Caesar, not of some Greek.

*12. What therefore will the lord of the vineyard do?

### Section B

1. πολλα ἐχω ὑμιν γραφειν ἀλλα ἐλπιζω γενεσθαι προς ὑμας και στομα προς στομα λαλησαι.

*2. και εἰπεν ὁ Ἰησους· Εἰς κριμα ἐγω εἰς τον κοσμον τουτον ἠλθον.

3. ὁ παις του διδασκαλου ἐμισει τα βιβλια του πατρος αὐτου.

*4. και προσελθων ἠγειρεν αὐτην κρατησας της χειρος.[6]

5. και ἐρχονται εἰς Ἱεροσολυμα· και εἰσελθων εἰς το ἱερον ἠρξατο ἐκβαλλειν τους ἀγοραζοντας ἐν τῳ ἱερῳ.
6. ὁ Φαρισαιος προς ἑαυτον ταυτα προσηυχετο· Ὁ θεος,[7] εὐχαριστω σοι ὁτι οὐκ εἰμι ὡσπερ οἱ ἀλλοι ἀνθρωποι, ἠ και ὡς οὑτος ὁ ἁμαρτωλος.
7. οἱ πρεσβυτεροι και οἱ διδασκαλοι ὀφειλουσιν διακονειν τοις προβατοις και προφητευειν τοις ἁμαρτωλοις και θεραπευειν τους

---

[6] Normally κρατεω does take an accusative. However, when the sense is 'take hold of someone <u>by</u> the hand', sometimes 'hand' occurs in the genitive (as in Mark 1.41).

[7] In practice ὁ θεος was normally used as the vocative of θεος, rather than ὠ θεε.

ἀσθενεις και μητε βλασφημειν τον θεον ἡμων μητε σκανδαλιζειν τα παιδια του κυριου.

*8. μη λεγετε ἐν ἑαυτοις· Πατερα ἐχομεν τον Ἀβρααμ. λεγω γαρ ὑμιν ὁτι δυναται [*is able*] ὁ θεος ἐκ των λιθων τουτων ἐγειραι τεκνα τῳ Ἀβρααμ.

*9. The ears of the sinners do not hear the seed which the sower sows.

*10. Judgement begins with[8] the household of God.

11. The elder prayed for James, and the lord, having heard, had mercy.

12. Touching the sinner, the one serving the Father in heaven healed her ears.

## Section C

**Mark 1.7-10** καὶ ἐκήρυσσεν λέγων, Ἔρχεται ὁ ἰσχυρότερός [*more powerful than*] μου ὀπίσω μου, οὗ οὐκ εἰμὶ ἱκανὸς [*worthy*] κύψας [κυπτω = *bend down*] λῦσαι τὸν ἱμάντα [*strap*] τῶν ὑποδημάτων [*sandals*] αὐτοῦ. 8 ἐγὼ ἐβάπτισα ὑμᾶς ὕδατι, αὐτὸς δὲ βαπτίσει ὑμᾶς ἐν πνεύματι ἁγίῳ. 9 Καὶ ἐγένετο ἐν ἐκείναις ταῖς ἡμέραις ἦλθεν Ἰησοῦς ἀπὸ Ναζαρὲτ [*Nazareth*] τῆς Γαλιλαίας καὶ ἐβαπτίσθη [*he was baptized*] εἰς τὸν Ἰορδάνην [*Jordan*] ὑπὸ Ἰωάννου. 10 καὶ εὐθὺς ἀναβαίνων ἐκ τοῦ ὕδατος εἶδεν σχιζομένους [*being split*] τοὺς οὐρανοὺς καὶ τὸ πνεῦμα ὡς περιστερὰν [*dove*] καταβαῖνον εἰς αὐτόν.

[8] For 'with' here use ἀπο (as in 1 Peter 4.17).

# The Passive and Voices

Rom. 11.26: και οὑτως πας Ἰσραηλ σωθησεται.
– and thus all Israel will be saved.

Luke 2.4: ἀνεβη δε και Ἰωσηφ ἀπο της Γαλιλαιας ... εἰς πολιν Δαυιδ ἡτις καλειται Βηθλεεμ. – Joseph also went up from Galilee to (the) city of David which is called Bethlehem.

Matt. 3.10: παν οὐν δενδρον μη ποιουν καρπον καλον ἐκκοπτεται και εἰς πυρ βαλλεται. – Therefore every tree not producing good fruit is cut down and is thrown into a fire.

Rom. 5.1: δικαιωθεντες οὐν ἐκ πιστεως εἰρηνην ἐχομεν προς τον θεον ... – Therefore having been justified through faith we have peace towards God . . .

In these sentences the verbs underlined are in the Passive (as opposed to the Active).

## 15.1 THE IDEA OF THE PASSIVE

Until now, all our sentences have been *active* in meaning – that is, the subject of the sentence is the one acting. However, in both English and Greek you can have *passive* sentences, in which the subject of the sentence is acted upon.

Active: Jesus heals the leper. Passive: The leper is healed.

A passive sentence does not indicate who *did* the action. However, this can be achieved by specifying an *agent* – 'the leper is healed *by Jesus*'. Greek expresses the *agent* by using the preposition ὑπο + gen (= 'by'). (See Chapter 4, section 4.3 for the distinction between animate *agents* and inanimate *instruments*.)

**Voices – Active and Passive?**
**See it in English**
Section 8
Page 247

Mark 1.9: ἐβαπτισθη εἰς τον Ἰορδανην ὑπο Ἰωαννου.
– He was baptised in the Jordan by John.

## 15.2 VOICES

There are **three** *Voices* in Greek – *Active, Middle* and *Passive.* As we learnt in Chapter 8, section 8.1.4, the deponent verbs (like ῥυομαι) use the *Middle Voice* to give an *Active* meaning. The *Middle Voice* will be discussed further later. For now, it is important to see that in both the Passive and Middle there is the whole range of moods and tenses that there is in the Active.

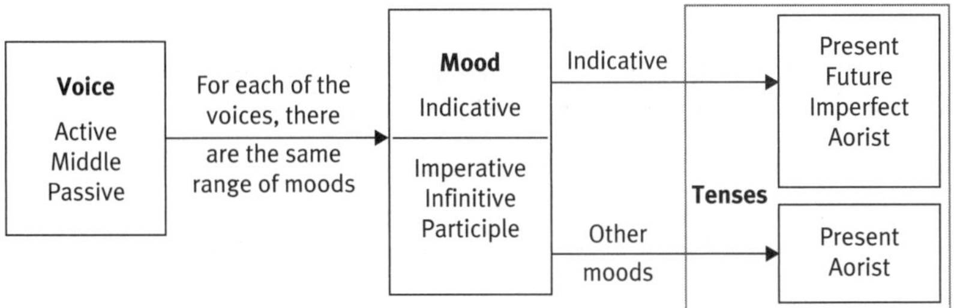


## 15.3 DISTINGUISHING THE TENSES

When we first met the tenses in Chapter 6 we saw that they could be distinguished by a pattern of ε prefixes and σ suffixes. The same pattern held when we met the Middle (deponent) verses in Chapter 8. In the Passive we can also be greatly helped by noticing a similar, though slightly different, pattern.

| | Indicative | | | Other Moods | | |
|---|---|---|---|---|---|---|
| | Active | Middle | Passive | Active | Middle | Passive |
| Present | λυ | ῥυ | λυ | λυ | ῥυ | λυ |
| Future | λυ σ | ῥυ σ | λυ θησ | | | |
| Imperfect | ἐ λυ | ἐ ῥυ | ἐ λυ | | | |
| Aorist | ἐ λυ σ | ἐ ῥυ σ | ἐ λυ θ | λυ σ | ῥυ σ | λυ θ |

Notes

- The pattern in the Active and in the Middle is the same.
- ῥυομαι is used as the exemplar in the Middle rather than λυω because the Middle is normally used only for the deponent verbs.
- In the Passive, the pattern of ἐ augments is the same as in the Active – the Imperfect and Aorist Indicative has an augment.

- The Aorist Passive is marked out by a θ suffix.
- The Future Passive is marked out by a θησ suffix.
- The Future Indicative is easily confused with the Aorist in the other moods in the Active and Middle (both have σ suffixes but no augment).

PRACTICE 15.3

**Give the possible tenses and voices of the following, and say whether they are indicative or other moods.**

| | | | |
|---|---|---|---|
| 1. ἐπιστευθη | 3. ἐλαμβανεν | 5. ἀπολυθησονται | 7. ποιηθητε |
| 2. πεμψατε | 4. ἀρξεται | 6. λογισασθαι | 8. ἐμισησαν |

## 15.4 THE MEANING OF THE PASSIVE

There is nothing unusual to learn about the meaning of the Passive. However, it can be helpful to see the basic English equivalents (compare Chapter 6, section 6.3 for the Active).

| | | |
|---|---|---|
| Indicative | Present | I am being untied, you are being untied, . . . |
| | Future | I will be untied, you will be untied, . . . |
| | Imperfect | I was being untied, you were being untied, . . . |
| | Aorist | I was untied, you were untied, . . . |
| Imperative | Present – process | Be untied! (continuously/repeatedly) |
| | Aorist – undefined | Be untied! |
| Infinitive | Present – process | To be untied (continuously/repeatedly) |
| | Aorist – undefined | To be untied |
| Participle | Present | Being untied (simultaneous) |
| | Aorist | Having been untied (sequence) |

## 15.5 THE PASSIVE ENDINGS

### *Indicative* Passive of λυω

| | Present | Future | Imperfect | Aorist |
|---|---|---|---|---|
| I | λυομαι | λυθησομαι | ἐλυομην | ἐλυθην |
| You (sing.) | λυῃ | λυθησῃ | ἐλυου | ἐλυθης |
| He, she, it | λυεται | λυθησεται | ἐλυετο | ἐλυθη |
| We | λυομεθα | λυθησομεθα | ἐλυομεθα | ἐλυθημεν |
| You (pl.) | λυεσθε | λυθησεσθε | ἐλυεσθε | ἐλυθητε |
| They | λυονται | λυθησονται | ἐλυοντο | ἐλυθησαν |

### *Other moods* Passive of λυω

| | | Present | Aorist |
|---|---|---|---|
| **Imperative** | 2nd Sing. | λυου | λυθητι |
| | 2nd Pl. | λυεσθε | λυθητε |
| **Infinitive** | | λυεσθαι | λυθηναι |
| **Participle** | | λυομενος | λυθεις[1] |

### 15.5.1 The Passive in the Present and Imperfect

If you look at the Present and Imperfect in the charts above, you will see that the endings are exactly the same as in the Present and Imperfect (Middle) of the deponent verbs. For example,

ῥυεται – 3rd Singular Present Middle Indicative of ῥυομαι
λυεται – 3rd Singular Present Passive Indicative of λυω

[1] λυθεις has a feminine nominative λυθεισα, a neuter nominative λυθεν, and a masculine and neuter stem λυθεντ-. It declines like λυων and λυσας (page 157). Thus, its declension in full is:

| | | Masc. | Fem. | Neuter |
|---|---|---|---|---|
| Singular | Nom. | λυθεις | λυθεισα | λυθεν |
| | Acc. | λυθεντα | λυθεισαν | λυθεν |
| | Gen. | λυθεντος | λυθεισης | λυθεντος |
| | Dat. | λυθεντι | λυθειση | λυθεντι |
| Plural | Nom. | λυθεντες | λυθεισαι | λυθεντα |
| | Acc. | λυθεντας | λυθεισας | λυθεντα |
| | Gen. | λυθεντων | λυθεισων | λυθεντων |
| | Dat. | λυθεισιν | λυθεισαις | λυθεισιν |

This obviously raises a question of how you tell the Middle and the Passive apart – we will deal with this later. For now, however, this is good news, since it means that there are no more endings to learn.

### 15.5.2 The Passive in the Future and the Aorist

If you look at the Future Passive in the chart on page 260, you will see that it has the same endings as the Future Middle (and hence the same as the Present Middle, and Present Passive). The distinguishing feature is the θησ suffix.

Looking at the Aorist, it is worth noting the surprising fact that its endings are far more similar to Active endings (in particular the -ημεν and -ητε and the participle not ending in -μενος) than the other Passive/Middle endings.

Both the Future and the Aorist Passive involve the addition of a θ to the end of the stem. Unsurprisingly, this can cause complications, just as adding a σ suffix can do (Chapter 6, section 6.6). The combinations that occur are given in the table on the right.

**KEY GRAMMAR**

| | | | | |
|---|---|---|---|---|
| π, β, φ | + | θ | → | φθ |
| τ, δ, θ, ζ | + | θ | → | σθ |
| κ, γ, χ, σσ | + | θ | → | χθ |

Plus, as you would expect, in -εω verbs the ε is lengthened into an η before the θ (just as it is before the σ in the Future/Aorist Active/ Middle).

Examples

ἀχθησομαι – Future Passive Indicative of ἀγω – I will be led
ἠχθην – Aorist Passive Indicative of ἀγω – I was led
λαληθεις – Aorist Passive participle of λαλεω – Having been spoken
βαπτισθηναι – Aorist Passive Infinitive of βαπτιζω – To be baptised

**PRACTICE 15.5.1 AND 15.5.2**

## Parse

1. ἠνοιγετο
2. θεραπευθησομαι
3. βαπτισθεις
4. διωκονται
5. ἐρχονται
6. ἐποιηθη

### 15.5.3 Irregular Future and Aorist Passives

All verbs use the standard endings for the Future and Aorist Passive, but there are a number of verbs that have irregular stems. However, at least they use the same stem for both the Future and the Aorist. In the table below the Aorist Passive Indicative is quoted, but the Future Passive can be reliably formed from this.[2] These five only have slight changes in the stem:

| | **Present** | **Aorist Passive** |
|---|---|---|
| I hear | ἀκουω | ἠκουσθην |
| I throw | βαλλω | ἐβληθην |
| I lift | ἐγειρω | ἠγερθην |
| I call | καλεω | ἐκληθην |
| I save | σωζω | ἐσωθην |

This one is quite difficult to recognise:

| | | |
|---|---|---|
| I take | λαμβανω | ἐλημφθην |

These five form a very awkward group, since they don't display the θ, which you normally rely on to indicate that the verb is Aorist or Future Passive.[3]

| | | |
|---|---|---|
| I send | ἀποστελλω | ἀπεσταλην |
| I write | γραφω | ἐγραφην |
| I sow | σπειρω | ἐσπαρην |
| I turn[4] | στρεφω | ἐστραφην |
| I shine[5] | φαινω | ἐφανην |

There are three whose Aorist Passive stems are formed from different verbs:

| | | |
|---|---|---|
| I say | λεγω | ἐρρεθην (or ἐρρηθην) |
| I see | ὁραω | ὠφθην |
| I carry | φερω | ἠνεχθην |

**PRACTICE 15.5.3**

## Parse

1. ἐσωθημεν
2. ἐγραφη
3. κληθησεται
4. βληθεις
5. ἐρρεθη
6. ἐλημφθησαν

---

[2] For example, βαλλω has the irregular Aorist Passive ἐβληθην. Its Future Passive is therefore βληθησομαι (remove augment, replace θ suffix with θησ and use Future Passive endings).

[3] These also have -ηθι in the 2nd singular Aorist Passive Imperative, rather than -ητι.

[4] Found most commonly in the compounds ἐπιστρεφω – I turn (back) and ὑποστρεφω – I return.

[5] φαινω frequently occurs in the Passive, where it means 'I appear'.

**HALF-WAY PRACTICE**

1. ἐλαληθη ὑπο των προφητων.
2. ὁ δουλος ἀπολυθεις εὐχαριστησεν τῳ θεῳ.
3. ὁ θεος βλεπεται ὑπο ἀγγελων.
4. ὁ Πετρος ἠρχετο εἰς την συναγωγην.
5. πειραζομενος[6] ἐγω οὐ πιπτω.
6. οἱ ἀποστολοι ἀποσταλησονται.
7. βλεψαντες τα πονηρα πραχθεντα ἐφυγον.
8. ἐκεινῃ τῃ ἡμερᾳ ὁ θεος ὀφθησεται.
9. The law will be written.
10. The old woman was carried by her sons.
11. After Jesus was arrested he said nothing.
12. Because they called, Lord, Lord, they were saved.[7]

## 15.6 UNDERSTANDING THE MIDDLE

The Middle Voice often ends up as a weak point for students – they understand the Active and the Passive (because they occur in English) but are then confused by what the Middle can mean. Soon we will learn a special meaning for the Middle, but this is very unusual. Normally, the Middle is used simply because the verb is a deponent verb, and deponent verbs use the *Middle* Voice when they want the *Active* meaning.

The following chart may help:

| | | Verb is | |
|---|---|---|---|
| | | Normal | Deponent |
| Meaning wanted | Active | Use **Active** | Use **Middle** |
| | Passive | Use **Passive** | Use **Passive** |

This chart illustrates that grammatically deponent verbs can be put into the Passive – when they want the Active meaning they use the Middle forms, when they want the Passive meaning they use the Passive forms. However, many deponent verbs are intransitive (i.e. they cannot have an object, for example 'I go')

[6] This is a concessive participle (see Chapter 14, section 14.4.2).

[7] Use a causal participle (see Chapter 14, section 14.4.2).

and so cannot occur in the Passive ('it was goed'?). Even those others which can occur in the Passive (ἀρχομαι – I begin) rarely do so. This is useful, because in the Present and Imperfect tenses the Middle and the Passive forms are identical, and so all you can say grammatically about, for example, ἀρχεται is that it is 3rd sing. Present *Middle* or *Passive* Indicative. In practice, however, it is far more likely to be Middle (with the Active meaning) than Passive (with the Passive meaning).

This can be summarised in the following chart:

| | | Verb is | |
|---|---|---|---|
| | | Normal | Deponent |
| Form on the page is | Active | Active → **Active** meaning | |
| | Middle or Passive | Passive → **Passive** meaning (or *very unusually* the special meaning of the Middle – see below) | Middle → **Active** meaning (or *quite unusually* it is actually in the Passive with Passive meaning) |

- Both of these charts only work if you know which verbs are deponent!

**Hint**

It often helps to be clear about why you find something confusing! For many students it is because the Middle seems to be Active *in meaning*, but very close to the Passive *in endings*. It is confusingly in the middle!

### 15.6.1 Special uses of the Middle

In Classical Greek (from which New Testament – Koine – Greek developed) the Middle was used much more widely to express actions that affected the subject (e.g. φερω – I carry, φερομαι – I carry off for myself = I win). There are remnants of this in Koine Greek.

(a) A small number of verbs still use the three Voices with different meanings.

ἐνδυει (Active) – He puts (clothes) on (someone else)
ἐνδυεται (Middle) – He puts (clothes) on himself
ἐνδυεται (Passive) – It is put on.

(b) Some writers (particularly the author of Luke and Acts) use the Middle as a stylistic device, imitating Classical Greek, which was thought at the time to be of greater literary quality (this is called 'archaizing').

Example

(φυλασσω in the Active – I guard; in the Middle – I am on my guard)

Luke 2.8: Και ποιμενες ἠσαν ἐν τῃ χωρᾳ τῃ αὐτῃ ... φυλασσοντες (Active) φυλακας της νυκτος ἐπι την ποιμνην αὐτων. – And in that region there were shepherds . . . keeping watch over their flock by night.

Luke 12.15: εἰπεν δε προς αὐτους· Ὁρατε και φυλασσεσθε (Middle) ἀπο πασης πλεονεξιας. – And he said to them, 'Look out and be on your guard against all kinds of greed.'

Acts 1.1: Τον μεν πρωτον λογον ἐποιησαμην περι παντων . . .
– I made a first account concerning all the things . . .
(There is no particular reason for the use of the Middle ποιεομαι here rather than the Active ποιεω, it is really just a matter of style.)

**Hint**

Be aware of these special uses; but remember, the vast majority of the time when you see a middle, it is a deponent verb conveying an active meaning.

## 15.7 PASSIVE DEPONENTS

The last straw for many students is to hear that there are Passive deponents – words that are Passive in form (not Middle) but Active in meaning! However, there are only four words in this category – and even some of those only when in the Aorist – so they can be thought of simply as an endearing idiosyncrasy. Since Middle and Passive only differ in form in the Future and the Aorist, it is only here that the difference between Middle and Passive deponents matters.

| Present | | Future | | Aorist | |
|---|---|---|---|---|---|
| I wish | βουλομαι | Passive | βουλησομαι | Passive | ἐβουληθην |
| I fear | φοβεομαι | Passive | φοβηθησομαι | Passive | ἐφοβηθην |
| I answer | ἀποκρινομαι | Middle | ἀποκρινεομαι | Passive | ἀπεκριθην |
| I go | πορευομαι | *Either* | πορευσομαι | Passive | ἐπορευθην |
| | | *or* | πορευθησομαι | | |

PRACTICE 15.7

## Translate

1. ἐβουληθημεν βλεψαι τον Ἰησουν.
2. ἐκεινῃ τῃ ἡμερᾳ φοβηθησεσθε;
3. δει πορευθηναι εἰς το ἱερον.
4. ἀποκριθητε οὐδεν.

## VOCAB FOR CHAPTER 15

Six more 2nd declension nouns
διαβολος (37) – the slanderer, the devil
*καρπος (66) – fruit
*ναος (45) – sanctuary, shrine, temple
Φιλιππος (36) – Philip
*φοβος (47) – fear
*χρονος (54) –time (period of)

Some verbs that are Passive deponents (at least in some tenses)
*ἀποκρινομαι (231) + dat. – I answer
*βουλομαι (37) – I wish
*πορευομαι (153) – I go
 ἐκπορευομαι (33) – I go out
*φοβεομαι (95) – I am afraid, fear

And many more (normal) verbs
*ἁγιαζω (28) – I make holy
*ἀσθενεω (33) – I am weak, sick
*βασταζω (27) – I take up
*γαμεω (28) – I marry
γνωριζω (25) – I make known
δουλευω (25) – I am a slave
ἐκχεω (27) – I pour out
*ἐνδυω (27) – I dress
*ἐπιστρεφω (36) – I turn (back)
ἡκω (26) – I have come, am present
*ἰσχυω (28) – I am strong
κελευω (25) – I command
*κλαιω (40) – I weep
κωλυω (23) – I hinder
λυπεω (26) – I grieve, pain
ὀμνυω (26) – I swear, take an oath
*περισσευω (39) – I exceed
*τελεω (28) – I finish, complete
*ὑποστρεφω (35) – I turn back, return
*φαινω (31) – I shine, appear
φρονεω (26) – I ponder

## Word helps

diabolical, phobia, chronology, hagiography, monogamy, endue, catastrophe, lupus, teleology, phenomenon/phantom/epiphany, schizophrenia.

## Exercises

### Section A

1. και ἠρξατο διδασκειν αὐτους ὁτι δει παθειν πολλα και διωχθηναι ὑπο των πρεσβυτερων και των ἀρχιερεων και των γραμματεων και ἀποκτανθηναι.

2. νυν ἡ κρισις ἐστιν του κοσμου τουτου, νυν ὁ ἀρχων του κοσμου τουτου ἐκβληθησεται ἐξω.
*3. ὁ δε Ἰησους εἰπεν αὐτοις· Το ποτηριον ὃ ἐγω πινω πιεσθε [= *irregular future of* πινω] και το βαπτισμα ὃ ἐγω βαπτιζομαι βαπτισθησεσθε.
4. μακαριοι οἱ ἐλεημονες [ἐλεημων = merciful; declines like πλειων] ὁτι αὐτοι ἐλεηθησονται.
*5. μακαριοι οἱ εἰρηνοποιοι [= εἰρηνη + ποιεω], ὁτι αὐτοι υἱοι θεου κληθησονται.
*6. και ἀποκριθεις[8] αὐτοις λεγει· Τίς ἐστιν ἡ μητηρ μου και οἱ ἀδελφοι μου;
*7. και ἀπεκριθη αὐτῳ εἱς ἐκ του ὀχλου· Διδασκαλε, ἠνεγκα τον υἱον μου προς σε, ἐχοντα πνευμα πονηρον.
8. ἠρξαντο λυπεισθαι και λεγειν αὐτῳ εἱς κατα (*by*) εἱς· Μητι ἐγω;
*9. And they were filled with great awe [*lit. 'they feared a great fear'*] and said to one another, 'Who then is this?'
*10. And having entered he said to them, 'Why are you afraid and weep? The child has not died.'
*11. He was afraid and answered the chief priest, 'They returned to the sanctuary.'
*12. For the husband not having faith is made holy through [*use* ἐν] his wife, and the wife not having faith is made holy through her husband.

## Section B

*1. ἐφανη ἀνηρ τις ἐκ της πολεως ἐχων δαιμονια και πολυν χρονον οὐκ ἐνεδυσατο ἱματιον και ἐν οἰκιᾳ οὐκ ἐμενεν.
2. Ἰδων δε ὁ Ἰησους ὀχλον περι αὐτον ἐκελευσεν τους μαθητας ἀπελθειν εἰς το περαν.
3. ὁ δε Ἰησους εἰπεν· Μη κωλυετε αὐτον. οὐδεις γαρ ἐστιν ὁς ποιησει δυναμιν ἐπι τῳ ὀνοματι μου και λαλησει κακως περι ἐμου.
4. ἀπεκριθη αὐτῳ ὁ ἀσθενων· Κυριε, ὑπηρετην οὐκ ἐχω βαλειν με εἰς το ὑδωρ· ὁτε εἰς αὐτο ἐρχομαι ἐγω, ἀλλος προ ἐμου καταβαινει.
*5. βουλομεθα οὐν γνωναι τίνα ταυτα ἐστιν.
6. Αὐτος γαρ ὁ Ἡρῳδης ἀποστειλας ἐκρατησεν τον Ἰωαννην και ἐδησεν αὐτον ἐν φυλακῃ [*prison*] δια την γυναικα του ἀδελφου αὐτου, ὁτι αὐτην ἐγαμησεν.
*7. και ἐφαγον τον καρπον παντες, και ἠρθη το περισσευσαν.

---

[8] Greek often uses the participle ἀποκριθεις alongside another verb of speaking (here λεγει). In many ways the ἀποκριθεις is redundant, although it helps to point out that the speaker has changed. The closest translations in English might be 'in reply' or 'answering' ('answering' seems wrong for an Aorist participle – but think of the sequence as being between the question in the previous sentence and the answer in this one).

8. ἡ γαρ ἀγαπη του θεου ἐκχειται ἐν ταις καρδιαις ἡμων δια πνευματος ἁγιου του λαμβανομενου ὑφ' ἡμων.
9. When the time of harvest [*lit. 'time of the fruits'*] came, he sent his slaves to receive the produce [*the fruits*] which was his.
10. Philip said, 'We were hindered by the devil but after a long time[9] we finished the sanctuary.
*11. So he sent one of his disciples, saying to him, 'Go into the city, and a man carrying a cup of water will serve you.'
12. For I make known to you, brothers and sisters, that the good news which was proclaimed by me is not according to a human being.

## Section C

**Matthew 11.2-5** ὁ δὲ Ἰωάννης ἀκούσας ἐν τῷ δεσμωτηρίῳ [*prison*] τὰ ἔργα τοῦ Χριστοῦ πέμψας διὰ τῶν μαθητῶν αὐτοῦ [3] εἶπεν αὐτῷ, Σὺ εἶ ὁ ἐρχόμενος ἢ ἕτερον προσδοκῶμεν [*we should wait for*]; [4] καὶ ἀποκριθεὶς ὁ Ἰησοῦς εἶπεν αὐτοῖς· Πορευθέντες ἀπαγγείλατε Ἰωάννῃ ἃ ἀκούετε καὶ βλέπετε· [5] τυφλοὶ ἀναβλέπουσιν καὶ χωλοὶ [*lame*] περιπατοῦσιν, λεπροὶ [*lepers*] καθαρίζονται [καθαριζω = *cleanse*] καὶ κωφοὶ [*deaf*] ἀκούουσιν, καὶ νεκροὶ ἐγείρονται καὶ πτωχοὶ [*poor*] εὐαγγελίζονται.

[9] For 'after a long time' use μετα πολυν χρονον (as in Matt. 25.19).

# The Perfect

Mark 1.2: καθως γεγραπται ἐν τῳ Ἠσαΐᾳ τῳ προφητῃ· Ἰδου ἀποστελλω ...
– Just as it is written in Isaiah the prophet, 'Look!, I am sending . . .'

John 19.30: ὁ Ἰησους εἰπεν· Τετελεσται – Jesus said, 'It is finished'.

1 John 5.10: ὁ μη πιστευων τῳ θεῳ ψευστην πεποιηκεν αὐτον, ὁτι οὐ πεπιστευκεν εἰς την μαρτυριαν ἡν μεμαρτυρηκεν ὁ θεος περι του υἱου αὐτου.
– The one who does not believe in God has made him a liar, because he has not believed in the testimony which God has testified concerning his son.

The underlined verbs are in the Perfect tense; the first two are Perfect Passive, those in 1 John 5.10 Perfect Active.

The Perfect tense communicates a past action with a present effect. The past action is seen as completed (the action itself is not continuing in the present), but it is not simply past history: it continues to have an effect in the present.

Thus Mark 1.2 could be translated as either 'it has been written' (stressing that it was written in the past) or 'it is written' (stressing that it bears witness in the present); either way, the writing of the text is a completed action that effects the present.

In John 19.30 the 'is . . .' wording seemed to fit best in English, in 1 John 5.10 the 'has . . .' wording, but however the Perfect is put into English, its meaning remains the same – a past completed action that has a present effect.

## 16.1 THE IDEA OF THE PERFECT

The Perfect tense is the fifth and final tense that we need to learn.[1] Since it is a tense, we will need to consider its form and meaning in the different voices and moods.

The essence of the Perfect is the idea of **completion**. This is an *aspect* – it conveys the nature of the action. If the Perfect is used, it conveys not a *process*, nor is it *undefined*, but rather that the action is now *completed*. Time is less important in the Perfect – the fact that the action is completed says something about the past (it was done in the past) but also something about the present (it is completed). 'Past event with present effect' is a useful slogan for the Perfect.

We can now complete the chart in Chapter 6, section 6.3 giving the meaning of the tenses:

| Greek tense | Time | Aspect | English equivalent |
|---|---|---|---|
| Present | Present | Process *or* Undefined | I am untying *or* I untie |
| Future | Future | Undefined | I will untie |
| Imperfect | Past | Process | I was untying |
| Aorist | Past | Undefined | I untied |
| **Perfect** | **Present and Past** | **Completed** | **I have untied** |

## 16.2 THE FORM OF THE PERFECT

| | | Active | Middle[2] | Passive |
|---|---|---|---|---|
| Indicative | I | λελυκα | ῥερυμαι | λελυμαι |
| | You (sing.) | λελυκας | ῥερυσαι | λελυσαι |
| | He, she, it | λελυκεν | ῥερυται | λελυται |
| | We | λελυκαμεν | ῥερυμεθα | λελυμεθα |
| | You (pl.) | λελυκατε | ῥερυσθε | λελυσθε |
| | They | λελυκασιν | ῥερυνται | λελυνται |
| Participle | | λελυκως | ῥερυμενος | λελυμενος |

[1] There is a variant on the Perfect called the Pluperfect, but this is very rare in the New Testament. It is mentioned briefly in section 16.4.

[2] As it happens, ῥυομαι never occurs in the Perfect, but it seems sensible to keep using the same 'pattern word'.

Notes

- The distinguishing mark of the Perfect, in all forms, is **reduplication** (see below).
- The Perfect Active also has a characteristic κ.
- The Perfect Indicative Active endings are similar to those in the Aorist.
- The Middle and the Passive share the same forms in the Perfect (as they also do in the Present and Imperfect).
- The Perfect Middle and Passive endings are similar to the Present Middle and Passive endings, but they lack any initial vowel (e.g. -ται not -εται, -μενος not -ομενος).
- λελυκως declines like πας with nominative singulars λελυκως, λελυκυια, λελυκος and 3rd declension stem λελυκοτ- (written in full on page 262).
- You can get Perfects in all of the other moods, where they convey a sense of completion (e.g. Perfect Infinitive Active λελυκεναι, Passive λελυσθαι). However, these are very rare.

## 16.2.1 Reduplication

Reduplication is the repeating of the first letter of the stem. This occurs in every form of the Perfect tense (and hence marks out Perfects very clearly). As you might expect, although all verbs have reduplication in the Perfect, the exact form it takes is dependent on what the first letter of the verb is.

### Starting with a consonant

Normally the consonant is repeated, followed by an ε.
E.g. λελυκα, πεπιστευκα.

χ, φ, θ (i.e. has an 'h' sound): The consonant is repeated without the 'h' sound, followed by an ε (κεχ-, πεφ- or τεθ-). E.g. τεθεραπευκα.

σ, ζ or ξ (i.e. has an 's' sound): The normal rule applies (thus σεσ-, ζεζ- or ξεξ) but normally the initial consonant is then dropped leaving, effectively, just the addition of an ε. E.g. ἐζητηκα, but also σεσωκα.

### Starting with a vowel

The doubling of the vowel is represented by its lengthening.

α → η    ε → η    ο → ω    E.g. ἠκολουθηκα

Notes

- Reduplication affects **the stem** – thus, in a compound verb the preposition will need to be removed, the stem reduplicated, and then the preposition rejoined (cf. augments). Thus the Perfect of ἀπολυω is ἀπολελυκα.

- When the effect of reduplication is only to add an ε or to lengthen a vowel it looks the same as adding an augment, but there is a crucial difference:

KEY GRAMMAR

Reduplication – Perfect – in all moods
Augmentation – Imperfect and Aorist – only in the Indicative

### 16.2.2 Stem changes

All forms of the Perfect result in a consonant being placed next to the end of the verb – either the κ for the Perfect Active, or the ending itself in the Middle or Passive. This can cause some complications, just as adding a σ or a θ for the Future or Aorist does.

-εω verbs are predictable – the ε is lengthened into an η before the consonant.

E.g. πεποιηκα is the 1st sing. Perfect Indicative Active of ποιεω
τετηρηται is the 3rd sing. Perfect Indicative Passive of τηρεω.

The stem changes in other verbs (i.e. those whose stems end in a consonant) are not worth learning because: (i) they are quite complicated, (ii) the Perfect is rare in the first place, and (iii) the words are normally still quite recognisable.

Basically what happens is that the consonant at the end of the stem changes to whichever consonant within its group sounds better next to the ending. The groups are the same as we have met before when considering additions of σ and θ:

KEY GRAMMAR

κ, γ, χ, σσ  π, β, φ  τ, δ, θ, ζ, σ

PRACTICE 16.2

### Parse

1. μεμισηκεν
2. κεκωλυμενους
3. πεπροφητευται
4. πεφιληκασιν
5. βεβλεπται
6. ἀπολελυμενην

HALF-WAY PRACTICE

1. οἱ δουλοι ἀπολελυνται.
2. μεμαρτυρηκα τῃ ἀληθειᾳ.
3. τί πεποιηκας;
4. πεπειρασμαι πολλα ἐτη.
5. οὐ προσκυνουμεν ἐν ἱερῳ ᾠκοδομημενῳ ὑπο ἀνθρωπων.
6. ὑποτετακται πονηρῳ κυριῳ.

7. σεσωμεθα δια της ἀγαπης του θεου.
8. οἱ στρατιωται κεκρατηκασιν τον Πετρον.
9. The sick woman has been healed.
10. The word has been sent (use πεμπω) into the world.
11. We have done good things.
12. Surely you have not believed in Jesus?

## 16.3 MORE ON THE MEANING OF THE PERFECT

The essence of the Perfect was given at the beginning of the chapter – *completion* – and the basic English equivalent of 'I have untied'. However, there are two further points worthy of note.

### 16.3.1 Participles

The meaning of the Perfect participles is as you would expect – they refer neither to sequence nor to simultaneous action but to a present state of affairs (resulting from completed action in the past).

E.g. Acts 16.34: ἠγαλλιασατο ... πεπιστευκως τῳ θεῳ.
– he rejoiced . . . because he had become a believer in God.
(i.e. he had believed and still believed in God.)

What is a little awkward is that there is no 'wooden translation' which can be used other than 'having believed', which is identical to the Aorist. Thus, you need to take care that you do express the true meaning of Perfect participles when you rephrase your 'wooden translation' into good English.

In practice, Perfect Active participles are very rare. Perfect Passive participles are more common and are often effectively equivalent to an adjective or a Present participle since they describe a present state.

E.g. Matt. 5.10: μακαριοι οἱ δεδιωγμενοι.
– Blessed are those who have been persecuted (i.e. the persecuted).

### 16.3.2 Difference between the Perfect and Aorist

The basic English equivalents 'I have untied' for the Perfect and 'I untied' for the Aorist are not always dependable. This is why you should try not to rely on these equivalents but rather think of the meaning of these tenses – Aorist is past undefined, Perfect is completed.

The difficulties are best highlighted by three examples:

1) ἡ πιστις σου σεσωκεν σε. (Mark 5.34)
2) οὐκ ἀνεγνωτε; (Mark 12.26)
3) ἐκαλεσεν αὐτους. (Mark 1.20)

1) is in the Perfect – the saving is complete – it happened in the past and is now being viewed as completed, giving rise to a state of salvation in the present.

2) and 3) are both in the Aorist – the actions are past, but without anything more being said about the nature of the action (process, completed etc.).

In English, though, we would probably translate these sentences as:

1. Your faith has saved you.
2. Have you not read?
3. He called them.

Thus, in English, we will probably use the word 'have' in sentence 2 (as an alternative to 'did you not read?') despite the fact that the Greek verb is Aorist and we associate the translation 'I have read' with the Perfect.

This displays the limitations of thinking of 'English equivalents'. 'Have you not read?' is a good translation of οὐκ ἀνεγνωτε; because translation is about conveying meaning, and both the Greek phrase and this translation convey a question about an action in the past the nature of which (process, completed etc.) is left undefined. The fact that order to convey this meaning English uses the word 'have' which you normally associate with the Perfect is merely unfortunate.[3]

**KEY GRAMMAR**
Focus on the meaning of the tenses, not their basic English equivalents

Conversely, sometimes it is impossible to convey in a reasonably fluent English translation the fact that the verb is Perfect, despite its importance for the meaning of the sentence. For example, take 1 Cor. 15.3-4: Χριστος ἀπεθανεν (Aorist) και ἐγηγερται (Perfect, irregular form) τῃ ἡμερᾳ τῃ τριτῃ. It is almost impossible to avoid translating this as 'Christ died and was raised on the third day', which would convey to an English reader that the two verbs 'died' and 'raised' are both in the same tense, pointing to actions in the past. However, this is not the meaning of the Greek, since ἀπεθανεν is Aorist while ἐγηγερται is Perfect, thus a difference is being drawn between the two verbs – the death was a past action but the resurrection has continuing effect today ('was raised, and is still in the state of being raised today').

---

[3] Technically, the problem is that in Greek action in indefinite past time uses the Aorist (past undefined), whereas English uses the Perfect. This can be represented thus:

|  |  |  |
|---|---|---|
| English Perfect | Present state resulting from past action<br>He has eaten it | Greek Perfect |
| English Perfect | Action in indefinite past<br>He has eaten many apples over the last year | Greek Aorist |
| English Past Simple | Action in definite past<br>He ate it | Greek Aorist |

**PRACTICE 16.3**

### Which tense is appropriate for the underlined verb?

1. I have learnt Greek.
2. I have learnt my vocab every day.
3. She has been helped by the teacher.
4. They have the books.
5. They spoke to those who had seen it all.

## 16.4 THE PLUPERFECT

The Pluperfect is very rare and is mentioned here more for the sake of completeness than for its importance. It is a variant on the Perfect which in effect moves the time of the events one stage further into the past.

| | |
|---|---|
| **Perfect** | *Present state arising from event in the past*<br>'I have broken the window' – past event, but it is still broken |
| **Pluperfect** | *Past state arising from event in the remote past*<br>'I had broken the window' – past event, created a state, but the state is now past (it was broken for a time, but now is fixed) |

However, it is misleading to think of 'I had untied' as an English equivalent of the Greek Pluperfect, because normally when there is a 'had' in English it would not be translated as a Pluperfect in Greek.

This is because the two most common occurrences of 'had' in English are in indirect statements and in temporal clauses, both of which are handled without the use of the Pluperfect in Greek.

### Indirect statements (see Chapter 10, section 10.3)

E.g. 'But he said that he had not destroyed the law.'

Greek uses the tense of the original words of the thought/speech, here 'I have not destroyed the law' and hence Perfect, not Pluperfect.

ὁ δε εἰπεν ὁτι οὐ καταλελυκεν τον νομον.

### Temporal clauses

E.g. 'When he had come, he spoke to the people'.

Greek would normally translate this with a participle, 'having come, he spoke to the people'. Alternatively, the word ὁτε ('when') followed by an Aorist could be used. Despite the 'had' in English, the Pluperfect would not be used in Greek, because the meaning wanted is not the meaning of the Pluperfect:

ἐλθων εἰπεν τῳ λαῳ *or* ὁτε ἠλθεν, εἰπεν τῳ λαῳ.

## Form of the Pluperfect

The Pluperfect only occurs in the Indicative. It has reduplication as in the Perfect and should have an augment (since it does refer to past time), although this is often omitted. The Active endings are similar to the Perfect Active, with the α of the ending replaced by ει. The Middle and Passive endings are very similar to the Aorist and Imperfect Middle endings, without the first vowel, and in fact are only marginally different from the Perfect endings.

| | Active | Middle and Passive |
|---|---|---|
| I | (ἐ)λελυκειν | (ἐ)λελυμην |
| You (sing.) | (ἐ)λελυκεις | (ἐ)λελυσο |
| He, she, it | (ἐ)λελυκει | (ἐ)λελυτο |
| We | (ἐ)λελυκειμεν | (ἐ)λελυμεθα |
| You (pl.) | (ἐ)λελυκειτε | (ἐ)λελυσθε |
| They | (ἐ)λελυκεισαν | (ἐ)λελυντο |

PRACTICE 16.4

## In which of the following would a Pluperfect be used?

1. When he had arrived, they began to eat.
2. The scribes said that the law had been broken.
3. I had believed but I do not any longer.
4. After I believed I was happy.
5. They thought that the temple had been destroyed.

## VOCAB FOR CHAPTER 16

More 1st declension (feminine) nouns
ἀκοη (24) – fame, report
ἀσθενεια (24) – weakness, disease
*διδαχη (30) – teaching (act and content)
ἑορτη (25) – festival
ἐπιστολη (24) – letter (correspondence)
*θυσια (28) – offering, sacrifice
*κωμη (27) – village
*μαχαιρα (29) – sword
νεφελη (25) – cloud
παρουσια (24) – presence, coming
*περιτομη (36) – circumcision
πορνεια (25) – sexual immorality

*προσευχη (36) – prayer
*ὑπομονη (32) – patience
*φυλη (31) – tribe, nation
*χηρα (26) – widow
*χωρα (28) – country(side)

Numbers
*τρεις (68) – three
(τρια with neuter nouns)
*τεσσαρες (41) – four
(τεσσαρα with neuter nouns)
πεντε (38) – five
ἑξ (13) – six
*ἑπτα (88) – seven
ὀκτω (8) – eight
ἐννεα (5) – nine
δεκα (25) – ten
*δωδεκα (75) – twelve
ἑκατον (17) – one hundred
χιλιας (23) – one thousand
*πρωτος (155) – first
*δευτερος (43) – second
*τριτος (56) – third
(Note: δυο – two, learnt in Chapter 6)

One exclamation
*οὐαι (46) – woe

Note two common words whose stems are irregular in the Perfect Active:
ἑωρακα – Perfect Active of ὁραω
ἀκηκοα – Perfect Active of ἀκουω

## Word helps

acoustic, didactic, epistle, atom, pornography, tripod/triangle, tetrahedron/Diatesseron, pentagon/Pentateuch, hexagon, heptathlon, octagon, Decalogue/decathlon, dodecahedron, chiliasm, prototype, Deuteronomy, Trito-Isaiah.

## Exercises

### Section A

*1. και λεγει αὐτοις· Γεγραπται, Ὁ οἰκος μου οἰκος προσευχης κληθησεται.
*2. κἀγω ἑωρακα, και μεμαρτυρηκα ὁτι οὑτος ἐστιν ὁ υἱος του θεου.
*3. ὁ πιστευων εἰς αὐτον οὐ κρινεται· ὁ δε μη πιστευων ἠδη κεκριται, ὁτι οὐ πεπιστευκεν εἰς το ὀνομα του μονογενους [*only*] υἱου του θεου.
*4. Ἰωαννης μεμαρτυρηκεν τῃ ἀληθειᾳ· ταυτα λελαληκεν ὑμιν.
*5. και ἡμεις πεπιστευκαμεν και ἐγνωκαμεν ὁτι συ εἶ ὁ ἁγιος του θεου.
*6. λεγει αὐτῳ· Ναι, κυριε, ἐγω πεπιστευκα ὁτι συ εἶ ὁ χριστος ὁ υἱος του θεου ὁ εἰς τον κοσμον ἐρχομενος.
*7. οὐδεις τον πατερα ἑωρακεν εἰ μη ὁ ὢν παρα του θεου, οὑτος ἑωρακεν τον πατερα.
8. και τοτε φανησεται το σημειον του υἱου του ἀνθρωπου ἐν οὐρανῳ, και ὀψονται [*irregular Future of* ὁραω] τον υἱον του ἀνθρωπου ἐρχομενον ἐπι των νεφελων του οὐρανου μετα δυναμεως και δοξης πολλης· οὑτως ἐσται ἡ παρουσια του υἱου του ἀνθρωπου.

*9. They said, 'Lord, look, here are two swords.'
10. At once his fame went out to the whole region of Galilee.
*11. The twelve have heard his teaching and have seen his sacrifice.
*12. The disciple has loved the holy ones in the seven churches.

## Section B

*1. το ἐργον μου τετελεκα, την πιστιν τετηρηκα.
*2. διο εἰσερχομενος εἰς τον κοσμον λεγει· Ἐλεος θελω και οὐ θυσιαν.
*3. ἀκουσας δε ὁ Ἰησους εἰπεν· Αὑτη ἡ ἀσθενεια οὐκ ἐστιν προς θανατον ἀλλ᾽ ὑπερ της δοξης του θεου, και δοξασθησεται ὁ υἱος του θεου δι᾽ αὐτης.
4. νυν δε οὐπω βλεπομεν αὐτῳ τα παντα ὑποτεταγμενα.
*5. ἑπτα ἀδελφοι ἠσαν· και ὁ πρωτος ἐλαβεν γυναικα και ἀπεθανεν.
6. ὁ δε λεγει αὐτοις· Ποσους ἀρτους ἐχετε; ὑπαγετε ἰδετε. και γνοντες λεγουσιν, Πεντε.
7. Ὃ ἠν ἀπ᾽ ἀρχης, ὃ ἀκηκοαμεν, ὃ πεπιστευκαμεν περι του λογου της ζωης, λελαληται ὑμιν ὑπο ἡμων.
*8. ὁ δε Ἰησους εἰπεν αὐτοις, Ἀμην λεγω ὑμιν ὁτι ὑμεις οἱ ἀκολουθησαντες μοι, ὁτε ὁ υἱος του ἀνθρωπου ἐστιν ἐπι θρονου δοξης αὐτου, και ὑμεις ἐσεσθε ἐπι δωδεκα θρονους κρινοντες τας δωδεκα φυλας του Ἰσραηλ.
9. For four days and four nights he prayed in the desert and saw a thousand angels in the clouds.
*10. The widow's son was healed/saved immediately by her faith.
11. Ten Greeks have believed the report about his coming.
12. In the second letter has been written teaching about patience, prayer, circumcision, immorality, and the feasts of the Lord.

## Section C

**Mark 5.25-34** καὶ γυνὴ οὖσα ἐν ῥύσει [*flow*] αἵματος δώδεκα ἔτη 26 καὶ πολλὰ παθοῦσα [*aor. act. part. f.s.* πασχω = *suffer*] ὑπὸ πολλῶν ἰατρῶν [*physicians*] καὶ δαπανήσασα [δαπαναω = *spend*] τὰ παρ᾽ αὐτῆς πάντα καὶ μηδὲν ὠφεληθεῖσα [ὠφελεω = *gain, benefit*] ἀλλὰ μᾶλλον [*rather, instead*] εἰς τὸ χεῖρον [*worse*] ἐλθοῦσα, 27 ἀκούσασα περὶ τοῦ Ἰησοῦ, ἐλθοῦσα ἐν τῷ ὄχλῳ ὄπισθεν [*from behind*] ἥψατο τοῦ ἱματίου αὐτοῦ· 28 ἔλεγεν γὰρ ὅτι Ἐὰν [*If*] ἅψωμαι [*I might touch*] κἂν [*even just*] τῶν ἱματίων αὐτοῦ σωθήσομαι. 29 καὶ εὐθὺς ἐξηράνθη [ξηραινω = *dry up, cease*] ἡ πηγὴ [*spring, flow*] τοῦ αἵματος αὐτῆς καὶ ἔγνω τῷ σώματι ὅτι ἴαται [*perf. pass of* ιαομαι – *I heal*] ἀπὸ τῆς μάστιγος [*disease*]. 30 καὶ εὐθὺς ὁ Ἰησοῦς ἐπιγνοὺς ἐν ἑαυτῷ τὴν ἐξ αὐτοῦ δύναμιν ἐξελθοῦσαν ἐπιστραφεὶς ἐν τῷ ὄχλῳ ἔλεγεν, Τίς μου ἥψατο τῶν ἱματίων; 31 καὶ ἔλεγον αὐτῷ οἱ μαθηταὶ αὐτοῦ, Βλέπεις τὸν ὄχλον

συνθλίβοντά [*press upon*] σε καὶ λέγεις, Τίς μου ἥψατο; 32 καὶ περιεβλέπετο
[περι + βλεπω] ἰδεῖν τὴν τοῦτο ποιήσασαν. 33 ἡ δὲ γυνὴ φοβηθεῖσα καὶ
τρέμουσα [τρεμω = *tremble*], εἰδυῖα [*knowing*] ὃ γέγονεν αὐτῇ, ἦλθεν καὶ
προσέπεσεν [προς + πιπτω] αὐτῷ καὶ εἶπεν αὐτῷ πᾶσαν τὴν ἀλήθειαν. 34 ὁ
δὲ εἶπεν αὐτῇ, Θυγάτηρ, ἡ πίστις σου σέσωκέν σε· ὕπαγε εἰς εἰρήνην καὶ
ἴσθι [*Pres. Imperative 2nd sing.*, εἰμι] ὑγιὴς [*healthy*] ἀπὸ τῆς μάστιγός σου.

# The Subjunctive

1 John 2.1: ταυτα γραφω ὑμιν ἱνα μη ἁμαρτητε.
– I am writing these things to you so that you may not sin.

1 Pet. 3.18: Χριστος ἁπαξ περι ἁματιων ἐπαθεν ... ἱνα ὑμας προσαγαγῃ τῳ θεῳ.
– Christ once for all suffered for sins . . . in order to bring you to God.

1 Cor. 11.27: ὁς ἀν ἐσθιῃ τον ἀρτον ἡ πινῃ το ποτηριον του κυριος ...
– Whoever eats the bread or drinks the cup of the Lord . . .

Mark 6.10: ὁπου ἐαν εἰσελθητε εἰς οἰκιαν, ἐκει μενετε.
– Wherever you enter a house, stay there.

Titus 3.12: ὁταν πεμψω Ἀρτεμαν προς σε ἡ Τυχικον, σπουδασον ἐλθειν προς με εἰς Νικοπολιν.
– When(ever) I send Artemas to you, or Tychicus, make every effort to come to me at Nicopolis.

Mark 1.38: και λεγει αὐτοις· Ἀγωμεν ἀλλαχου ...
– And he said to them, 'Let us go elsewhere . . .'

Mark 6.24: ἐξελθουσα εἰπεν τῃ μητρι αὐτης· Τί αἰτησωμαι;
– When she had gone out, she said to her mother, 'What should I ask (for)?'.

Heb. 10.35: μη ἀποβαλητε οὐν την παρρησιαν ὑμων ...
– do not throw away your boldness . . .

Rev. 18.21: βληθησεται Βαβυλων ἡ μεγαλη πολις και οὐ μη εὑρεθῃ ἐτι.
– Babylon the great city will be thrown down and will never be found again.

All of the verbs underlined in these verses are in the Subjunctive mood. As you can see the Subjunctive does not have a single meaning but it used in a range of different situations, often preceded by a particular word, such as ἱνα or ὁταν.

## 17.1 THE IDEA OF THE SUBJUNCTIVE

The Subjunctive is the fifth and final mood to learn – by the end of this chapter you will know the whole of the verb (as well as all the nouns and adjectives).

The Subjunctive is only used in set constructions, never just because the writer thought it would be fun. Thus there is no 'meaning' of the Subjunctive to learn – it only occurs as one part of a broader construction, and it is that construction which has a meaning (such as expressing purpose).[1] However, it can be hard to learn something if you can't summarise the 'meaning' of what you are learning. Therefore, it may help to think of the Subjunctive as the '*mood of doubtful assertion*'. A rough parallel in English would be the use of 'may' or 'might'.

Subjunctives occur in all three of the Voices (Active, Middle or Passive), but only in the Present or the Aorist tense. Thus it is similar to the Imperative and Infinitive – indeed the difference between the Present and the Aorist in the Subjunctive is the same as in the Infinitive and Imperative (process or default). Like the Indicative it occurs in the first, second and third person, singular and plural.

## 17.2 THE FORMATION OF THE SUBJUNCTIVE

The Subjunctive is easy to form. It differs from the Indicative only in the lack of augment and in having different endings. But those endings are in fact only a simple permutation on the Indicative ones, and only come in two patterns.

> KEY GRAMMAR
> 1. Remove any augment
> 2. Replace the Indicative endings with the Subjunctive ones

### 17.2.1 Present Active, Aorist Active, Aorist Passive

The Subjunctive endings are the same as the Present Indicative Active of λυω with the initial vowels lengthened.

-ω, -ῃς, -ῃ, -ωμεν, -ητε, -ωσιν

Thus:

| | |
|---|---|
| Present Active | λυω, λυῃς, λυῃ, λυωμεν, λυητε, λυωσιν |
| 1st Aorist Active | λυσω, λυσῃς, λυσῃ, λυσωμεν, λυσητε, λυσωσιν |

---

[1] Although it is not an exact parallel, what does the English word 'be' mean? You can't answer the question, because 'be' is used as an essential part of many different grammatical forms such as, 'I may be', 'You will be taught', 'To be taught', 'Be helpful!'

| | |
|---|---|
| 2nd Aorist Active | βαλω, βαλῃς, βαλῃ, βαλωμεν, βαλητε, βαλωσιν |
| Aorist Passive | λυθω, λυθῃς, λυθῃ, λυθωμεν, λυθητε, λυθωσιν |

### 17.2.2 Present Middle, Present Passive, Aorist Middle

The Subjunctive endings are the same as the Present Indicative Middle of ῥυομαι / Passive of λυω with the initial vowels lengthened.

-ωμαι, -ῃ, -ηται, -ωμεθα, -ησθε, -ωνται

Thus:

| | |
|---|---|
| Present Middle | ῥυωμαι, ῥυῃ, ῥυηται, ῥυωμεθα, ῥυησθε, ῥυωνται |
| Present Passive | λυωμαι, λυῃ, λυηται, λυωμεθα, λυησθε, λυωνται |
| 1st Aorist Middle | ῥυσωμαι, ῥυσῃ, ῥυσηται, ῥυσωμεθα, ῥυσησθε, ῥυσωνται |
| 2nd Aorist Middle | γενωμαι, γενῃ, γενηται, γενωμεθα, γενησθε, γενωνται |

Notes

- The -εω verbs are easy in the Subjunctive – the endings always begin with a long vowel, so the ε will always be absorbed and the endings left identical to those of λυω. Thus, the Present Active Subjunctive of φιλεω is φιλω, φιλῃς, φιλῃ, φιλωμεν, φιλητε, φιλωσιν.
- εἰμι uses the same endings without any stem – its Present Subjunctive is ὠ, ᾐς, ᾐ, ὠμεν, ἠτε, ὠσιν.

PRACTICE 17.2

**Parse**

| | | | |
|---|---|---|---|
| 1. ἀγωμεν | 4. ἐρχωνται | 7. ἀρξωμαι | 10. ἀκουσητε |
| 2. πεμψωσιν | 5. λυθῃς | 8. βαλληται | 11. ἰδωμεν |
| 3. τελῃ | 6. εἰπωσιν | 9. διδασκῃ | 12. φιλουμεν |

## 17.3 THE USES OF THE SUBJUNCTIVE

There are seven different constructions in which the Subjunctive is used. The Subjunctive has to occur in these constructions, and will not occur elsewhere. The first two of the constructions are far more common than the others. Whichever construction is being used, the difference between the tenses is the same – the Present if the action is being viewed as part of a process (continuous or repeated), otherwise the Aorist, just as in the Infinitive and Imperative.

KEY GRAMMAR
Present Subjunctive – Process
Aorist Subjunctive – Default

### 17.3.1 Indefinite clauses

Clauses that refer to a person, place or time that is not definite use the word (technically a 'particle') ἀν plus the Subjunctive, to express this indefiniteness.

KEY GRAMMAR
ἀν + Subjunctive = indefinite

Often, this indefiniteness is expressed in English by the word 'ever'.

| | |
|---|---|
| ὁς – who | ὁς ἀν + Subjunctive – whoever |
| ὁπου – where | ὁπου ἀν + Subjunctive – wherever |
| ὁτε – when | ὁταν + Subjunctive – whenever |

#### Examples

Mark 3.35: ὁς ἀν ποιηση το θελημα του θεου ...
– whoever does the will of God . . .
Matt. 6.6: συ δε ὁταν προσευχη ... – But whenever you pray . . .
Rev. 14.4: οὑτοι οἱ ἀκολουθουντες τῳ ἀρνιῳ ὁπου ἀν ὑπαγη.
– These ones follow the lamb wherever he goes.

#### Notes

- Sometimes ἐαν is used in place of ἀν.
  Col. 3.23: ὁ ἐαν ποιητε, ἐκ ψυχης ἐργαζεσθε ὡς τῳ κυριῳ και οὐκ ἀνθρωποις. – whatever you do, work at it wholeheartedly as (a task for) the Lord and not for humans.
- Often the meaning of a sentence is indefinite, and hence Greek will use an indefinite construction, when the use of 'ever' seems inappropriate in English. For example, Matt. 6.6 ὁταν προσευχη means 'whenever you pray' – what follows is a general rule, not an instruction for a particular occasion. However, in English this might be translated as 'when you pray'. Similarly Mark 6.10 μενετε ἑως ἀν ἐξελθητε means 'remain until ever you leave' – i.e. remain until whenever it happens to be that you leave – but would normally be translated in English simply as 'remain until you leave'.

### 17.3.2 Purpose clauses

We have already seen that purpose can be expressed simply by the use of an Infinitive. For example, ἠλθεν γραψαι βιβλιον. – She came to write a book.

An alternative to this is to use ἱνα plus the Subjunctive. The negative of this is ἱνα μη although sometimes μη is used on its own.

> KEY GRAMMAR
> ἱνα + Subjunctive = purpose

#### Examples

John 8.59: ἠραν οὐν λιθους ἱνα βαλωσιν ἐπ᾽ αὐτον.
– Therefore they took stones in order that they might throw (them) at him.

Matt. 7.1: μη κρινετε, ἱνα μη κριθητε.
– Do not judge, in order that you might not be judged.

Phil. 1.9: και τουτο προσευχομαι, ἱνα ἡ ἀγαπη ὑμων ... περισσευη ...
– And I pray this that your love may overflow . . .

It is important to understand that any of the Greek ways of expressing purpose can be translated by any of the English ways.[2]

| Thus, either of these: ἠραν οὐν λιθους | ἱνα βαλωσιν<br>βαλειν | ἐπ᾽ αὐτον |
|---|---|---|

could be translated by any of the following:

| Therefore they took stones | in order that they might throw<br>to throw<br>in order to throw<br>so that they might throw | (them) at him. |
|---|---|---|

**Note:** ὁπως + Subjunctive is a more unusual alternative for ἱνα + Subjunctive.[3]

---

[2] Many students find it easier to think of the Greek purpose with the Infinitive matching the English purpose with an Infinitive, and the Greek purpose with ἱνα + Subjunctive matching English, 'in order that . . . may/might'. This is fine as an aid to memory, as long as it is understood that Greek and English purpose clauses do not need to match in this way.

[3] ἱνα + Subjunctive sometimes introduces clauses that might be better categorised as 'noun clauses' rather than 'purpose clauses'. However, if you approach them as purpose clauses, their meaning soon becomes clear. E.g. John 4.34: ἐμον βρωμα ἐστιν ἱνα ποιω το θελημα του πεμψαντος με – My food is to do the will of the one who sent me.

**Hint**

We have looked at the two most common uses of the Subjunctive. Notice that each has a 'flag word' – ἀν (ἐαν) or ἱνα (ὁπως) – which alerts you to the fact that a Subjunctive is on the way.

**HALF-WAY PRACTICE**

1. ἠλθες ἱνα ἀκουῃς;
2. οἱ προφηται ἀπεσταλησαν ἱνα λεγωσιν ὑπερ του θεου.
3. ὁς ἀν βλεπῃ με, βλεπει τον πατερα.
4. ἐκρατησαν τον Παυλον ἱνα μη φυγῃ.
5. ὁταν πορευησθε, φοβουμαι.
6. ὁπου πορευονται;
7. ὁ ἀποστολος ἐγραψεν ὑμιν ἱνα πιστευσητε.
8. ὁπου ἀν ἐλθῃ ὁ Ἰησους, μεγας ὀχλος συνηχθη.
9. Jesus cast out the demons in order that he might be saved.
10. Whoever entered the city died.
11. I called to her so she would hear.
12. Whenever I look I see the mountains.

### 17.3.3 Exhortations (Hortatory Subjunctive)

The Subjunctive can be used on its own in the 1st person plural form to express an exhortation, when the speaker is exhorting others to join him or her in an action.

**KEY GRAMMAR**
1st plural Subjunctive = 'let us'

### Examples

Mark 4.35: διελθωμεν εἰς το περαν. – Let us go to the other side.
Rom. 14.19 ἀρα οὐν τα της εἰρηνης διωκωμεν.
– So therefore let us pursue the things of peace.
Heb. 10.22 προσερχωμεθα μετα ἀληθινης καρδιας ἐν πληροφορια̨ πιστεως.
– Let us approach with a true heart in full assurance of faith.

### 17.3.4 Deliberation (Deliberative Subjunctive)

The Subjunctive is used when the speaker is deliberating – 'What should I do?', 'Where should we go?'

**KEY GRAMMAR**
1st person Subjunctive = deliberation

## Examples

Luke 3.10: τί οὐν ποιησωμεν; – What then should we do?
Heb. 11.32: και τί ἐτι λεγω; – And what more should I say?
Rom. 6.15: τί οὐν; ἁμαρτησωμεν, ὁτι οὐκ ἐσμεν ὑπο νομον ἀλλα ὑπο χαριν; – What then? Should we sin, because we are not under law but under grace?

### 17.3.5 Prohibitions

We have already learnt that a command uses the Imperative mood, and that the negative for the *other moods* is μη. Thus, you might imagine that prohibitions (negative commands) are straightforward. Unfortunately, this is not the case.

KEY GRAMMAR
Aorist Subjunctive replaces Aorist Imperative in prohibitions

| | | |
|---|---|---|
| Process | Positive | Present Imperative |
| | Negative | μη + Present Imperative |
| Default | Positive | Aorist Imperative |
| | Negative | μη + Aorist **Subjunctive** |

As we have learnt, the difference between the Present and the Aorist in Imperatives and Subjunctives is that between process and default. In Imperatives and prohibitions this often means the difference between attitudes and conduct (Present) and specific actions (Aorist).[4]

## Examples[5]

Luke 11.4: μη εἰσενεγκης ἡμας εἰς πειρασμον. – Do not bring us to testing.
Rom. 10.6: μη εἰπης ἐν τῃ καρδιᾳ σου· τίς ἀναβησεται εἰς τον οὐρανον; – Do not say in your heart, 'Who will go up to heaven?'
Matt. 10.5: τουτους τους δωδεκα ἀπεστειλεν ὁ Ἰησους ... λεγων· Εἰς ὁδον ἐθνων μη ἀπελθητε και εἰς πολιν Σαμαριτων μη εἰσελθητε. – Jesus sent out these twelve . . . saying, 'Do not go out into the road of the Gentiles, and do not enter a city of the Samaritans.'

---

[4] You should be aware that the difference between prohibitions with the Present Imperative and the Aorist Subjunctive is still a matter of some debate among scholars.

[5] In addition, one sometimes finds οὐ + Future Indicative for a prohibition. This is not really Greek, but is the literal translation into Greek of a Hebrew idiom for an emphatic prohibition. E.g. Matt. 5.27: ἠκουσατε ὁτι ἐρρεθη· Οὐ μοιχευσεις – You heard that it was said, 'Do not commit adultery' (lit: you shall not commit adultery).

### 17.3.6 Emphatic negative future

The standard way to make negative statements about the future is simply to use the Future Indicative with οὐ. However, it is more emphatic to use the double negative οὐ μη plus the Aorist Subjunctive.

> KEY GRAMMAR
> οὐ μη + Aorist Subjunctive = emphatic negative future

#### Examples

Mark 13.30: ἀμην λεγω ὑμιν ὁτι οὐ μη παρελθῃ ἡ γενεα αὑτη ...
– Truly I tell you that this generation will (definitely) not pass away . . .

John 6.37: τον ἐρχομενον προς ἐμε οὐ μη ἐκβαλω ἐξω.
– The one who comes to me I will (definitely) not drive away outside.

- Sometimes, we find οὐ μη + Future Indicative with a similar meaning:

Matt. 26.35: λεγει αὐτῳ ὁ Πετρος· ... οὐ μη σε ἀπαρνησομαι.
– Peter said to him, '. . . I will never deny you.'

### 17.3.7 Conditions

Certain conditions use the Subjunctive (those after ἐαν). These will be discussed in Chapter 20.

**PRACTICE 17.3.3–17.3.7**

### Translate

1. ὁπου ἐλθω;
2. μη ἐξελθητε.
3. οὐ μη ὑπαγαγωσιν.
4. δοξαζωμεν τον του κοσμου κυριον.
5. τί ἀκουσωμεν του διδασκαλου;
6. ζητωμεν ἁγιαν ζωην.

## VOCAB FOR CHAPTER 17

*ἀν (166) – conditional particle
ἀχρι (49) + gen. – until
*ἱνα (663) + subj. – in order that
ὁπως (53) + subj. – in order that
ὁταν (123) + subj. – whenever
*ἐαν (351) + subj. – alternative for ἀν (also can mean 'if' – see Chapter 20)

Six more 2[nd] declension nouns
*ἀγρος (36) – field
ἀνεμος (31) – wind
*διακονος (29) – servant
*ἐχθρος (32) – enemy
ἡλιος (32) – sun
*οἰνος (34) – wine

And three more verbs
*ἀναιρεω (24) – I take away, kill
κατηγορεω (23) – I accuse
ὁμολογεω (26) – I promise, confess

Yet more feminine 1[st] declension nouns
*γενεα (43) – family, generation
*γλωσσα (50) – tongue, language
*γραφη (50) – writing, scripture
διαθηκη (33) – covenant, last will and testament
διακονια (34) – service, ministry
*ἐπαγγελια (52) – promise
ἐπιθυμια (38) – desire
θυρα (39) – door
Ἰουδαια (43) – Judea
*μαρτυρια (37) – testimony, witness
ὀργη (36) – anger, wrath
*σοφια (51) – wisdom
*σωτηρια (46) – salvation
τιμη (41) – price, value, honour
*φυλακη (47) – watch (guards), prison
χρεια (49) – need

An adjective that often functions as a noun: *πτωχος (34) – poor

### Word helps

agriculture, animate, heliotropic/helium, categorical, homily, genealogy, glossolalia/glossary, deacon/diaconate, martyr, orgy, philosophy, soteriology, Timothy, phylactery/prophylactic.

## Exercises

### Section A

*1. οὐ γαρ ἀπεστειλεν ὁ θεος τον υἱον εἰς τον κοσμον ἱνα κρινῃ τον κοσμον, ἀλλ᾽ ἱνα σωθῃ ὁ κοσμος δι᾽ αὐτου.
2. και ἀποκριθεις αὐτῳ ὁ Ἰησους εἰπεν· Τί σοι θελεις ποιησω; ὁ δε τυφλος εἰπεν αὐτῳ, Ῥαββι, ἱνα ἀναβλεψω.
3. Και λεγει αὐτοις ἐν ἐκεινῃ τῃ ἡμερᾳ· Διελθωμεν εἰς το περαν.
4. ὁ δε στρατιωτης ἰδων ἀνεῳγμενας (Perfect Passive Participle from ἀνοιγω) τας θυρας της φυλακης, ἠμελλεν ἑαυτον ἀναιρειν μαχαιρᾳ δοκων ὁτι πεφευγασιν οἱ μαθηται.

*5. ὁς γαρ ἀν ποιησῃ το θελημα του θεου, οὑτος ἀδελφος μου και ἀδελφη και μητηρ ἐστιν.

*6. και ἐξελθουσα εἰπεν τῃ μητρι αὐτης· Τί αἰτησωμαι; ἡ δε εἰπεν· Την κεφαλην Ἰωαννου του βαπτιζοντος.

*7. οὑτος ἠλθεν εἰς μαρτυριαν, ἱνα μαρτυρησῃ περι του φωτος, ἱνα παντες πιστευσωσιν δι᾽ αὐτου. οὐκ ἠν ἐκεινος το φως, ἀλλ᾽ ἱνα μαρτυρησῃ περι του φωτος.

8. οὑτοι δ᾽ εἰσιν οἱ παρα την ὁδον· ὁπου σπειρεται ὁ λογος, και ὁταν ἀκουσωσιν, εὐθυς ἐρχεται ὁ Σατανας και αἰρει τον λογον τον ἐσπαρμενον (Perfect Passive Participle of σπειρω) εἰς αὐτους.

*9. And having gone out into the fields they preached so that the people would repent.

*10. His mercy is for [use εἰς] generations and generations to those who fear him.

11. According to the writings, there will be signs in the sun and stars, and on the earth suffering and need of the nations.

12. And they were bringing children to him so that he might touch them.

## Section B

*1. ὁς ἀν ἑν των τοιουτων παιδιων δεξηται ἐπι τῳ ὀνοματι μου, ἐμε δεχεται· και ὁς ἀν ἐμε δεχηται, οὐκ ἐμε δεχεται ἀλλα τον ἀποστειλαντα με.

*2. λεγει ἡ μητηρ αὐτου τοις διακονοις· Ὅ τι ἀν λεγῃ ὑμιν ποιησατε.

3. οἱ δε εἰπαν· Τί ἐτι ἐχομεν μαρτυριας χρειαν; αὐτοι γαρ ἠκουσαμεν ἀπο του στοματος αὐτου.

*4. και ἀπεστειλεν αὐτον εἰς οἰκον αὐτου λεγων· Μη εἰς την κωμην εἰσελθῃς.

5. και λεγει αὐτοις· Ἀγωμεν εἰς τας ἀλλας πολεις και κωμας, ἱνα και ἐκει κηρυξω· εἰς τουτο γαρ ἐξηλθον.

6. ὁ πιστευων εἰς τον υἱον ἐχει ζωην αἰωνιον· ὁ δε ἀρνουμενος τον υἱον οὐκ ὀψεται (irregular Future of ὁραω) ζωην, ἀλλ᾽ ἡ ὀργη του θεου μενει ἐπ᾽ αὐτῳ.

*7. ὁ μεν υἱος του ἀνθρωπου ὑπαγει καθως γεγραπται περι αὐτου, οὐαι δε τῳ ἀνθρωπῳ ἐκεινῳ ὁς ἀν ᾐ ὁ ἐχθρος τῳ υἱῳ του ἀνθρωπου.

*8. ἐγω δε οὐ παρα ἀνθρωπου την μαρτυριαν λαμβανω, ἀλλα ταυτα λεγω ἱνα ὑμεις σωθητε.

9. The servants of God say 'Wisdom and honour and power and glory be (omit the verb to be) to the lamb.'

10. The promises of God and the covenant are salvation for this generation.

11. The leaders of Judea listened to his testimony until the end in order that they might accuse him.
*12. The servant asked his masters, 'What do you wish that I might do for you (pl.)?'

## Section C

**John 6.28-30** εἶπον οὖν πρὸς αὐτόν, Τί ποιῶμεν ἵνα ἐργαζώμεθα τὰ ἔργα τοῦ
θεοῦ; [29] ἀπεκρίθη ὁ Ἰησοῦς καὶ εἶπεν αὐτοῖς, Τοῦτό ἐστιν τὸ ἔργον τοῦ θεοῦ,
ἵνα πιστεύητε εἰς ὃν ἀπέστειλεν ἐκεῖνος. [30] εἶπον οὖν αὐτῷ, Τί οὖν ποιεῖς
σὺ σημεῖον, ἵνα ἴδωμεν καὶ πιστεύσωμέν σοι; τί ἐργάζῃ;

# Using verbs

We have now learnt all of the basic forms and uses of verbs in Greek. However, there are a number of more unusual or particular uses that are worth looking at.

## 18.1 δυναμαι, καθημαι, κειμαι AND οἰδα

These four verbs all describe states that can be thought of as arising from past situations. For example, if you are sitting now it is because you have sat down in the past. Similarly you know something now because you have learnt it in the past.

δυναμαι – I am able (to)
καθημαι – I sit
κειμαι – I lie

οἰδα – I know

Therefore these verbs use the endings of the Perfect and Pluperfect tense for the Present and Past (Imperfect).

KEY GRAMMAR

Present: Current state arising from past action – use Perfect endings
Past: Past state arising from action in further past – use Pluperfect endings

**Note:** the Past tense of these verbs is called their Imperfect (when, for example, you are parsing) because it describes an ongoing situation in the past (as opposed to the Aorist, which would more describe an action in the past).

• δυναμαι, καθημαι, κειμαι

These are deponent, and hence have the Middle endings.

| Present | | | Imperfect | | |
|---|---|---|---|---|---|
| δυνα-μαι | καθη-μαι | κει-μαι | ἐδυνα-μην | ἐκαθη-μην | ἐκει-μην |
| δυνα-σαι | καθη-σαι | κει-σαι | ἐδυνα-σο | ἐκαθη-σο | ἐκει-σο |
| δυνα-ται | καθη-ται | κει-ται | ἐδυνα-το | ἐκαθη-το | ἐκει-το |
| δυνα-μεθα | καθη-μεθα | κει-μεθα | ἐδυνα-μεθα | ἐκαθη-μεθα | ἐκει-μεθα |
| δυνα-σθε | καθη-σθε | κει-σθε | ἐδυνα-σθε | ἐκαθη-σθε | ἐκει-σθε |
| δυνα-νται | καθη-νται | κει-νται | ἐδυνα-ντο | ἐκαθη-ντο | ἐκει-ντο |
| | Infinitives | δυνασθαι, καθησθαι, κεισθαι | | | |
| | Participles | δυναμενος, καθημενος, κειμενος | | | |

• οἰδα

This uses the Active endings.

| Present | Imperfect |
|---|---|
| οἰδ-α | ᾐδ-ειν |
| οἰδ-ας | ᾐδ-εις |
| οἰδ-εν | ᾐδ-ει |
| οἰδ-αμεν | ᾐδ-ειμεν |
| οἰδ-ατε | ᾐδ-ειτε |
| οἰδ-ασιν | ᾐδ-εισαν |

| Infinitive | εἰδεναι |
|---|---|
| Participle | εἰδως[1] |

**Hint**

Some of the forms of οἰδα are easily confused with εἰδον the 2nd Aorist of ὁραω (I see).[2] Remember that there are no augments in the *other moods*.

| | Indicative | Infinitive | Participle |
|---|---|---|---|
| I see – 2nd Aorist[3] | εἰδον | ἰδειν | ἰδων |
| I know | ᾐδειν (Imperfect) | εἰδεναι | εἰδως |

[1] εἰδως declines like the perfect participle λελυκως – feminine nominative singular εἰδυια, neuter nominative singular εἰδος, masculine and neuter stem εἰδοτ-.

[2] This because they are both in fact using parts of the same basic verb.

[3] Note also ἰδου meaning look!/behold! which is related to but not directly part of εἰδον (the actual Imperatives from εἰδον being ἰδε and ἰδετε).

Examples

Jas. 2.14: μη δυναται ἡ πιστις σωσαι αὐτον; – Faith is not able to save him, is it?

Acts 2.34: εἰπεν ὁ κυριος τῳ κυριῳ μου· Καθου ἐκ δεξιων μου. – The lord said to my lord, 'Sit at my right.'

Matt. 28.6: οὐκ ἐστιν ὡδε, ἠγερθη γαρ καθως εἰπεν· δευτε ἰδετε τον τοπον ὁπου ἐκειτο. – He is not here, for he has been raised just as he said; come see the place where he lay.

Rev. 4.2: εὐθεως ἐγενομην ἐν πνευματι, και ἰδου θρονος ἐκειτο ἐν τῳ οὐρανῳ, και ἐπι τον θρονον καθημενος. – Immediately I was in the spirit, and behold a throne lying in heaven, and one sitting on the throne.

3 John 12: και ἡμεις δε μαρτυρουμεν, και οἰδας ὁτι ἡ μαρτυρια ἡμων ἀληθης ἐστιν. – We also testify, and you know that our testimony is true.

2 Cor. 4.14: εἰδοτες ὁτι ὁ ἐγειρας τον κυριον Ἰησουν και ἡμας συν Ἰησου ἐγερεῖ. – Knowing that the one who raised the Lord Jesus will raise us also with Jesus.

PRACTICE 18.1

## Parse

| | | |
|---|---|---|
| 1. δυνανται | 4. ἐκειτο | 7. ἰδειν |
| 2. καθημενοις | 5. οἰδατε | 8. ἰδων |
| 3. δυνασθαι | 6. ᾐδειν | 9. εἰδως |

## 18.2 USE OF INFINITIVES

We have already learnt the forms of the Infinitive, and the distinction between the Present and Aorist Infinitives. However, we have not yet studied carefully the different uses of the Infinitive in Greek – only noting that it is used as in English after certain verbs (e.g. θελω – I wish) and for purpose.

### 18.2.1 After certain verbs

An Infinitive often comes after the following verbs.[4]

| | | | |
|---|---|---|---|
| δει[5] | It is (was) necessary | ἐξεστιν | It is lawful |
| δυναμαι | I am able | θελω | I wish |
| ἐστιν | It is | μελλω | I intend / am about (to) |

[4] Plus, in fact, all verbs of 'commanding', telling someone *to do* something.

[5] The imperfect of δει is ἐδει ('it was necessary').

Examples

Rev. 1.19: γραψον οὖν ἁ εἶδες και ἁ εἰσιν και ἁ μελλει γενεσθαι μετα ταυτα. – Therefore write what you see and what is and what is about to happen after these things.

Gal. 4.21: λεγετε μοι, οἱ ὑπο νομον θελοντες εἶναι, τον νομον οὐκ ἀκουετε; – Tell me, you who wish to be under the law, don't you listen to the law?

1 Cor. 10.23: παντα ἐξεστιν ἀλλ' οὐ παντα οἰκοδομει. – Everything is permitted but not everything builds up.

## The 'subject' of an Infinitive

Often when these verbs are used with an Infinitive there is a 'second subject'.

For example, in the sentence 'I want the messenger to depart' the subject of the sentence is 'I'. But what is 'messenger'? From one point of view it is the object of 'I want', from another it is the subject of 'to depart'. There is a simple rule in Greek that any such 'subject of an Infinitive' goes in the accusative.[6]

- I want the messenger to depart – θελω τον ἀγγελον ἀπελθειν

KEY GRAMMAR

The 'subject of an Infinitive' goes in the accusative

Examples

Mark 8.31: δει τον υἱον του ἀνθρωπου πολλα παθειν. – The son of man must suffer greatly (lit: it is necessary the son of man to suffer greatly).

Rom. 16.19: θελω δε ὑμας σοφους εἶναι εἰς το ἀγαθον . . . – I want you to be wise towards the good . . .

Notes

- ἐξεστιν is irregular, in that when combined with an Infinitive the 'subject' of the Infinitive is normally in the dative, not the accusative. For example: Matt. 14.4: Οὐκ ἐξεστιν σοι ἐχειν αὐτην. – 'It is not lawful for you to have her.'
- When translating δει it is often sensible to rephrase 'it is necessary' (which you hardly ever say in English) to some form of 'must'. (N.B. there is no word in Greek for 'must' – δει is used instead.)

[6] This may seem annoying ('If it is a type of subject, why not put it in the nominative?'), but it has the advantage of strictly reserving the nominative for the subject of the main verb in the sentence, which helps when trying to analyse a complicated sentence.

### 18.2.2 Result clauses

Greek expresses result very easily, simply by the word ὥστε and the Infinitive.

KEY GRAMMAR
ὥστε + Infinitive = result

- This is a little different from English, which uses an Indicative.
- Often there is a second subject, in which case it goes in the accusative.
- To get the meaning right you should first translate ὥστε as 'with the result that', but this sounds clumsy in English, so then you need to rephrase it, often using the English word 'so' or even just 'and'.

Examples

Matt. 15.30-1: και ἐθεραπευσεν αὐτους· ὥστε τον ὀχλον θαυμασαι.
– And he healed them, with the result that the crowd was amazed.
(or 'so the crowd was amazed' or 'and the crowd was amazed').

Mark 15.5: ὁ δε Ἰησους οὐκετι οὐδεν ἀπεκριθη, ὥστε θαυμαζειν τον Πιλατον.
– But Jesus answered nothing further, with the result that Pilate was amazed. (or 'so Pilate was amazed' or 'and Pilate was amazed').

**PRACTICE 18.2.1 AND 18.2.2**

### Translate

1. θελω αὐτον γαμειν με.
2. δει διδασκαλον διδασκειν.
3. προσηλθεν ὥστε αὐτους ὑπαγαγειν.
4. δυνασθε ἐσθιειν ἀρτον ἐν τῳ ἱερῳ;
5. φιλω την σοφιαν ὥστε ἀκουειν του διδασκαλου μου.

### 18.2.3 Purpose

As we have already learnt, purpose is expressed in Greek either by just using the Infinitive or by ἱνα plus the Subjunctive.

Examples

Jude 14: ἰδου ἠλθεν κυριος ... ποιησαι κρισιν κατα παντων.
– Behold, the Lord is coming . . . to execute (lit: do) judgement against all.

Mark 3.14-15: ἐποιησεν δωδεκα ἱνα ὡσιν μετ' αὐτου και ἱνα ἀποστελλῃ αὐτους κηρυσσειν και ἐχειν ἐξουσιαν ἐκβαλλειν τα δαιμονια.
– He made (the) twelve in order (for them) to be with him and so that he might send them to preach and to have authority to cast out the demons.

## 18.2.4 Articular Infinitive

The neuter singular of the article (το, το, του, τῳ) can be put in front of an Infinitive to make a noun denoting the activity of the verb, or the fact of that activity happening (this is called the *articular Infinitive*).

κρινειν – to judge → το κρινειν – (the activity of/the fact of) judging
ἐσθιειν – to eat → το ἐσθιειν – (the activity of/the fact of) eating

The *articular Infinitive* is mainly used with a preposition. The Infinitive itself does not decline, but the article does. The most common prepositions used with the articular Infinitive are:

| | |
|---|---|
| δια + acc. | because of |
| μετα + acc. | after |
| εἰς + acc. *or* προς + acc. | with a view to / aiming at / leading to[7] |
| προ + gen. | before |
| ἐν + dat. | during / while |

Examples

Jas. 4.2: οὐκ ἐχετε δια το μη αἰτεισθαι ὑμας.
– you do not have because you do not ask.
(lit: on account of the fact of you not asking)

Matt. 26.32: μετα δε το ἐγερθηναι με προαξω ὑμας εἰς την Γαλιλαιαν.
– after I have been raised I will go head of you into Galilee.
(lit: after the activity of me being raised)

2 Cor. 1.4: ὁ παρακαλων ἡμας ἐπι παση τη θλιψει ἡμων εἰς το δυνασθαι ἡμας παρακαλειν τους ἐν παση θλιψει. – the one encouraging us in all our suffering so that we might be able to encourage those who are in any suffering. (lit: with a view to the activity of us being able)

Gal. 2.12: προ του γαρ ἐλθειν τινας ἀπο Ἰακωβου μετα των ἐθνων συνησθιεν.
– for before some people came from James, he used to eat with the Gentiles. (lit: before the fact of some people coming)

Mark 4.4: και ἐγενετο ἐν τῳ σπειρειν ὁ μεν ἐπεσεν παρα την ὁδον.
– And as he sowed some fell alongside the path.
(lit: in the activity of sowing . . .)

---

[7] Alternatively, εἰς το + Infinitive and προς το + Infinitive can be thought of as a form of purpose clause. Indeed, there is another similar form – sometimes rather than just the Infinitive for purpose, του + Infinitive is used. Thus one can summarise the different ways of expressing purpose as follows.
*Either* **1.** Infinitive: (i) alone, (ii) preceded by του, (iii) preceded by εἰς το / προς το
*or* **2.** ἱνα + Subjunctive

**HALF-WAY PRACTICE**

1. ἐδυναμεθα λεγειν αὐτῳ.
2. θελω εἰδεναι τον θεον.
3. μετα το προσευχεσθαι ἐξηλθον ἐκ της συναγωγης.
4. ἡ χηρα ἠν πτωχη ὡστε μη ἐχειν πολλα.
5. εἰδον ὁτι δει αὐτην ἀποθανειν.
6. οἰδατε τας ἐπαγγελιας τας αἰωνιους;
7. ἠλθες προς το προσκυνησαι τῳ θεῳ;
8. οἱ μαθηται ἐφυγον ὡστε τους στρατιωτας μη εὑρειν μηδενα.
9. Did you know him?
10. Before sitting down they gave thanks.
11. They were so amazed that they worshipped him.
12. You must be a slave.

## 18.3 THIRD PERSON IMPERATIVES

We have already learnt the normal Imperatives – commands to 'you' (singular or plural). These are called 2nd person Imperatives. Now we need to learn the 3rd person Imperatives. These are quite rare. They mean 'let him/her/it/them [untie]' in the sense of 'he/she/it/they should' (**not** 'allow them to').

KEY GRAMMAR
3rd person Imperatives = 'Let . . .'

The forms are as follows.

| | Present Active | 1st Aorist Active | Present Middle or Passive | 1st Aorist Middle | Aorist Passive |
|---|---|---|---|---|---|
| Sing. | λυετω | λυσατω | ῥυεσθω | ῥυσασθω | λυθητω |
| Pl. | λυετωσαν | λυσατωσαν | ῥυεσθωσαν | ῥυσασθωσαν | λυθητωσαν |

Notes

- The endings are distinctive: -τω/θω for 3rd sing., -τωσαν/-θωσαν for 3rd pl.
- The standard distinguishing marks are visible: -σα in the 1st Aorist Active and Middle, θ in the Aorist Passive.

Examples

Mark 4.23: εἰ τις ἐχει ὠτα ἀκουειν ἀκουετω.
– If someone has ears to hear, he should hear!

Rom. 6.12: μη οὐν βασιλευετω ἡ ἁμαρτια ἐν τῳ θνητῳ ὑμων σωματι.
– Therefore sin should not reign in your mortal body.

PRACTICE 18.3

## Translate

1. μη λεγετω τῳ πονηρῳ.
2. ἐλθετω ἡ βασιλεια σου.
3. δει την βασιλειαν ἐλθειν.
4. προσκυνωμεν τῳ θεῳ.
5. προσκυνειτωσαν τῳ θεῳ.
6. τα δαιμονια ἐκβληθητω.

## 18.4 PRINCIPAL PARTS

In the previous chapters we have learnt all the different parts of the verb. In the process we have seen that **endings** are perfectly regular, but various verbs have irregularities in their **stems** (beyond those which are just the result of the standard combinations of letters such as π + σ → ψ).

There is a standard format for presenting this information about **stems** called the 'principal parts' of the verb. This consists of six parts of the verb, from which all of the tenses and voices can be constructed. In the reference section (pages 253–4), the principal parts of the common verbs that have irregularities in their stems are listed.

Look at page 253. There we see the following information about βαλλω.

| Present | Future | Aorist Active | Perfect Active | Perfect Passive | Aorist Passive |
|---|---|---|---|---|---|
| βαλλω | βαλεω | ἐβαλον | βεβληκα | βεβλημαι | ἐβληθην |

This tells us all that we need to know to work out all the forms of βαλλω, given that we know the standard endings (for λυω) in the different tenses. For while you wouldn't be able to work out that the Perfect Active of βαλλω is βεβληκα, once you know this you can just add the standard endings of λυω in the Perfect to βεβληκα to form the Perfect of βαλλω.

Teachers differ as to how much they stress the importance of learning the principal parts of these common verbs – it is certainly very useful, but it is quite a chore. However, what is undoubtedly essential is being able to form the different parts of the verb once you have been given the principal parts (whether from this list, or from a dictionary).

The way in which each one of the principal parts relates to a number of different parts of the verbs (and vice versa) is set out below.

| **Principal parts** | | | **All the parts of the verb** | |
|---|---|---|---|---|
| Present Active | λυω | → | Present Active<br>Imperfect Active<br>Present Middle/Passive<br>Imperfect Middle/Passive | λυω<br>ἐλυον<br>λυομαι<br>ἐλυομην |
| Future Active | λυσω | → | Future Active<br>Future Middle | λυσω<br>λυσομαι |
| Aorist Active | ἐλυσα | → | Aorist Active<br>Aorist Middle | ἐλυσα<br>ἐλυσαμην |
| Perfect Active | λελυκα | → | Perfect Active<br>Pluperfect Active | λελυκα<br>(ἐ)λελυκειν |
| Perfect Middle/Passive | λελυμαι | → | Perfect Middle/Passive<br>Pluperfect Middle/Passive | λελυμαι<br>ἐλελυμην |
| Aorist Passive | ἐλυθην | → | Aorist Passive<br>Future Passive | ἐλυθην<br>λυθησομαι |

Example

- βαλλω is given as:

| Present | Future | Aorist Active | Perfect Active | Perfect Passive | Aorist Passive |
|---|---|---|---|---|---|
| βαλλω | βαλεω | ἐβαλον | βεβληκα | βεβλημαι | ἐβληθην |

| | | | |
|---|---|---|---|
| βαλλω | | the 1st sing. Imperfect Passive is | ἐβαλλομην |
| βαλεω[8] | tells you | the 2nd plural Future Active is | βαλειτε |
| ἐβαλον | that, for | the 3rd sing. Aorist Active is | ἐβαλεν |
| | example, | (and -ον ending points out that it has a 2nd Aorist) | |
| βεβληκα | | the Perfect participle is | βεβληκως |
| βεβλημαι | | the 3rd plural Perfect Passive is | βεβληνται |
| ἐβληθην | | the 1st plural Future Passive is | βληθησομεθα |

- Imagine you need to translate οἱ ἐπι την γην την καλην σπαρεντες. (Mark 4.20)

You guess from the context that the final word is something to do with σπειρω (I sow). You look up the principal parts of σπειρω and find the sixth form is ἐσπαρην. This tells you that the Aorist Passive participle will be σπαρεις (declined like λυθεις; no augment for the participle, and the principal part has told you that it, unusually, does not have a θ). Given this, you can see that σπαρεντες is the masc. nom. plural of the Aorist Passive participle of σπειρω. Hence the phrase means, 'the ones having been sown on the good soil'.

**PRACTICE 18.4**

## Translate

1. ἠρθησαν.
2. πολλα εἰληφαμεν.
3. ἠκουσα το ῥηθεν.
4. σωσεις τον ἐσχηκοτα δαιμονιον;
5. οἱ ἀρχιερεις εἰληφασιν τας γραφας.
6. εἰδον ἀνεῳγμενον οὐρανον.

## 18.5 ASPECT AND TIME IN TENSES

As we have learnt the different moods and tenses we have encountered the ideas of time and aspect. Now it is time to look again at what is meant by the tenses. The student should be aware that the degree to which Greek tense is primarily about aspect or primarily about time is a matter of some dispute among scholars. It is perhaps fair to say that traditionally tense has been seen as being mainly about time, but more recently there has been a reassessment of this, stressing aspect. The learner is best to follow the famous Greek proverb 'moderation in all things' (μηδεν ἀγαν) and to understand both the time and

[8] Thus the future of βαλλω is βαλεω using the -εω endings, which is what one would expect in the Future of a liquid verbs (Chapter 11, section 11.2). Thus 'I will throw' will be βαλῶ.

the aspect side of the tenses, and to be suspicious of those saying it is all of one or all of the other.

The building blocks of an understanding of tenses can be summarised as follows.

- Three time distinctions: future, present, past
- Three 'aspects': process – the action is in progress
  undefined – the action is considered in itself, without reference to continuation or completion
  completed – the action is completed
- The tenses function differently in the different moods
  - Indicatives – time and aspect
  - Participles – relative time (relative to the main verb)
  - Other moods – aspect only

| | Indicative | | | Participles | Imperative Infinitive Subjunctive |
|---|---|---|---|---|---|
| Present | Present | + | Process (or Undefined) | Simultaneous | Process |
| Future | Future | + | Undefined | – | – |
| Imperfect | Past | + | Process | – | – |
| Aorist | Past | + | Undefined | Sequence | Undefined |
| Perfect | (Present) | + | Completed | – | – |

## Notes

- The meaning of the participles is closely related to that of the other moods – action is normally *simultaneous* with the main verb because it is seen as an ongoing *process*, and action is prior to the main verb in *sequence* because it is seen as an action with an *undefined* relationship to the main verb. However, thinking in terms of being simultaneous or in sequence tends to make it easier for beginners to make a start on reading the New Testament.
- There are occasions when the time element of the Indicative seems to be absent and aspect dominates (e.g. Rom. 3.23: παντες γαρ ἡμαρτον. – ἡμαρτον is Aorist here, but clearly this does not mean 'for all sinned on one particular occasion in the past' but rather 'for all sin' – a general, 'undefined' statement). However, normally time (*alongside* aspect) is very important to tense in the Indicative.
- The augment marks out past time – hence it occurs in the Imperfect and Aorist *in the Indicative only.*

## VOCAB FOR CHAPTER 18

A host of extra adjectives
ἀξιος (41) – worthy
*δεξιος (54) – right (hand)
*δυνατος (32) – powerful, capable, able
ἐλευθερος (23) – free
*ἐσχατος (52) – last, least
*ἱκανος (39) – sufficient
ἰσχυρος (29) – strong
λευκος (25) – white, bright
*λοιπος (55) – remaining
*μεσος (58) – middle
νεος (23) – new, young
*ὀλιγος (40) – small, little (pl. few)
πλουσιος (28) – rich
πνευματικος (26) – spiritual
*φιλος (29) – loved, friendly, friend

A couple more nouns
*μαρτυς, μαρτυρος, ὁ (35) – witness
*μισθος (29) – pay, wages
*σταυρος (27) – cross

Some more verbs
αὐξανω (23) – I grow
καθαριζω (31) – I make/declare clean
*καθιζω (46) – I cause to sit down
*δυναμαι (210) – I can, I am able
*καθημαι (91) – I sit (down)
κειμαι (24) – I lie, recline
*οἰδα (318) – I know
παρειμι (24) – I am present

In a category of its own
*ὡστε + Infinitive (83) – with the result that

A number of words with an α prefix to make them negative
*ἀδικεω (28) – I do wrong
ἀδικια (25) – wrongdoing
*καθαρος (27) – clean, pure
*ἀκαθαρτος (32) – impure, unclean[9]
ἀπιστος (23) – unbelieving, faithless[9]

## Word helps

axiom, dexterity, dynamic, eschatology, leukaemia, Mesopotamia, neologism/Neolithic, oligarchy, plutocratic, pneumatic, philosophy/philanthropic, martyr, auction, cathartic/Katharine, cathedral.

## Exercises

### Section A

*1. ὁ Χριστος ὁ βασιλευς Ἰσραηλ καταβατω νυν ἀπο του σταυρου, ἱνα ἰδωμεν και πιστευσωμεν.

*2. και ἐλεγον· Οὐχ οὑτος ἐστιν Ἰησους ὁ υἱος Ἰωσηφ, οὑ ἡμεις οἰδαμεν τον πατερα και την μητερα; πως νυν λεγει ὁτι Ἐκ του οὐρανου καταβεβηκα;

[9] Note: compound adjectives only occur with the masculine endings (for masculine and feminine) or the neuter.

*3. ὁ δε Ἰησους εἰπεν αὐτοις· Οὐκ οἰδατε τί αἰτεισθε. δυνασθε πιειν το ποτηριον ὃ ἐγω πινω ἢ το βαπτισμα ὃ ἐγω βαπτιζομαι βαπτισθηναι;

*4. ὁ ἀφ᾽ ἑαυτου λαλων ζητει την δοξαν την ἰδιαν· ὁ δε ζητων την δοξαν του πεμψαντος αὐτον οὑτος ἀληθης ἐστιν και ἀδικια ἐν αὐτῳ οὐκ ἐστιν.

*5. Τοτε ὁ Ἰησους εἰπεν τοις μαθηταις αὐτου· Εἰ τις θελει ὀπισω μου ἐλθειν, ἀρνησασθω ἑαυτον και ἀρατω τον σταυρον αὐτου και ἀκολουθειτω μοι.

6. και Μαρια θεωρει δυο ἀγγελους ἐν λευκοις καθιζομενους, ἑνα προς τῃ κεφαλῃ και ἑνα προς τοις ποσιν, ὁπου ἐκειτο το σωμα του Ἰησου.

7. λεγοντες δε φωνῃ μεγαλῃ εἰπαν· Ἀξιον ἐστιν το ἀρνιον καθημενον ἐπι τῳ θρονῳ ἐν δεξιᾳ του θεου λαβειν την δυναμιν και σοφιαν και τιμην και δοξαν.

*8. ὁ μεν οὐν κυριος Ἰησους μετα το λαλησαι αὐτοις ἀνεβη εἰς τον οὐρανον και ἐκαθητο ἐκ δεξιων του θεου.

*9. Blessed are the pure in heart, because they will see God.

10. The power of God was there with a view to healing the sick and cleansing those with unclean spirits.

11. We are working now in order to read the New Testament.

12. Our knowledge is growing with the result that we are able to learn from the writings: first, the gospel according to Mark.

## Section B

1. πορευθεντες δε μαθετε τί ἐστιν· Δει τον υἱον του ἀνθρωπου πολλα παθειν.

*2. και παλιν ἠρξατο διδασκειν παρα την θαλασσαν· και συναγεται προς αὐτον ὀχλος πολυς, ὡστε αὐτον εἰς πλοιον ἐμβαντα καθησθαι ἐν τῃ θαλασσῃ, και πας ὁ ὀχλος προς την θαλασσαν ἐπι της γης ἠσαν.[10]

*3. δυναμεις και σημεια ἐποιησεν δι᾽ αὐτου ὁ θεος ἐν μεσῳ ὑμων καθως αὐτοι οἰδατε.

4. ὁ θεριζων [harvester/reaper] μισθον λαμβανει και συναγει καρπον εἰς ζωην αἰωνιον, ἱνα ὁ σπειρων ὁμου χαιρῃ και ὁ θεριζων.

*5. ἐνδυσασθε το ἱματιον το καθαρον προς το δυνασθαι εἰναι μετα του βασιλεως και των φιλων αὐτου.

---

[10] You would expect to have the singular ἠν here agreeing with ὀχλος but in fact Mark 4.1 has the plural, presumably because the crowd is thought of as many individuals. Note ἐμβαινω = ἐν-βαινω.

6. οἱ δε ἀρχιερεις και παντες οἱ λοιποι ἐζητουν κατα του Ἰησου μαρτυριαν εἰς το ἀποκτεινειν αὐτον, και οὐχ ηὑρισκον.
7. και ἐν τῳ κατηγορεισθαι αὐτον ὑπο των ἀρχιερεων και πρεσβυτερων οὐδεν ἀπεκρινατο.[11]
8. ὁ δε Ἡρῳδης ἰδων τον Ἰησουν ἐχαρη [*irreg. Aorist 3rd sing. of* χαιρω], ἠν γαρ ἐξ ἱκανων χρονων θελων ἰδειν αὐτον δια το ἀκουειν περι αὐτου και ἠλπιζεν τι σημειον ἰδειν ὑπ' αὐτου γινομενον.
9. It is necessary that servants of God be spiritual, worthy, and capable, free from impure desire, not new in the faith, and not unfaithful.

*10. He is treating you unjustly with the result that you are not able to receive your wages.

*11. For do you rich not have homes for the purpose of eating and drinking in?

12. The strong, because they are free, are able to sit and eat with the unclean nations.

## Section C

**Matthew 6.9-13** Οὕτως οὖν προσεύχεσθε ὑμεῖς· Πάτερ ἡμῶν ὁ ἐν τοῖς οὐρανοῖς, ἁγιασθήτω τὸ ὄνομά σου· 10 ἐλθέτω ἡ βασιλεία σου· γενηθήτω τὸ θέλημά σου, ὡς ἐν οὐρανῷ καὶ ἐπὶ γῆς· 11 Τὸν ἄρτον ἡμῶν τὸν ἐπιούσιον [*for today, for the coming day*] δὸς [*give!*] ἡμῖν σήμερον· 12 καὶ ἄφες [*forgive*, ἀφιημι] ἡμῖν τὰ ὀφειλήματα [*debts, from* ὀφειλω] ἡμῶν, ὡς καὶ ἡμεῖς ἀφήκαμεν [ἀφιημι] τοῖς ὀφειλέταις [*debtors*] ἡμῶν· 13 καὶ μὴ εἰσενέγκῃς [εἰσφερω = εἰς+φερω] ἡμᾶς εἰς πειρασμόν [*time of testing*], ἀλλὰ ῥῦσαι ἡμᾶς ἀπὸ τοῦ πονηροῦ.

[11] You would expect ἀπεκριθη since ἀποκρινομαι is a Passive deponent in the Aorist (see Chapter 15, section 15.7). However, seven times in the New Testament it does occur in the Aorist Middle (as opposed to 195 times in the Aorist Passive).

# Extra verbs

## 19.1 -μι VERBS

The-μι verbs (so called because they end in -μι in their 1st singular Present Indicative Active) are a separate class of verbs from the normal -ω verbs (e.g. λυω). The bad news is that their full pattern is awkward to learn. The good news, however, is that only three of them are common, and you don't need to be able to form them yourself, only to recognise and translate them.

Matt. 27.60: και ἐθηκεν αὐτο ἐν τῳ καινῳ αὐτου μνημειῳ.
– and he placed it in his new tomb.
Acts 20.35: μακαριον ἐστιν μαλλον διδοναι ἠ λαμβανειν.
– It is more blessed to give than to receive.
Rev. 3.20: ἰδου ἑστηκα ἐπι την θυραν και κρουω.
– Behold, I stand at the door and knock.

### 19.1.1 Characteristics of -μι verbs

The essential feature of -μι verbs is that they use a different, longer stem in the Present (and thus also for the Imperfect) than for the rest of the verb (compare λυω, where the one stem λυ- is used throughout). It is crucial to recognise which of the two stems a particular occurrence of a -μι verb is using.

| The Three -μι Verbs | | Verbal Stem | Present Stem (for Present and Imperfect) |
|---|---|---|---|
| τιθημι | I place | θε | τιθε |
| διδωμι | I give | δο | διδο |
| ἱστημι | I cause to stand | στα | ἱστα |

Note

The Present stem is formed from the verbal stem by a form of reduplication – the first consonant is repeated (or an 'h' sound for those beginning with vowels or σ) together with an ι. Note the difference between this and proper reduplication (for the Perfect) which uses an ε vowel.

KEY GRAMMAR

In -μι verbs the Present stem is longer than the verbal stem

### 19.1.2 Parsing -μι verbs – the survival guide

The endings of the -μι verbs are slightly different from those of λυω. They are discussed more in the next section. However, they are similar enough to those of λυω that their person and number are normally recognisable, as is their voice (the context will often supply this as well). Hence the key issue in parsing is identifying tense. Fortunately, once you grasp the pattern that the changing stems form, the tense can easily be deduced without attention to the endings.

| | |
|---|---|
| Present stem | Present |
| Present stem + augment | Imperfect |
| Verbal stem + σ suffix | Future Indicative (or 1st Aorist other mood) |
| Verbal stem + augment + σ suffix | 1st Aorist Active Indicative |
| Verbal stem + augment | 2nd Aorist Active Indicative |
| Verbal stem | 2nd Aorist Active other mood |
| Verbal stem + θ[1] | Aorist Passive (+ augment in Indicative) |
| Verbal stem + θησ[1] | Future Passive |
| Reduplicated verbal stem | Perfect |

Notes

- διδωμι and τιθημι both use a 1st Aorist in the Indicative, and a 2nd Aorist in the other moods. Thus, verbal stem plus σ must be the Future Indicative (since there are no 1st Aorist other moods). For ἱστημι, where there is a 1st Aorist in the other moods, the Future Indicative has to be distinguished by its endings, which are always the same as the Future Indicative of λυω.

---

[1] The Aorist Passive of τιθημι should be ἐθεθην, the θ for the Aorist Passive added to the verbal stem θε. However, to avoid two θ on the run, this was written as ἐτεθην etc. Similarly the Future Passive is τεθησομαι.

- The reduplication in the Perfect is proper reduplication with an ε: δεδο-, τεθε-, ἑστα-.

## Examples

| | | | |
|---|---|---|---|
| τιθετε | – Present stem | – Present | – you place |
| ἐθηκεν | – Verbal stem + ε | – 2nd Aorist Indicative | – she placed |
| τιθεναι | – Present stem | – Present | – to place (Infinitive) |
| θειναι | – Verbal stem | – 2nd Aorist other mood | – to place (Infinitive) |
| δεδοται | – reduplication | – Perfect | – it has been given |
| ἱστας | – Present stem | – Present | – standing (participle) |
| στας | – Verbal stem | – 2nd Aorist other mood | – having stood (participle) |
| δωσετε | – Verbal stem + σ | – Future Indicative | – you will give |
| ἐστησεν | – Verbal stem + ε + σ | – 1st Aorist Indicative | – he stood |

PRACTICE 19.1.2

### Which tense are the following?

(Have an intelligent guess at the rest of the parsing as well.)

1. ἐδωκεν
2. ἐδιδου
3. δεδοται
4. τιθεμεν
5. τεθησεται
6. διδωσιν
7. θωμεν
8. δοντας
9. ἱστησιν
10. σταθησονται
11. στησατε
12. ἐστησατε

Examples

John 2.10: και λεγει αὐτῳ· Πας ἀνθρωπος πρωτον τον καλον οἰνον <u>τιθησιν</u> ...
– And he said to him, 'Every person <u>puts (out)</u> the fine wine first . . .'

Matt. 12.18: <u>θησω</u> το πνευμα μου ἐπ' αὐτον. – <u>I will place</u> my spirit on him.

John 19.19: ἐγραψεν δε και τιτλον ὁ Πιλατος και <u>ἐθηκεν</u> ἐπι του σταυρου.
– Pilate also wrote a notice and <u>placed</u> (it) on the cross.

2 Tim. 1.11: εἰς ὃ <u>ἐτεθην</u> ἐγω κηρυξ και ἀποστολος και διδασκαλος.
– for which <u>I was appointed</u> a herald, and apostle and teacher.

Eph. 1.22: και αὐτον ἐδωκεν κεφαλην ὑπερ παντα τῃ ἐκκλησιᾳ. – and he gave him as head (or 'made him head') over all things for the church.

Mark 4.11: ἐλεγεν αὐτοις· Ὑμιν το μυστηριον δεδοται της βασιλειας του θεου. – He said to them, 'The secret of the kingdom of God has been given to you'.

Matt. 20.18: και ὁ υἱος του ἀνθρωπου παραδοθησεται τοις ἀρχιερευσιν ... – And the son of man will be handed over to the chief priests . . .

2 Pet. 3.15: καθως και ὁ ἀγαπητος ἡμων ἀδελφος Παυλος κατα την δοθεισαν αὐτῳ σοφιαν ἐγραψεν ὑμιν. – Just as our beloved brother Paul also wrote to you according to the wisdom given to him.

### 19.1.3 The meaning of ἱστημι

ἱστημι is basically a transitive verb (i.e. one which can take an object) meaning 'I cause to stand' or 'I stand something up.' However, particular tenses of ἱστημι are used to convey an intransitive meaning (i.e. one which cannot take an object) – 'I stand (myself) up.' The full pattern is as follows:

| If you want . . . | | | Then use . . . | |
|---|---|---|---|---|
| Transitive: | Present | I cause to stand | Present Active | ἱστημι |
| | Future | I will cause to stand | Future Active | στησω † |
| | Past | I caused to stand | 1st Aorist Active | ἐστησα † |
| Intransitive: | Present | I stand | Perfect Active | ἑστηκα † |
| | Future | I will stand | Future Middle | στησομαι † |
| | Past | I stood | *Either* 2nd Aorist Active | ἐστην |
| | | | *or* AoristPassive | ἐσταθην † |

Notes

- Forms marked † conjugate identically to the corresponding part of λυω.
- Since the Perfect Active is used for a Present intransitive meaning, the Pluperfect Active (εἱστηκειν †) is used for an Imperfect intransitive meaning.
- Since ἱστημι has both a 1st and 2nd Aorist, watch the forms of the participles (and the other moods) – ἱστας (Present participle), στησας (σ suffix – 1st Aorist participle – transitive), στας (no suffix – 2nd Aorist participle – intransitive).

### Examples

Transitive:

Mark 9.36: και λαβων παιδιον ἐστησεν αὐτο ἐν μεσῳ αὐτων.

– And he took a child and stood him in their midst.

Matt. 25.33: και στησει τα μεν προβατα ἐκ δεξιων αὐτου ...

– and he will stand (or 'put') the sheep on his right . . .

Intransitive:

Matt. 20.32: και στας ὁ Ἰησους ἐφωνησαν αὐτους και εἰπεν ...

– And Jesus stood still (lit: 'having stood') and called them and said . . .

2 Cor. 1.24: συνεργοι ἐσμεν της χαρας ὑμων· τῃ γαρ πιστει ἑστηκατε.

– We are fellow-workers of your joy, because you stand in the faith.

## 19.1.4 The pattern of endings

It is not necessary to learn all of the endings of the -μι verbs. In practice the endings are similar enough to those of λυω that if you understand the principle of the Present and verbal stems, you should be able to recognise the forms. However, for completeness the Present and Aorist endings are given below (more detail on the -μι verbs can be found on pages 265–8).

**Note:** Basically, the three different -μι verbs have the same endings, but with a different vowel dominating – ε for τιθημι, α for ἱστημι and ο for διδωμι.

| Present Active | | | | | |
|---|---|---|---|---|---|
| **Indicative** | | | **Subjunctive** | | |
| τιθημι | ἱστημι | διδωμι | τιθω | ἱστω | διδω |
| τιθης | ἱστης | διδως | τιθῃς | ἱστῃς | διδῳς |
| τιθησι(ν) | ἱστησι(ν) | διδωσι(ν) | τιθῃ | ἱστῃ | διδῳ |
| τιθεμεν | ἱσταμεν | διδομεν | τιθωμεν | ἱστωμεν | διδωμεν |
| τιθετε | ἱστατε | διδοτε | τιθητε | ἱστητε | διδωτε |
| τιθεασι(ν) | ἱστασι(ν) | διδοασι(ν) | τιθωσι(ν) | ἱστωσι(ν) | διδωσι(ν) |
| **Imperative** | | | **Infinitive** | | |
| | | | τιθεναι | ἱσταναι | διδοναι |
| τιθει | ἱστη | διδου | **Participle** | | |
| τιθετω | ἱστατω | διδοτω | τιθεις -εισα- εν, stem τιθεντ- | | |
| τιθετε | ἱστατε | διδοτε | ἱστας -ασα, -αν, stem ἱσταντ- | | |
| τιθετωσαν | ἱστατωσαν | διδοτωσαν | διδους -ουσα -ον, stem διδοντ- | | |

| Aorist Active |
|---|
| **Indicative** – 1st Aorists ἐθηκα, ἐστησα, ἐδωκα (conjugates regularly).<br>– ἱστημι also has intransitive 2nd Aorist, ἐστην (endings as ἐλυθην).<br>**Other moods** – As in the Present but using the verbal stem (i.e. missing the initial τι, δι or ἱ), except 2nd sing. Imperative which are θες, στηθι, δος and Infinitives θειναι, στηναι, δουναι. |

## 19.1.5 Other similar verbs

There are a few other verbs which share some of the same characteristics as these three 'proper' -μι verbs.

ἱημι (literally 'send' but only found in compounds such as ἀφιημι – I leave, forgive, dismiss, and συνιημι – I understand). This follows the same pattern as τιθημι with the Present stem ἱε and verbal stem ἑ.

**Verbs in -υμι** (such as δεικνυμι – I show, ἀπολλυμι – I destroy, ῥηγνυμι – I break). These have -μι verb endings in the Present tense (with the υ vowel dominating), but then use an altered stem for the other tenses along with the normal λυω endings (see the principal parts on page 253 for the details).

φημι **(I say)** This only appears in the following Indicative Active forms: Present: φημι, I say; φησιν, he says; φασιν, they say; Imperfect: ἐφη, he said.

εἰμι **(I am)** If you look back at the Present of εἰμι (Chapter 5, section 5.3) you will see that it has some similarities with the Present of the -μι verbs.

### Examples

Luke 5.21: τίς δυναται ἁμαρτιας ἀφειναι εἰ μη μονος ὁ θεος;
– Who is able to forgive sins except God alone?

Rev. 2.4: ἀλλα ἐχω κατα σου ὁτι την ἀγαπην σου την πρωτην ἀφηκες.
– But I have (this) against you that you abandoned your first love.

Matt. 4.7: ἐφη αὐτῳ ὁ Ἰησους· Παλιν γεγραπται ...
– Jesus said to him, 'Again it is written . . .'

Jas. 2.18: δειξον μοι την πιστιν σου χωρις των ἐργων, κἀγω σοι δειξω ἐκ των ἐργων μου την πιστιν. – Show me your faith without works, and I will show you my faith through my works.

**HALF-WAY PRACTICE**

1. διδοασιν τον μισθον αὐτων τοις στρατιωταις.
2. ὁ Ἰησους ἀνεστησεν τον νεκρον.
3. ἑστημεν μετα του κυριου ἐπι τῳ ὀρει.
4. ἀφεντες οὐκ ὑπεστρεψαν.
5. ἐφη ὁτι ἑστηκεν ἐκει.
6. ... ἑως ἀν θω τους ἐχθρους σου ὑπο των ποδων σου.
7. δος μοι τον ἀρτον της ζωης.
8. στας ὁ ἀποστολος ἐκηρυσσεν τῳ ὀχλῳ.
9. They handed over the teaching to the elders.
10. He made the sick man stand up in the synagogue.
11. After she had dismissed the crowd she began to pray.
12. While he was giving them the wine, he taught them.

## 19.2 αω AND οω VERBS

There are two other groups of contracting verbs similar to the -εω group (e.g. φιλεω). These follow the same general pattern as the -εω verbs, but the short α or ο at the end of their stems undergo slightly different contractions.

KEY GRAMMAR

Present and Imperfect – Contractions take place
Other tenses – Short vowel lengthens[2]

| | -εω<br>φιλεω – I love | -αω<br>τιμαω – I honour | -οω<br>πληροω – I fulfil |
|---|---|---|---|
| Present and Imperfect | ε + ε → ει<br>ε + ο → ου<br>ε + diphthong or long vowel drops out | α + ε or η → α<br>α + any ο → ω<br>α + any ι → ᾳ | ο + short vowel or ου → ου<br>ο + long vowel → ω<br>ο + any ι → οι |
| Other tenses | ε becomes η | α becomes η | ο becomes ω |

[2] Really, contractions occur when the α, ε, or ο is followed by a vowel (as in the Present and Imperfect), lengthening when followed by a consonant (as in the other tenses).

Notes

- The Present Infinitives of -αω and -οω verbs behave as if the Infinitive ending is -εν not -ειν, hence τιμαν and πληρουν.
- In the 3rd Sing. Imperfect Active Indicative of -εω, -αω and -οω verbs the 'optional ν' was not used. Thus the ending is ε giving: ἐφιλει, ἐτιμα, ἐπληρου.
- A few -εω verbs keep the ε in the other tenses e.g. καλεσω.

## Examples

- ἐφιλει – He was loving
- πεφιλημαι – I have been loved
- ἐτιμα – She was honouring
- τιμᾳς – You are honouring
- τιμησω – I will honour
- πληροι – It is fulfilling
- πληρουται – It is being fulfilled
- πεπληρωται – It has been fulfilled

2 Thes. 2.1: ἐρωτωμεν δε ὑμας, ἀδελφοι, ... – We ask you, brothers,

Eph. 6.2: τιμα τον πατερα σου και την μητερα – Honour your father and mother.

Gal. 2:20: ζω δε οὐκετι ἐγω, ζῃ δε ἐν ἐμοι Χριστος· ὃ δε νυν ζω ἐν σαρκι, ἐν πιστει ζω τῃ του υἱου του θεου του ἀγαπησαντος με και παραδοντος ἑαυτον ὑπερ ἐμου.
– It is no longer I who live, but Christ lives in me. What I now live in flesh I live by faith in the son of God who loved (lit: 'the one having loved') me and handed himself over for me.

Matt. 12.16-17: και ἐπετιμησεν αὐτοις ἱνα μη φανερον αὐτον ποιησωσιν, ἱνα πληρωθῃ το ῥηθεν δια Ἠσαϊου του προφητου ...
– And he rebuked them so that they would not make him known, in order that what was spoken through Isaiah the prophet might be fulfilled . . .

1 Tim. 3.16: ὃς ἐφανερωθη ἐν σαρκι, ἐδικαιωθη ἐν πνευματι ...
– who was revealed in flesh, justified in spirit . . .

PRACTICE 19.2

## Parse

1. πλανανται
2. πεπληρωμενος
3. ζω
4. ἐδικαιουν
5. μισησεις
6. ἀγαπαν
7. ἐνικησαν
8. τιμησουσιν
9. ἠρωτησεν
10. τιμᾳς
11. σταυρουται
12. πεινᾳ

## VOCAB FOR CHAPTER 19

-μι verbs
*διδωμι (415) – I give
ἀποδιδωμι (48) – I give away
*παραδιδωμι (119) – I hand over, entrust
*ἱστημι (155) – I cause to stand, stand
*ἀνιστημι (108) – I raise
παριστημι (41) – I place beside
*τιθημι (100) – I put, place
ἐπιτιθημι (39) – I put, place upon
ἀφιημι (143) – I leave, forgive, dismiss
*συνιημι (26) – I understand
*ἀπολλυμι (90) – I ruin, destroy[7]
δεικνυμι (33) – I point out, show
πιμπλημι (24) – I fulfil
φημι (66) – I say

-αω verbs
*ἀγαπαω (143) – I love
*γενναω (97) – I bear (beget)[3]
διψαω (16) – I thirst (for)
*ἐρωταω (63) – I ask[4]
ἐπερωταω (56) – I ask (for)[4]
*ζαω (140) – I live[5]
ἰαομαι (26) – I heal[6]
κοπιαω (23) – I labour
νικαω (28) – I overcome
πειναω (23) – I hunger
*πλαναω (39) – I deceive, lead astray
*τιμαω (21) – I honour, value
ἐπιτιμαω (29) – I rebuke
(plus ὁραω which we learnt in Chapter 11 because it has the 2nd Aorist εἰδον)

-οω verbs
δικαιοω (39) – I justify
*πληροω (86) – I fulfil, fill, complete
*σταυροω (46) – I crucify
τελειοω (23) – I accomplish, complete
*φανεροω (49) – I reveal, make known

### Word helps

donate/donor, stand, thesis/antithesis, affirm/euphemism, dipsomania, pediatrics/psychiatry, Nike™, planet, Timothy, indict, pleroma/plenary, teleology.

[3] In the Passive γενναω means 'I am born'.
[4] Like αἰτεω (Chapter 6), ἐρωταω and its compounds are followed by a double accusative – both the person asked and what is asked for occur in the accusative.
[5] ζαω behaves differently from other -αω verbs, contracting to an η rather than an α. Thus, for example, the Present Infinitive is ζην not ζαν.
[6] In the 'other tenses' (Future, Aorist and Perfect) the α in ἰαομαι remains an α rather than becoming an η. Thus, for example, the Future is ἰασομαι.
[7] The Middle of ἀπολλυμι (ἀπολλυμαι) means 'I perish.'

## Exercises

### Section A

*1. και ἀφεντες τον πατερα αὐτων Ζεβεδαιον ἐν τῳ πλοιῳ μετα των ἀλλων ἀπηλθον ὀπισω αὐτου.

*2. ὁ δε ἀποκριθεις εἰπεν αὐτοις· Δοτε αὐτοις ὑμεις φαγειν.

3. μακαριοι οἱ πεινωντες και διψωντες την δικαιοσυνην.

*4. ὁ δε ποιων την ἀληθειαν ἐρχεται προς το φως, ἱνα φανερωθῃ αὐτου τα ἐργα.

*5. ... ἱνα παντες τιμωσι τον υἱον καθως τιμωσι τον πατερα. ὁ μη τιμων τον υἱον οὐ τιμᾳ τον πατερα τον πεμψαντα αὐτον.

6. εἰπεν αὐτοις ὁ Ἰησους· Ἐγω εἰμι ὁ ἀρτος της ζωης· ὁ ἐρχομενος προς ἐμε οὐ μη πειναση, και ὁ πιστευων εἰς ἐμε οὐ μη διψηση.

*7. τουτο δε ἐστιν το θελημα του πεμψαντος με, ἱνα παν ὃ δεδωκεν μοι μη ἀπολεσω ἐξ αὐτου, ἀλλα ἀναστησω αὐτο ἐν τῃ ἐσχατῃ ἡμερᾳ.

8. οὑτος ἀκουσας ὁτι Ἰησους ἡκει ἐκ της Ἰουδαιας εἰς την Γαλιλαιαν ἀπηλθεν προς αὐτον και ἠρωτα ἱνα καταβῃ και ἰασηται αὐτου τον υἱον, ἠμελλεν γαρ ἀποθνῃσκειν.

*9. After he perished, he rose again.

10. A strong man will win – he labours and lives to win. (For 'win' use νικαω.)

*11. He asked where she was born.

12. We have led them astray from the path; who can justify us?

### Section B

1. ἀγαπητοι, ἀγαπωμεν ἀλληλους, ὁτι ἡ ἀγαπη ἐκ του θεου ἐστιν, και πας ὁ ἀγαπων ἐκ του θεου γεγεννηται και γινωσκει τον θεον.

2. μετα τουτο εἰδως ὁ Ἰησους ὁτι ἠδη παντα τετελεσται, ἱνα πληρωθῃ ἡ γραφη, λεγει· Διψω.

*3. και ἐνεδυσαν αὐτον τα ἱματια αὐτου και ἀπηγαγον [=ἀπ-ἀγω] αὐτον εἰς το σταυρωσαι αὐτον.

*4. οἱ δε εἰπαν αὐτῳ· Δος ἡμιν ἱνα εἱς σου ἐκ δεξιων και εἱς ἐξ ἀριστερων [*left*] καθισωμεν ἐν τῃ δοξῃ σου.

*5. τί οὐν ποιησει ὁ κυριος του ἀμπελωνος; ἐλευσεται και ἀπολεσει τους διακονους και δωσει τον ἀμπελωνα ἀλλοις.

*6. ὁ δε Ἰησους προσεκαλεσατο αὐτους λεγων· Ἀφετε τα παιδια ἐρχεσθαι προς με· των γαρ τοιουτων ἐστιν ἡ βασιλεια του θεου.

7. ἐντολην καινην διδωμι ὑμιν, ἱνα ἀγαπατε ἀλληλους· καθως ἠγαπησα ὑμας ἱνα και ὑμεις ἀγαπατε ἀλληλους.

*8. ἐν τῳ λαλειν τους μαθητας αὐτος ὁ Ἰησους ἐστη ἐν μεσῳ αὐτων και λεγει αὐτοις· Εἰρηνη ὑμιν.

*9. He knows to give good things in order to honour his friends.

10. The child, filled with wisdom, said [*use* φημι], 'I am standing where you left me.'
*11. His promise was fulfilled and he appeared standing before me.
12. He placed his hands on the sick child with the result that the child was healed.

## Section C

**Mark 3.24-30** καὶ ἐὰν βασιλεία ἐφ' ἑαυτὴν μερισθῇ [μεριζω = *divide*], οὐ
δύναται σταθῆναι ἡ βασιλεία ἐκείνη· [25] καὶ ἐὰν οἰκία ἐφ' ἑαυτὴν μερισθῇ,
οὐ δυνήσεται ἡ οἰκία ἐκείνη σταθῆναι. [26] καὶ εἰ ὁ Σατανᾶς ἀνέστη ἐφ'
ἑαυτὸν καὶ ἐμερίσθη, οὐ δύναται στῆναι ἀλλὰ τέλος ἔχει. [27] ἀλλ' οὐ
δύναται οὐδεὶς εἰς τὴν οἰκίαν τοῦ ἰσχυροῦ εἰσελθὼν τὰ σκεύη αὐτοῦ
διαρπάσαι [διαρπαζω = *plunder*], ἐὰν μὴ πρῶτον τὸν ἰσχυρὸν δήσῃ, καὶ τότε
τὴν οἰκίαν αὐτοῦ διαρπάσει. [28] Ἀμὴν λέγω ὑμῖν ὅτι πάντα ἀφεθήσεται τοῖς
υἱοῖς τῶν ἀνθρώπων τὰ ἁμαρτήματα [*sins*] καὶ αἱ βλασφημίαι [*blasphemies*]
ὅσα ἐὰν βλασφημήσωσιν· [29] ὃς δ' ἂν βλασφημήσῃ εἰς τὸ πνεῦμα τὸ ἅγιον,
οὐκ ἔχει ἄφεσιν [*forgiveness*] εἰς τὸν αἰῶνα, ἀλλὰ ἔνοχός [*guilty*] ἐστιν
αἰωνίου ἁμαρτήματος. [30] ὅτι ἔλεγον, Πνεῦμα ἀκάθαρτον ἔχει.

# Final pieces

## 20.1 CONDITIONS

Conditional sentences (those containing an 'if') are basically intuitive – you have been translating senses with εἰ ('if') in them since Chapter 5. However, it is possible to classify conditional sentences into a number of different groups, each with further sub-groups, with ever tighter definitions of exactly what is conveyed. This can be of some value, although a book on the *elements* of New Testament Greek is not the place for this level of detail. Furthermore, such analysis can be counter-productive, since sometimes it is rather doubtful whether writers were using conditionals quite so precisely. However, it is worth learning a little more about conditional sentences.

### 20.1.1 The basic conditional sentence[1]

Any conditional sentence has two parts:

| | *Protasis* – the 'if' clause | *Apodosis* – the 'then' clause |
|---|---|---|
| Gal. 5.18: | εἰ δε πνευματι ἀγεσθε | οὐκ ἐστε ὑπο νομον |
| | if you are led by the spirit | you are not under law |

The logic of any conditional sentence is:

If the Protasis is true, then the Apodosis is true.[2]

- E.g. 'If you like Greek (then) you are wise.'

When your teacher says this sentence, it conveys nothing about whether you do or don't like Greek. What it conveys is that (in the teacher's opinion) *IF* it is true that you like Greek *THEN* it is automatically true that you are wise.

[1] Sometimes called a fulfilled conditional or an 'assumed true' conditional.

[2] Strictly speaking we should say 'then the apodosis follows', since the apodosis is not always a statement that can be true or not. For example, it could be a command: 'If you like Greek, buy this book' means if the protasis is true ('you like Greek'), then the apodosis follows ('you should buy this book').

These conditional sentences are expressed in Greek simply by the use of the word εἰ corresponding to the English 'if', as you have been doing since Chapter 5.

### 20.1.2 Two variations on the basic conditional

There are two ways in which Greek alters the basic conditional sentence to give a different flavour.

#### (a) Indefinite conditions (ἐαν + Subjunctive)

Sometimes Greek will use ἐαν + Subjunctive rather than εἰ + Indicative in the protasis. In such a condition, it is still the case that *IF* the protasis is true *THEN* the apodosis follows. However, the Subjunctive conveys the sense that there is something 'indefinite', not completely defined, about the protasis.[3]

Often this indefiniteness is merely because the condition speaks about the future, which is by definition somewhat undefined, and thus this whole group of conditions are often called 'future conditions'.

- E.g. 'If you like Greek, you will learn it.'

However, sometimes, ἐαν + Subjunctive is used to highlight the fact that the protasis is indefinite because it addresses a generic situation, without a particular occasion being in mind.

- E.g. 'If someone enjoys rules and patterns, they like Greek.'

(The speaker does not have a particular person or occasion in mind – it is a generalised statement.)

#### (b) 'Contrary to fact' conditions (ἀν in apodosis)

Sometimes Greek will put the word ἀν in the apodosis. In such a condition, it is still the case that *IF* the protasis is true *THEN* the apodosis follows. However, the writer is deliberately expressing that they believe that the protasis is not true. These conditions are sometimes called 'unfulfilled conditions'.

- E.g. 'If you had liked Greek, you would have learnt it.'

---

[3] Useful parallels can be drawn between these indefinite conditions and indefinite clauses (Chapter 17, section 17.3.1). Indefinite clauses can be seen as normal (definite) clauses to which ἀν + Subjunctive are added to express the indefiniteness.
*Definite*: ὁτε ἐσθιεις – when you eat – ὁτε (when) + Indicative.
*Indefinite*: ὁταν ἐσθιῃς – whenever you eat – ὁταν (=ὁτε + ἀν) + Subjunctive – suggesting a level of indefiniteness; a generic situation, not a particular occasion.
Similarly with conditions the basic form is (a) εἰ + Indicative, but one can use (b) ἐαν (=εἰ + ἀν) + Subjunctive to suggest a level of indefiniteness.

Here the speaker is saying two things: (1) that if you like Greek you will learn it (a basic condition) and (2) that you didn't like Greek (the force of the ἀν).[4]

**Hint**

In English, *contrary to fact conditions* have the word 'would' in the *apodosis.*

## 20.1.3 The form of conditionals in Greek

| | Protasis | Apodosis |
|---|---|---|
| Basic conditions | εἰ + Indicative | Any mood or tense |
| Indefinite conditions | ἐαν + Subjunctive | Any mood or tense |
| 'Contrary to fact' conditions | εἰ + Indicative[5] | ἀν + Indicative[5] |

The key principles of conditional sentences can be summarised thus:

**KEY GRAMMAR**

Protasis: εἰ + Indicative = If
ἐαν + Subjunctive = If (*future/generalised/hypothetical*)

Apodosis: ἀν = Would (*protasis seen as untrue*)

Examples

Basic conditions (fulfilled)

Gal. 3.29: εἰ δε ὑμεις Χριστου, ἀρα του Ἀβρααμ σπερμα ἐστε.
– If you are Christ's, then you are Abraham's offspring.

1 Cor. 8.3: εἰ δε τις ἀγαπᾳ τον θεον, οὑτος ἐγνωσται ὑπ' αὐτου.
– If someone loves God, he is known by him.

Luke 23.37: εἰ συ εἶ ὁ βασιλευς των Ἰουδαιων, σωσον σεαυτον.
– If you are the king of Israel, save yourself!

Luke 11.19: εἰ δε ἐγω ἐν Βεελζεβουλ ἐκβαλλω τα δαιμονια, οἱ υἱοι ὑμων ἐν τίνι ἐκβαλλουσιν; – If I cast out demons by Beelzeboul, by whom do your sons cast them out?

[4] Being precise, the 'contrary to fact' condition does not convey that the protasis is false, but only that the speaker thinks that it is false. E.g. Luke 7.39: οὑτος εἰ ἠν προφητης, ἐγινωσκεν ἀν ... 'If this man were a prophet he would know. . . '. The speaker thinks that Jesus is not a prophet, but the author of the gospel may well think that he is.

[5] In both the protasis and apodosis the Imperfect is used for references to present time, and the Aorist for references to past time. Note also that if the protasis of an 'contrary to fact' condition is negative μη is used (strangely, given the verb is in the Indicative).

Indefinite conditions

Matt. 9.21: ἐαν μονον ἁψωμαι του ἱματιου αὐτου, σωθησομαι.
– If only I touch his cloak, I will be saved.

John 14.14: ἐαν τι αἰτησητε με ἐν τῳ ὀνοματι μου, ἐγω ποιησω.
– If you ask me for anything in my name, I will do it.

1 Cor. 14.14: ἐαν γαρ προσευχωμαι γλωσσῃ, το πνευμα μου προσευχεται.
– because if I pray in a tongue, my spirit prays.

1 John 2.15: ἐαν τις ἀγαπᾳ τον κοσμον, οὐκ ἐστιν ἡ ἀγαπη του πατρος ἐν αὐτῳ. – If someone loves the world, the love of the father is not in him.

Unfulfilled conditions

John 5.46: εἰ γαρ ἐπιστευετε Μωϋσει, ἐπιστευετε ἀν ἐμοι.
– For if you believed Moses, you would believe me.

1 Cor. 2.8: εἰ γαρ ἐγνωσαν, οὐκ ἀν τον κυριον της δοξης ἐσταυρωσαν
– For if they had known, they would not have crucified the lord of glory.

Heb. 8.4: εἰ μεν οὐν ἠν ἐπι γης, οὐδ᾽ ἀν ἠν ἱερευς.
– Therefore if he were on earth, he would not even be a priest.

**PRACTICE 20.1**

## Translate

1. εἰ φιλεις τον θεον, σοφος εἶ.
2. εἰ ἠκουσεν οὐκ ἀν ἀπεθανεν.
3. ἐαν ὁ βασιλευς ἐξελθῃ, οἱ δουλοι ἀπολυθησονται.
4. εἰ το εὐαγγελιον κηρυσσεται, χαιρετε.
5. εἰ ἀκαθαρτοι ἠμεν, οὐκ ἀν ἐν τῳ ἱερῳ ἐκαθημεθα.
6. ἐαν ἐγω δω σοι, δωσεις οὐν συ ἀλλοις;

## 20.2 THE GENITIVE ABSOLUTE

Mark 14.17: και ὀψιας γενομενης ἐρχεται μετα των δωδεκα.
– When it was evening, he comes (came) with the twelve.
(lit: 'evening having happened')

Here the word evening ὀψια is in the genitive, and γενομενης (Aorist participle of γινομαι – 'having happened') is gen. fem. sing. to agree with it. But why is ὀψια in the genitive? It is not a possessor, nor is it governed by a preposition. What place does it have in the sentence? It is not subject or object. This is an example of a particular construction using participles called the *genitive absolute*.

The genitive absolute is a noun with a participle agreeing with it which is 'separated off' from the rest of the sentence (this is what 'absolute' means, from the Latin ab-solutus – 'separated off' – it has nothing to do with 'absolutely'). This separation is in meaning – the noun does not have a place in the main sentence – which is then expressed by the noun and participle occurring in the genitive (which makes sure you can't confuse them with the subject or object of the main sentence).

Up to now, you have been able to represent every sentence, however complex, by a map of interconnected units, based round a skeleton of subject, verb and (normally) object. For example, the sentence 'While he was passing along the sea, he saw Simon and Andrew casting (nets) in the sea' (Mark 1.28) could be represented in the diagram on this page.

Here the main sentence is shaded grey, and all the rest of the sentence connects to it, and hence the *case* of the other pieces of the sentence can be determined: 'passing' agrees with 'he', the subject of the sentence, and so is nominative; 'casting' agrees with 'Simon and Andrew', the object of the sentence, and so is accusative.

However, if we take our example from Mark 14.17: 'Evening having happened, he comes with the twelve', the diagram would look rather different, for there is no connection between 'evening having happened' and 'he comes with the twelve'. Thus, 'evening having happened' is a 'separated-off' clause, which does not connect to the main sentence.

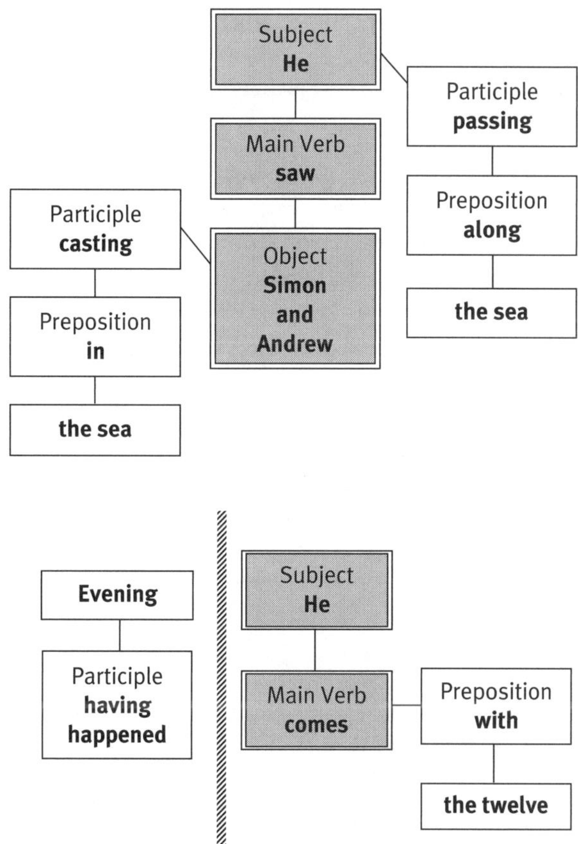

Therefore in Greek it will be a genitive absolute, and thus 'evening' and 'having happened' will be in the genitive.[6]

**Hint**

- Genitive absolutes normally occur at the beginning of sentences – so if the first word in a sentence is in the genitive, 'think genitive absolute'.
- Very often genitive absolutes give some 'background information', such as the time or circumstances at which something happened.

Examples

Mark 14.66: και ὀντος του Πετρου κατω ἐν τῃ αὐλῃ ἐρχεται μια των παιδισκων.
– While Peter was below in the Hall, one of the servant-girls came.

Matt. 26.21: και ἐσθιοντων αὐτων εἰπεν· Ἀμην λεγω ὑμιν ...
– While they were eating, Jesus said, 'Amen I say to you. . .'

Rom. 5.13: ἁμαρτια δε οὐκ ἐλλογειται μη ὀντος νομου.
– Sin is not counted when there is no law.

**HALF-WAY PRACTICE**

1. ἐλθοντος δε Ἰησου οἱ διδασκαλοι ἐθαυμαζον.
2. εἰ γαρ ἐβλεπον ἐπιστευον ἀν.
3. του δε βασιλεως ἀποθανοντος ἠλθον εἰς την Γαλιλαιαν.
4. ἡμερας γενομενης ἐλαλει τῳ ὀχλῳ.
5. ἐαν τα δαιμονια ἐκβληθῃ εὐχαριστησομεν.
6. του γαρ λογου κηρυσσομενου οἱ ἀκουοντες ἐπιστευσαν.
7. αὐτου δε ὀντος ἁγιου παντες ἐφοβουντο.
8. εἰ ὁ νομος οὐκ ἐδωθη, οὐκ ἀν ἐγνωσαν την ἁμαρτιαν.
9. As she came in the angel said to her, '. . .
10. If he is holy he will worship God.
11. If it were day we would not be afraid.
12. When he had been raised everyone was amazed.

[6] In the Greek of the time this rule was breaking down, and we will often find a genitive absolute used when the noun involved does in fact turn up elsewhere in the sentence, but the use of a genitive absolute avoids creating a rather complex sentence. E.g. Mark 9.28: και εἰσελθοντος αὐτου εἰς οἰκον οἱ μαθηται αὐτου κατ' ἰδιαν ἐπηρωτων αὐτον . . . – 'And as he was going into a house his disciples asked him privately . . . '. Here εἰσελθοντος could have been made to agree with the αὐτον but the use of the genitive absolute breaks the sentence into smaller blocks, making it easier to understand.

## 20.3 PERIPHRASTICS

As we already know, Greek forms tenses by adding suffixes and prefixes to the verb, while English forms them by adding auxiliary words (e.g. I was going – ἠγον). However, Greek does upon occasion use a construction similar to English using an auxiliary word plus a participle. This is called a periphrastic construction.[7]

| Tense | Periphrastic Construction |
|---|---|
| Present | Present of εἰμι + Present participle |
| Imperfect | Imperfect of εἰμι + Present participle |
| Future | Future of εἰμι + Present participle |
| Perfect | Present of εἰμι + Perfect participle |
| Pluperfect[8] | Imperfect of εἰμι + Perfect participle |
| Future Perfect[8] | Future of εἰμι + Perfect participle |

In Classical Greek the periphrastic constructions emphasised the continuous force of the participle (either continuous occurrence – Present participle, or the continuation of the completed state – Perfect participle). This is why the Aorist participle is never used in periphrastic constructions. However, it is doubtful that any such emphasis is present in the periphrastic constructions in the New Testament, and for two reasons. First, as Greek developed from the Classical period to the New Testament period, this emphasis seems to have waned. Second, in Aramaic, Imperfects are always expressed using a periphrastic construction, and this idiom may have influenced the occurrences in the New Testament writings.

### Examples

Mark 2.18: ἠσαν οἱ μαθηται Ἰωαννου και οἱ Φαρισαιοι νηστευοντες.
– The disciples of John and the Pharisees were fasting.
Eph. 2.5: χαριτι ἐστε σεσωσμενοι – By grace you have been saved.
2 John 12: ... ἱνα ἡ χαρα ἡμων πεπληρωμενη ᾐ.
– . . . in order that our joy might be complete.
(Note: here the periphrastic uses the Present Subjunctive of εἰμι after ἱνα.)

---

[7] The name derives from περι (around, about) and φραζω (I explain), since they explain their meaning in a round-about fashion.

[8] English 'equivalents': Pluperfect 'I had loosened'; Future Perfect 'I will have loosened'.

**PRACTICE 20.3**

## Translate

1. ὁ διδασκαλος ἠν καθημενος μετ᾽ αὐτων.
2. ἐν τῳ προφητῃ ἐστιν γεγραμμενον.
3. και ἠν Ἰωσηφ ἐνδεδυμενος καλον ἱματιον.
4. τιμωμενος δε ἐσται ὁ προφητης.

## 20.4 COMPARISON AND FORMATION OF ADJECTIVES AND ADVERBS

From any adjective you can form a corresponding adverb, and from an adjective or adverb, you can form two variants – the comparative and the superlative.

As in English, there is a pattern by which these are normally formed, but some of the more common adjectives and adverbs have irregular forms. There is a further slight variation – if the last letter of the adjective or adverb's stem is short, ω is used as the joining vowel in the comparative and superlative, while if it is long or a diphthong, ο is used.

For example: σοφος has a short vowel at the end of the stem: σοφ-
δικαιος has a diphthong at the end of the stem: δικαι-

| | | Example | |
|---|---|---|---|
| | | Short Vowel | Long Vowel or Diphthong |
| Adjective | wise | σοφος | δικαιος |
| *Comparative* adjective | wiser, more wise | σοφωτερος | δικαιοτερος |
| *Superlative* adjective | wisest, most/very wise | σοφωτατος | δικαιοτατος |
| Adverb | wisely | σοφως | δικαιως |
| *Comparative* adverb | more wisely | σοφωτερον | δικαιοτερον |
| *Superlative* adverb | most/very wisely | σοφωτατα | δικαιοτατα |

## Common irregular forms

**Adjectives**

| | | | | | | | |
|---|---|---|---|---|---|---|---|
| ἀγαθος | good | → | κρεισσων | better | | | |
| κακος | bad | → | χειρων | worse | | | |
| μεγας | great | → | μειζων | greater | | | |
| πολυς | much | → | πλειων | more | | | |
| μικρος | small | → | μικροτερος | smaller | → | ἐλαχιστος | smallest |

| Adjective | | | Adverbs | | | | |
|---|---|---|---|---|---|---|---|
| ἀγαθος | good | → | εὐ | well | | | |
| Unused root | | → | μαλλον | more | → | μαλιστα | most |
| πολυς | much | → | πολλα | greatly | | | |

Notes

- We learnt in Chapter 12, section 12.4 that comparison is expressed in Greek either by a genitive or by the use of the word ἤ with the second noun in the same case as the first.
- μαλλον is the *adverb* 'more' (qualifying a verb), while πλειων is the *adjective* 'more' (qualifying a noun).
- The superlative was gradually falling out of use, and often the comparative was used in its place.

**Hint**

It is helpful to remember that words ending in -ως are adverbs. You should now understand how the forms καλως, ὁμοιως and οὑτως, which you learnt earlier, have been formed from καλος, ὁμοιος and οὑτος.

Examples

- ἀξιως – in a worthy manner
- παντως – by all means
- ὀντως – really
- πρωτως – for the first time

Mark 1.32: ἐφερον προς αὐτον παντας τους <u>κακως</u> ἐχοντας.
– They were bringing to him all those who were sick (lit: the ones 'having <u>badly</u>').

Mark 5.23: λεγων ὁτι Το θυγατριον μου <u>ἐσχατως</u> ἐχει.
– saying, 'My daughter is dying' (lit: has <u>finally</u>).

1 Cor. 7.40: <u>μακαριωτερα</u> δε ἐστιν ἐαν <u>οὑτως</u> μεινῃ.
– She is <u>more blessed</u> if she remains as she is (lit: <u>thus</u>).

---

PRACTICE 20.4

## Parse

1. ἁγιωτατα
2. ἐλαχιστοις
3. κακωτερου
4. πονηροτατοι
5. μειζοντα
6. ἱκανως

## 20.5 THE OPTATIVE

In Classical Greek there was a sixth mood, called the optative, which is best thought of as an even less certain form of the subjunctive. However, by the New Testament period its use was rare, except among those writers trying to imitate the style of writing of the past (cf. non-deponent use of the Middle – Chapter 15, section 15.6.1). It does occur, though, in a famous phrase of Paul – μη γενοιτο – 'may it not be!'

The optative was used:

1. For wishes
2. For indirect questions (i.e. questions within reported speech).

The optatives were formed in a similar way to subjunctives, but rather than being marked out be a long η or ω, they have the diphthongs οι or αι.

Examples

Rom. 6.1-2: ἐπιμενωμεν τῃ ἁμαρτιᾳ, ἱνα ἡ χαρις πλεονασῃ; <u>μη γενοιτο</u>.
– Should we remain in sin in order that grace abounds? <u>By no means</u>!

Luke 1.38: <u>γενοιτο</u> μοι κατα το ῥημα σου.
– <u>May it be</u> to me according to your word.

## VOCAB FOR CHAPTER 20

Important adverbs, comparatives and superlatives
*ἀληθως (18) – truly
*ἐλαχιστος (14) – smallest
εὐ (5) – well
*κρεισσων (19) – better

μαλιστα (12) – most of all
*μαλλον (81) – more, rather
*μικρον (16) – a little, a short time
*μικρος (46) – small
χειρων (11) – worse

A final few more nouns
*ζῳον (23) – living thing
*θυσιαστηριον (23) – altar
ποιμην, ποιμενος, ὁ (18) – shepherd

and verbs
θεαομαι (22) – I see, look at
*καυχαομαι (37) – I boast
*μιμνῃσκομαι (23) + gen. – I remember
νιπτω (17) – I wash

### Word helps

<u>eu</u>phemism/<u>eu</u>logy/<u>eu</u>thanasia, <u>micro</u>scope/o<u>micro</u>n, <u>zoo</u>, <u>thea</u>tre, <u>mne</u>monic.

## Exercises

### Section A

*1. και τοτε ἐαν τις ὑμιν εἰπῃ· Ἰδε ὡδε ὁ Χριστος, Ἰδε ἐκει, μη πιστευετε.

*2. και προελθων μικρον ἐπιπτεν ἐπι της γης και προσηυχετο ἱνα εἰ δυνατον ἐστιν παρελθῃ ἀπ᾽ αὐτου ἡ ὡρα.

*3. ἀπεκριθη Ἰησους· Ἀμην ἀμην λεγω σοι, ἐαν μη τις γεννηθῃ ἐξ ὑδατος και πνευματος, οὐ δυναται εἰσελθειν εἰς την βασιλειαν του θεου.

4. μετα ταυτα εὑρισκει αὐτον ὁ Ἰησους ἐν τῳ ἱερῳ και εἰπεν αὐτῳ· Ἰδε ὑγιης [*well*] γεγονας. μηκετι ἁμαρτανε, ἱνα μη χειρον σοι τι γενηται.

5. ὁ γαρ πατηρ φιλει τον υἱον και παντα δεικνυσιν αὐτῳ ἃ αὐτος ποιει, και μειζονα τουτων δειξει αὐτῳ ἐργα, ἱνα ὑμεις θαυμαζητε.

6. ἐγω δε ἐχω την μαρτυριαν μειζονα του Ἰωαννου· τα γαρ ἐργα ἃ δεδωκεν μοι ὁ πατηρ ἱνα τελειωσω αὐτα, αὐτα τα ἐργα ἃ ποιω μαρτυρει περι ἐμου ὁτι ὁ πατηρ με ἀπεσταλκεν.

*7. και ἐθαυμαζον ἐπι τῃ διδαχῃ αὐτου ἐτι μαλλον· ἠν γαρ διδασκων αὐτους ὡς ἐξουσιαν ἐχων και οὐχ ὡς οἱ γραμματεις.

8. και γενομενου σαββατου ἠρξατο διδασκειν ἐν τῃ συναγωγῃ, και πολλοι ἀκουοντες ἐθαυμασαν λεγοντες· Ποθεν τουτῳ ταυτα, και τίς ἡ σοφια, και αἱ δυναμεις τοιαυται δια των χειρων αὐτου γινομεναι;

9. Let us remember the shepherd of our souls.

10. If the son makes you free, you will be truly [*really*] free.

*11. He was teaching [*use periphrastic*] them about love for the least of the brothers and for all living things.

12. Will I crucify again the one who washed me from sin? May it never be!

### Section B

1. ἠσαν δε τινες των γραμματεων ἐκει καθημενοι και λογιζομενοι ἐν ταις καρδιαις αὐτων.

*2. ἐαν ἐγω μαρτυρω περι ἐμαυτου, ἡ μαρτυρια μου οὐκ ἐστιν ἀληθης.

3. Ἐγω εἰμι ὁ ποιμην ὁ καλος και εὐ γινωσκω τα ἐμα και γινωσκει με τα ἐμα.

4. και ἐθεασαμεθα την δοξαν αὐτου και μιμνῃσκομεθα μαλιστα του κυριου της δοξης νιπτοντος τους ποδας ἡμων.

*5. αὐτη ἐγερθησεται ἐν τῃ κρισει μετα των ἀνδρων της γενεας ταυτης και κατακρινεῖ [κατα + κρινω = *I condemn*] αὐτους, ὁτι ἠλθεν ἀκουσαι την σοφιαν του βασιλεως, και ἰδου πλειον του βασιλεως ὡδε.

*6. Ἐγενετο δε ἐν τῳ βαπτισθηναι ἁπαντα τον λαον και Ἰησου βαπτισθεντος και προσευχομενου ἀνεῳχθηναι τον οὐρανον.

*7. και ἐρχεται το τριτον και λεγει αὐτοις· Καθευδετε το λοιπον; ἠλθεν ἡ ὡρα, ἰδου παραδιδοται ὁ υἱος του ἀνθρωπου εἰς τας χειρας των ἁμαρτωλων.

8. ἐαν οὐν προσφερῃς τι ἐπι το θυσιαστηριον και μνησθῃς ἐκει ὁτι ὁ ἀδελφος σου ἐχει τι κατα σου, ὑποστρεφε εὐθυς προς αὐτον και ἐρωτα εἰρηνην.

*9. If we live, it is better to live well and to love one another.

10. When the shepherds had arrived, they saw the sleeping child.

*11. He who has given you all things in Christ, will he not also give you his love?

*12. I have a beautiful and very wise wife.

## Section C

**1 Corinthians 13.1-3** Ἐὰν ταῖς γλώσσαις τῶν ἀνθρώπων λαλῶ καὶ τῶν ἀγγέλων, ἀγάπην δὲ μὴ ἔχω, γέγονα χαλκὸς [*brass*] ἠχῶν [ἠχεω *be noisy*] ἢ κύμβαλον [*cymbal*] ἀλαλάζον [ἀλαλαζω *clang*]. [2] καὶ ἐὰν ἔχω προφητείαν [*prophecy*] καὶ εἰδῶ τὰ μυστήρια πάντα καὶ πᾶσαν τὴν γνῶσιν καὶ ἐὰν ἔχω πᾶσαν τὴν πίστιν ὥστε ὄρη μεθιστάναι [μεθιστημι *remove*], ἀγάπην δὲ μὴ ἔχω, οὐθέν [=οὐδεν] εἰμι. [3] κἂν ψωμίσω [*feed, give away*] πάντα τὰ ὑπάρχοντά μου καὶ ἐὰν παραδῶ τὸ σῶμά μου ἵνα καυχήσωμαι, ἀγάπην δὲ μὴ ἔχω, οὐδὲν ὠφελοῦμαι [ὠφελεω *gain, profit, benefit*]

- - - - - - - - - - - - - - - - - - - - - - - - - - -

χαιρε·
νυν γαρ οἰδας την γλωσσαν των Ἑλληνων.
το βιβλιον ἠν κακον και το ἐργον μεγα,
ἀλλα τετελειωται· συ νενικηκας.
ὀλιγον δε μισθον μιμνῃσκου δουναι τῳ διδασκαλῳ σου,
τοτε ὑπαγαγων ἀναγνω την καινην διαθηκην.

- - - - - - - - - - - - - - - - - - - - - - - - - - -

# Going further

The aim of this book was: 'To help you learn enough Greek to read the New Testament.' If you have completed the twenty chapters, have a reasonable (not perfect) grasp of their main points, and have practised with the sentences and passages along the way, then you have reached this goal. All you now need is more practice. To begin with you will find reading the New Testament quite slow, but soon your reading will become faster and more fluent, and far more enjoyable.

There are a wide variety of tools designed to help you become more fluent and reference works that provide more depth than has been possible in this book. I list some of these below grouped into various categories. Remember, though, your goal was not to be able to progress to more complicated Greek books, but to read the New Testament. So do that – make a start today! And if at all possible, don't read alone – find a couple of others who will join you. That way you can encourage each other, and what you have forgotten someone else will probably have remembered, so you will go much faster. Quite quickly you will find the commonly occurring vocabulary and grammar becomes very familiar, allowing you to focus your energies on the more unusual or complicated words and phrases. Enjoy it!

## The basics

**A Copy of the Greek New Testament** – You will need one of these. Older copies may have a slightly different text owing to developments in textual criticism. The best option is probably the United Bible Society's (4$^{th}$ edn) *The Greek New Testament* (Stuttgart: Deutsche Bibelgesellschaft, 2001). The other possibility is the *Novum Testamentum Graece* (27$^{th}$ edn, 2001) also from the Deutsche Bibelgesellschaft (known as Nestle-Aland after the names of its editors). These two give the same text, but differ in the 'apparatus' (notes) they give for textual criticism.

**A Dictionary** – The dictionary at the back of this book lists only the most common words in the New Testament. As you start to read, you will encounter others, so you will need a dictionary (or 'lexicon'). There are various available, but for a relatively cheap, easy-to-use dictionary try W.C. Trenchard's *A Concise Dictionary of the New Testament* (Cambridge: Cambridge University Press, 2003). The standard dictionary for scholarly work (far more detailed but also more expensive, and more bulky) is *A Greek-English Lexicon of the New Testament and Other Early Christian Literature* edited by F.W. Danker (and others)(Chicago: University of Chicago Press, 3rd edn, 2000). Some editions of the United Bible Society's Greek text come with a dictionary in the back, which can also be very useful.

## Helps

There are all sorts of books produced to help you read the Greek New Testament.

**Verse-by-verse helps** – These comment on each verse in order for you not to need to keep searching though reference works, which makes them ideal companions when reading. S. Kubo's *A Reader's Greek-English Lexicon of the New Testament* (Grand Rapids, MI: Zondervan, 1975) focuses on vocabulary, while M. Zerwick and M. Grosvenor's *A Grammatical Analysis New Testament* (Rome: Editrice Pontificio Istituto Biblico, 5th edn, 1996) also parses unusual grammatical forms. Into this category also come *interlinears*, where the Greek text is given on one line, and an English translation below. These can be useful, but do little to help you *understand* the Greek.

**Vocab-builders** – These categorise Greek words in various ways to help you expand your working vocabulary as easily and as memorably as possible. Current options include B.M. Metzger's *Lexical Aids for Students of New Testament Greek* (Grand Rapids, MI: Baker Books, 3rd edn, 1993) and W.C. Trenchard's *The Student's Complete Vocabulary Guide to the Greek New Testament* (Grand Rapids, MI: Zondervan, 1997).

**Analytical dictionaries** – These list every form that occurs in the New Testament, and tells you what basic word it has come from (e.g. it would list ἐλυσαν and not just λυω). Current options include those by B. and T. Friberg, W.D. Mounce and W.J. Pershbacher.

## Further reference tools

You may want to look at a more detailed analysis of **Greek grammar**. For this D.B. Wallace's *Greek Grammar Beyond the Basics* (Grand Rapids, MI: Zondervan, 2000) is good but daunting (he has produced a shorter version called *The Basics of New Testament Syntax* [Grand Rapids, MI: Zondervan, 2000]). An older standard is *A Greek Grammar of the New Testament and Other Early Christian*

*Literature* edited by F. Blass and A. Debrunner (translated by R. Funk) (Chicago: University of Chicago Press, 1961).

A **Greek concordance** can be useful – some quote the word's usage in English (such as the one by J.R. Kohlenberger III), others quote it in Greek (such as the one by W.F. Moulton, A.S. Geden, H.K. Moulton, and I.H. Marshall).

## New skills

You may want learn about **textual criticism** – the process by which our printed modern texts of the Greek New Testament are produced from the many ancient copies we have. On this see *The Text of the New Testament* either by K. and B. Aland (Grand Rapids, MI: Eerdmans, 2nd edn, 1996) or by B.M. Metzger (Oxford: Oxford University Press, 3rd edn, 1992) (whose *A Textual Commentary on the Greek New Testament* [Stuttgart: Deutsche Bibelgesellschaft, 2nd edn, 1995] is also very useful, commenting on all the most important passages).

If you are going on in academic work, you may need to learn to use **Greek accents**. For this see D.A. Carson's *Greek Accents: A Student's Manual* (Grand Rapids, MI: Baker Books, 1985).

## Computers

There are a growing number of useful computer tools for Greek, in particular *Bibleworks* and *Gramcord*, both of which allow you to conduct extensive investigations and searches for grammatical constructions or occurrences of particular words. The Internet contains a constantly expanding range of information and resources – links can be found on this book's website: www.nt-greek.net.

# Comparative English grammar

## Why a section on English grammar?

The aim of this textbook is to help you learn Greek, not English. You already know English perfectly well and are already using English grammar all the time. However, many readers will be using English grammar implicitly, without realising it, because many people today learn English without any focus on formal grammar. Whether this matters or not is a moot point and not an argument to be gone into here. However, it can be unfortunate when you start to learn a foreign language, particularly a language like Greek whose structure and grammar are actually very similar to English. Often Greek grammar is best explained by reference to English. For example, Greek sentences have subjects and objects just as English does. If you already understand what a subject and an object is (from English), then all you need to learn about Greek is that the subject is put in the *nominative* case and the object in the *accusative* case. This explanation does not work, though, if you have never met the terms 'subject' and 'object' before. In these situations it can be helpful first to understand what 'subject' and 'object' are in English, and then to learn how they are pressed in Greek. This is why there is a section on English grammar in a Greek textbook.

## How to use this guide

This guide does not intend to give an overview of English grammar. Rather, it contains explanations of English grammar that may help with your learning of the Greek covered in this book. You may wish to read through the whole of this guide, to familiarise yourself with the grammatical terminology used, and the aspects of English grammar that are highlighted. However, the guide is intended to be a reference tool – at various points within Chapters 1–20 you will be referred to the appropriate part of this guide. For example, when in Chapter 2 you meet the idea of subjects and objects in Greek, you are referred to section 3 of this guide, which explains subjects and objects in English. In a similar way, when grammatical terms occur in the index, they refer both to where they are taught in Greek and to where the English parallel is given in this guide.

## Contents



## 1. The parts of speech

An obvious first question to ask of any word is 'What type of word is it?' For example, 'put' is a different sort of word from 'coat', and 'on' is very different again. They are called different *parts of speech*. There are eight different *parts of speech*: that is, eight different types of word. Many of the chapters of this book are focused on explaining how Greek handles a particular part of speech, e.g. Chapter 5 looks at *adjectives*, while Chapter 2 introduces basic *verbs* and *nouns*. Being clear as to what the different parts of speech are in English is vital if you are to grasp how they are formed and used in Greek.

### 1.1 Noun

A noun is the name of any person or thing. For example, 'coat', 'Jim', 'peace'.

Most nouns are in fact the name given to the common link between a number of things or people. 'Cup' is the name given to all cups, which expresses the fact that although I have one cup that is large and another that is old, they are both part of the same group of things – they are both cups. Therefore formally many nouns are called *common nouns*.[1]

[1] The more you think about this, the more complicated it becomes. It was the Greek philosopher Plato (c. 427–347 BC) who was first recorded as debating what it is about a cup that makes it a cup, when they can come in many different types and sizes.

Another type of noun is a *proper noun.* This is the name given to a particular person, place or thing. For example – Jeremy, Oxford, Wycliffe Hall. In English and in Greek we mark out proper nouns by giving them capital letters.

A third type of noun is an *abstract noun.* This is the name of a quality, state or action rather than a person or thing. For example – love, peace, destruction.

### 1.2 Verb

A verb is a word describing an action. For example – sing, learn, eat.

Sometimes 'action' needs to be interpreted loosely. In the sentence 'he is hot', or 'it exists in my dreams', 'is' and 'exists' are verbs, although you might not think of them as actions. Nevertheless you could say that 'being hot' is what 'he' is doing, or 'existing' is what 'it' is doing.

### 1.3 Pronoun

A pronoun is a word used to replace a noun. For example – she, this, who.

Whenever a pronoun is used, you should be able to identify what noun it is replacing. This noun is called the *antecedent*, and it affects the choice of pronoun. Consider the two sentences: 'Mary eats the cake. Mary likes the cake.' In English this sounds strange. You would normally replace the second occurrence of the word Mary with a pronoun. Because the antecedent of the pronoun is Mary, you would use the pronoun 'she' (if the antecedent were John you would use 'he' or if it were 'the children' you would say 'they'). Similarly you would replace the second occurrence of 'cake' with 'it'. Thus you would actually say 'Mary eats the cake. She likes it.' The sentence 'she likes it', contains two pronouns, 'she' and 'it', each of which is replacing a particular noun.

There are many subdivisions of pronouns, but they all share the same function of replacing a noun. For example, 'who' is a 'relative pronoun' because it relates together what could be two independent sentences. Rather than writing 'John envies Mary. Mary ate the cake', you write 'John envies Mary who ate the cake' ('Mary' is the antecedent of 'who').

### 1.4 Adjective

An adjective is a word that is joined to a noun to qualify its meaning (that is, to add something to it). For example – new, my, three.

Most adjectives answer the questions 'What kind of?' or 'How many?' (adjectives of *quality* or *quantity*). However, there are some other types of adjective that are slightly different. *Demonstrative* adjectives such as 'this' or 'those' answer the question 'Which?'; *possessive* adjectives such as 'my' or 'our' answer the question 'Whose?'; *interrogative* adjectives *ask* questions, such as 'Which?' Nevertheless, all adjectives are joined to a noun. In the sentences '*This* cake is good', '*My* cake has gone' '*Which* cake was eaten?' 'this', 'my' and 'which' all qualify 'cake' and so are adjectives.

The word 'the' is a special type of adjective. It is called the '*definite article*' and is sometimes considered a separate part of speech (alongside its partner the 'indefinite article' – 'a'). However, it is joined to a noun to qualify its meaning, so it can be seen as an adjective. For example, consider the sentences – 'Mary likes cake' and 'Mary likes the cake.' The word 'the' in the second sentence qualifies 'cake' and tells us that it is a particular cake that is being referred to, not cake in general.

## 1.5 Prepositions

A preposition is a word (or phrase) joined to a noun (or pronoun) that indicates the relationship between the noun / pronoun and another part of the sentence: for example – into, with, on behalf of.

In English as in Greek, the noun (pronoun) that a preposition is joined to normally comes immediately after it. In the sentence 'He went into the house', 'into' is a preposition joined to 'house' (or *governing* 'house'), indicating the relationship between 'the house' and 'he went'. The relationship would be different if the preposition 'out of' had been used, or 'on to'. Similarly 'he went <u>with</u> them' or 'Christ died <u>on behalf of</u> sin'.

## 1.6 Adverb

An adverb is a word joined to a verb to qualify its meaning. For example – slowly, carefully, not. Adverbs can also be used to qualify an adjective or another adverb (e.g. 'extremely' is an adverb that can be used to qualify an adverb – he worked *extremely* carefully – or an adjective – the drink was *extremely* hot).

Adverbs and adjectives are closely related to each other. Adjectives qualify nouns, while adverbs qualify verbs (or adjectives or adverbs). In English you can often form an adverb by adding –ly to the end of the adjective word: for example 'slow' and 'slowly'.

## 1.7 Conjunction

A conjunction is a word that joins together two sentences, clauses or words: for example – and, but, because.

## 1.8 Interjection

An interjection is a word that stands complete on its own, expressing a feeling directly: for example – alas, thanks, hello.

## 1.9 Words that can be more than one part of speech

In English the same word can be more than one *part of speech*, depending on how it is used in a sentence. For example, 'talk' can be both a verb ('At lunch we talk about the class') and a noun ('I enjoyed listening to the talk'); and 'free' can be an adjective ('He had a free ticket') or a verb ('They free the slave'). This almost never happens in Greek.[2] Therefore when, for example, you want to translate the word 'talk' you need to be sure whether it is a noun (Greek λογος) or a verb (Greek λεγω).

## 1.10 Example

Then Peter quickly opened the large window next to the door and said, 'Hello!'

| | | |
|---|---|---|
| **Then** | Connects this sentence to the previous one | Conjunction |
| **Peter** | The name of a particular thing/person | (Proper) Noun |
| **quickly** | Qualifies (further describes) 'opened' | Adverb |
| **opened** | An action | Verb |
| **the** | Qualifies (further describes) 'window' | Adjective (article) |
| **large** | Qualifies (further describes) 'window' | Adjective |
| **window** | The name of something | Noun |
| **next to** | Indicates how 'door' relates to 'window' | Preposition |
| **the** | Qualifies (further describes) 'door' | Adjective (article) |
| **door** | The name of something | Noun |
| **and** | Connects the two clauses together | Conjunction |
| **said** | An action | Verb |
| **Hello** | Expresses a complete idea or feeling | Interjection |

## 2. Sentences, clauses and phrases

A sentence is a group of words that make complete sense on their own. Grammatically they do not need to be part of a larger whole. In English, a sentence is marked out by beginning with a capital letter and finishing with a full stop (or period). This paragraph contains four sentences, each of which makes complete sense on its own.

A clause or phrase is a group of words that makes sense but is not complete. Technically a clause is a group of words that contains a finite verb (that is, a verb in the indicative, imperative or subjunctive mood – see section 9 below), otherwise it is a phrase. For example, 'They ate the cake which they liked in the house' is a sentence. Within this, 'which they liked' is a clause (it is not complete

[2] Occasionally in Greek the same word can be an adjective and an adverb.

on its own so it is not a sentence, but it does have a finite verb, so it is a clause). 'In the house' is a phrase.

## 3. Subject and object

The *subject* is the noun (or pronoun) that is uppermost in mind when the sentence is formed and is the focus of attention. In English it is normally the first noun (or pronoun) in the sentence. For example, the boy arrived, she is singing, the cake was eaten, later they went away. In most sentences (*active* sentences – see section 8 below) the subject does the action expressed by the verb.

Some verbs refer to actions that do not directly affect something else – they do not have *objects*. These are called *intransitive* verbs: for example – I remain, I die, I sleep.

Most verbs, however, naturally have an *object* as well as a subject. These are called *transitive* verbs. The object specifies who or what is directly affected by the verb. For example, in the sentence 'I love him' – 'love' is a transitive verb and 'him' is the object; in 'she eats the cake' – 'the cake' is the object.

An important distinction is made between objects that are *directly* affected by the action of the verb and those that are *indirectly* affected, or secondarily affected. Such objects are called *indirect objects* (as opposed to *direct objects*) and are normally shown in English by the use of a preposition. For example, 'I gave the cake to her' – 'the cake' is the *direct object*, and 'her' is an *indirect object* (notice the 'to').

Note that some verbs can be used intransitively or transitively. For example, 'I sang' is complete in itself – 'sang' can be used intransitively – but it can also be used transitively – 'I sang the national anthem'.

## 4. Complements

The previous section has highlighted a distinction between transitive verbs, which have an object, and intransitive verbs, which do not.

However, some intransitive verbs are not complete in themselves. For example, 'He becomes' is not complete. You need to specify what he becomes (e.g. 'He becomes angry'). Most intransitive verbs can be used on their own but are more often completed by another word. For example, 'She appears' is complete when it means 'She was not there before but then she appears', but needs completing when used in the sense 'She appears happy'. Similarly the verb 'to be' can be used on its own to mean 'exists' (e.g. 'Are you there?', 'I am') but normally needs completing ('I am sad').

The word that 'completes' such a sentence is called a *complement*. It can be a noun, adjective or a pronoun – 'He is a shepherd', 'He is good', 'He is mine.' When learning Greek it is important to understand that a complement is *not* an object. An *object* is a separate person or thing from the subject that receives the action of the verb. A *complement* is a further description of the subject.

## 5. Person

*Person* indicates the relationship between the one who is speaking[3] the sentence, and the one who is doing the action in the sentence.

When the person speaking is the same as the one doing the action, it is 'first person' – in the sentence 'I hit the dog', 'I' is a first-person pronoun, and 'hit' is a verb in the first person.

When the person spoken to is the one doing the action, it is 'second person' – in the sentence 'You like the dog', 'you' is a second-person pronoun, and 'like' is a verb in the second person.

When the person spoken about is the one doing the action, it is 'third person' – in the sentence 'She carries the dog', 'she' is a third-person pronoun, and 'carries' is a verb in the third person.

For example – 'The waiter brought your meal to me' – 'brought' is a verb in the third person ('he brought'); 'your' is an adjective in the second person and 'me' is a pronoun in the first person.

## 6. Inflection

*Inflection* is when the form of a word is altered to express more precisely the meaning of the word or its function in the sentence, or in order to match with other words in the sentence. The part of the word that remains unchanged is called the *stem.*

In Greek inflection is very common – almost every word you ever meet is inflected. However, in English inflection occurs only to a limited extent.

*Nouns* are inflected in English to show *number* – that is whether they are singular (one) or plural (more than one). For example, one house, two houses; one child, five children; one box, two boxes. They are also inflected to show possession – Peter, Peter's. Certain nouns that express 'occupations' can be inflected to show gender – that is whether the noun refers to a male or female person. For example, prince and princess, actor and actress.

*Verbs* are inflected in English to show tense, voice and mood (sections 7, 8 and 9 below). For example, love, loved, loving. Verbs are also inflected in the third person singular in the Present tense – I talk, he talks; you see, she sees; they go, it goes.[4]

---

[3] Or writing, thinking, feeling etc.

[4] The verb to be is more inflected – I am, you are, he/she/it is.

*Pronouns* are the most inflected part of English. For example, 'he' or 'him' depending on the function of the pronoun in the sentence (subject or object – he saw Mary; Mary saw him); or depending on gender (who is first; what is first).

Inflections appear to be gradually falling out of use in English. Several centuries ago the second person singular of verbs was also inflected – I talk, thou (you) talkest, he talks – and verbs such as 'shall' had a 't' in the third person singular – I shall, he shalt. In modern English it is still generally considered correct to inflect 'who' to 'whom' when it is not the subject (e.g. Who hit me? Whom did you hit?), although the distinction is frequently ignored (e.g. personally I would normally say 'who did you hit' rather than 'whom did you hit').

## 7. Tense

The tense of a verb indicates the *time* at which the verb takes place and the *aspect* or nature of the action.

English has an elaborate structure of tenses constructed by the use of auxiliary verbs (parts of 'to be' and 'to have'). Greek has fewer different tenses and distinguishes between them by inflection.[5]

| | | Time<br>Past | Present | Future |
|---|---|---|---|---|
| Aspect | Continuous | *Imperfect*<br>I was loving | *Present Continuous*<br>I am loving | *Future Continuous*<br>I will be loving |
| | Simple | *Simple Past*<br>I loved | *Simple Present*<br>I love | *Simple Future*<br>I will love |
| | Complete | *Pluperfect*<br>I had loved | *Perfect*<br>I have loved | *Future Perfect*<br>I will have loved |

## 8. Voice

There are two Voices in English – *Active* and *Passive*. These indicate whether the subject is carrying out the action of the verb, or whether the action of the verb is being done to the subject. For example, 'She broke the jar' is an *active* sentence: the subject 'she' is carrying out the action 'break'. However, 'The jar is broken' is a *passive* sentence: the action 'break' is being done to the jar.

[5] The verb 'to be' is used in Greek as an auxiliary in the periphrastic forms, but these are rare (Chapter 20, Section 20.3).

*Voice* is closely related to the categories of *subject* and *object* (section 3 above).

| | |
|---|---|
| Intransitive verbs – | *Active* only: Subject does the action. No object. |
| Transitive verbs – | *Active*: Subject does the action to the object. |
| | *Passive*: Subject has the action done to it. |

It is best to think of Active sentences as the basic type of sentence, and indeed they are far more common than Passive sentences. A Passive sentence is a special type of sentence in which (compared with an Active sentence) the *object* has become the *subject*. The reason for using a Passive sentence is that (a) the person or thing doing the action does not need to be specified, and (b) the stress or focus is directed on the person or thing to which the action is done.

For example, 'The woman ate the cake' is an Active sentence. 'Woman' is the subject. 'Cake' is the object. However, the sentence can be changed into a Passive sentence – 'the cake is eaten', in which 'cake' is the subject. This changes the focus onto the cake, not the woman, and indeed the woman is no longer mentioned.

## 9. Mood

The *mood* of a verb indicates the manner in which the action of the verb is to be regarded. These can be classified into two groups: the moods of finite verbs, and those of infinite verbs. The difference between these is that a finite verb refers to a particular action, and so can make a sentence complete (see section 3 above). An infinite verb expresses the idea of the verb more generally and hence is not complete in itself but needs to be part of a larger sentence.

### Moods of finite verbs

*Indicative* – A verb in the Indicative mood makes a statement or asks a question. For example – 'He went in', 'They will arrive soon', 'Why are you here?' Most verbs are in the Indicative mood.

*Imperative* – A verb in the Imperative mood gives a command or request. For example – 'Sit down', 'Come', 'Pick up your mat!'

*Subjunctive* – A verb in the Subjunctive expresses a thought or wish rather than an actual fact: for example – 'Your will be done', 'I may go', 'If I were you.'

### Moods of infinite verbs[6]

*Infinitive* – The Infinitive is a verbal noun, expressing in a noun the action of the verb generally. It is normally preceded in English by 'to'. For example – 'I want to learn', 'I love to sing'. The fact that the Infinitive is a verbal *noun* is made clear

[6] Often these are not considered as 'moods' in English, but that is how they are labelled in Greek, and so it is convenient to label them as such here.

by the fact that 'to learn' or 'to sing' in the examples could be replaced with a noun – 'I want a drink', 'I love water.' The fact that it is a *verbal* noun is shown by the fact that the Infinitive can have its own object – 'I want to learn a language', 'I love to sing the national anthem.'

*Participle* – The participle is a verbal adjective, expressing in an adjective the action of the verb generally. In English there are two participles – an Active participle ending in -ing (e.g. singing, drinking) and a Passive participle normally ending in -ed (e.g. loved, cooked). In English participles are mainly used in the formation of the various tenses (e.g. I am singing). Greek participles are rarely used in this way. In English they can also be used simply as adjectives, for example – 'I saw the singing policeman', 'You are my loved son', 'I ate the cooked fish.' Greek uses participles extensively in this way.

## 10. Gender

There is no concept of grammatical gender in English. If a word refers to a male it is considered masculine and hence will use the masculine pronouns he, him and his. If it refers to a female it is considered feminine and hence will use the feminine pronouns she, her and hers. Otherwise it is considered neuter and will use the neuter pronouns it and its. This means that every noun that is not referring to a person or animal is considered neuter.[7] This approach of reflecting real gender in the pronoun used has its difficulties, in particular when referring to people whose gender is unknown (e.g. in the sentence 'I am going to see my new doctor, I hope that *** will be helpful') or in referring to entities seen as people (and therefore not neuter) but not gendered (e.g. 'I believe in the Holy Spirit. *** is a gift from God').

Greek is different. As in many European languages, the idea of gender is used in Greek to define different patterns of words. Thus, speaking very roughly, a third of Greek words are said to be 'masculine' words, a third 'feminine' and a third 'neuter'. Naturally, those words that do refer to males will be masculine, but in addition thousands of words which to an English speaker are neuter are also 'masculine' – e.g. field, river, heaven. Similarly words such as sword, hope and power are 'feminine' in Greek. Thus it is important when learning Greek to understand that references to gender will normally be references to 'grammatical gender', i.e. which pattern of words the word in question belongs to, rather than implying something about its real or natural gender (as if Greeks thought of a river as a male thing, and a sword as a female thing).

---

[7] In more poetic language there are some exceptions, e.g. ships are often referred to as if they were female – 'When the new ship was launched, her decks were full of sailors.'

# Parsing guide

When reading a language, you can often understand a sentence without working out precisely every grammatical form within it. This is to be encouraged – after all you do not normally analyse the grammar of a sentence in your own language. However, when you are just starting out, or if a sentence is particularly difficult, or if there is a complicated exegetical argument about its meaning, you will need to *parse* each word and then very precisely fit together the meaning of the sentence.

| Noun | Adjective<br>Pronoun<br>Article | Verb | | |
|---|---|---|---|---|
| | | Indicative<br>Imperative<br>Subjunctive | Infinitive | Participle |
| (Gender) | Gender | | | Gender |
| *(Masculine)* | *Feminine* | | | *Neuter* |
| Case | Case | | | Case |
| *Genitive* | *Accusative* | | | *Dative* |
| Number | Number | | | Number |
| *Singular* | *Plural* | | | *Plural* |
| | | Person | | |
| | | *2nd person* | | |
| | | Number | | |
| | | *Singular* | | |
| | | Tense | Tense | Tense |
| | | *Present* | *Aorist* | *Perfect* |
| | | Voice | Voice | Voice |
| | | *Active* | *Middle* | *Passive* |
| | | Mood | Mood | Mood |
| | | *Imperative* | *Infinitive* | *Participle* |

*Parsing* a word means explaining its grammatical form. For example, τον is the accusative masculine singular of the definite article. What information you need to given when parsing depends on the type of word you are parsing.

The table on page 250 sets out what pieces of information you should give when parsing, and gives an example (in italics).

## Notes

- It is not strictly necessary to give the gender of a noun, because for any given noun it cannot change. However, your teacher may encourage you to state the gender of nouns when parsing to help you ensure that you make any articles or adjectives correctly agree with it.
- The Middle and Passive often share the same endings. In these cases, *from a grammatical point of view* all you can say is that it is 'middle or passive'; the meaning of the rest of the sentence should make clear which it is.
- Sometimes a form can be one of several options. In these cases, give all the options. For example, ἀγαθου is masculine or neuter, genitive, singular.
- It can be helpful to say 'deponent' or 'middle deponent' when parsing a deponent verb such as ἐρχομαι.

**Hint**

- The augment (ἐ) can only occur when a verb is in the *Indicative* – therefore if a verb has the augment, it must be in the *Indicative*.
- The *Imperative* and *Infinitive* only occur (except extremely rarely) in the *Present* and the *Aorist*.
- The *participle* only occurs (except extremely rarely) in the *Present*, *Aorist* or *Perfect*.
- When parsing verbs, look for the distinctive patterns:

| | Indicative | | Other Moods | |
|---|---|---|---|---|
| | Active and Middle | Passive | Active and Middle | Passive |
| Present | — | — | — | — |
| Future | — σ | — θησ | | |
| Imperfect | ἐ — | ἐ — | | |
| Aorist | ἐ — σ | ἐ — θ | — σ | — θ |
| Perfect | Reduplication | | | |

- Watch out for compound verbs, and verbs which begin with vowels.
- A participle is parsed as a combination of an adjective and a verb.

## Examples

| | |
|---|---|
| λογον | Accusative, Singular |
| καλαις | Feminine, Dative, Plural |
| ἐλυετο | 3rd Person Singular, Imperfect, Passive, Indicative |
| λυσαι | Aorist, Active, Infinitive |
| λυθεντας | Masculine Accusative Plural, Aorist Passive participle |

## THE PARSING FLOW CHART

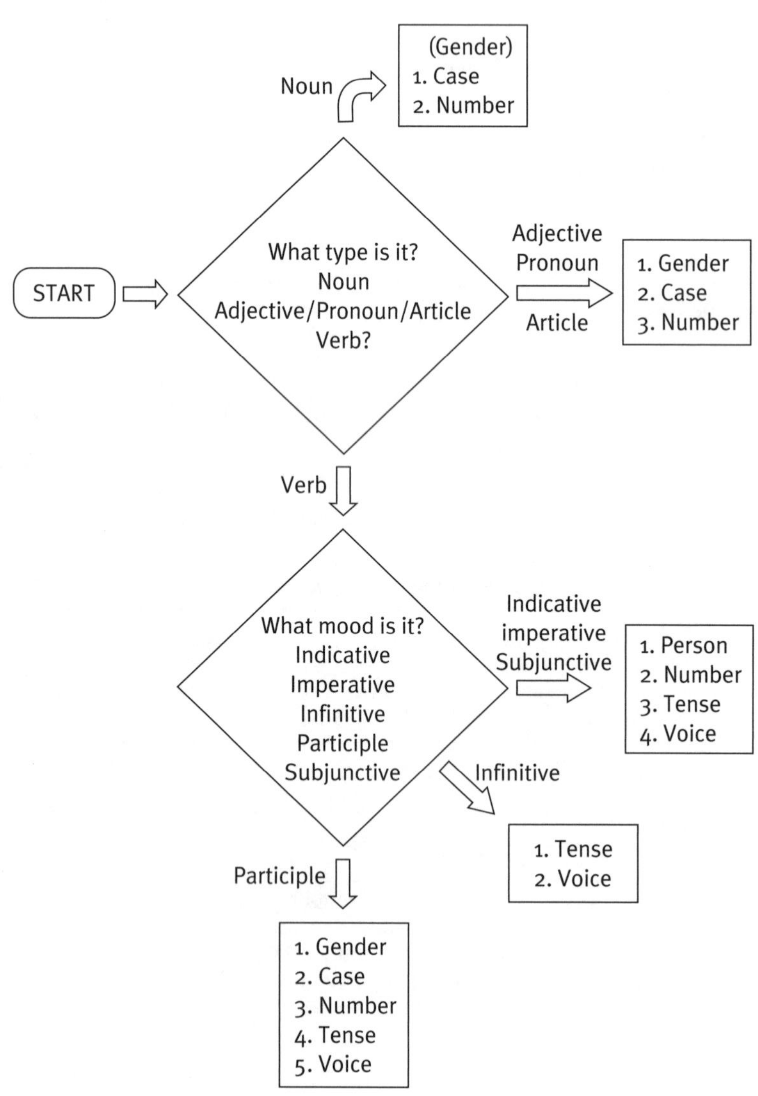

# Principal parts

Hint

- Refer back to Chapter 18, section 18.4 (page 207) for guidance on how to construct any part of a verb from its principal parts.
- Notice that various verbs use the -εω endings in the future. These are given here in their uncontracted form for clarity (i.e. the future of βαλλω is given as βαλεω, although this will contract to βαλῶ).

| Present | Future | Aorist Active (or Middle) | Perfect Active | Perfect Passive | Aorist Passive | |
|---|---|---|---|---|---|---|
| **Most verbs have the same principal parts as λυω:** | | | | | | |
| λυω | λυσω | ἐλυσα | λελυκα | λελυμαι | ἐλυθην | **untie** |
| **The principal parts of the three types of contracted verbs:** | | | | | | |
| φιλεω | φιλησω | ἐφιλησα | πεφιληκα | πεφιλημαι | ἐφιληθην | **love** |
| τιμαω | τιμησω | ἐτιμησα | τετιμηκα | τετιμημαι | ἐτιμηθην | **honour** |
| πληροω | πληρωσω | ἐπληρωσα | πεπληρωκα | πεπληρωμαι | ἐπληρωθην | **fulfil** |
| **These two are regular except for the χ in the Perfect Active:** | | | | | | |
| κηρυσσω | κηρυξω | ἐκηρυξα | κεκηρυχα | κεκηρυγμαι | ἐκηρυχθην | **proclaim** |
| πρασσω | πραξω | ἐπραξα | πεπραχα | πεπραγμαι | ἐπραχθην | **do** |
| **The following have various irregularities:** | | | | | | |
| ἀγγελλω | ἀγγελεω | ἠγγειλα | ἠγγελκα | ἠγγελμαι | ἠγγελην | **announce** |
| ἀγω | ἀξω | ἠγαγον | | ἠγμαι | ἠχθην | **lead** |
| αἱρω | ἀρεω | ἠρα | ἠρκα | ἠρμαι | ἠρθην | **take (away)** |
| ἀκουω | ἀκουσω | ἠκουσα | ἀκηκοα | | ἠκουσθην | **hear** |
| ἁμαρτανω | ἁμαρτησω | ἡμαρτον | ἡμαρτηκα | | | **sin** |
| ἀνοιγω | ἀνοιξω | ἠνοιξα *or* ἀνεῳξα | ἀνεῳγα | ἀνεῳγμαι | ἠνοιχθην | **open** |
| -βαινω | -βησομαι | -ἐβην | -βεβηκα | | | **go** |
| βαλλω | βαλεω | ἐβαλον | βεβληκα | βεβλημαι | ἐβληθην | **throw** |
| γινομαι | γενησομαι | ἐγενομην | γεγονα | γεγενημαι | ἐγενηθην | **become** |
| γινωσκω | γνωσομαι | ἐγνων | ἐγνωκα | ἐγνωσμαι | ἐγνωσθην | **know** |
| γραφω | γραψω | ἐγραψα | γεγραφα | γεγραμμαι | ἐγραφην | **write** |
| δεχομαι | δεξομαι | ἐδεξαμην | | δεδεγμαι | ἐδεχθην | **receive** |
| ἐγειρω | ἐγερεω | ἠγειρα | | ἐγηγερμαι | ἠγερθην | **raise up** |
| εὑρισκω | εὑρησω | εὑρον | εὑρηκα | | εὑρεθην | **find** |
| θελω | θελησω | ἠθελησα | | | | **wish** |

| Present | Future | Aorist Active (or Middle) | Perfect Active | Perfect Passive | Aorist Passive | |
|---|---|---|---|---|---|---|
| -θνησκω | -θανεομαι | -εθανον | -τεθνηκα | | | **die** |
| καλεω | καλεσω | ἐκαλεσα | κεκληκα | κεκλημαι | ἐκληθην | **call** |
| κραζω | κραξω | ἐκραξα | κεκραγα | | | **cry out** |
| κρινω | κρινεω | ἐκρινα | κεκρικα | κεκριμαι | ἐκριθην | **judge** |
| λαμβανω | λημψομαι | ἐλαβον | εἰληφα | εἰλημμαι | ἐλημφθην | **take** |
| -λειπω | -λειψω | -ἐλιπον | | | | **leave behind** |
| μανθανω | | ἐμαθον | μεμαθηκα | | | **learn** |
| πασχω | | ἐπαθον | πεπονθα | | | **suffer** |
| πειθω | πεισω | ἐπεισα | πεποιθα | πεπεισμαι | ἐπεισθην | **persuade** |
| πινω | πιομαι | ἐπιον | πεπωκα | | ἐποθην | **drink** |
| πιπτω | πεσεομαι | ἐπεσον | πεπτωκα | | | **fall** |
| σπειρω | σπερεω | ἐσπειρα | | ἐσπαρμαι | ἐσπαρην | **sow** |
| -στελλω | -στελεω | -ἐστειλα | -ἐσταλκα | -ἐσταλμαι | -ἐσταλην | **send** |
| σωζω | σωσω | ἐσωσα | σεσωκα | σεσωσμαι | ἐσωθην | **save** |
| φευγω | φευξομαι | ἐφυγον | πεφευγα | | | **flee** |

**These have stems derived from more than one verb:**

| | | | | | | |
|---|---|---|---|---|---|---|
| ἐρχομαι | ἐλευσομαι | ἠλθον | ἐληλυθα | | | **come** |
| ἐσθιω | φαγομαι | ἐφαγον | | | | **eat** |
| ἐχω | ἑξω | ἐσχον | ἐσχηκα | | | **have** |
| λεγω | ἐρεω | εἰπον | εἰρηκα | εἰρημαι | ἐρρηθην *or* ἐρρεθην | **say** |
| ὁραω | ὀψομαι | εἰδον | ἑωρακα *or* ἑορακα | | ὠφθην | **see** |
| φερω | οἰσω | ἠνεγκον | ἐνηνοχα | ἐνηνεγμαι | ἠνεχθην | **carry** |

**The -μι verbs:**

| | | | | | | |
|---|---|---|---|---|---|---|
| τιθημι | θησω | ἐθηκα | τεθεικα | τεθειμαι | ἐτεθην | **place** |
| διδωμι | δωσω | ἐδωκα | δεδωκα | δεδομαι | ἐδοθην | **give** |
| ἱστημι | στησω | ἐστησα | | | | **cause to stand** |
| | | ἐστην | ἑστηκα | | ἐσταθην | **stand** |
| ἀφιημι | ἀφησω | ἀφηκα | | ἀφεωμαι | ἀφεθην | **leave** |
| ἀπολλυμι | ἀπολεσω | ἀπωλεσα | | | | **ruin** |
| ἀπολλυμαι | ἀπολεομαι | ἀπωλομην | ἀπολωλα | | | **perish** |
| δεικνυμι | δειξω | ἐδειξα | δεδειχα | | ἐδειχθην | **show** |

# Grammar reference tables

## NOUNS

### First and Second Declension

| | Mainly Masc. (2nd) | Neuter (2nd) | Feminine (1st) | | | Masculine (1st) | |
|---|---|---|---|---|---|---|---|
| Nom. | λογος | ἐργον | ἀρχη | ἡμερα | δοξα | προφητης | Ἰουδας |
| Voc. | λογε | ἐργον | ἀρχη | ἡμερα | δοξα | προφητα | Ἰουδα |
| Acc. | λογον | ἐργον | ἀρχην | ἡμεραν | δοξαν | προφητην | Ἰουδαν |
| Gen. | λογου | ἐργου | ἀρχης | ἡμερας | δοξης | προφητου | Ἰουδα |
| Dat. | λογῳ | ἐργῳ | ἀρχῃ | ἡμερᾳ | δοξῃ | προφητῃ | Ἰουδᾳ |
| Nom. | λογοι | ἐργα | ἀρχαι | ἡμεραι | δοξαι | προφηται | |
| Acc. | λογους | ἐργα | ἀρχας | ἡμερας | δοξας | προφητας | |
| Gen. | λογων | ἐργων | ἀρχων | ἡμερων | δοξων | προφητων | |
| Dat. | λογοις | ἐργοις | ἀρχαις | ἡμεραις | δοξαις | προφηταις | |

### Third Declension

| | Masc. & Feminine | Family Group | Neuter | Neuter Contract. | Vowel Stems Fem. | Vowel Stems Masculine |
|---|---|---|---|---|---|---|
| Nom. | ἀστηρ | πατηρ | σωμα | ἐθνος | πολις | βασιλευς |
| Voc. | ἀστηρ | πατερ | σωμα | ἐθνος | πολις | βασιλευ |
| Acc. | ἀστερα | πατερα | σωμα | ἐθνος | πολιν | βασιλεα |
| Gen. | ἀστερος | πατρος | σωματος | ἐθνους | πολεως | βασιλεως |
| Dat. | ἀστερι | πατρι | σωματι | ἐθνει | πολει | βασιλει |
| Nom. | ἀστερες | πατερες | σωματα | ἐθνη | πολεις | βασιλεις |
| Acc. | ἀστερας | πατερας | σωματα | ἐθνη | πολεις | βασιλεις |
| Gen. | ἀστερων | πατερων | σωματων | ἐθνων | πολεων | βασιλεων |
| Dat. | ἀστερσιν | πατρασιν | σωμασιν | ἐθνεσιν | πολεσιν | βασιλευσιν |

## PRONOUNS AND THE DEFINITE ARTICLE

| | Definite Article | | | Relative Pronoun | | | Interog./Indef. | |
|---|---|---|---|---|---|---|---|---|
| | Masc. | Fem. | Neut. | Masc. | Fem. | Neut. | M/F | Neut. |
| Nom. | ὁ | ἡ | το | ὅς | ἥ | ὅ | τις | τι |
| Acc. | τον | την | το | ὅν | ἥν | ὅ | τινα | τι |
| Gen. | του | της | του | οὗ | ἧς | οὗ | τινος | τινος |
| Dat. | τῳ | τῃ | τῳ | ᾧ | ᾗ | ᾧ | τινι | τινι |
| Nom. | οἱ | αἱ | τα | οἵ | αἵ | ἅ | τινες | τινα |
| Acc. | τους | τας | τα | οὕς | ἅς | ἅ | τινας | τινα |
| Gen. | των | των | των | ὧν | ὧν | ὧν | τινων | τινων |
| Dat. | τοις | ταις | τοις | οἷς | αἷς | οἷς | τισι | τισι |

| | 1st Person | 2nd Person | 3rd Person | | |
|---|---|---|---|---|---|
| | | | Masc. | Fem. | Neuter |
| Nom. | ἐγω | συ | αὐτος | αὐτη | αὐτο |
| Acc. | ἐμε, με | σε | αὐτον | αὐτην | αὐτο |
| Gen. | ἐμου, μου | σου | αὐτου | αὐτης | αὐτου |
| Dat. | ἐμοι, μοι | σοι | αὐτῳ | αὐτῃ | αὐτῳ |
| Nom. | ἡμεις | ὑμεις | αὐτοι | αὐται | αὐτα |
| Acc. | ἡμας | ὑμας | αὐτους | αὐτας | αὐτα |
| Gen. | ἡμων | ὑμων | αὐτων | αὐτων | αὐτων |
| Dat. | ἡμιν | ὑμιν | αὐτοις | αὐταις | αὐτοις |

| | That | | | This | | |
|---|---|---|---|---|---|---|
| | Masc. | Fem. | Neuter | Masc. | Fem. | Neuter |
| *Nom.* | ἐκεινος | ἐκεινη | ἐκεινο | οὑτος | αὑτη | τουτο |
| *Acc.* | ἐκεινον | ἐκεινην | ἐκεινο | τουτον | ταυτην | τουτο |
| *Gen.* | ἐκεινου | ἐκεινης | ἐκεινου | τουτου | ταυτης | τουτου |
| *Dat.* | ἐκεινῳ | ἐκεινῃ | ἐκεινῳ | τουτῳ | ταυτῃ | τουτῳ |
| *Nom.* | ἐκεινοι | ἐκειναι | ἐκεινα | οὑτοι | αὑται | ταυτα |
| *Acc.* | ἐκεινους | ἐκεινας | ἐκεινα | τουτους | ταυτας | ταυτα |
| *Gen.* | ἐκεινων | ἐκεινων | ἐκεινων | τουτων | τουτων | τουτων |
| *Dat.* | ἐκεινοις | ἐκειναις | ἐκεινοις | τουτοις | ταυταις | τουτοις |

# ADJECTIVES

## Second Declension

| | Masc. | Fem.[1] | Neuter |
|---|---|---|---|
| *Nom.* | ἀγαθος | ἀγαθη | ἀγαθον |
| *Voc.* | ἀγαθε | ἀγαθη | ἀγαθον |
| *Acc.* | ἀγαθον | ἀγαθην | ἀγαθον |
| *Gen.* | ἀγαθου | ἀγαθης | ἀγαθου |
| *Dat.* | ἀγαθῳ | ἀγαθῃ | ἀγαθῳ |
| *Nom.* | ἀγαθοι | ἀγαθαι | ἀγαθα |
| *Acc.* | ἀγαθους | ἀγαθας | ἀγαθα |
| *Gen.* | ἀγαθων | ἀγαθων | ἀγαθων |
| *Dat.* | ἀγαθοις | ἀγαθαις | ἀγαθοις |

| | Masc. | Fem. | Neuter | Masc. | Fem. | Neuter |
|---|---|---|---|---|---|---|
| *Nom.* | πολυς | πολλη | πολυ | μεγας | μεγαλη | μεγα |
| *Acc.* | πολυν | πολλην | πολυ | μεγαν | μεγαλην | μεγα |
| *Gen.* | πολλου | πολλης | πολλου | μεγαλου | μεγαλης | μεγαλου |
| *Dat.* | πολλῳ | πολλῃ | πολλῳ | μεγαλῳ | μεγαλῃ | μεγαλῳ |
| *Nom.* | πολλοι | πολλαι | πολλα | μεγαλοι | μεγαλαι | μεγαλα |
| *Acc.* | πολλους | πολλας | πολλα | μεγαλους | μεγαλας | μεγαλα |
| *Gen.* | πολλων | πολλων | πολλων | μεγαλων | μεγαλων | μεγαλων |
| *Dat.* | πολλοις | πολλαις | πολλοις | μεγαλοις | μεγαλαις | μεγαλοις |

[1] 2nd declension adjectives whose stem ends in a vowel or ρ (such as ἁγιος) decline with an α throughout the feminine singular – ἁγια, ἁγιαν, ἁγιας, ἁγιᾳ.

## Third Declension

| | Masc. & Fem. | Neuter | Masc. & Fem. | Neuter |
|---|---|---|---|---|
| *Nom.* | πλειων | πλειον | ἀληθης | ἀληθες |
| *Acc.* | πλειονα | πλειον | ἀληθη | ἀληθες |
| *Gen.* | πλειονος | πλειονος | ἀληθους | ἀληθους |
| *Dat.* | πλειονι | πλειονι | ἀληθει | ἀληθει |
| *Nom.* | πλειονες | πλειονα | ἀληθεις | ἀληθη |
| *Acc.* | πλειονας | πλειονα | ἀληθεις | ἀληθη |
| *Gen.* | πλειονων | πλειονων | ἀληθων | ἀληθων |
| *Dat.* | πλειοσιν | πλειοσιν | ἀληθεσιν | ἀληθεσιν |

## Mixed Form

| | Masc. | Fem. | Neuter |
|---|---|---|---|
| *Nom.* | πας | πασα | παν |
| *Acc.* | παντα | πασαν | παν |
| *Gen.* | παντος | πασης | παντος |
| *Dat.* | παντι | πασῃ | παντι |
| *Nom.* | παντες | πασαι | παντα |
| *Acc.* | παντας | πασας | παντα |
| *Gen.* | παντων | πασων | παντων |
| *Dat.* | πασι(ν) | πασαις | πασι(ν) |

## Comparison of Adjectives

| | | | |
|---|---|---|---|
| *Regular* | σοφος | σοφωτερος | σοφωτατος |
| | δικαιος | δικαιοτερος | δικαιοτατος |
| *Irregular* | ἀγαθος | κρεισσων | |
| | κακος | χειρων | |
| | μεγας | μειζων | |
| | πολυς | πλειων | |
| | μικρος | μικροτερος | ἐλαχιστος |

### Comparison of Adverbs

| | | | |
|---|---|---|---|
| *Regular* | σοφως<br>δικαιως | σοφωτερον<br>δικαιοτερον | σοφωτατα<br>δικαιοτατα |
| *Irregular* | εὐ | κρεισσον<br>μαλλον | <br>μαλιστα |

### One

| | Masc. | Fem. | Neuter |
|---|---|---|---|
| *Nom.* | εἱς | μια | ἑν |
| *Acc.* | ἑνα | μιαν | ἑν |
| *Gen.* | ἑνος | μιας | ἑνος |
| *Dat.* | ἑνι | μιᾳ | ἑνι |

## THE VERB

### Indicative

| Active | | | | |
|---|---|---|---|---|
| Present | Future | Imperfect | Aorist | Perfect |
| λυω | λυσω | ἐλυον | ἐλυσα | λελυκα |
| λυεις | λυσεις | ἐλυες | ἐλυσας | λελυκας |
| λυει | λυσει | ἐλυε(ν) | ἐλυσε(ν) | λελυκεν |
| λυομεν | λυσομεν | ἐλυομεν | ἐλυσαμεν | λελυκαμεν |
| λυετε | λυσετε | ἐλυετε | ἐλυσατε | λελυκατε |
| λυουσι (ν) | λυσουσι(ν) | ἐλυον | ἐλυσαν | λελυκασι(ν) |

| Middle | | | | |
|---|---|---|---|---|
| Present | Future | Imperfect | Aorist | Perfect |
| ῥυομαι | ῥυσομαι | ἐρυομην | ἐρυσαμην | ῥερυμαι |
| ῥυῃ | ῥυσῃ | ἐρυου | ἐρυσω | ῥερυσαι |
| ῥυεται | ῥυσεται | ἐρυετο | ἐρυσατο | ῥερυται |
| ῥυομεθα | ῥυσομεθα | ἐρυομεθα | ἐρυσαμεθα | ῥερυμεθα |
| ῥυεσθε | ῥυσεσθε | ἐρυεσθε | ἐρυσασθε | ῥερυσθε |
| ῥυονται | ῥυσονται | ἐρυοντο | ἐρυσαντο | ῥερυνται |

| Passive | | | | |
|---|---|---|---|---|
| Present | Future | Imperfect | Aorist | Perfect |
| λυομαι | λυθησομαι | ἐλυομην | ἐλυθην | λελυμαι |
| λυῃ | λυθησῃ | ἐλυου | ἐλυθης | λελυσαι |
| λυεται | λυθησεται | ἐλυετο | ἐλυθη | λελυται |
| λυομεθα | λυθησομεθα | ἐλυομεθα | ἐλυθημεν | λελυμεθα |
| λυεσθε | λυθησεσθε | ἐλυεσθε | ἐλυθητε | λελυσθε |
| λυονται | λυθησονται | ἐλυοντο | ἐλυθησαν | λελυνται |

Plus, the very rare Pluperfect:

Active: (ἐ)λελυκειν, (ἐ)λελυκεις, (ἐ)λελυκει, (ἐ)λελυκειμεν, (ἐ)λελυκειτε, (ἐ)λελυκεισαν.

Middle and Passive: (ἐ)λελυμην, (ἐ)λελυσο, (ἐ)λελυτο, (ἐ)λελυμεθα, (ἐ)λελυσθε, (ἐ)λελυντο.

**Imperatives, Infinitives and Subjunctives**

| | Present Active | Aorist Active | Present Middle or Passive | Aorist Middle | Aorist Passive |
|---|---|---|---|---|---|
| *Subjunctive* | | | | | |
| 1st Sing. | λυω | λυσω | ῥυωμαι | ῥυσωμαι | λυθω |
| 2nd Sing. | λυῃς | λυσῃς | ῥυῃ | ῥυσῃ | λυθῃς |
| 3rd Sing. | λυῃ | λυσῃ | ῥυηται | ῥυσηται | λυθῃ |
| 1st Pl. | λυωμεν | λυσωμεν | ῥυωμεθα | ῥυσωμεθα | λυθωμεν |
| 2nd Pl. | λυητε | λυσητε | ῥυησθε | ῥυσησθε | λυθητε |
| 3rd Pl. | λυωσι(ν) | λυσωσι(ν) | ῥυωνται | ῥυσωνται | λυθωσι(ν) |
| *Imperative* | | | | | |
| 2nd Sing. | λυε | λυσον | ῥυου | ῥυσαι | λυθητι |
| 3rd Sing. | λυετω | λυσατω | ῥυεσθω | ῥυσασθω | λυθητω |
| 2nd Pl. | λυετε | λυσατε | ῥυεσθε | ῥυσασθε | λυθητε |
| 3rd Pl. | λυετωσαν | λυσατωσαν | ῥυεσθωσαν | ῥυσασθωσαν | λυθητωσαν |
| *Infinitive* | | | | | |
| | λυειν | λυσαι | ῥυεσθαι | ῥυσασθαι | λυθηναι |

Plus the rare Perfect Infinitive: Active – λελυκεναι<br>Middle and Passive – λελυσθαι

## Participles

| | | Declines like | Nom. Sing. | Masc./Neuter Stem |
|---|---|---|---|---|
| *Active* | | | | |
| Present | λυων | πας | λυων, λυουσα, λυον | λυοντ- |
| Aorist | λυσας | πας | λυσας, λυσασα, λυσαν | λυσαντ- |
| Perfect | λελυκως | πας | λελυκως, λελυκυια, λελυκος | λελυκοτ- |
| *Middle* | | | | |
| Present | ῥυομενος | ἀγαθος | | |
| Aorist | ῥυσαμενος | ἀγαθος | | |
| Perfect | ῥερυμενος | ἀγαθος | | |
| *Passive* | | | | |
| Present | λυομενος | ἀγαθος | | |
| Aorist | λυθεις | πας | λυθεις, λυθεισα, λυθεν | λυθεντ- |
| Perfect | λελυμενος | ἀγαθος | | |

| | Present Active | | | Aorist Active | | |
|---|---|---|---|---|---|---|
| | Masc. | Fem. | Neuter | Masc. | Fem. | Neuter |
| *Nom.* | λυων | λυουσα | λυον | λυσας | λυσασα | λυσαν |
| *Acc.* | λυοντα | λυουσαν | λυον | λυσαντα | λυσασαν | λυσαν |
| *Gen.* | λυοντος | λυουσης | λυοντος | λυσαντος | λυσάσης | λυσαντος |
| *Dat.* | λυοντι | λυουσῃ | λυοντι | λυσαντι | λυσασῃ | λυσαντι |
| *Nom.* | λυοντες | λυουσαι | λυοντα | λυσαντες | λυσασαι | λυσαντα |
| *Acc.* | λυοντας | λυουσας | λυοντα | λυσαντας | λυσασας | λυσαντα |
| *Gen.* | λυοντων | λυουσων | λυοντων | λυσαντων | λυσασων | λυσαντων |
| *Dat.* | λυουσι(ν) | λυουσαις | λυουσι(ν) | λυσασι(ν) | λυσασαις | λυσασι(ν) |

| | Aorist Passive | | | Perfect Active | | |
|---|---|---|---|---|---|---|
| | Masc. | Fem. | Neuter | Masc. | Fem. | Neuter |
| *Nom.* | λυθεις | λυθεισα | λυθεν | λελυκως | λελυκυια | λελυκος |
| *Acc.* | λυθεντα | λυθεισαν | λυθεν | λελυκοτα | λελυκυιαν | λελυκος |
| *Gen.* | λυθεντος | λυθεισης | λυθεντος | λελυκοτος | λελυκυιας | λελυκοτος |
| *Dat.* | λυθεντι | λυθειση | λυθεντι | λελυκοτι | λελυκυιᾳ | λελυκοτι |
| *Nom.* | λυθεντες | λυθεισαι | λυθεντα | λελυκοτες | λελυκυιαι | λελυκοτα |
| *Acc.* | λυθεντας | λυθεισας | λυθεντα | λελυκοτας | λελυκυιας | λελυκοτα |
| *Gen.* | λυθεντων | λυθεισων | λυθεντων | λελυκοτων | λελυκυιων | λελυκοτων |
| *Dat.* | λυθεισι(ν) | λυθεισαις | λυθεισι(ν) | λελυκοσι(ν) | λελυκυιαις | λελυκοσι(ν) |

## CONTRACTING VERBS

## -εω Verbs

### Present and Imperfect have contractions

ε + ε → ει
ε + ο → ου
ε + diphthong or long vowel drops out

| *Indicative* | | | |
|---|---|---|---|
| Present Active | Imperfect Active | Present Middle/Passive | Imperfect Middle/Passive |
| φιλω | ἐφιλουν | φιλουμαι | ἐφιλουμην |
| φιλεις | ἐφιλεις | φιλῃ | ἐφιλου |
| φιλει | ἐφιλει | φιλειται | ἐφιλειτο |
| φιλουμεν | ἐφιλουμεν | φιλουμεθα | ἐφιλουμεθα |
| φιλειτε | ἐφιλειτε | φιλεισθε | ἐφιλεισθε |
| φιλουσι(ν) | ἐφιλουν | φιλουνται | ἐφιλουντο |

| *Imperative* | | *Subjunctive* | |
|---|---|---|---|
| Present Active | Present Middle/Passive | Present Active | Present Middle/Passive |
| | | φιλω | φιλωμαι |
| φιλει | φιλου | φιλῃς | φιλῃ |
| φιλειτω | φιλεισθω | φιλῃ | φιληται |
| | | φιλωμεν | φιλωμεθα |
| φιλειτε | φιλεισθε | φιλητε | φιλησθε |
| φιλειτωσαν | φιλεισθωσαν | φιλωσιν | φιλωνται |

| | Present Active | Present Middle/Passive |
|---|---|---|
| *Infinitive* | φιλειν | φιλεισθαι |
| *Participle* | φιλων, φιλουσα, φιλουν (Masc./Neuter stem: φιλουντ-) | φιλουμενος |

### Other tenses as λυω with the stem φιλη-

**Note:** Some -εω verbs keep the short ε at the end of the stem e.g. καλεσω.

## -αω Verbs

### Present and Imperfect have contractions

α + ε or η → α
α + any ο → ω
α + any ι → ᾳ

| *Indicative* | | | |
|---|---|---|---|
| Present Active | Imperfect Active | Present Middle/Passive | Imperfect Middle/Passive |
| τιμω | ἐτιμων | τιμωμαι | ἐτιμωμην |
| τιμᾳς | ἐτιμας | τιμᾳ | ἐτιμω |
| τιμᾳ | ἐτιμα | τιμαται | ἐτιματο |
| τιμωμεν | ἐτιμωμεν | τιμωμεθα | ἐτιμωμεθα |
| τιματε | ἐτιματε | τιμασθε | ἐτιμασθε |
| τιμωσι(ν) | ἐτιμων | τιμωνται | ἐτιμωντο |

| *Imperative* | | *Subjunctive* | |
|---|---|---|---|
| Present Active | Present Middle/Passive | Present Active | Present Middle/Passive |
| | | τιμω | τιμωμαι |
| τιμα | τιμω | τιμᾳς | τιμᾳ |
| τιματω | τιμασθω | τιμᾳ | τιμαται |
| | | τιμωμεν | τιμωμεθα |
| τιματε | τιμασθε | τιματε | τιμασθε |
| τιματωσαν | τιμασθωσαν | τιμωσιν | τιμωνται |

| | Present Active | Present Middle/Passive |
|---|---|---|
| *Infinitive* | τιμαν | τιμασθαι |
| *Participle* | τιμων, τιμωσα, τιμων (Masc./Neuter stem: τιμωντ-) | τιμωμενος |

### Other tenses as λυω with the stem τιμη-

**Note:** ζαω has the Present Indicative: ζω, ζῃς, ζῃ, ζωμεν, ζητε, ζωσιν
Present Infinitive: ζην

## -οω Verbs

### Present and Imperfect have contractions

ο + short vowel or ου → ου
ο + long vowel → ω
ο + any ι → οι

| *Indicative* | | | |
|---|---|---|---|
| Present Active | Imperfect Active | Present Middle/Passive | Imperfect Middle/Passive |
| πληρω | ἐπληρουν | πληρουμαι | ἐπληρουμην |
| πληροις | ἐπληρους | πληροι | ἐπληρου |
| πληροι | ἐπληρου | πληρουται | ἐπληρουτο |
| πληρουμεν | ἐπληρουμεν | πληρουμεθα | ἐπληρουμεθα |
| πληρουτε | ἐπληρουτε | πληρουσθε | ἐπληρουσθε |
| πληρουσι(ν) | ἐπληρουν | πληρουνται | ἐπληρουντο |

| *Imperative* | | *Subjunctive* | |
|---|---|---|---|
| Present Active | Present Middle/Passive | Present Active | Present Middle/Passive |
| | | πληρω | πληρωμαι |
| πληρου | πληρου | πληροις | πληροι |
| πληρουτω | πληρουσθω | πληροι | πληρωται |
| | | πληρωμεν | πληρωμεθα |
| πληρουτε | πληρουσθε | πληρωτε | πληρωσθε |
| πληρουτωσαν | πληρουσθωσαν | πληρωσιν | πληρωνται |

| | Present Active | Present Middle/Passive |
|---|---|---|
| *Infinitive* | πληρουν | πληρουσθαι |
| *Participle* | πληρων, πληρουσα, πληρουν (Masc./Neuter Stem: πληρουντ-) | πληρουμενος |

## Other tenses as λυω with the stem πληρω-

## μι VERBS

### Present Active

| *Indicative* | | | *Subjunctive* | | |
|---|---|---|---|---|---|
| τιθημι | ἱστημι | διδωμι | τιθω | ἱστω | διδω |
| τιθης | ἱστης | διδως | τιθῃς | ἱστῃς | διδῳς |
| τιθησι(ν) | ἱστησι(ν) | διδωσι(ν) | τιθῃ | ἱστῃ | διδῳ |
| τιθεμεν | ἱσταμεν | διδομεν | τιθωμεν | ἱστωμεν | διδωμεν |
| τιθετε | ἱστατε | διδοτε | τιθητε | ἱστητε | διδωτε |
| τιθεασι(ν) | ἱστασι(ν) | διδοασι(ν) | τιθωσι(ν) | ἱστωσι(ν) | διδωσι(ν) |

| *Imperative* | | | *Infinitive* | | |
|---|---|---|---|---|---|
| | | | τιθεναι | ἱσταναι | διδοναι |
| τιθει | ἱστη | διδου | *Participle* | | |
| τιθετω | ἱστατω | διδοτω | τιθεις -εισα -εν; stem τιθεντ- | | |
| τιθετε | ἱστατε | διδοτε | ἱστας -ασα, -αν; stem ἱσταντ- | | |
| τιθετωσαν | ἱστατωσαν | διδοτωσαν | διδους -ουσα -ον; stem διδοντ- | | |

**Present Middle/Passive**

| *Indicative* | | | *Subjunctive* | | |
|---|---|---|---|---|---|
| τιθεμαι | ἱσταμαι | διδομαι | τιθωμαι | ἱστωμαι | διδωμαι |
| τιθεσαι | ἱστασαι | διδοσαι | τιθῃ | ἱστῃ | διδῳ |
| τιθεται | ἱσταται | διδοται | τιθηται | ἱστηται | διδωται |
| τιθεμεθα | ἱσταμεθα | διδομεθα | τιθωμεθα | ἱστωμεθα | διδωμεθα |
| τιθεσθε | ἱστασθε | διδοσθε | τιθησθε | ἱστησθε | διδωσθε |
| τιθενται | ἱστανται | διδονται | τιθωνται | ἱστωνται | διδωνται |

| *Imperative* | | | *Infinitive* | | |
|---|---|---|---|---|---|
| τιθεσο | ἱστασο | διδοσο | τιθεσθαι | ἱστασθαι | διδοσθαι |
| τιθεσθω | ἱστασθω | διδοσθω | *Participle* | | |
| τιθεσθε | ἱστασθε | διδοσθε | | | |
| τιθεσθωσαν | ἱστασθωσαν | διδοσθωσαν | τιθεμενος | ἱσταμενος | διδομενος |

**Imperfect**

| *Indicative Active* | | | *Indicative Middle/Passive* | | |
|---|---|---|---|---|---|
| ἐτιθην | ἱστην | ἐδιδουν | ἐτιθεμην | ἱσταμην | ἐδιδομην |
| ἐτιθεις | ἱστης | ἐδιδους | ἐτιθεσο | ἱστασο | ἐδιδοσο |
| ἐτιθει | ἱστη | ἐδιδου | ἐτιθετο | ἱστατο | ἐδιδοτο |
| ἐτιθεμεν | ἱσταμεν | ἐδιδομεν | ἐτιθεμεθα | ἱσταμεθα | ἐδιδομεθα |
| ἐτιθετε | ἱστατε | ἐδιδοτε | ἐτιθεσθε | ἱστασθε | ἐδιδοσθε |
| ἐτιθεσαν | ἱστασαν | ἐδιδοσαν | ἐτιθεντο | ἱσταντο | ἐδιδοντο |

**Future Active/Middle/Passive**
Formed directly from the principal parts, following the pattern of λυω.

**Aorist Active** διδωμι **and** τιθημι

*Indicative*
ἐθηκα and ἐδωκα following the pattern of λυω

| *Imperative* | | *Infinitive* | |
|---|---|---|---|
| θες<br>θετω<br>θετε<br>θετωσαν | δος<br>δοτω<br>δοτε<br>δοτωσαν | θειναι | δουναι |

*Subjunctive and Participle*
As in Present, but using the verbal stems (θ not τιθ, δ not διδ).

**Aorist Active** ἱστημι

*1st Aorist (Transitive)*
All moods formed from ἐστησα following the pattern of λυω.

*2nd Aorist (Intransitive)*
*Indicative*: ἐστην, ἐστης, ἐστη, ἐστημεν, ἐστητε, ἐστησαν
*Imperative*: στηθι, στητω, στητε, στητωσαν
*Infinitive*: στηναι
*Subjunctive and Participle*: As in Present, but using the verbal stem (στ not ἱστ).

**Aorist Middle**

| *Indicative* | | | *Imperative* | | |
|---|---|---|---|---|---|
| ἐθεμην | ἐσταμην | ἐδομην | | | |
| ἐθου | ἐστω | ἐδου | θου | στω | δου |
| ἐθετο | ἐστατο | ἐδοτο | θεσθω | στασθω | δοσθω |
| ἐθεμεθα | ἐσταμεθα | ἐδομεθα | | | |
| ἐθεσθε | ἐστασθε | ἐδοσθε | θεσθε | στασθε | δοσθε |
| ἐθεντο | ἐσταντο | ἐδοντο | θεσθωσαν | στασθωσαν | δοσθωσαν |

*Infinitive, Subjunctive and Participle*
As in Present, but using the verbal stems (θ not τιθ, δ not διδ, στ not ἱστ).

**Aorist Passive**
Formed directly from the principal parts, following the pattern of λυω.

**Perfect Active/Middle/Passive**
Formed directly from the principal parts, following the pattern of λυω.
(ἱστημι uses both ἑστηκως and ἑστως for the Perfect Active participle)

**Meaning of ἱστημι**

| Meaning | | Form | |
|---|---|---|---|
| *Transitive:* | | | |
| Present | I cause to stand | Present Active | ἱστημι |
| Imperfect | I was causing to stand | Imperfect Active | ἱστην† |
| Future | I will cause to stand | Future Active | στησω† |
| Aorist | I caused to stand | 1st Aorist Active | ἐστησα† |
| Perfect | I have caused to stand | Perfect Active | ἑστηκα† |
| *Intransitive* | | | |
| Present | I stand | Perfect Active | ἑστηκα† |
| Imperfect | I was standing | Pluperfect Active | εἱστηκειν† |
| Future | I will stand | Future Middle | στησομαι† |
| Past | I stood | 2nd Aorist Active *or* | ἐστην |
| | | Aorist Passive | ἐσταθην† |
| Perfect | I have stood | Perfect Middle/Passive | ἑσταμαι† |

† conjugate identically to the corresponding part of λυω.

**Verbs in** -υμι

*Present Active Indicative*: δεικνυμι, δεικνυεις, δεικνυσι(ν), δεικνυμεν, δεικνυτε, δεικνυασιν.

*All other Present forms*: As διδωμι but δεικνυ replacing διδο / διδου

*All non-Present forms*: Formed directly from the principal parts, following the pattern of λυω.

ἱημι

As τιθημι with the Present stem ἱε and verbal stem ἑ.

φημι

This only appears in the following forms:

*Present Indicative Active*: φημι, I say; φησιν, he says; φασιν, they say.

*Imperfect Indicative Active*: ἐφη, he said.

εἰμι

| Indicative | | | Imperative | Subjunctive |
|---|---|---|---|---|
| Present | Future | Imperfect | | |
| εἰμι | ἐσομαι | ἠμην | | ὠ |
| εἶ | ἐσῃ | ἠς (or ἠσθα) | ἰσθι | ἠς |
| ἐστι(ν) | ἐσται | ἠν | ἐστω | ἠ |
| ἐσμεν | ἐσομεθα | ἠμεν (or ἠμεθα) | | ὠμεν |
| ἐστε | ἐσεσθε | ἠτε | ἐστε | ἠτε |
| εἰσι(ν) | ἐσονται | ἠσαν | ἐστωσαν | ὠσιν |

| *Present Infinitive* | εἰναι |
|---|---|
| *Present participle* | ὠν, οὐσα, ὀν (M/N stem ὀντ-) |

**Note:** Usually the Imperative of γινομαι is used instead of the Imperative of εἰμι.

## PATTERNS OF LETTER CHANGES

**Addition of σ**

*In general (verbs and nouns)*

| | | | | |
|---|---|---|---|---|
| κ, γ, χ, σσ | | | | ξ |
| π, β, φ | + | σ | → | ψ |
| τ, δ, θ, ζ | | | | σ |

*Plus, for dative plural of 3rd declension nouns/adjectives/participles*

εντ + σιν → εισιν     οντ + σιν → ουσιν

**Note:** κραζω has Future κραξω and Aorist ἐκραξα.
ἀνηρ has dative plural ἀνδρασιν and χειρ has dative plural χερσιν.

**Augments**

| | | | |
|---|---|---|---|
| | α | becomes | η |
| ἐ plus | ε | becomes | η |
| | ο | becomes | ω |
| | η, ι, υ and ω | remain | η, ι, υ and ω |

## COMMON 2ND AORISTS

| 2nd Aorist | Present | | Present | 2nd Aorist | |
|---|---|---|---|---|---|
| ἀπεθανον | ἀποθνῃσκω | I die | ἀγω | ἠγαγον | I lead |
| ἐβαλον | βαλλω | I throw | ἁμαρτανω | ἡμαρτον | I sin |
| ἐβην | βαινω | I go | ἀποθνῃσκω | ἀπεθανον | I die |
| ἐγενομην | γινομαι | I become | βαινω | ἐβην | I go |
| ἐγνων | γινωσκω | I know | βαλλω | ἐβαλον | I throw |
| εἰδον | ὁραω | I see | γινομαι | ἐγενομην | I become |
| εἰπον | λεγω | I say | γινωσκω | ἐγνων | I know |
| ἐλαβον | λαμβανω | I take | ἐρχομαι | ἠλθον | I come |
| ἐμαθον | μανθανω | I learn | ἐσθιω | ἐφαγον | I eat |
| ἐπαθον | πασχω | I suffer | εὑρισκω | εὑρον | I find |
| ἐπεσον | πιπτω | I fall | ἐχω | ἐσχον | I have |
| ἐπιον | πινω | I drink | καταλειπω | κατελιπον | I leave |
| ἐσχον | ἐχω | I have | λαμβανω | ἐλαβον | I take |
| εὑρον | εὑρισκω | I find | λεγω | εἰπον | I say |
| ἐφαγον | ἐσθιω | I eat | μανθανω | ἐμαθον | I learn |
| ἐφυγον | φευγω | I flee | ὁραω | εἰδον | I see |
| ἠγαγον | ἀγω | I lead | πασχω | ἐπαθον | I suffer |
| ἠλθον | ἐρχομαι | I come | πινω | ἐπιον | I drink |
| ἡμαρτον | ἁμαρτανω | I sin | πιπτω | ἐπεσον | I throw |
| ἠνεγκον | φερω | I carry | φερω | ἠνεγκον | I bring |
| κατελιπον | καταλειπω | I leave | φευγω | ἐφυγον | I flee |

| 2nd Aorist participles (Masc. Nom. Sing.)[2] | Present | 2nd Aorist participles (Masc. Nom. Sing.)[2] | Present |
|---|---|---|---|
| ἀγαγων | ἀγω | ἰδων | ὁραω |
| ἁμαρτων | ἁμαρτανω | καταλιπων | καταλειπω |
| ἀποθανων | ἀποθνησκω | λαβων | λαμβανω |
| βαλων | βαλλω | μαθων | μανθανω |
| βας | βαινω | παθων | πασχω |
| γενομενος | γινομαι | πεσων | πιπτω |
| γνους | γινωσκω | πιων | πινω |
| εἰπων | λεγω | σχων | ἐχω |
| ἐλθων | ἐρχομαι | φαγων | ἐσθιω |
| ἐνεγκων | φερω | φυγων | φευγω |
| εὑρων | εὑρισκω | | |

[2] Given to display the un-augmented forms.

## PREPOSITIONS

***Note:*** *These lists include some prepositions which were not given in Chapter 4. Some occur elsewhere in the book. A few are not sufficiently common to occur in the vocabulary lists but are here for completeness.*

**Greek prepositions with their meaning with different cases**

| | **+ accusative** | **+ genitive** | **+ dative** |
|---|---|---|---|
| ἀνα | upwards, again | | |
| ἀντι | | instead of | |
| ἀπο | | (away) from | |
| ἀχρι | | until | |
| δια | because of | through | |
| εἰς | to, into | | |
| ἐκ | | (out) from | |
| ἐμπροσθεν | before (place) | | |
| ἐν | | | in (or rarely 'by/with') |
| ἑνεκα | | for the sake of | |
| ἐνωπιον | | before (place) | |
| ἐξω | | outside | |
| ἐπι | onto | on, in the time of | on/in, on the basis of |
| ἑως | | until | |
| κατα | according to | against | |
| μετα | after | with | |
| ὀπισω | | after (place) | |
| παρα | (motion) beside | from beside (a person) | (location) beside |
| περαν | | on the other side of | |
| περι | approximately, around | concerning, about | |
| προ | | before (time) | |
| προς | to, towards, against | | |
| συν | | | with |
| ὑπερ | above | on behalf of | |
| ὑπο | under | by | |
| χωρις | | apart from | |

## Time expressions

Time expressions do not normally use prepositions.

**Time word +**

| | | | |
|---|---|---|---|
| **accusative:** | Time 'how long' | δυο ἡμερας | for two days |
| **genitive:** | Time 'during' | της νυκτος | during the night |
| **dative:** | Time 'at which' | ἐκεινῃ τῃ ἡμερᾳ | on that day |

Notes

- In practice in the New Testament ἐν is often used together with the dative for time 'at which' – ἐν ἐκεινῃ τῃ ἡμερᾳ – on that day.
- Generally when words such as 'during', 'while', 'when' or 'after' occur in English, they would be communicated in Greek by the correct tense of the participle ('during' and 'while' – Present; 'when' and 'after' – Aorist).

**English prepositions with their equivalents in Greek**

| | |
|---|---|
| about | περι + gen. |
| above | ὑπερ + acc. |
| according to | κατα + acc. |
| after | *time* – it happened after – μετα + acc.<br>*place* – he followed after – ὀπισω + gen. |
| again | ἀνα + acc. |
| against | κατα + gen. |
| apart from | χωρις + gen. |
| approximately | περι + acc. |
| around | περι + acc. |
| because of | δια + acc. |
| before | *place* – before the throne – ἐμπροσθεν + gen.; ἐνωπιον + gen.<br>*time* – before that day – προ + gen. |
| beside | *location* – walking beside the sea – παρα + dat.<br>*motion* – sitting beside the sea – παρα + acc.<br>*from a person* – from beside the king – παρα + gen. |
| by | *instrument (inanimate)* – by a word – dative (rarely ἐν + dat.)<br>*agent (animate)* – by a messenger – ὑπο + gen.<br>*time 'during which'* – by night – genitive |
| concerning | περι + gen. |
| during | *time 'during which'* – during the night – genitive |

| | |
|---|---|
| for | *indirect object* – I work for the Lord – dative<br>*on behalf of* – he died for us – ὑπερ + gen.<br>*for the sake of* – for the sake of righteousness – ἑνεκα + gen.<br>*time 'how long'* – for forty days – accusative |
| from | *away from* – away from the sea – ἀπο + gen.<br>*out of* – what comes out of the heart – ἐκ + gen.<br>*beside a person* – from beside the king – παρα + gen. |
| in<br>in the time of<br>instead of<br>into | ἐν + dat. (rarely ἐπι + dat.)<br>ἐπι + gen.<br>ἀντι + gen.<br>εἰς + acc. |
| on | *location* – on the earth – ἐπι + gen.; ἐπι + dat.<br>*time 'at which'* – on that day – dative; ἐν + dat. |
| on behalf of<br>on the basis of<br>on the other side of<br>onto<br>(out) from<br>outside<br>through | ὑπερ + gen.<br>ἐπι + dat.<br>περαν + gen.<br>ἐπι + acc.<br>ἐκ + gen.<br>ἐξω + gen.<br>δια + gen. |
| to | *indirect object* – she spoke to me – dative<br>*motion into* – he went into the sea – εἰς + acc.<br>*motion towards* – he went towards the sea – προς + acc. |
| towards<br>under<br>until<br>upwards | προς + acc.<br>ὑπο + acc.<br>ἀχρι + gen. or ἑως + gen.<br>ἀνα + acc. |
| with | *instrument* – with a word – dative (rarely ἐν + dat.)<br>*in company of* – with him – μετα + gen. or συν + dat. |

## WORDS DISTINGUISHED BY ACCENTS

1. εἰ (page 57)
no accent (εἰ) = if; circumflex (εἶ) = you (singular) are

2. ἀλλα (page 103)
accent on first syllable (ἄλλα) = neuter nom./acc. pl. of ἀλλος (other things)
accent on second syllable (ἀλλὰ) = but

3. ἡ, ὁ, οἱ, αἱ (page 113)
no accent (e.g. ὁ) = from ὁ, ἡ, το meaning 'the', accent (e.g. ὃ) = from ὅς meaning 'who'

4. **liquid verbs** (pages 130–31)
circumflex (e.g. μενεῖς) = future (you will stay); no circumflex (e.g. μένεις) = present (you are staying)

5. τις **in all its forms** (pages 140–1)
accent on first syllable (e.g.) τίς = interrogative (who))
no accent or accent on second syllable (e.g. τις, τινὰς) = indefinite (someone)

## OTHER EASILY CONFUSED WORDS

| | |
|---|---|
| ἀρα / ἀρ- | so / *(liquid) aorist* of αἰρω |
| ἀρτι / ἀχρι | now, just now / until |
| γενν- / γεν- / γν- | I bear / 2nd *aorist* of γινομαι / 2nd *aorist* of γινωσκω |
| δε / δει | but / it is necessary |
| δια / διο / δυο | because of, through / therefore / two |
| εἰδον / εἰπον / ἐπιον | 2nd *aorist* of ὁραω / 2nd *aorist* of λεγω / 2nd *aorist* of πινω |
| εἰδον / εἰδως | 2nd *aorist* of ὁραω / *participle* from οἰδα |
| εἰς / εἱς | into / one |
| ἐξ / ἑξ | from (before vowel) / six |
| ἐν / ἑν | in / one |
| ἐπει / ἐπι | since / onto, on |
| καθως / καλως | just as / appropriately, well |
| ὁτε / ὁτι | when / that, because, " (marking beginning of speech) |
| οὐ / οὑ / οὗ | not / where / whose, of whom |
| ποτε / τοτε | once / then |
| σημειον / σημερον | sign, miracle / today |
| ὑπερ / ὑπο | above, on behalf of / under, by |
| ὡς / ὡσπερ / ὡστε | as, like / just as / with the result |

# Answers to practice questions and section A exercises

## CHAPTER 1

### 1.1

A.

| α | β | γ | δ | ε | ζ | η | θ | ι | κ | λ | μ | ν | ξ | ο | π | ρ | σ | τ | υ | φ | χ | ψ | ω |
|---|---|---|---|---|---|---|---|---|---|---|---|---|---|---|---|---|---|---|---|---|---|---|---|
| a | b | g | d | e | z | ē | th | i | k | l | m | n | x | o | p | r | s | t | u | ph or f | ch | ps | ō |

B.

| a | b | c | d | e | f | g | h | i | j | k | l | m | n | o | p | q | r | s | t | u | v | w | x | y | z |
|---|---|---|---|---|---|---|---|---|---|---|---|---|---|---|---|---|---|---|---|---|---|---|---|---|---|
| α | β | κ | δ | ε | φ | γ | | ι | ι | κ | λ | μ | ν | ο | π | | ρ | σ or ς | τ | υ | | | ξ | υ | ζ |

C. 1.baptisma – baptism 2. thronos – throne 3. kosmos – cosmos, world 4. megas – great 5. mikros – small 6. mustērion *or* mystērion – mystery 7. parabolē – parable 8. paralutikos *or* paralytikos – paralytic 9. sabbaton – Sabbath

D. 1. βλασφημη – blasphemy 2. καρδια – heart 3. λογικος – rational, spiritual 4. μητηρ – mother 5. πατηρ – father 6. πνευματικος – spiritual 7. προφητης – prophet 8. πυρ – fire 9. φωνη – voice

### 1.2

Errors in: 1 (should be ἀγω), 2 (should be βλεπω), 4 (should be λεγω).

### 1.3 and 1.4

A. 1. Paulos (Paul) 2. Maria (Mary) 3. Abraam (Abraham) 4. Joseph 5. Simon 6. Heroides (Herod) 7. Jerusalem 8. Caesar

B. 1. Βαρναβας 2. Πετρος 3. Φιλιππος 4. Πιλατος 5. Τιμοθεος 6. Ἰουδαια 7. Σατανας 8. Φαρισαιος

C. pater hēmōn ho en tois ouranois / hagiasthētō to onoma sou / elthetō hē basileia sou / genēthētō to thelēma sou / hōs en ouranō (i) kai epi gēs

### 1.5

Smooth breathings on 2 (ἀγω) and 5 (ἰωτα).

### 1.6

1 and 4 are questions.

## Exercises

1. [1] en archē(i) ēn ho logos, kai ho logos ēn pros ton theon, kai theos ēn ho logos.
[2] houtos ēn en archē(i) pros ton theon. [3] panta di’ autou egeneto, kai chōris autou
egeneto oude hen. ho gegonen [4] en autō(i) zōē ēn, kai hē zōē ēn to phōs tōn
anthrōpōn; [5] kai to phōs en tē(i) skotia(i) phainei, kai hē skotia auto ou katelaben.
[6] egeneto anthrōpos apestalmenos para theou, onoma autō(i) Iōannēs; [7] houtos
ēlthen eis marturian, hina marturēsē(i) peri tou phōtos, hina pantes pisteusōsin di’
autou. [8] ouk ēn ekeinos to phōs, all’ hina marturēsē(i) peri tou phōtos. [9] ēn to
phōs to alēthinon, ho phōtizei panta anthrōpon, erchomenon eis ton kosmon. [10] en
tō(i) kosmō(i) ēn, kai ho kosmos di’ autou egeneto, kai ho kosmos auton ouk egnō.
[11] eis ta idia ēlthen, kai hoi idioi auton ou parelabon. [12] hosoi de elabon auton,
edōken autois exousian tekna theou genesthai tois pisteuousin eis to onoma
autou, [13] hoi ouk ex haimatōn oude ek thelēmatos sarkos oude ek thelēmatos
andros all’ ek theou egennēthēsan. [14] kai ho logos sarx egeneto kai eskēnōsen en
hēmin, kai etheasametha tēn doxan autou, doxan hōs monogenous para patros,
plērēs charitos kai alētheias.

2. [15] Ἰωαννης μαρτυρει περι αὐτου και κεκραγεν λεγων, Οὑτος ἠν ὁν
εἰπον, Ὁ ὀπισω μου ἐρχομενος ἐμπροσθεν μου γεγονεν, ὁτι πρωτος μου ἠν.
[16] ὁτι ἐκ του πληρωματος αὐτου ἡμεις παντες ἐλαβομεν και χαριν ἀντι
χαριτος· [17] ὁτι ὁ νομος δια Μωϋσεως ἐδοθη, ἡ χαρις και ἡ ἀληθεια δια
Ἰησου Χριστου ἐγενετο. [18] θεον οὐδεις ἑωρακεν πωποτε· μονογενης θεος ὁ
ὠν εἰς τον κολπον του πατρος ἐκεινος ἐξηγησατο.

[19] Και αὑτη ἐστιν ἡ μαρτυρια του Ἰωαννου, ὁτε ἀπεστειλαν προς αὐτον
οἱ Ἰουδαιοι ἐξ Ἱεροσολυμων ἱερεις και Λευιτας ἱνα ἐρωτησωσιν αὐτον, Συ
τις εἰ; [20] και ὡμολογησεν και οὐκ ἠρνησατο, και ὡμολογησεν ὁτι Ἐγω οὐκ
εἰμι ὁ Χριστος. [21] και ἠρωτησαν αὐτον, Τι οὐν; Συ Ἠλιας εἰ; και λεγει, Οὐκ
εἰμι. Ὁ προφητης εἰ συ; και ἀπεκριθη, Οὐ. [22] εἰπαν οὐν αὐτῳ, Τις εἰ; ἱνα
ἀποκρισιν δωμεν τοις πεμψασιν ἡμας· τι λεγεις περι σεαυτου; [23] ἐφη, Ἐγω
φωνη βοωντος ἐν τῃ ἐρημῳ, Εὐθυνατε την ὁδον κυριου, καθως εἰπεν
Ἠσαϊας ὁ προφητης.

# CHAPTER 2

## 2.1

1. he (she, it) is taking (receiving) 2. we are teaching 3. they are hearing 4. you (pl.) have 5. I see 6. you (s.) untie 7. βαλλει 8. ἐχουσιν (or ἐχουσι) 9. ἀγομεν

## 2.2

1. they love 2. you (pl.) are doing 3. he (she, it) is calling 4. we are keeping 5. I am seeking 6. you (s.) are speaking 7. λαλουσιν (or λεγουσιν) 8. ποιει 9. ζητειτε

## 2.3.1

1. accusative singular 2. nominative plural 3. accusative plural 4. nominative plural 5. nominative singular 6. accusative plural 7. nominative plural 8. accusative singular

## 2.3.3

1. A brother is teaching crowds. 2. We are seeking bread. 3. You (s.) are untying slaves. 4. A lord says a word. 5. People are calling. 6. Angels are keeping laws. 7. ἀδελφος βλεπει οἰκον. 8. ἀνθρωποι βλεπουσιν. 9. φιλουμεν κοσμον. 10. θεος ἀγει.

## 2.4 and 2.5

1. The sons have a house. 2. You (pl.) call the brother. 3. God is making the heavens. 4. An angel is leading crowds. 5. The lord is listening. 6. ζητουμεν τον Χριστον. 7. οἱ υἱοι λαλουσιν (or λεγουσιν) λογους. 8. ὁ λαος φιλει τον θεον (or οἱ ἀνθρωποι φιλουσιν τον θεον).

## Exercise Section A

1. I have a son. 2. The person calls a slave. 3. You (s.) love the law. 4. Amen amen, I say (am saying) . . . 5. The Messiah is teaching the crowd. (Christ teaches the crowd.) 6. God makes the world and the heaven. 7. Joseph receives the brothers. 8. We hear (are listening to) and love the message/word. 9. ὁ Χριστος λεγει τους λογους. 10. ὁ ὀχλος ἀκουει τον νομον. 11. λυεις τους δουλους. 12. (οἱ) ἀνθρωποι ποιουσιν (τον) ἀρτον.

## CHAPTER 3

### 3.1

1. Accusative 2. Genitive 3. Dative 4. Nominative 5. Genitive 6. Dative 7. Accusative 8. Nominative 9. Genitive Singular 10. Dative Plural 11. Accusative Plural 12. Dative Singular 13. Genitive Plural 14. Genitive Singular 15. Nominative Plural 16. Accusative Singular

### 3.2

1. I hear the Lord. 2. She sees the angel of God (or She sees God's angel). 3. We have faith in the Messiah. 4. You hear the words. 5. ἀκουουσιν του θεου. 6. πιστευω τῳ κυριῳ.

### Half-way Practice

1. We have the law of God. 2. The slaves are speaking to the Lord. 3. I am seeking the house of Christ. 4. You are making bread for the brothers. 5. The crowd hears the word of the Lord. 6. She sees the angel and she listens to (hears) the angel. 7. He has faith in the son of God. 8. The brother unties a slave for the Lord. 9. διδασκω τον λογον του θεου. 10. ἀκουουσιν του υἱου. 11. τηρουμεν τον νομον (του) οὐρανου. 12. λεγεις (or λεγετε) τῳ ὀχλῳ.

### 3.3.2

1. Accusative Singular 2. Dative Singular 3. Nominative *or* Accusative Plural 4. Genitive Singular 5. Dative Plural 6. Genitive Plural 7. Nominative Singular 8. Genitive Singular

### 3.3.3

1. τον 2. τῃ 3. των 4. ἡ 5. τα 6. τοις 7. την 8. τα

### 3.3.4 and 3.3.5

1. Nominative *or* Accusative Plural 2. Genitive Plural 3. Genitive Singular 4. Dative Singular Masculine *or* Neuter 5. Dative Plural 6. Accusative Singular Feminine 7. Dative Singular 8. Dative Plural 9. Accusative Singular 10. No 11. Yes 12. Yes 13. Yes 14. No 15. No 16. No 17. Yes 18. No

### 3.4

2, 4 and 5 could be vocatives (1 accusative, 3 nominative).

### 3.6

1. I love him. 2. She is teaching his words. 3. They have it. 4. I hear her voice. 5. Paul is calling them. 6. βλεπουσιν τον δουλον. 7. τηρει το τεκνον αὐτου. 8. ὁ Ἰησους φιλει τα τεκνα αὐτων.

### Exercise Section A

1. The sister is saying to Jesus: 'Lord, I believe.' 2. I am doing the works of God. 3. God loves the son and speaks to him. 4. We are receiving and keeping his books. 5. The crowd is saying to Jesus, 'You have a demon.' 6. Peter, you are teaching the kingdom of God. 7. The sisters and brothers are keeping the laws and the Sabbath. 8. Does the son of man keep the Sabbath? 9. ἡ ἐκκλησια αὐτων ζητει την δοξαν του θεου. 10. ὁ Παυλος διδασκει την οἰκιαν του κυριου. 11. ἀδελφοι και ἀδελφαι, λαμβανετε την ἀγαπην του θεου. 12. τα τεκνα βαλλει γην.

## CHAPTER 4

### 4.1

1. in the world 2. into the heavens 3. towards the boats 4. out of (from) the house 5. (away) from the temple 6. in the church (assembly) 7. ἐκ της καρδιας 8. εἰς τους ὀχλους 9. ἀπο αὐτου

### 4.2

1. with them 2. because of the law 3. against God 4. on behalf of the lord 5. from God 6. through Christ 7. περι (της) ἀγαπης 8. ἐκ της θαλασσης 9. ὑπο την γην

### Half-way Practice

1. I believe because of the word of the Lord. 2. Jesus is leading the brothers towards the boats. 3. They are speaking to him about the temple. 4. The master of the household speaks on behalf of the child. 5. The son takes the bread with him. 6. God loves the deeds according to the law. 7. Paul speaks to the people against God's messiah. 8. They are leading the children into the house. 9. βλεπω αὐτο ἐν τῃ καρδιᾳ αὐτης. 10. ὁ Ἰησους διδασκει τον ὀχλον ἐξω του ἱερου. 11. ὁ θεος φιλει τους λαους ὑπο (τον) οὐρανον. 12. ὁ θεος λεγει τον νομον δια ἀγγελων (δι᾽ ἀγγελων).

### 4.3

Instrumental datives in 2 and 4 (in 1 'with' = 'in company of' hence μετα + gen.; in 3 'her' being a person, not an inanimate object, is classed as an agent and not an instrument, hence ὑπο + gen.).

### 4.5 and 4.6

1. Does God hear? 2. God does not hear. 3. How does God speak? 4. I do not believe him. 5. Where are you leading the crowd? 6. Do you keep the law?

### Exercise Section A

1. I am not receiving glory from people. 2. Do you (s.) believe in the son of man? 3. The Lord is saying to them, 'Where are you leading them? 4. Peter is teaching them about the kingdom beside the boats. 5. We are looking up into heaven in front of the temple. 6. Jesus is casting demons out of the person with a word. 7. I am living under sin and against God's law. 8. Peter is gathering the church into (in) the house of Jacob's sister. 9. ὑπαγομεν προς την θαλασσαν. 10. παρακαλειτε τους ἀδελφους ἐν κυριῳ.[1] 11. τηρεις το σαββατον δια τον νομον; 12. οἱ ἀνθρωποι ἐν τῳ πλοιῳ προσκυνουσιν τῳ κυριῳ.

## CHAPTER 5

### 5.1

1. Masc. Nom. Pl. 2. Masc./Fem./Neut. Gen. Pl. 3. Masc. Acc. Sing. *or* Neut. Nom./Acc. Sing. 4. Fem. Nom. Sing. 5. Fem. Dat. Pl. 6. Fem. Acc. Sing. 7. Fem. Nom. Sing. *or* Neut. Nom./Acc. Pl. 8. Masc. Dat. Pl.

### 5.2

1. We are keeping the good law. 2. The holy brother is listening. 3. He has a blind slave. 4. A holy people loves God. 5. The lord does not have a beautiful son. 6. She is casting out the wicked demons 7. You (pl.) are calling the good sisters. 8. ζητω πονηραν ζωην. 9. πιστευει τῃ ἰδιᾳ καρδιᾳ. 10. ὁ ὀχλος ζητει τον μονον θεον.

### 5.3

1. you (pl.) are 2. I am 3. they are 4. you (sing.) are 5. he/she/it is

---

[1] Interestingly, in the New Testament ἐν κυριῳ is used far more frequently than ἐν τῳ κυριῳ (forty-eight occurrences as against one).

## 5.4

1. Are you (pl.) good? 2. The law of God is holy. 3. The children are Jewish. 4. Is the blind sister dead? 5. Is holy Jerusalem eternal? 6. ἀγαθον ἡ πονηρον (ἐστιν) το εὐαγγελιον; 7. ὁ θεος ὁ μονος (ἐστιν) ἐν οὐρανῳ. (or οὐρανοις). 8. ἐσμεν ἐν τῃ συναγωγῃ.

## Half-way Practice

1. Peter loves the dead child. 2. The blind son sees the messiah. 3. They call the lord holy. 4. He throws it into the good earth. 5. We do not believe (in) a different gospel. 6. The slave of God is blessed. 7. Is the kingdom of Jesus holy? 8. The good brother is not alone. 9. πονηρος ὀχλος ζητει σημεια. 10. ὁ θεος (ἐστιν) νεκρος; 11. ὑπαγομεν εἰς (or προς) τους ἰδιους οἰκους (or τας ἰδιας οἰκιας). 12. ἡ ἀδελφη ἡ Ἰουδαια (ἐστιν) ἀγαθη.

## 5.5

1. God loves the Jews. 2. The good (people/men) teach. 3. Paul speaks to the holy ones. 4. The blind man departs.

## 5.6

1. πολλαι 2. πολλα 3. πολλων 4. πολλην 5. πολλοις 6. μεγαν 7. μεγαλων 8. μεγαλην 9. μεγαλῃ 10. μεγα

## 5.7 and 5.8

1. Is there a god in heaven? 2. Abraham's child is a sign. 3. There are many holy Jews. 4. The word of Jesus is good news.

## Exercise Section A

1. Jesus is saying to her, 'I am life and peace.' 2. And Peter is saying to him, 'You are the Messiah, the son of God.' 3. I receive the kingdom of God like a child. 4. He is not a god of dead people. / He is not a god of the dead. 5. The demon is saying, 'Jesus, you are the holy one of God.' 6. She sees God's new heaven and new earth. 7. Beloved, I am not teaching a different law, but the one from (the) beginning. 8. The great (loud) voice from heaven (the heavens) says, 'You are my beloved son.' 9. αἱ ἡμεραι πονηραι εἰσιν και (οἱ ἀνθρωποι) οἱ πονηροι τα πονηρα ποιουσιν. 10. δικαιος (ἐστιν) ὁ νομος, ἀλλα ἐστιν ὁ καιρος του εὐαγγελιου. 11. ἑκαστος ἐχει τον ἰδιον οἰκον. 12. ὁ Χριστος (ἐστιν) κεφαλη της ἐκκλησιας.

## CHAPTER 6

### 6.2

1. Future 2. Imperfect 3. Aorist 4. Imperfect 5. Future 6. Present

### 6.3

1. Future 2. Imperfect 3. Imperfect 4. Present 5. Aorist 6. Present 7. I will hear 8. I take 9. I was sending 10. I was baptizing 11. I believed 12. I have.

### 6.4

1. we were throwing 2. we untied 3. you (pl.) will hear 4. you (s.) are throwing out 5. they believed 6. they will set free 7. γραφομεν 8. πιστευσουσιν 9. ἐλαμβανετε

### Half-way Practice

1. She was teaching the crowd. 2. God will hear him. 3. The holy ones have the law. 4. We will untie the boat. 5. Did you believe because of the word? 6. I/they were speaking about the kingdom. 7. How will you divorce her? 8. The brothers did not believe. 9. ἐλαμβανομεν το πλοιον. 10. ἐπιστευσαν τῳ θεῳ. 11. ὁ ἀγαθος κυριος ἀπολυσει τους δουλους. 12. ἐλεγον ἀλλα νυν ἀκουσω.

### 6.5

1. ἠγον 2. ὑπηγον 3. ἐβλεπον 4. ἀνεβλεπον 5. παρελαμβανον 6. ἀπεκαλυπτον 7. ἠνοιγον 8. ἐδιδασκον

### 6.6

1. ἐβαπτισα 2. ἐπεμψα 3. ἠκουσα 4. ἀπελυσα 5. ἐκηρυξα 6. ἀνεβλεψα 7. ἀπεκαλυψα 8. ἐδοξασα

### 6.7

1. Imperfect 2. Aorist 3. Future 4. Aorist 5. Imperfect 6. Imperfect 7. Future 8. Aorist.

### 6.8

1. they did 2. she will love 3. we were worshipping 4. they will ask 5. he kept 6. I/they were seeking 7. you gave thanks 8. they built

## Exercise Section A

1. Once I baptized, but now he will baptize. 2. A voice from heaven proclaimed, 'And I glorified it and will glorify (it) again.' 3. And he was casting out many demons in each place. 4. He called and saved them; then they worshipped him. 5. Jesus was receiving the children and the children listened to Jesus. 6. The holy angel was opening the heavens. 7. And you (s.) will call the child 'Jesus': he will save his people from their sins. 8. And they spoke the message (word) of the Lord to the faithful brothers in his house. 9. νυν εὐλογησομεν τον κυριον. 10. ἠδη ἐγραψα αὐτοις, ἀλλα νυν παλιν γραψω. 11. ἀπεκαλυψεν την ἀγαπην αὐτου ὁτε ἐγραψεν αὐτῃ. 12. ᾐτησαν σημεια και ἐκραξαν φωνῃ μεγαλῃ τῳ Ἰησου.

## CHAPTER 7

### 7.2

1. Throw out! (continuously) 2. Repent! (default) 3. Keep (pl.) the law! (continuously) (or 'you are keeping the law') 4. Write to her! (default) 5. Hear (pl.) the voice/sound! (continuously) (or 'you are hearing the voice/sound') 6. Seek (pl.) God! (default) 7. You (pl.) will seek God. 8. ἀνοιξον τους οὐρανους. 9. διδασκετε αὐτην. 10. λυσατε τα τεκνα.

### 7.3

1. Do you (s.) wish to see? 2. We were seeking to hear. 3. It is necessary to walk about (live). 4. You were about to write. 5. θελετε μετανοησαι; 6. δει φιλειν τον θεον.

## Half-way Practice

1. Baptise the brothers! (or 'you are baptising the brothers.') 2. Listen to him! 3. It is permitted to speak? (or 'Is speaking allowed?') 4. It is necessary to speak to Timothy. 5. Worship the holy God! (or 'you are worshipping the holy God'.) 6. Listen to him! 7. I want to send a messenger. 8. Do not seek to divorce. 9. θελετε εὐχαριστησαι; (or possibly εὐχαριστειν;) 10. ζητειτε το εὐαγγελιον. 11. μη περιπατει ἐν τῳ ἱερῳ. 12. μελλουσιν κραξαι· Ἀμην.

### 7.4.1

Note: all are masculine nominative 1. Present Plural 2. Aorist Singular 3. Aorist Plural 4. Aorist Singular 5. Present Singular 6. Present Singular 7. Present Plural 8. Aorist Singular

### 7.4.2

1. As they looked they were going away. 2. He cried out (while) saying. 3. When he saw (him), he says to him. 4. They were living keeping the law. 5. After I heard the message, I glorified God. 6. When they believed, they repented.

### 7.4.3

1. After they opened their eyes, they saw the sea. 2. While speaking to the crowd the apostle was looking at heaven. 3. When he had written the book, Peter sent it for the church. 4. κηρυξαντες τον λογον προσεκυνησαν τῳ θεῳ.

### 7.5

1. The one who sent him saves. 2. The one who sees God is blessed. 3. The ones who bear witness (or 'the witnesses') will preach. 4. The believer speaks peace.

## Exercise Section A

1. And he says to the Pharisees, 'Is it lawful on the Sabbath to do good or to do evil, to save a life or not to save it?' 2. Amen amen I say, (or 'truly truly I say') the one who believes has eternal life. 3. His commandment is eternal life. 4. And the sheep hear his voice and his own sheep follow after him. 5. The faithful sister was crying out to Jesus, 'Have mercy, Lord, son of David!' 6. And Jesus proclaimed, saying, 'Repent and believe (in) the good news. 7. He says to the crowd with his apostles, 'If you wish to follow after the Lord, it is necessary to have boldness.' 8. I am a man under authority, and I say to a slave, 'Do it,' and he does. 9. ἐλεγεν παραβολην περι (της) χαρας. 10. Μη ἀναγετε τυφλα θηρια εἰς το ἱερον. 11. θεωρειτε το μνημειον; 12. ὁ Ἰησους ἐλεγεν ἐν παραβολαις ἀλλα κατ᾽ ἐξουσιαν.

# CHAPTER 8

### 8.1.1

All the verbs are deponent
1. Present Indicative 3rd Plural 2. Imperfect Indicative 3rd Singular 3. Imperfect Indicative 1st Singular 4. Aorist Participle Singular (masculine nominative) 5. Future Indicative 3rd Singular 6. Present Imperative 2nd Singular 7. Present Participle Plural (masculine nominative) 8. Present Participle Singular (masculine nominative) 9. Present Indicative 2nd Plural *or* Present Imperative 2nd Plural

## 8.1.3

1. βλεπουσιν 2. ἐρχεται 3. ἐδεχεσθε 4. ἀρξαμενοι 5. γραψομεν 6. ἐξερχεσθε 7. ἐλογισαντο 8. πειθων 9. προσευχεσθαι 10. ἠρνουντο (ἀρνεομαι goes through the same contractions as φιλεω thus what should be ἠρνεοντο becomes ἠρνουντο [ε + ο = ου])

## Half-way Practice

1. They are coming into the temple. 2. I wish to rescue him. 3. You (pl.) are receiving the word. (or 'Receive the word!') 4. After they heard, they began to go. 5. As he was leaving, he was glorifying God. 6. I am about to pray, saying: 7. The Jews are leaving the synagogue. 8. Do not preach the good news! 9. οἱ Φαρισαιοι ἠρξαντο ἐργασασθαι (ἐργαζεσθαι). 10. ἠσπαζοντο τους πονηρους. 11. ἀρνησομαι τηρειν τον νομον. 12. δει εἰσερχεσθαι εἰς το ἱερον.

## 8.2

1. The commandments were holy. 2. David was great. 3. I wish to be with them. 4. The one who loves God will be blessed. 5. Being holy, he was praying. 6. τα τεκνα ἠν μονα. 7. νεκροι ἐσονται οἱ δουλοι. 8. Ἰουδαιοι ὀντες θελομεν εἰσερχεσθαι εἰς την συναγωγην.

## 8.3.

1. His disciples are going/coming. 2. He was speaking to Judas. 3. The brother will receive John. 4. Many soldiers were approaching. 5. ὁ Ἰησους ἐκηρυσσεν την ὁδον. 6. οἱ προφηται οὐκ ἠσαν ἁγιοι.

## Exercise Section A

1. Jesus comes and takes the bread. 2. And the crowd was going again to him along the sea and he was teaching them. 3. From then Jesus began to preach and say, 'Repent! The kingdom of heaven is approaching.' 4. He was telling them in a parable: 'It is necessary to pray at all times.' 5. And the crowd was seeking to touch him; signs of authority were coming out from him. 6. John will be great before the Lord, like Elijah; but Herod (is, will be) evil. 7. The son of man is about to come in the glory of God with his angels, and then each person will receive according to his life. 8. He was saying to the disciples, 'If you (pl.) wish to come after the son of man, deny Satan and follow the Lord daily. 9. ὁ οἰκος (του) Ἰουδα προσηυξατο· Κυριε, ῥυσαι τον Ἰσραηλ ἐκ της Αἰγυπτου. 10. ὁ Ἠλιας ἠν μεγας προφητης. 11. ἀπηρχοντο ἀπο της συναγωγης ὁτε εἰσηρχομεθα. 12. ὁ Βαρναβας και ὁ Παυλος

εὐηγγελιζοντο ἐν τῃ ὁδῳ ἀπο Ἱεροσολυμων μετα των πιστων μαθητων (συν τοις πιστοις μαθηταις).

## CHAPTER 9

### 9.1.1

1. Feminine Nominative Plural 2. Masculine *or* Neuter Genitive Singular 3. Neuter Nominative *or* Accusative Plural 4. Neuter Nominative *or* Accusative Plural 5. Masculine Nominative Plural (of αὐτος) 6. Masculine Nominative Plural 7. Neuter Nominative *or* Accusative Singular 8. Feminine Nominative Singular.

### 9.1.2

1. This was the place. 2. The sheep of these people are dead. 3. The whole crowd was listening. 4. He is speaking in those parables. 5. His prophets are coming. 6. These disciples are blind.

### Half-way Practice

1. They are denying themselves. 2. I love that disciple. 3. She is gathering these sheep. 4. He used to teach in other parables. 5. On the same day Mary saw the Lord. 6. Because of these things the crowd were saying to one another. 7. Jesus himself was praying. 8. He was a servant of this temple. 9. προσευχομεθα τῳ αὐτῳ θεῳ. 10. αὐτος ὁ Πετρος ἠρνησατο τον Ἰησουν. 11. μετα τουτο ἠρξαντο ἀκουσαι (or just ἠκουον). 12. ἐκεινα τα δαιμονια (ἠν) πονηρα.

### 9.3

1. Your law saves. 2. God saves you. 3. We believed, but you did not listen. 4. You will save yourself, but I (will save) others. 5. σωσον σεαυτον. 6. κηρυξω τα ἐργα ὑμων.

### 9.4

1. Many believed because (for) the disciples were proclaiming the good news. 2. God sent the prophets, but the people were blind. 3. Does God love even (the) evil people? 4. Joseph is speaking to him, but he (the other one) will not listen. 5. Some are approaching, others are departing for their homes. 6. ζητησομεν οὐν τον κυριον.

## Exercise Section A

1. But as for Jesus (or 'Jesus himself'), he did not entrust (trust) himself to them. 2. And he was saying to them, 'You (pl.) are of this world; I am not of this world.' 3. And with/in many such parables he was speaking the word to them. 4. They go again to Jerusalem. And Jesus is walking in the temple and the Jews are coming to him. 5. Therefore the Jews were saying to themselves, 'Where is this man about to go?' 6. We are from God and the whole world is in (under the power of) the evil one. 7. And he was saying to them, 'To you (pl.) I teach the mystery of the kingdom of God; but to them outside, I say these things in parables.' 8. For John was saying to Herod, 'It is not lawful for you to have your brother's wife.' 9. αὑτη ἐστιν ἡ ἐντολη μου (or ἡ ἐμη ἐντολη), Ἐχετε ἀγαπην ἀλληλοις διοτι ἐστε οἱ μαθηται μου (or οἱ ἐμοι μαθηται). 10. ἐγω εἰμι ὁ ἀρτος της ζωης. 11. ὁ Ἰησους λεγει αὐτοις· Οὐκ (ἐγω) λεγω ὑμιν ἐν ποιᾳ ἐξουσιᾳ ταυτα ποιω. 12. ἀναβλεψας ἐλεγεν· Βλεπω ἀνθρωπους ἀλλα ὡς δενδρα περιπατουσιν.

## CHAPTER 10

### 10.1.1

Antecedents are:
1. demon 2. man 3. meal 4. sacrifice 5. Messiah 6. soldiers

### 10.1.2

1. Neuter Nominative *or* Accusative Singular 2. Masculine Accusative Singular 3. Masculine *or* Neuter Genitive Singular 4. Feminine Dative Singular 5. Feminine Nominative Plural 6. Feminine Nominative Plural (of the article) 7. Masculine Accusative Plural 8. Feminine Accusative Singular (of the article) 9. Masculine, Feminine *or* Neuter Genitive Plural 10. Masculine *or* Neuter Dative Plural.

## Half-way Practice

1. I see the slave whom he called. 2. Depart from the house in which you are. 3. Where are the cups which we love? 4. For they believed the good news which the apostles were preaching. 5. Greet (pl.) the ones who are coming to you (pl.). 6. This is the Lord through whom we will pray. 7. I am saying to you what I heard (what I heard, this I am saying to you). 8. Greet Timothy on whose behalf the church is praying. 9. τηρει τον ἀρτον ὁν ἐποιησεν. 10. δει φιλειν τον θεον ὁς σωζει ἡμας. 11. πιστευεις τῳ εὐαγγελιῳ ὃ ἠκουσας; 12. ὁ μαθητης ὁς ἠρνησατο τον Ἰησουν μετενοησεν;

### 10.2

1. Surely you don't see? / You don't see, do you? 2. Surely you love me? / You love me, don't you? 3. I do not love you. 4. Surely not I? / It is not me, is it?

### 10.3

1. Indirect – Present 2. Direct 3. Indirect – Imperfect 4. Indirect – Aorist 5. Direct 6. Indirect – Present

### 10.4

1. Dative 2. Accusative 3. Genitive 4. Accusative 5. Dative 6. Genitive

## Exercise Section A

1. Am I not an apostle? Did I not see Jesus our Lord? Listen to what I am saying to you (pl.). 2. Some of the Pharisees heard these things and were amazed, saying to him, 'Surely we are not also blind, are we?' 3. And not only (that), but we are coming near to God through our Lord Jesus Christ, through whom we now are receiving peace with God. 4. Others were saying, 'This man is the Messiah,' but others were saying, 'Surely the Messiah does not come from Galilee, does he?' 5. And David says, 'Blessed is the person to whom the Lord reckons righteousness apart from works.' 6. For many days the people were in Egypt just as God had said to Abraham. 7. The soldier denied (it), saying, 'I am not a Jew, am I?' 8. And we are in the one who is true, in his son Jesus Christ. (This one) He is the true God and eternal life. 9. λεγει αὐτῳ ὁ Ἰησους· Ἐγω εἰμι ἡ ὁδος και ἡ ἀληθεια και ἡ ζωη. 10. ὁ Πιλατος ἐκαθευδεν περαν της θαλασσης της Γαλιλαιας. 11. ἃ δε ἐγραψα ὑμιν, ἐνωπιον του θεου μαρτυρω. 12. μη θαυμαζετε δια τουτο, ὁτι ἐρχεται ὡρα ἐν ᾗ οἱ νεκροι ἀκουσουσιν την φωνην αὐτου.

## CHAPTER 11

### 11.1.4

1. we fell 2. I/they took 3. you (pl.) were throwing 4. he said 5. it happened 6. I/they came 7. she was fleeing 8. you (s.) saw

### 11.1.5

1. Aorist Infinitive 2. Masc. Nom. Sing. Aorist Participle 3. Present Infinitive 4. Singular Aorist Imperative 5. Masc. Nom. Pl. Aorist Participle 6. Masc. Nom. Sing. Aorist Participle 7. Plural Aorist Imperative 8. Aorist Infinitive

### 11.1.6

1. having gone down 2. he went up 3. they came 4. you (pl.) knew 5. having known

## Half-way Practice

1. Many died. 2. I was/they were leading it. 3. I/they ate the bread. 4. When they came, they saw him. 5. See the road! 6. It is necessary to go to Jerusalem. 7. After Jesus had said these things he left. 8. When he had gone up to the temple he died. 9. οἱ προφηται εἰπον. 10. τον υἱον ἐφιλησα (ἐφιλουν if you wish to stress continuity). 11. θελω ἰδειν (βλεψαι) την θαλασσαν. 12. εὑρων ἐλαβον αὐτο.

### 11.2.2

1. They remained. 2. We will announce 3. He raised (in fact ἠγειρεν could also be imperfect – he was raising). 4. They killed. 5. He will judge the world. 6. Having sent, he went out. 7. I wish to sow. 8. After they lifted, they brought. 9. ἀπαγγελουσιν 10. βαλειτε 11. ἐγειρον τον νεκρον. 12. ἀπεκτεινεν αὐτην.

## Exercise Section A

1. The disciples came to him, saying, 'This is a desert place and the hour has already gone by; dismiss the crowds.' 2. And a voice came from heaven (the heavens), 'You are my beloved son.' 3. And when he came home from the crowd, his disciples found him and spoke to him about the parable. 4. For I proclaimed to you that which I also received, that Christ died on behalf of our sins according to the good news. 5. For through the law I have died to the law. 6. Therefore he says to the apostle, 'Do not always be blind in your heart, but (be) believing.' 7. He was in the world, and the world came about through him, and the world did not know him. 8. Righteous Lord, the world did not know you, but I knew you, and these knew that you sent me. 9. και ἀνεβη εἰς το πλοιον μετ᾽ αὐτων και ἐφυγον. 10. Μετα τουτο κατεβη εἰς την Γαλιλαιαν και ἡ Μαρια και οἱ ἀδελφοι αὐτου και οἱ μαθηται αὐτου, και ἐκει ἐμειναν οὐ πολλας ἡμερας. 11. ἰδου ὁ υἱος του ἀνθρωπου ἀποστελει τους ἀγγελους αὐτου. 12. ἐκεινος ὁ λογος ὁν εἰπον κρινεῖ αὐτον ἐν τῃ ἡμερᾳ του κυριου.

## CHAPTER 12

### 12.2

1. Genitive Singular 2. Nominative Plural 3. Dative Singular 4. Genitive Plural 5. Accusative Singular 6. Genitive Singular 7. Dative Plural 8. Accusative Singular 9. ἀνδρων 10. γυναιξιν 11. ποδα 12. χειρας 13. σαρκι 14. χαριτος 15. θυγατερες 16. αἰωσιν

### 12.3

1. Dative Singular 2. Genitive Singular 3. Nominative/Accusative Plural 4. Genitive Plural 5. αἱμα 6. πνευματων 7. σωμασιν 8. ὀνοματα

## Half-way Practice

1. Is Jesus the saviour? 2. The father's son fled. 3. I have a good mother. 4. They saw their fathers. 5. He baptizes with water. 6. The men left. 7. Christ died on behalf of men and women. 8. Do the will of God. 9. φιλει δυο γυναικας. 10. το πνευμα οὐ φιλει την σαρκα. 11. ἐχω μεγαλους ποδας. 12. εἰδον το φως.

### 12.4

1. More soldiers are coming. 2. You have a bigger head than I. 3. Did Jesus have more disciples than John? 4. I am a prophet of a greater temple.

### 12.5

1. Who is coming? 2. I want some bread. 3. Why do you (pl.) love Christ? 4. About what (or whom – both plural) did he speak? 5. Some fathers are wicked. 6. Whom are you (pl.) seeking? 7. τί προσευχῃ; 8. τίνι εἰπετε; 9. προφηται τινες καλουσιν. 10. τίνα νομον τηρειτε;

## Exercise Section A

1. Father, glorify your name. 2. I baptized you (pl.) with water, but he will baptize you in (the) Holy Spirit. 3. But he said to her, 'Daughter, your faith saved you; go in peace.' 4. In him was life, and the life was the light of men (humanity). 5. And the word became flesh. 6. The woman said to him, 'I do not have a husband.' Jesus said to her, 'You spoke appropriately, "I don't have a husband."' 7. Jesus said to them, 'I told you (pl.) and you do not believe; these works which I do in the name of my father witness about me.' 8. Simon Peter said to him, 'Lord, whom shall we follow? You have words of eternal life.' 9. εἰπον αὐτῳ οἱ Φαρισαιοι· Τί οἱ μαθηται σου οὐ καλως χερσιν ἐσθιουσιν;

10. ἀλλ᾽ ἐν κυριῳ οὔτε γυνη χωρις ἀνδρος οὔτε ἀνηρ χωρις γυναικος. 11. χαρις ὑμιν και εἰρηνη ἀπο (του) θεου πατρος ἡμων και (του) κυριου Ἰησου Χριστου του σωτηρος ἡμων. 12. καθως ἐλαλησεν δια στοματος των ἁγιων προφητων αὐτου, τουτο ποιησει.

## CHAPTER 13

### 13.1

1. Nominative *or* Accusative Plural 2. Accusative Singular 3. Genitive Plural 4. Accusative Singular 5. Dative Plural 6. Nominative Singular 7. ἱερεις 8. ἀναστασεως 9. γραμματευσιν 10. πιστιν

### 13.2

1. Dative Singular 2. Nominative *or* Accusative Plural 3. Genitive Singular 4. Nominative *or* Accusative Plural Masculine *or* Feminine 5. Genitive Plural 6. Nominative *or* Accusative Singular 7. πληθη 8. ἀσθενει 9. σκευων 10. ἐθνεσιν

### Half-way Practice

1. Depart to the Gentiles. 2. In that year the king died. 3. The scribes spoke against Jesus. 4. Peter does not pay attention to the high priest. 5. The true disciples are in the city. 6. Through faith we have hope of glory. 7. I have a share of the kingdom. 8. The one who seeks truth also receives power. 9. ὁ πατηρ του βασιλεως εἰπεν τῳ ἀρχιερει. 10. δια το ἐλεος αὐτου ὁ θεος ῥυεται ἡμας. 11. περιεπατουμεν ποτε ὑπο κρισιν. 12 (ἡ) πιστις εὑρεν το ἀληθες τελος αὐτης.

### 13.3

1. Masculine Nominative Plural 2. Feminine Dative Plural 3. Masculine *or* Neuter Genitive Singular 4. Feminine Accusative Singular 5. Neuter Nominative *or* Accusative Singular 6. Masculine *or* Neuter Dative Singular 7. All the fathers died. 8. I will preach the good news in all nations. 9. Everyone was amazed because of all the things which he was doing. 10. The saviour of all is praying.

### 13.4

1. Is no one good? 2. I/they saw one city. 3. Didn't you find anything? 4. Say nothing to anyone (lit: 'nothing to nobody') 5. He said that there was one Lord and one church. 6. I have one sheep.

## Exercise Section A

1. Therefore the chief priests of the Jews were saying to Pilate, 'Do not write: "The King of the Jews," but that which that man said: "I am the king of the Jews." ' 2. But Jesus said to him, 'Why do you say I am good? No one is good, except God alone.' (or 'except one [person] – God') 3. The grace of the Lord Jesus Christ and the love of God and the fellowship of the Holy Spirit (be) with you all. 4. Do not call someone 'Rabbi', for you (pl.) have one teacher, and all of you are brothers. 5. And Peter says (said) to Jesus, 'Rabbi, it is good that we are here, and we shall build three tents for you (pl.), one for you, and one for Moses, and one for Elijah.' 6. And the two will be (made) into one flesh; thus they are no longer two but one flesh. 7. And all the crowd was seeking to touch him, because power was coming out from him and he was healing them all. 8. And the disciples left and went to the city and found (it) just as he had told them. 9. και προσελθων εἱς (ἐκ) των γραμματεων εἰπεν αὐτῳ· Ῥαββι, ἀκολουθησω σοι. 10. και βασιλευς ἐσται ἐπι τον οἰκον (του) Ἰακωβ εἰς τους αἰωνας (εἰς τον αἰωνα) και της βασιλειας αὐτου οὐκ ἐσται τελος. 11. ἐν τουτῳ τῳ κοσμῳ θλιψιν ἐχετε, ἀλλα ἐν ἐμοι εἰρηνην ἐχετε. 12. οἱ μεν ἐξερχονται εἰς ἀναστασιν ζωης, οἱ δε εἰς ἀναστασιν κρισεως.

## CHAPTER 14

### 14.1

1. γραψας 2. ποιουντες 3. ἐρχομενος 4. φιλησαντες 5. λογισαμενος 6. προσευχομενοι

### 14.2

All are participles
1. Present Active Masculine Plural Nominative 2. Aorist Active Masculine Singular Nominative 3. Present Deponent Feminine Plural Dative 4. Aorist Active Neuter Singular Nominative *or* Accusative 5. Aorist Active Masculine *or* Neuter Singular Dative 6. Aorist Active Masculine *or* Neuter Genitive Plural 7. Present Active Feminine Singular Accusative. 8. Aorist Active Masculine Plural Accusative 9. Present Deponent Masculine Plural Nominative 10. ἀνοιγουσας 11. ποιησας 12. κηρυξαντων 13. ἁπτομενῳ 14. ἐλθοντα 15. πιστευσασας

## Half-way Practice

1. When he had come, he healed him. 2. While he was going up, he saw the spirit. 3. When they fled, they went into a temple. 4. He was baptizing the

wicked people who had repented. 5. We spoke to the children as they came. 6. Did you see the scribes who had gone into the temple? 7. I am seeking the coming kingdom 8. After she departed she saw her father speaking. 9. ὁ Ἰησους ἠσπασατο τον προσερχομενον ὀχλον. 10. ἰδουσα ἐπιστευσεν. 11. ὁ Φαρισαιος ἐδιδαξεν τους ἀκουοντας Ἰουδαιους. 12. ἀκουσας τουτο ὁ βασιλευς ἀπεστειλεν (ἐπεμψεν) τους στρατιωτας αὐτου εὑρειν το τεκνον (παιδιον).

### 14.4

1. Love those who hate you. 2. Because Moses was holy he used to speak to God. 3. I want to go into the synagogue and listen to the Rabbi. 4. They were speaking to each other about what had happened. 5. εἰδον τους φεροντας τον ἀσθενη. 6. Singular: ὑπαγαγων κηρυξον το εὐαγγελιον. Plural: ὑπαγαγοντες κηρυξατε το εὐαγγελιον.[2]

## Exercise Section A

1. The one who loves his life will not save it, and the one who hates his life in this world will guard it into eternal life. 2. And when he came out he saw a large crowd and he had mercy on them, because they were like sheep without a shepherd, and he began to teach them many things. 3. Amen amen, I say to you (pl.), that the one who hears my word and believes the one who sent me has eternal life and does not come to judgement. 4. Everyone who sees the son and believes in him has eternal life. 5. Therefore the Jews were talking about him with one another because he said, 'I am the bread which came down from heaven.' 6. For this is the word through Isaiah the prophet, who said, 'A voice of someone crying out in the wilderness, "Prepare the way of the Lord!"' 7. And he said to them, 'Men of Israel, pay attention to yourselves, what you are about to do to these people.' 8. And Satan was tempting him in the desert for many days, and Jesus was with the animals, and the angels were serving him. 9. ὁ γαρ πατηρ παντα ὑπεταξεν ὑπο τους ποδας του υἱου. 10. τεκνα (παιδια) ἀγαπητα, φυλασσετε ἑαυτα ἀπο των μισουντων την ψυχην ὑμων. (or παιδες ἀγαπητες, φυλασσετε ἑαυτους ...) 11. ἐκεινος ὁ λιθος ἐχει την εἰκονα του Καισαρος, οὐτε Ἑλληνος τινος. 12. τί οὐν ποιησει ὁ κυριος του ἀμπελωνος;

[2] Or one might prefer the Present Imperative of κηρυσσω if this is establishing a general, ongoing command – κηρυσσε or κηρυσσετε; or one could use εὐαγγελιζομαι to mean 'preach the gospel', giving singular ὑπαγαγων εὐαγγελισαμενος / εὐαγγελιζομενος plural: ὑπαγαγοντες εὐαγγελισαμενοι / εὐαγγελιζομενοι.

## CHAPTER 15

### 15.3

1. Aorist Passive Indicative 2. Future Active Indicative *or* Aorist Active Other Mood (ending shows that it is Aorist Active Imperative) 3. Imperfect Active Indicative 4. Future Middle Indicative *or* Aorist Middle Other Mood (ending shows that it is Future Middle Indicative) 5. Future Passive Indicative 6. Future Middle Indicative *or* Aorist Middle Other Mood (ending shows that it is Aorist Middle Infinitive) 7. Aorist Passive Other Mood (ending shows that it is Imperative) 8. Aorist Active Indicative.

### 15.5.1 and 15.5.2.

1. Imperfect Middle/Passive Indicative 3rd Singular 2. Future Passive Indicative 1st Singular 3. Aorist Passive Participle Masculine Singular Nominative 4. Present Middle/Passive Indicative 3rd Plural 5. Present Middle/Passive Indicative 3rd Plural. 6. Aorist Passive Indicative 3rd Singular

### 15.5.3

1. Aorist Passive Indicative 1st Plural 2. Aorist Passive Indicative 3rd Singular 3. Future Passive Indicative 3rd Singular 4. Aorist Passive Participle Masculine Nominative Singular 5. Aorist Passive Indicative 3rd Singular 6. Aorist Passive Indicative 3rd Plural

### Half-way Practice

1. It was said by the prophets. 2. After the slave was set free he gave thanks to God. 3. God is seen by angels. 4. Peter was going into the synagogue. 5. Although I am tempted I do not fall. 6. The apostles will be sent. 7. When they saw the evil things which had been done they fled. 8. On that day God will be seen. 9. ὁ νομος γραφησεται. 10. ἡ πρεσβυτερα (γυνη) ἠνεχθη ὑπο των υἱων αὐτης. 11. κρατηθεις ὁ Ἰησους (οὐκ) εἰπεν οὐδεν. 12. καλησαντες· Κυριε, κυριε, ἐσωθησαν.

### 15.7

1. We wished to see Jesus. 2. On that day will you be afraid? 3. It is necessary to go into temple. 4. Answer nothing ('give no answer', 'say nothing in reply').

### Exercise Section A

1. And he began to teach them that it was necessary to suffer many things and to be persecuted by the elders and the chief priests and the scribes and to be killed.

2. Now is the judgement of this world, now the ruler of this world will be thrown out. 3. Jesus said to them, 'The cup which I drink, you will drink, and the baptism with which I am baptized, you will be baptized.' 4. Blessed are the merciful, because they will receive mercy. 5. Blessed are the peacemakers, because they will be called sons of God. 6. And answering them he said, 'Who is my mother and (who are) my brothers?' 7. And one of the crowd answered him, 'Teacher, I brought to you my son because he has an evil spirit.' 8. They began to be grieved and one by one they said to him, 'It isn't me, is it?' 9. και ἐφοβηθησαν φοβον μεγαν και εἰπον ἀλληλοις (προς ἀλληλους)· Τίς ἀρα οὑτος ἐστιν; 10. και εἰσελθων εἰπεν αὐτοις· Τί φοβεισθε και κλαιετε; το παιδιον οὐκ ἀπεθανεν. 11. ἐφοβηθη και ἀπεκριθη τῳ ἀρχιερει ὁτι Ὑπεστρεψαν προς τον ναον. 12. ὁ γαρ ἀνηρ μη ἐχων πιστιν ἁγιαζεται ἐν τῃ γυναικι και ἡ γυνη μη ἐχουσα πιστιν ἁγιαζεται ἐν τῳ ἀνδρι.

## CHAPTER 16

### 16.2

1. Perfect Active Indicative 3rd Singular 2. Perfect Middle/Passive Participle Masculine Plural Accusative 3. Perfect Middle/Passive Indicative 3rd Singular 4. Perfect Active Indicative 3rd Plural 5. Perfect Middle/Passive Indicative 3rd Singular 6. Perfect Middle/Passive Participle Feminine Singular Accusative

### Half-way Practice

1. The slaves have been freed. 2. I have borne witness to the truth. 3. What have you done? 4. I have been tempted for many years. 5. We do not worship in a temple which has been built by men (humans). 6. He has been subjected to a wicked master. 7. We have been saved through the love of God. 8. The soldiers have arrested Peter. 9. ἡ ἀσθενης τεθεραπευται. 10. ὁ λογος πεπεμπται εἰς τον κοσμον (or ἐν τῳ κοσμῳ or just τῳ κοσμῳ). 11. πεποιηκαμεν τα ἀγαθα. 12. μη πεπιστευκας τῳ Ἰησου;

### 16.3

1. Perfect 2. Aorist 3. Perfect 4. Present 5. Aorist

### 16.4

1. No (Aorist participle) 2. No (Indirect statement using Perfect) 3. Yes. 4. No (Aorist participle) 2. No (Indirect statement using Perfect)

## Exercise Section A

1. And he says to them, 'It is written, "My house will be called a house of prayer." ' 2. I have seen and have given witness that this one is the son of God. 3. The one who believes in him is not judged; the one who does not believe has been judged already, because he has not believed in the name of the only son of God. 4. John has borne witness to the truth; these things he has told you (pl.). 5. And we have believed and have come to know that you are the holy one of God. 6. And she said to him, 'Yes, Lord, I have believed that you are the Christ, the son of God, the one who is coming into the world.' 7. No one has seen the Father except the one who is from God – this one has seen the Father. 8. And then the sign of the son of man will appear in heaven, and they will see the son of man coming on the clouds of heaven with power and much glory; thus will the coming of the son of man be. 9. οἱ δε εἰπον· Κυριε, ἰδου μαχαιραι ὡδε δυο. 10. εὐθυς ἐξηλθεν ἡ ἀκοη αὐτου εἰς ὁλην την χωραν της Γαλιλαιας. 11. οἱ δωδεκα την διδαχην αὐτου ἀκηκοασιν και ἑωρακαν την θυσιαν αὐτου. 12. ὁ μαθητης πεφιληκεν τους ἁγιους (τους) ἐν ταις ἑπτα ἐκκλησιαις.

## CHAPTER 17

### 17.2

1. Present Active Subjunctive 1st Plural 2. Aorist Active Subjunctive 3rd Plural 3. Present Active Subjunctive 3rd Singular 4. Present <u>Middle</u>/Passive Subjunctive 3rd Plural 5. Aorist Passive Subjunctive 2nd Singular 6. Aorist Active Subjunctive 3rd Plural 7. Aorist Middle Subjunctive 1st Singular 8. Present Middle/<u>Passive</u> Subjunctive 3rd Singular 9. Present Active Subjunctive 3rd Singular 10. Aorist Active Subjunctive 2nd Plural 11. Aorist Active Subjunctive 1st Plural 12. Present Active Indicative 1st Plural

## Half-way Practice

1. Did you come so that you might hear? 2. The prophets were sent in order that they might speak on behalf of God. 3. Whoever sees me, sees the father. 4. They seized Paul so that he would not flee. 5. Whenever you go, I am afraid. 6. Where are they going? 7. The apostle wrote to you in order that you might believe (come to believe). 8. Wherever Jesus went a great crowd gathered. 9. ὁ Ἰησους ἐξεβαλεν τα δαιμονια ἱνα σωθῃ. 10. ὁς ἀν εἰσελθῃ την πολιν ἀπεθανεν. 11. ἐκαλεσα αὐτῃ ἱνα ἀκουσῃ. 12. ὁταν βλεπω τα ὀρη βλεπω.

### 17.3.3 – 17.3.7

1. Where should I go? 2. Do not leave! 3. They will never depart. 4. Let us glorify the lord of the world. 5. Why should we listen to the teacher? 6. Let us seek a holy life.

### Exercise Section A

1. For God did not send the son into the world so that he might judge the world, but that the world might be saved through him. 2. And answering him Jesus said, 'What do you wish me to do for you?' And the blind man said to him, 'Rabbi, that I might receive my sight.' 3. And he said to them on that day, 'Let us go across to the other side.' 4. But the soldier, having seen the doors of the prison had been opened, was about to kill himself with a sword, since he thought the disciples had fled. 5. Whoever does the will of God, this one is my brother and my sister and my mother. 6. And after she left, she said to her mother, 'What should I ask for?' And she (her mother) said, 'The head of John the Baptizer.' 7. He (this one) came for witness (as a witness), so that he might bear witness about the light, so that all might believe through him. He (that one) was not the light, but (he came) so that he might witness about the light. 8. These are the ones along the road where the word is sown, and whenever they hear, immediately Satan comes and takes away the word which had been sown in them. 9. Και ἐξελθοντες εἰς τους ἀγρους ἐκηρυξαν ἱνα (οἱ ἀνθρωποι) μετανοησωσιν. 10. το ἐλεος αὐτου εἰς γενεας και γενεας τοις φοβουμενοις αὐτον. 11. κατα τας γραφας ἐσονται σημεια ἐν ἡλιῳ και ἀστερσιν, και ἐπι τῃ γῃ θλιψις και χρεια ἐθνων. 12. Και προσεφερον αὐτῳ παιδια ἱνα αὐτων ἁψηται.

## CHAPTER 18

### 18.1

1. 3rd Plural Present Middle Indicative 2. Masculine/Neuter Dative Plural, Present Middle Participle 3. Present Middle Infinitive 4. 3rd Singular Imperfect Middle Indicative 5. 2nd Plural Present Active Indicative (οἰδα) 6. 1st Singular Imperfect Active Indicative (οἰδα) 7. Aorist Active Infinitive (ὁραω) 8. Masculine Nominative Singular, Aorist Active Participle (ὁραω) 9. Masculine Nominative Singular, Present Active Participle (οἰδα).

### 18.2.2 and 18.2.3

1. I want him to marry me. 2. A teacher must teach. 3. He approached so they departed. 4. Are you able to eat bread in the temple? 5. I love wisdom so I listen to my teacher.

## Half-way Practice

1. We were able to speak to him. 2. I want to know God. 3. After praying I/they left the synagogue. 4. The widow was poor so she did not have much. 5. I/they saw that it was necessary for her to die. 6. Do you know the eternal promises? 7. Did you come to worship (with the aim of worshipping) God? 8. The disciples fled so the soldiers found nobody. 9. ᾔδεις αὐτον; 10. προ του καθησθαι εὐχαριστησαν. 11. (οὑτως) ἐθαυμαζον ὡστε προσκυνησαι αὐτῳ. 12. δει σε δουλευειν (or δει σε εἰναι δουλον).

## 18.3

1. She should not speak to the evil man. 2. Let your kingdom come! / May your kingdom come! 3. The kingdom must come. 4. Let us worship God. 5. They should worship God. 6. The demons should be cast out.

## 18.4

1. They were taken (away). 2. We have received many things. 3. I heard what was said. 4. Will you save the man who has a demon? 5 The chief priests have taken the scriptures. 6. I saw heaven open.

## Exercise Section A

1. Let Christ the King of Israel come down now from the cross, so that we might see and might believe. 2. And they were saying, 'Isn't this Jesus the son of Joseph, whose father and mother we know? How now does he say, "I have come down from heaven"?' 3. Jesus said to them, 'You (pl.) do not know what you are asking. Can you drink the cup which I drink or be baptized with the baptism with which I am baptized?' 4. The one who speaks from himself is seeking his own glory; but the one who seeks the glory of the one who sent him, this one is true and injustice is not in him. 5. Then Jesus said to his disciples, 'If anyone wishes to come after me, let him deny himself and take up his cross and follow me.' 6. And Mary sees two angels in white sitting where the body of Jesus had been lying, one at the head and one at the feet. 7. (Speaking) in a loud voice they said, 'Worthy is the lamb sitting on the throne at the right (side/hand) of God to receive power and wisdom and honour and glory.' 8. Therefore the Lord Jesus, after speaking to them, went up into heaven and sat at the right hand of God. 9. μακαριοι οἱ καθαροι τῃ καρδιᾳ, ὁτι αὐτοι τον θεον ὀψονται. 10. δυναμις θεου ἠν ἐκει εἰς (or προς) το θεραπευειν τους ἀσθενεις και καθαριζειν τους ἐχοντας πνευματα ἀκαθαρτα. 11. ἐργαζομεθα νυν ἱνα ἀναγινωσκωμεν (or εἰς/προς το ἀναγινωσκειν) την καινην διαθηκην. 12. ἡ γνωσις ἡμων αὐξανει ὡστε ἡμας δυνασθαι μανθανειν ἀπο των γραφων· πρωτον (ἀπο) του εὐαγγελιου κατα Μαρκον.

## CHAPTER 19

### 19.1.2

1. Aorist (Active Indicative 3$^{rd}$ Singular) 2. Imperfect (Active Indicative 3$^{rd}$ Singular) 3. Perfect (Passive Indicative 3$^{rd}$ Singular) 4. Present (Active Indicative 1$^{st}$ Plural) 5. Future (Passive Indicative 3$^{rd}$ Singular) 6. Present (Active Indicative 3$^{rd}$ Singular) 7. Aorist (Active Subjunctive 1$^{st}$ Plural) 8. Aorist (Active Participle Masculine Plural Accusative) 9. Present (Active Indicative 3$^{rd}$ Singular) 10. Future (Passive Indicative 3$^{rd}$ Plural) 11. Aorist (Active Imperative 2$^{nd}$ Plural) 12. Aorist (Active Indicative 2$^{nd}$ Plural)

## Half-way Practice

1. They are giving the soldiers their pay. 2. Jesus raised the dead person. 3. We stood with the lord on the mountain. 4. When they had left they did not turn back. 5. He said that he was standing there. 6. . . . until I place your enemies under your feet. 7. Give me the bread of life. 8. After he had stood up, the apostle began to preach to the crowd. 9. παρεδωκαν την διδαχην τοις πρεσβυτεροις. 10. ἐστησεν τον ἀσθενη ἐν τῃ συναγωγῃ. 11. ἀφεισα τον ὀχλον προσηυχετο (or ἠρξατο προσευχεσθαι). 12. διδους τον οἰνον αὐτοις ἐδιδαξεν (αὐτους).

### 19.2

1. Present Middle/<u>Passive</u> Indicative 3$^{rd}$ Singular 2. Perfect Middle/<u>Passive</u> Participle Masculine Nominative Singular 3. Present Active Indicative 1$^{st}$ Singular 4. Imperfect Active Indicative 3$^{rd}$ Plural *or* 1$^{st}$ Singular 5. Future Active Indicative 2$^{nd}$ Singular 6. Present Active Infinitive 7. Aorist Active Indicative 3$^{rd}$ Plural 8. Future Active Indicative 3$^{rd}$ Plural 9. Aorist Active Indicative 3$^{rd}$ Singular 10. Present Active Indicative 2$^{nd}$ Singular 11. Present Middle/<u>Passive</u> Indicative 3$^{rd}$ Singular 12. Present Active Indicative 3$^{rd}$ Singular

## Exercise Section A

1. And after they left their father Zebedee in the boat with the others, they went away after him. 2. He answered them, saying, 'You give them (something) to eat.' 3. Blessed are those who hunger and thirst for righteousness. 4. The one who does the truth (does what is true) comes to the light, so that his works might be revealed. 5. So that all might honour the son just as they honour the father. The one who does not honour the son does not honour the father who sent him. 6. Jesus said to them, 'I am the bread of life; the one who comes to me will never hunger, and the one who believes in me will never thirst.' 7. This is the will of the one who sent me, that I should not lose anything of all that he

has given to me, but I will raise it up on the last day. 8. When this one heard that Jesus had come from Judea to Galilee, he went to him and asked him to come down and heal his son, for he was about to die. 9. μετα το ἀπολεσθαι (ἀπολομενος) ἀνεστη παλιν. 10. ὁ ἰσχυρος νικησει· κοπιᾳ και ζῃ νικαν. 11. ἠρωτησεν ὁπου ἐγεννηθη. 12. πεπλανηκαμεν αὐτους ἀπο της ὁδου· τίς δυναται ἡμας δικαιουν;

## CHAPTER 20

### 20.1

1. If you (s.) love God, you are wise. 2. If he had heard, he would not have died. 3. If the king goes out, the slaves will be released. 4. If the gospel is preached, rejoice! 5. If we were unclean, then we would not sit in the temple. 6. If I give to you (s.), will you therefore give to others?

### Half-way Practice

1. When Jesus came, the teachers were amazed. 2. For if they see they would believe. 3. After the king died, they went into Galilee. 4. When day came (happened) he was talking (began to talk) to the crowd. 5. If the demons are thrown out, we will rejoice. 6. For while the word was being preached, those who were listening believed. 7. Since he was holy, they all were afraid. 8. If the law had not been given, they would not have known sin. 9. αὐτης εἰσερχομενης, ὁ ἀγγελος εἰπεν αὐτῃ· ... 10. ἐαν ᾖ ἁγιος προσκυνησει τῳ θεῳ. 11. εἰ ἡμερα ἠν οὐκ ἀν ἐφοβουμεθα. 12. αὐτου ἐγερθεντος παντες ἐθαυμαζον.

### 20.3

1. The teacher was sitting with them. 2. It is written in the prophet. (Perfect participle – it stands written, it has been written.) 3. And Joseph was wearing a beautiful garment. 4. The prophet will be honoured.

### 20.4

1. Superlative Adverb *or* Adjective Neuter Nominative *or* Accusative Plural 2. Superlative Adjective Neuter *or* Masculine Dative Plural 3. Comparative Adjective Neuter *or* Masculine Genitive Singular 4. Superlative Adjective Masculine Nominative Plural 5. Comparative Adjective Masculine Accusative Singular *or* Neuter Nominative *or* Accusative Plural. 6. Adverb

## Exercise Section A

1. And if anyone should say to you then, 'Look, here is the Christ,' or 'Look, there,' do not believe (him). 2. And having gone forward a little, he fell on the ground and prayed that, if it was possible, the hour would pass from him. 3. Jesus answered, 'Amen amen, I say to you, if someone is not born of water and the spirit, he is not able to enter the kingdom of God.' 4. After these things, Jesus finds him in the temple and said to him, 'See, you have become well. Do not sin any longer, so that something worse does not happen to you.' 5. For the father loves the son and shows him all that he himself is doing, and he will show him greater works than these, so that you (pl.) might be amazed. 6. But I have a testimony greater than John; for the works which the father has given to me so that I might complete them, the works themselves which I do bear witness about me, that the father has sent me. 7. And they were yet more amazed at his teaching; for he was teaching them as one having authority and not as the scribes. 8. And when the Sabbath had come, he began to teach in the synagogue, and many who heard were amazed, saying, 'From where did these things (come) to this one, and what is this wisdom, and such miracles that come about through his hands?' 9. μιμνησκωμεθα του ποιμενος των ψυχων ἡμων. 10. ἐαν οὐν ὁ υἱος ὑμας ἐλευθερους ποιησῃ, ὀντως ἐλευθεροι ἐσεσθε. 11. διδασκων ἠν αὐτους περι της ἀγαπης τῳ ἐλαχιστῳ των ἀδελφων και πασιν ζῳοις. 12. σταυρωσω παλιν τον ἐμε ἀπο της ἁμαρτιας νιψαντα; μη γενοιτο.

# Greek – English dictionary

*N.B. The number following each Greek word gives the number of times it occurs in the New Testament. The number following the English word gives the chapter in which it is introduced.*

Α α

Ἀβρααμ (73) – Abraham 1

ἀγαγ- *part of 2nd Aorist* from ἀγω

*ἀγαθος (102) – good 5

*ἀγαπαω (143) – I love 19

*ἀγαπη (116) – love 3

ἀγαπητος (61) – beloved 5

ἀγγελλω (1) – I announce 11

*ἀγγελος (175) – messenger, angel 2

*ἁγιαζω (28) – I make holy 15

*ἁγιος (233) – holy 5

ἀγοραζω (30) – I buy 14

*ἀγρος (36) – field 17

*ἀγω (67) – I lead, bring 2

*ἀδελφη (26) – sister 3

*ἀδελφος (343) – brother 2

*ἀδικεω (28) – I do wrong 18

ἀδικια (25) – wrongdoing 18

Αἰγυπτος, ἡ (25) – Egypt 8

*αἱμα, αἱματος, το (97) – blood 12

*αἰρω (101) – I take (away), lift up 11

*αἰτεω (70) – I ask for (+ acc. of person asked, + acc. of thing asked for) 6

*αἰων, αἰωνος, ὁ (122) – age (long time) 12

*αἰωνιος (71) – eternal 5

*ἀκαθαρτος (32) – impure, unclean 18

ἀκηκοα – Perfect Active of ἀκουω

ἀκοη (24) – fame, report 16

*ἀκολουθεω (90) + dat. – I follow 7

*ἀκουω (428) – I hear, listen to (+ acc. of thing heard, + gen. of person heard) 2

*ἀληθεια (109) – truth 10

*ἀληθης, ἀληθους (26) – truthful, true, genuine 13

ἀληθινος (28) – true, genuine, real 10

*ἀληθως (18) – truly 20

*ἀλλα (638) – but 5

*ἀλληλος (100) – each other, one another 9

*ἀλλος (155) – other 9

ἁμαρτανω (43) – I do wrong, sin 11

*ἁμαρτια (173) – sin 3

ἁμαρτ- *part of 2nd Aorist* from ἁμαρτανω

*ἁμαρτωλος (47) – sinner 14

ἀμην (129) – amen, truly 1

*ἀμπελων, ἀμπελωνος, ὁ (23) – vineyard 14

*ἀν (166) – conditional particle 17
*ἀναβαινω (82) – I go up 11
ἀνεβην – 2nd *Aorist* from ἀναβαινω
ἀναβλεπω (25) – I look up, receive sight 4
ἀναγινωσκω (32) – I read 11
ἀναγω (23) – I lead up, restore 7
*ἀναιρεω (24) – I take away, kill 17
ἀναστασις, ἀναστασεως, ἡ (42) – resurrection 13
ἀνεμος (31) – wind 17
*ἀνηρ, ἀνδρος, ὁ (216) – man (male), husband 12
*ἀνθρωπος (550) – human being, person 2
*ἀνιστημι (108) – I raise 19
*ἀνοιγω (77) – I open 6
ἀξιος (41) – worthy 18
ἀπαγγελλω (45) – I report, announce 11
ἁπας (34) – every, all 13
ἀπεθανον – 2nd *Aorist* from ἀποθνῃσκω
*ἀπερχομαι (117) – I depart, go away 8
ἀπιστος (23) – unbelieving, faithless 18
*ἀπο (646) + gen. – (away) from 4
ἀποδιδωμι (48) – I give away 19
ἀποθαν- *part of 2nd Aorist* from ἀποθνῃσκω
*ἀποθνῃσκω (111) – I die 11
ἀποκαλυπτω (26) – I reveal, uncover 6
*ἀποκρινομαι (231) – I answer 15
ἀποκτεινω (74) – I kill 11
ἀπολλυμαι (90) – I perish (mid. of ἀπολλυμι) 19
*ἀπολλυμι (90) – I ruin, destroy (mid. ἀπολλυμαι – I perish) 19
*ἀπολυω (66) – I set free, divorce, dismiss 4
*ἀποστελλω (132) – I send (out) 11
*ἀποστολος (80) – apostle 7
ἁπτομαι (39) + gen. – I touch 8
ἀρα (49) *postpositive* – so 9
*ἀρνεομαι (33) – I refuse, deny 8
*ἀρνιον (30) – lamb, sheep 9
ἀρτι (36) – now, just now 6
*ἀρτος (97) – bread 2
ἀρχη (55) – beginning 3
*ἀρχιερευς, ἀρχιερεως, ὁ (122) – high priest, chief priest 13
*ἀρχομαι (86) – I begin 8
ἀρχων, ἀρχοντος, ὁ (37) – ruler, leader 12
ἀσθενεια (24) – weakness, disease 16
*ἀσθενεω (33) – I am weak, sick 15
*ἀσθενης, ἀσθενους (26) – weak, sick 13
*ἀσπαζομαι (59) – I greet 8
ἀστηρ, ἀστερος, ὁ (24) – star 12
αὐξανω (23) – I grow 18
*αὐτος η ο (5597) – he, she, it, they 3; himself, herself, itself, themselves (emphatic); same 9
*ἀφιημι (143) – I leave, dismiss, forgive 19
ἀχρι (49) + gen. – until 17

Β β

*βαλλω (122) – I throw 2
βαλ- *part of 2nd Aorist* from βαλλω
*βαπτιζω (77) – I baptise, dip 6
Βαρναβας, ὁ (28) – Barnabas 8
*βασιλεια (162) – reign, kingship, kingdom 3
*βασιλευς, βασιλεως, ὁ (115) – king 13
*βασταζω (27) – I take up 15

βιβλιον (34) – book, scroll 3
βλασφημεω (34) – I blaspheme 14
*βλεπω (133) – I see, watch 2
*βουλομαι (37) – I wish 15

Γ γ
Γαλιλαια (61) – Galilee 5
*γαμεω (28) – I marry 15
*γαρ (1041) *postpositive* – for, because 9
γε (25) – indeed 9
*γενεα (43) – family, generation 17
*γενναω (97) – I bear (beget) (Pass. 'I am born') 19
γεν- *part of 2nd Aorist* from γινομαι
*γη (250) – earth, soil, land 3
*γινομαι (669) – I become, happen 11
*γινωσκω (222) – I know 11
*γλωσσα (50) – tongue, language 17
γν- *part of 2nd Aorist* from γινωσκω
γνωριζω (25) – I make known 15
γνωσις, γνωσεως, ἡ (29) – knowledge 13
γραμματευς, γραμματεως, ὁ (63) – clerk, scribe 13
*γραφη (50) – writing, Scripture 17
*γραφω (191) – I write 6
*γυνη, γυναικος, ἡ (215) – woman, wife 12

Δ δ
*δαιμονιον (63) – demon 3
Δαυιδ (59) – David 1
*δε (2792) *postpositive* – but 9
*δει (101) – it is necessary (impers.) 7
δεικνυμι (33) – I point out, show 19
δεκα (25) – ten 16
δενδρον (25) – tree 9
*δεξιος (54) – right (hand) 18
*δευτερος (43) – second 16
*δεχομαι (56) – I receive 8
δεω (43) – I bind, tie up 7
*δια (667) + acc. – because of 4 + gen. – through 4
διαβολος (37) – the slanderer, the devil 15
διαθηκη (33) – covenant, last will and testament 17
*διακονεω (37) + dat. – I serve 14
διακονια (34) – service 17
*διακονος (29) – servant 17
διαλογιζομαι (16) – I consider, argue, discuss 14
*διδασκαλος (59) – teacher 14
*διδασκω (97) – I teach 2
*διδαχη (30) – teaching (act and content) 16
*διδωμι (415) – I give 19
διερχομαι (43) – I cross over 8
δικαιος (79) – upright, just 5
*δικαιοσυνη (92) – righteousness 7
δικαιοω (39) – I justify 19
*διο (53) – therefore 9
διοτι (23) – because 9
διψαω (16) – I thirst (for) 19
διωκω (45) – I persecute, pursue 6
*δοκεω (62) – I think, seem 7
*δοξα (166) – splendour, glory 3
*δοξαζω (61) – I praise, glorify 6
δουλευω (25) – I am a slave 15
*δουλος (124) – slave 2
*δυναμαι (210) – I can, I am able 18
*δυναμις, δυναμεως, ἡ (119) – power, miracle 13
*δυνατος (32) – powerful, capable, able 18
*δυο (135) – two 6
*δωδεκα (75) – twelve 16

Ε ε

*ἐαν (351) + subj. – if, alternative for ἀν 17

*ἑαυτος (319) – himself, herself, itself, themselves (reflexive) 9

ἐβαλον – 2nd *Aorist* from βαλλω

*ἐγγιζω (42) + dat. – I approach, come near 10

ἐγγυς (31) – near 10

*ἐγειρω (144) – I raise up, wake 11

ἐγενομην – 2nd *Aorist* from γινομαι

ἐγνων – 2nd *Aorist* from γινωσκω

*ἐγω; ἡμεις (2666) – I, we 9

*ἐθνος, ἐθνους, το (162) – nation (pl. Gentiles) 13

εἰ (502) – if 5

εἰδον – 2nd *Aorist* from ὁραω

εἰκων, εἰκονος, ἡ (23) – image 14

*εἰμι (2462) – I am 5

εἰπον – 2nd *Aorist* from λεγω

*εἰρηνη (92) – peace 5

*εἰς (1767) + acc. – into 4

*εἱς μια ἑν (345) – one, a single 13

*εἰσερχομαι (194) – I go into, enter 8

*εἰτε (65) – if 9

εἰτε ... εἰτε – if . . . if, whether . . . or 9

*ἐκ (914) + gen. – (out of) from 4

ἑκαστος (82) – each 5

ἑκατον (17) – one hundred 16

*ἐκβαλλω (81) – I drive out (cast out, throw out) 4

*ἐκει (105) – there, in that place 10

ἐκειθεν (37) – from there 10

*ἐκεινος (265) – that, pl. those 9

*ἐκκλησια (114) – assembly (hence later 'church') 3

ἐκπορευομαι (33) – I go out 15

ἐκχεω (27) – I pour out 15

ἐλαβον – 2nd *Aorist* from λαμβανω

*ἐλαχιστος (14) – smallest 20

ἐλεεω (29) – I have mercy on, pity 7

*ἐλεος, ἐλεους, το (27) – mercy 13

ἐλευθερος (23) – free 18

ἐλθ- *part of* 2nd *Aorist* from ἐρχομαι

Ἑλλην, Ἑλληνος, ὁ (25) – Greek 14

ἐλπιζω (31) – I hope 14

*ἐλπις, ἐλπιδος, ἡ (53) – hope 12

ἐμαθον – 2nd *Aorist* from μανθανω

ἐμαυτος (37) – myself 9

ἐμος (76) – my, mine 9

*ἐμπροσθεν (48) + gen. – in front of 10

*ἐν (2752) + dat. – in (rarely, 'by' or 'with') 4

ἑν (εἱς μια ἑν) (345) – one, a single 13

*ἐνδυω (27) – I dress 15

ἐνεγκ- *part of* 2nd *Aorist* from φερω

ἑνεκα (26) + gen. – for the sake of 10

ἐννεα (5) – nine 16

*ἐντολη (67) – commandment 7

ἐνωπιον (94) + gen. – in front of, in the presence of 4

ἑξ (13) – six 16

*ἐξερχομαι (218) – I go out, go away 8

ἐξεστι (31) – it is permitted (impers.) 7

*ἐξουσια (102) – authority 7

ἐξω (63) + gen. – outside 4

ἑορτη (25) – festival 16

*ἐπαγγελια (52) – promise 17

ἐπαθον – 2nd *Aorist* from πασχω

ἐπει (26) – since 9

ἐπερωταω (56) – I ask (for) (+ acc. of person asked, + acc. of thing asked for) 19

ἐπεσον – 2nd *Aorist* from πιπτω

*ἐπι (890) + acc. – onto 4
+ gen. – on, in the time of 4
+ dat. – on/in, on the basis of 4
ἐπιγινωσκω (44) – I recognise 11
ἐπιθυμια (38) – desire 17
ἐπικαλεω (30) – I call upon, name 4
ἐπιον – 2nd *Aorist* from πινω
ἐπιστολη (24) – letter (correspondence) 16
*ἐπιστρεφω (36) – I turn (back) 15
ἐπιτιθημι (39) – I put upon 19
ἐπιτιμαω (29) – I rebuke 19
*ἑπτα (88) – seven 16
*ἐργαζομαι (41) – I work 8
*ἐργον (169) – work, deed 3
*ἐρημος, ἡ (48) – wilderness, desolate land 8
*ἐρχομαι (634) – I come, go 8
*ἐρωταω (63) – I ask (+ acc. of person asked, + acc. of thing asked for) 19
*ἐσθιω (158) – I eat 11
*ἐσχατος (52) – last, least 18
ἐσχον – 2nd *Aorist* from ἐχω
*ἑτερος (98) – another, different 5
*ἐτι (93) – still, yet 6
*ἑτοιμαζω (40) – I prepare, make ready 14
*ἐτος, ἐτους, το (49) – year 13
εὐ (5) – well 20
*εὐαγγελιζομαι (54) – I proclaim good news 8
*εὐαγγελιον (76) – good news, gospel 3
*εὐθυς (51) – immediately 10
*εὐλογεω (42) – I speak well of, bless, praise 6
*εὑρισκω (176) – I find 11
*εὑρον – 2nd *Aorist* from εὑρισκω
*εὐχαριστεω (38) – I give thanks 6
ἐφαγον – 2nd *Aorist* from ἐσθιω
ἐφυγον – 2nd *Aorist* from φευγω
*ἐχθρος (32) – enemy 17
*ἐχω (708) – I have, hold 2
ἑωρακα – Perfect Active of ὁραω
ἑως (146) + gen. – until 4

Ζ ζ
*ζαω (140) – I live 19
*ζητεω (117) – I seek 2
*ζωη (135) – life 3
*ζῳον (23) – living thing 20

Η η
ἠ (343) – or 5
ἠγαγον – 2nd *Aorist* from ἀγω
ἡγεομαι (28) – I lead 10
*ἠδη (61) – already 6
ἡκω (26) – I have come, am present 15
ἠλθον – 2nd *Aorist* from ἐρχομαι
*Ἠλιας, ὁ (29) – Elijah 8
ἡλιος (32) – sun 17
ἡμαρτον – 2nd *Aorist* from ἁμαρτανω
*ἡμεις; ἐγω (2666) – we, I 9
*ἡμερα (389) – day 3
ἠνεγκον – 2nd *Aorist* from φερω
Ἡρῳδης, ὁ (43) – Herod 8

Θ θ
*θαλασσα (91) – sea, lake 3
*θανατος (120) – death 7
*θαυμαζω (43) – I am amazed 10
θεαομαι (22) – I see, look at 20
*θελημα, θεληματος, το (62) – will 12
*θελω (208) – I wish, want 7
*θεος (1317) – god, God 2
*θεραπευω (43) – I heal 10
*θεωρεω (58) – I look at 7

*θηριον (46) – animal, beast 7
*θλιψις, θλιψεως, ἡ (45) – oppression, suffering 13
*θρονος (62) – throne 14
θυγατηρ, θυγατρος, ἡ (28) – daughter 12
θυρα (39) – door 17
*θυσια (28) – offering, sacrifice 16
*θυσιαστηριον (23) – altar 20

Ι ι
Ἰακωβ (27) – Jacob 1
Ἰακωβος (42) – James 14
ἰαομαι (26) – I heal 19
*ἰδιος (114) – one's own 5
ἰδ- *part of 2nd Aorist* from ὁραω
*ἰδου (200) – Look!, Behold! 11
ἱερευς, ἱερεως, ὁ (31) – priest 13
*ἱερον (71) – temple 3
*Ἱεροσολυμα, τα (77) – Jerusalem 5
*Ἰερουσαλημ, ἡ (63) – Jerusalem 5
*Ἰησους (917) – Jesus 3
*ἱκανος (39) – sufficient 18
*ἱματιον (60) – garment 7
*ἱνα + subj. (663)– in order that 17
*Ἰουδαιος (195) – Jewish, a Jew 5
Ἰουδαια (43) – Judea 17
*Ἰουδας, ὁ (44) – Judah, Judas 8
Ἰσραηλ (68) – Israel 1
*ἱστημι (155) – I cause to stand, stand 19
ἰσχυρος (29) – strong 18
*ἰσχυω (28) – I am strong 15
*Ἰωαννης or Ἰωανης, ὁ (135) – John 8
Ἰωσηφ (35) – Joseph 1

Κ κ
*κἀγω (84) – and I 9
καθαριζω (31) – I make/declare clean 18
*καθαρος (27) – clean, pure 18
*καθευδω (22) – I sleep 10
*καθημαι (91) – I sit (down) 18
*καθιζω (46) – I cause to sit down 18
*καθως (182) – just as 10
*και (9161) – and 1; also, even 9
καινος (42) – new 5
καιρος (85) – time, season 5
*Καισαρ, Καισαρος, ὁ (29) – Caesar 14
κακος (50) – bad 5
*καλεω (148) – I call 2
*καλος (100) – beautiful, good 5
καλως (37) – appropriately, well 10
*καρδια (156) – heart 3
*καρπος (66) – fruit 15
*κατα (473) + acc. – according to 4
+ gen. – against, 4
*καταβαινω (81) – I go down 11
καταλειπω (24) – I leave (behind) 11
καταργεω (27) – I make ineffective, abolish 7
κατεβην – *2nd Aorist* from καταβαινω
κατελιπον – *2nd Aorist* from καταλειπω
κατηγορεω (23) – I accuse 17
κατοικεω (44) – I dwell, inhabit, live 4
*καυχαομαι (37) – I boast 20
κειμαι (24) – I lie, recline 18
κελευω (25) – I command 15
*κεφαλη (75) – head 5
*κηρυσσω (61) – I proclaim, preach 6
*κλαιω (40) – I weep 15
κοπιαω (23) – I labour 19
*κοσμος (186) – world 2
*κραζω (56) – I cry out 6
*κρατεω (47) – I grasp, arrest 14
*κρεισσων (19) – better 20
*κριμα, ατος, το (27) – judgement 14

*κρινω (114) – I judge, decide 11
*κρισις, κρισεως, ἡ (47) – judgement 13
*κυριος (717) – lord, master, sir 2
κωλυω (23) – I hinder 15
*κωμη (27) – village 16

Λ λ
λαβ- *part of 2nd Aorist* from λαμβανω
*λαλεω (296) – I speak, say 2
*λαμβανω (258) – I take, receive 2
*λαος (142) – people (as in 'a people'), nation 2
*λεγω (2354) – I say, speak, tell 2
λευκος (25) – white, bright 18
*λιθος (59) – stone 14
λογιζομαι (40) – I calculate, consider 8
*λογος (330) – word, message 2
*λοιπος (55) – remaining 18
λυπεω (26) – I grieve (pain) 15
*λυω (42) – I untie 2

Μ μ
*μαθητης, ὁ (261) – disciple 8
μαθ- *part of 2nd Aorist* from μανθανω
*μακαριος (50) – blessed, happy 5
μαλιστα (12) – most of all 20
*μαλλον (81) – more, rather 20
μανθανω (25) – I learn 11
Μαρια *or* Μαριαμ (27) – Mary 3
*μαρτυρεω (76) – I bear witness, testify 7
*μαρτυρια (37) – testimony, witness 17
*μαρτυς, μαρτυρος, ὁ (35) – witness 18
*μαχαιρα (29) – sword 16
*μεγας μεγαλη μεγα (243) – large, great 5
μειζων (48) – larger, greater 12
*μελλω (109) – I intend, am about (to) 7
μελος, μελους, το (34) – member, part, limb 13
*μεν (179) *postpositive* – on the one hand 9
*μενω (118) – I remain 11
*μερος, μερους, το (42) – part, share 13
*μεσος (58) – middle 18
*μετα (469) + acc. – after 4
+ gen. – with 4
*μετανοεω (34) – I repent, change my mind 7
*μη (1042) – not 7
*μηδε (56) – and not, but not 7
μηδεις (90) – no, no one, nothing 13
μηκετι (22) – no longer 7
μηποτε (25) – never 9
μητε (34) – and not, nor 7
*μητηρ, μητρος, ἡ (83) – mother 12
μια (εἱς, μια, ἑν) (345) – one, a single 13
*μικρον (16) – a little, a short time 20
*μικρος (46) – small 20
*μιμνῃσκομαι (23) + gen. – I remember 20
*μισεω (40) – I hate 14
*μισθος (29) – pay, wages 18
μνημειον (40) – tomb, monument 7
*μονος (114) – only, alone 5
μυστηριον (28) – mystery, secret 9
*Μωϋσης, Μωϋσεως, ὁ (80) – Moses 13

Ν ν
ναι (33) – yes, of course 10
*ναος (45) – sanctuary, shrine, temple 15
*νεκρος (128) – dead 5

νεος (23) – new, young 18
νεφελη (25) – cloud 16
νικαω (28) – I overcome, conquer 19
νιπτω (17) – I wash 20
*νομος (194) – law 2
νους, νοος, ὁ (24) – mind 13
*νυν (147) – now 6
νυξ, νυκτος, ἡ (61) – night 12

Ξ ξ
(None)

Ο ο
*ὁ ἡ το (19867) – the 2
*ὁδος, ἡ (101) – way, road 8
*οἰδα (318) – I know 18
*οἰκια (93) – house, household 3
*οἰκοδομεω (40) – I build (up) 6
*οἰκος (114) – household, house 2
*οἰνος (34) – wine 17
ὀκτω (8) – eight 16
*ὀλιγος (40) – small, little (pl. few) 18
*ὁλος (109) – whole, entire 9
ὀμνυω (26) – I swear, take an oath 15
ὁμοιος (45) – similar, like 10
*ὁμοιως (30) – likewise 10
ὁμολογεω (26) – I promise, confess 17
*ὀνομα, ατος, το (231) – name 12
*ὀπισω (35) + gen. – behind 7
*ὁπου (82) – where 10
ὁπως + subj. (53) – in order that 17
*ὁραω (454) – I see 11
ὀργη (36) – anger, wrath 17
*ὀρος, ὀρους, το (63) – mountain, hill 13
*ὁς ἥ ὅ (1398) – who, which, what 10
*ὁσος (110) – as/how great, as/how much 5
ὁστις (153) – who 12
ὁταν + subj. (123) – whenever 17
*ὁτε (103) – when 6
*ὁτι (1296) – that, because, “ (marking beginning of speech) 10
οὑ (24) – where 10
*οὐ οὐκ οὐχ (1606) – not 4
*οὐαι (46) – woe 16
*οὐδε (143) – and not 10
*οὐδεις (234) – no, no one, nothing 13
οὐκετι (47) – no longer 6
*οὐν (499) *postpositive* – therefore, consequently 9
οὐπω (26) – not yet 6
*οὐρανος (273) – heaven 2
*οὐς, ὠτος, το (36) – ear 14
*οὐτε (87) – neither 10
οὐτε ... οὐτε – neither . . . nor 10
*οὑτος αὑτη τουτο (1387) – this, pl. these 9
*οὑτως (208) – in this manner, thus 10
*οὐχι (54) – not, no 10
ὀφειλω (35) – I owe 11
*ὀφθαλμος (100) – eye 7
*ὀχλος (175) – crowd 2

Π π
παθ- *part of 2nd Aorist* from πασχω
*παιδιον (52) – child, infant 14
*παις, παιδος, ὁ (24) – child, servant 14
*παλιν (141) – back, again 6
παντοτε (41) – always 6
*παρα (194) + acc. – alongside 4
+ gen. – from beside 4
+ dat. – beside 4
*παραβολη (50) – parable 7
παραγγελλω (32) + dat. – I order 11
παραγινομαι (37) – I arrive, stand by 11

*παραδιδωμι (119) – I entrust, hand over 19
*παρακαλεω (109) – I exhort, request, comfort, encourage 4
παρακλησις, παρακλησεως, ἡ (29) – encouragement 13
παραλαμβανω (49) – I take, receive 4
παρειμι (24) – I am present 18
παρερχομαι (29) – I go by, pass by 8
παριστημι (41) – I place beside 19
παρουσια (24) – presence, coming 16
παρρησια (31) – outspokenness, boldness 7
*πας, πασα, παν (1243) – every, all, whole 13
*πασχα (29) – Passover 14
πασχω (42) – I suffer 11
*πατηρ, πατρος, ὁ (413) – father, ancestor 12
*Παυλος (158) – Paul 3
πειθω (52) – I convince, persuade 6
πειναω (23) – I hunger 19
*πειραζω (38) – I test, tempt 14
*πεμπω (79) – I send 6
πεντε (38) – five 16
περαν (23) + gen. – on the other side of 10
*περι (333) + acc. – around, approximately 4
+ gen. – concerning, about 4
*περιπατεω (95) – I walk about, live 4
*περισσευω (39) – I exceed 15
*περιτομη (36) – circumcision 16
πεσ- *part of 2nd Aorist* from πιπτω
*Πετρος (156) – Peter 3
πι- *part of 2nd Aorist* from πινω
*Πιλατος (55) – Pilate 10
πιμπλημι (24) – I fulfil 19
*πινω (73) – I drink 11
*πιπτω (90) – I fall (down) 11
*πιστευω (241) + dat. – I believe (in), trust, have faith in 3
*πιστις, πιστεως, ἡ (243) – faith 12
πιστος (67) – faithful, believing 5
*πλαναω (39) – I lead astray, deceive 19
*πλειων (55) – more 12
πληθος, πληθους, το (31) – multitude, large amount 13
πλην (31) – however, yet 10
*πληροω (86) – I fulfil, fill, complete 19
*πλοιον (68) – boat 3
πλουσιος (28) – rich 18
*πνευμα, πνευματος, το (379) – spirit, wind 12
πνευματικος (26) – spiritual 18
ποθεν; (29) – from where? 10
*ποιεω (568) – I do, make 2
ποιμην, ποιμενος, ὁ (18) – shepherd 20
ποιος; (33) – of what kind? 9
*πολις, πολεως, ἡ (162) – city, town 13
*πολυς πολλη πολυ (416) – much, many 5
*πονηρος (78) – evil, wicked 5
*πορευομαι (153) – I go 15
πορνεια (25) – sexual immorality 16
ποσος; (37) – how great? how much? 9
*ποτε (29) *postpositive* – once (at some time) 6
*ποτηριον (31) – cup 9
που; (48) – where? 4
*πους, ποδος, ὁ (93) – foot 12
*πρασσω (39) – I do 14
*πρεσβυτερος (66) – elder, old person 14
προ (47) + gen. – before 4

*προβατον (39) – sheep 7
*προς (700) + acc. – to, towards 4
*προσερχομαι (86) – I come to, go to, approach 8
*προσευχη (36) – prayer 16
*προσευχομαι (85) – I pray 8
*προσεχω (24) + dat. – I pay attention to, take heed (of) 6
προσκαλεομαι (29) – I summon 8
*προσκυνεω (60) + dat. – I worship 4
προσφερω (47) – I bring to, offer 11
*προσωπον (76) – face 3
προφητευω (28) – I prophesy 14
*προφητης, ὁ (144) – prophet 8
*πρωτος (155) – first 16
*πτωχος (34) – poor 17
πυρ, πυρος, το (71) – fire 12
*πως; (103) – how? 4

Ρ ρ

ῥαββι (15) – rabbi 1
ῥημα, ατος, το (68) – word, saying 12
*ῥυομαι (17) – I rescue 8

Σ σ

σαββατον (68) – Sabbath 3
*σαρξ, σαρκος, ἡ (147) – flesh 12
Σατανας, ὁ (36) – Satan 8
*σεαυτος (43) – yourself 9
*σημειον (77) – sign, miracle 3
σημερον (41) – today 6
Σιμων, Σιμωνος, ὁ (75) – Simon 12
σκανδαλιζω (29) – I cause to fall/sin 14
σκευος, σκευους, το (23) – object (pl. property) 13
σκοτος, σκοτους, το (31) – darkness 13
σος (27) – your, yours (sing.) 9
*σοφια (51) – wisdom 17
σπειρω (52) – I sow 11
*σπερμα, ατος, το (43) – seed 14
*σταυρος (27) – cross 18
*σταυροω (46) – I crucify 19
στομα, στοματος, το (78) – mouth 12
*στρατιωτης, ὁ (26) – soldier 8
*συ; ὑμεις (2907) – you (sing); you (pl.) 9
συν (128) + dat. – together with 4
*συναγω (59) – I gather, bring together 4
*συναγωγη (56) – synagogue 5
συνειδησις, συνειδησεως, ἡ (30) – conscience 13
συνερχομαι (30) – I come together 8
συνιημι (26) – I understand 19
σχ- *part* of 2nd *Aorist* from ἐχω
*σωζω (106) – I save, rescue, heal 6
*σωμα, σωματος, το (142) – body 12
*σωτηρ, σωτηρος, ὁ (24) – saviour 12
*σωτηρια (46) – salvation 17

Τ τ

*τε (215) *postpositive* – and 9
*τεκνον (99) – child 3
τελειοω (23) – I accomplish, complete 19
*τελεω (28) – I finish, complete 15
*τελος, τελους, το (40) – end, goal 13
*τεσσαρες (41) – four (τεσσαρα with neuter nouns) 16
*τηρεω (70) – I keep 2
*τιθημι (100) – I put/place 19
*τιμαω (21) – I honour, value 19
τιμη (41) – price, value, honour 17
*Τιμοθεος (24) – Timothy 6
*τί; (556) – why? 12
*τις τι (525) – someone, something 12

*τίς; τί; (556) – who?, which?, what? 12
τοιουτος (57) – of such a kind, such 9
*τοπος (94) – place 6
*τοτε (160) – then 6
*τρεις (68) – three (τρια with neuter nouns) 16
*τριτος (56) – third 16
*τυφλος (50) – blind 5

Υ υ
*ὑδωρ, ὑδατος, το (76) – water 12
*υἱος (377) – son 2
*ὑμεις; συ (2907) – you (pl.); you (sing.) 9
ὑπαγω (79) – I depart 4
ὑπαρχω (60) – I exist, am 6
*ὑπερ (150) + acc. – above 4
+ gen. – on behalf of 4
ὑπηρετης, ὁ (20) – servant 8
*ὑπο (220) + acc. – under 4
+ gen. – by (at the hands of) 4
*ὑπομονη (32) – patience 16
*ὑποστρεφω (35) – I turn back, return 15
*ὑποτασσω (38) – I subject 14

Φ φ
φαγ- *part of 2nd Aorist* from ἐσθιω
*φαινω (31) – I shine, appear 15
*φανεροω (49) – I reveal, make known 19
*Φαρισαιος (98) – Pharisee 7
*φερω (66) – I bear, carry 11
*φευγω (29) – I flee 11
φημι (66) – I say 19
*φιλεω (25) – I love, like 2
Φιλιππος (36) – Philip 15
*φιλος (29) – loved, friendly, friend 18
*φοβεομαι (95) – I am afraid, fear 15
*φοβος (47) – fear 15
φρονεω (26) – I ponder 15
φυγ- *part of 2nd Aorist* from φευγω
*φυλακη (47) – watch (guards), prison 17
φυλασσω (31) – I guard 14
*φυλη (31) – tribe, nation 16
*φωνεω (43) – I call (out) 14
*φωνη (139) – sound, voice 3
*φως, φωτος, το (73) – light 12

Χ χ
*χαιρω (74) – I rejoice (in the Imperative – 'Greetings!') 11
χαρα (59) – joy 7
χαριζομαι (23) – I give freely 14
*χαρις, χαριτος, ἡ (155) – grace 12
*χειρ, χειρος, ἡ (177) – hand 12
χειρων (11) – worse 20
*χηρα (26) – widow 16
χιλιας (23) – one thousand 16
*χρεια (49) – need 17
*Χριστος (529) – Christ, Messiah 2
*χρονος (54) – time (period of) 15
*χωρα (28) – country(side) 16
*χωρις (41) + gen. – separate from, apart from 10

Ψ ψ
ψυχη (103) – soul, self 3

Ω ω
*ὡδε (61) – here 10
ὡρα (106) – hour, occasion 3
ὡσπερ (36) – just as 12
*ὡστε + Infinitive (83) – with the result that 18
*ὡς (504) – as, like 5

# English – Greek dictionary

*N.B. The number in brackets following each Greek word gives the number of times it occurs in the New Testament. The following number outside brackets gives the chapter in which it is introduced.*

**A a**

I abolish (make ineffective) – καταργεω (27) 7
able (powerful, capable) – δυνατος (32) 18
I am able (can) – δυναμαι (210) 18
I am about to (intend) – μελλω (109) 7
about (concerning) – περι (333) + gen. 4
above – ὑπερ (150) + acc. 4
Abraham – Ἀβρααμ (73) 1
I accomplish (complete) – τελειοω (23) 19
according to – κατα (473) + acc. 4
I accuse – κατηγορεω (23) 17
I am afraid (fear) – φοβεομαι (95) 15
after – μετα (469) + acc. 4
again (back) – παλιν (141) 6
against (down from) – κατα (473) + gen. 4
age (long time) – αἰων, αἰωνος, ὁ (122) 12
all (every, whole) – πας, πασα, παν (1243), ἁπας, ἁπασα, ἁπαν (34) 13
alone (only) – μονος (114) 5
alongside – παρα (194) + acc. 4
already – ἠδη (61) 6
also (even) – και (9161) 9
altar – θυσιαστηριον (23) 20
always – παντοτε (41) 6
I am – εἰμι (2462) 5
I am (exist) – ὑπαρχω (60) 6
I am able (can) – δυναμαι (210) 18
I am about to (intent) – μελλω (109) 7
I am amazed – θαυμαζω (43) 10
I am born – Pass. of γενναω (97) 19
amen (truly) – ἀμην (129) 1
ancestor (father) – πατηρ, πατρος, ὁ (413) 12
and – και (9161) 1
and – τε *postpositive* (215) 9
and I – κἀγω (84) 9
and not (but not) – μηδε (56) 7
and not (nor) – μητε (34) 7
and not – οὐδε (143) 10
angel (messenger) – ἀγγελος (175) 2

anger (wrath) – ὀργη (36) 17
animal (beast) – θηριον (46) 7
I announce (report) – ἀπαγγελλω (45) 11
I announce – ἀγγελλω (1) 11
another (different) – ἑτερος (98) 5
one another (each other) – ἀλληλος (100) 9
I answer – ἀποκρινομαι (231) 15
apart from (separate from) – χωρις (41) + gen. 10
apostle – ἀποστολος (80) 7
I appear (shine) – φαινω (31) 15
I approach (come near) – ἐγγιζω (42) + dat. 10
I approach (go to, come to) – προσερχομαι (86) 8
appropriately (well) – καλως (37) 10
approximately (around) – περι (333) + acc. 4
I argue (consider, discuss) – διαλογιζομαι (16) 14
around (approximately) – περι (333) + acc. 4
I arrest (grasp) – κρατεω (47) 14
I arrive (stand by) – παραγινομαι (37) 11
as (like) – ὡς (504) 5
as great (how great, as/how much) – ὁσος (110) 5
as much (how much, as/how great) – ὁσος (110) 5
I ask – ἐρωταω (63) (+ acc. of person asked, + acc. of thing asked for) 19
I ask (for) – ἐπερωταω (56) (+ acc. of person asked, + acc. of thing asked for) 19
I ask for – αἰτεω (70) (+ acc. of person asked, + acc. of thing asked for) 6
assembly (church) – ἐκκλησια (114) 3
at some time (once) – ποτε (29) 6
I pay attention to (take head of) – προσεχω + dat. (24) 6
authority – ἐξουσια (102) 7
(away) from – ἀπο (646) + gen. 4
I go away – ἐξερχομαι (218) 8
I go away – ἀπερχομαι (117) 8

**B b**

back (again) – παλιν (141) 6
bad – κακος (50) 5
Barnabas – Βαρναβας, ὁ (28) 8
I baptize (dip) – βαπτιζω (77) 6
on the basis of – ἐπι (890) + dat. 4
I bear (carry) – φερω (66) 11
I bear (beget)– γενναω (97) 19
I bear witness (testify) – μαρτυρεω (76) 7
beast (animal) – θηριον (46) 7
beautiful (good) – καλος (100) 5
because – διοτι (23) 9
because (for) – γαρ *postpositive* (1041) 9
because (that, ")– ὁτι (1296) 10
because of – δια (667) + acc. 4
I become (happen) – γινομαι (669) 11
before – προ (47) + gen. 4
I beget (bear) – γενναω (97) 19
I begin – ἀρχομαι (86) 8
beginning – ἀρχη (55) 3
behind – ὀπισω (35) + gen. 7
Behold! (Look!) – ἰδου (200) 11
I believe (in) (trust, have faith in) – πιστευω (241) (+ dat.) 3
believing (faithful) – πιστος (67) 5
beloved – ἀγαπητος (61) 5
beside – παρα (194) + dat. 4
better – κρεισσων (19) 20

I bind (tie up) – δεω (43) 7
I blaspheme – βλασφημεω (34) 14
I bless (speak well of, praise) – εὐλογεω (42) 6
blessed (happy) – μακαριος (50) 5
blind – τυφλος (50) 5
blood – αἱμα, ατος, το (97) 12
I boast – καυχαομαι (37) 20
boat – πλοιον (68) 3
body – σωμα, ατος, το (142) 12
boldness (outspokenness) – παρρησια (31) 7
book (scroll) – βιβλιον (34) 3
I am born – Pass. of γενναω (97) 19
bread – ἀρτος (97) 2
bright (white) – λευκος (25) 18
I bring (lead) – ἀγω (67) 2
I bring to (offer) – προσφερω (47) 11
I bring together (gather) – συναγω (59) 4
brother – ἀδελφος (343) 2
I build (up) – οἰκοδομεω (40) 6
but – ἀλλα (638) 5
but – δε *postpositive* (2792) 9
but not (and not) – μηδε (56) 7
I buy – ἀγοραζω (30) 14
by (at the hands of) – ὑπο (220) + gen. 4

**C c**

Caesar – Καισαρ, Καισαρος, ὁ (29) 14
I calculate (consider) – λογιζομαι (40) 8
I call – καλεω (148) 2
I call (out) – φωνεω (43) 14
I call upon (name) – ἐπικαλεω (30) 4
I can (am able) – δυναμαι (210) 18
capable (able, powerful) – δυνατος (32) 18
I carry (bear) – φερω (66) 11
I cast out (drive out, throw out) – ἐκβαλλω (81) 4
I cause to sit down – καθιζω (46) 18
I cause to stand – ἱστημι (155) 19
I change my mind (repent) – μετανοεω (34) 7
chief priest (high priest) – ἀρχιερευς, ἀρχιερεως, ὁ (122) 13
child – τεκνον (99) 3
child (infant) – παιδιον (52) 14
child (servant) – παις, παιδος, ὁ (24) 14
Christ (Messiah) – Χριστος (529) 2
church (assembly) – ἐκκλησια (114) 3
circumcision – περιτομη (36) 16
city (town) – πολις, πολεως, ἡ (162) 13
clean (pure) – καθαρος (27) 18
I make/declare clean – καθαριζω (31) 18
clerk (scribe) – γραμματευς, γραμματεως, ὁ (63) 13
cloud – νεφελη (25) 16
I come (go) – ἐρχομαι (634) 8
I come near (approach) – ἐγγιζω (42) 10
I have come (am present) – ἡκω (26) 15
I come to (go to, approach) – προσερχομαι (86) 8
I come together – συνερχομαι (30) 8
I comfort (exhort, request, encourage) – παρακαλεω (109) 4
coming (presence) – παρουσια (24) 16
I command – κελευω (25) 15

commandment – ἐντολη (67) 7
I complete (fulfil, fill) – πληροω (86) 19
I complete (accomplish) – τελειοω (23) 19
I complete (finish) – τελεω (28) 15
I confess (promise) – ὁμολογεω (26) 17
I conquer (overcome) – νικαω (28) 19
concerning (about) – περι (333) + gen. 4
conscience – συνειδησις, συνειδησεως, ἡ (30) 13
consequently (therefore) – οὐν *postpositive* (499) 9
I consider (argue, discuss) – διαλογιζομαι (16) 14
I consider (calculate) – λογιζομαι (40) 8
I convince (persuade) – πειθω (52) 6
country(side) – χωρα (28) 16
covenant (last will and testament) – διαθηκη (33) 17
cross – σταυρος (27) 18
I cross over – διερχομαι (43) 8
crowd – ὀχλος (175) 2
I crucify – σταυροω (46) 19
I cry out – κραζω (56) 6
cup – ποτηριον (31) 9

**D d**

darkness – σκοτος, σκοτους, το (31) 13
daughter – θυγατηρ, θυγατρος, ἡ (28) 12
David – Δαυιδ (59) 1
day – ἡμερα (389) 3
dead – νεκρος (128) 5
death – θανατος (120) 7
I deceive (lead astray) – πλαναω (39) 19
I decide (judge) – κρινω (114) 11
deed (work) – ἐργον (169) 3
demon – δαιμονιον (63) 3
I deny (refuse) – ἀρνεομαι (33) 8
I depart (go away) – ἀπερχομαι (117) 8
I depart – ὑπαγω (79) 4
desire – ἐπιθυμια (38) 17
desolate land (wilderness) – ἐρημος, ἡ (48) 8
I destroy (ruin) – ἀπολλυμι (90) 19
the devil (slanderer) – διαβολος (37) 15
I die – ἀποθνῃσκω (111) 11
different (another) – ἑτερος (98) 5
I dip (baptize) – βαπτιζω (77) 6
disciple – μαθητης, ὁ (261) 8
I discuss (consider, argue) – διαλογιζομαι (16) 14
disease (weakness) – ἀσθενεια (24) 16
I dismiss (leave, forgive) – ἀφιημι (143) 19
I dismiss (set free, divorce) – ἀπολυω (66) 4
I divorce (set free, dismiss) – ἀπολυω (66) 4
I do (make) – ποιεω (568) 2
I do – πρασσω (39) 14
I do wrong (sin) – ἁμαρτανω (43) 11
door – θυρα (39) 17
down from (against) – κατα (473) + gen. 4
I dress – ἐνδυω (27) 15
I drink – πινω (73) 11
I drive out (cast out, throw out) – ἐκβαλλω (81) 4
I dwell (inhabit, live) – κατοικεω (44) 4

**E e**

each – ἑκαστος (82) 5

each other (one another) – ἀλληλος (100) 9

ear – οὐς, ὠτος, το (36) 14

earth (land, soil) – γη (250) 3

I eat – ἐσθιω (158) 11

Egypt – Αἰγυπτος, ἡ (25) 8

eight – ὀκτω (8) 16

elder (old person) – πρεσβυτερος (66) 14

Elijah – Ἠλιας, ὁ (29) 8

I encourage (exhort, request, comfort) – παρακαλεω (109) 4

encouragement – παρακλησις, παρακλησεως, ἡ (29) 13

end (goal) – τελος, τελους, το (40) 13

enemy – ἐχθρος (32) 17

I enter (go into) – εἰσερχομαι (194) 8

entire (whole) – ὁλος (109) 9

I entrust (hand over)– παραδιδωμι (119) 19

eternal – αἰωνιος (71) 5

even (also) – και (9161) 9

every (all, whole) – πας, πασα, παν (1243), ἁπας, ἁπασα, ἁπαν (34) 13

evil (wicked) – πονηρος (78) 5

I exceed – περισσευω (39) 15

I exhort (request, comfort, encourage) – παρακαλεω (109) 4

I exist (am) – ὑπαρχω (60) 6

eye – ὀφθαλμος (100) 7

**F f**

face – προσωπον (76) 3

faith – πιστις, πιστεως, ἡ (243) 12

I have faith in (believe in, trust) – πιστευω (241) (+ dat.) 3

faithful (believing) – πιστος (67) 5

faithless (unbelieving) – ἀπιστος (23) 18

I fall (down) – πιπτω (90) 11

I cause to fall (sin) – σκανδαλιζω (29) 14

fame (report) – ἀκοη (24) 16

family (generation) – γενεα (43) 17

father (ancestor) – πατηρ, πατρος, ὁ (413) 12

fear – φοβος (47) 15

I fear (am afraid) – φοβεομαι (95) 15

festival – ἑορτη (25) 16

few (little, small) – ὀλιγος (40) (pl.) 18

field – ἀγρος (36) 17

I fill (fulfil, complete) – πληροω (86) 19

I find – εὑρισκω (176) 11

I finish (complete) – τελεω (28) 15

fire – πυρ, πυρος, το (71) 12

first – πρωτος (155) 16

five – πεντε (38) 16

I flee – φευγω (29) 11

flesh – σαρξ, σαρκος, ἡ (147) 12

I follow – ἀκολουθεω (90) + dat. 7

foot – πους, ποδος, ὁ (93) 12

for (because) – γαρ *postpositive* (1041) 9

for the sake of – ἑνεκα (26) + gen 10

I forgive (leave, dismiss) – ἀφιημι (143) 19

four – τεσσαρες (τεσσαρα with neuter nouns) (41) 16

I set free (divorce, dismiss) – ἀπολυω (66) 4

free – ἐλευθερος (23) 18

friend, friendly (loved) – φιλος (29) 18

(away) from – ἀπο (646) + gen. 4
(out of) from – ἐκ (914) + gen. 4
from besides – παρα (194) + gen. 4
from there – ἐκειθεν (37) 10
from where? – ποθεν; (29) 10
in front of – ἐμπροσθεν (48) + gen. 10
fruit – καρπος (66) 15
I fulfil (fill, complete) – πληροω (86), πιμπλημι (24) 19

**G g**

Galilee – Γαλιλαια (61) 5
garment – ἱματιον (60) 7
I gather (bring together) – συναγω (59) 4
generation (family) – γενεα (43) 17
genuine (truthful, true) – ἀληθης, ἀληθους (26) 13
genuine (true, real) – ἀληθινος (28) 10
Gentiles – τα ἐθνη (pl.; sing. = nation) (162) 13
I give – διδωμι (415) 19
I give away – ἀποδιδωμι (48) 19
I give freely – χαριζομαι (23) 14
I give thanks – εὐχαριστεω (38) 6
I glorify (praise) – δοξαζω (61) 6
glory (splendour) – δοξα (166) 3
I go (come) – ἐρχομαι (634) 8
I go – πορευομαι (153) 15
I go away (depart) – ἀπερχομαι (117) 8
I go away (go out) – ἐξερχομαι (218) 8
I go by (pass by) – παρερχομαι (29) 8
I go down – καταβαινω (81) 11
I go into (enter) – εἰσερχομαι (194) 8
I go out (go away) – ἐκπορευομαι (33) 15
I go to (come to, approach) – προσερχομαι (86) 8
I go up – ἀναβαινω (82) 11
goal (end) – τελος, τελους, το (40) 13
god, God – θεος (1317) 2
good – ἀγαθος (102) 5
good (beautiful) – καλος (100) 5
good news (gospel) – εὐαγγελιον (76) 3
gospel (good news) – εὐαγγελιον (76) 3
grace – χαρις, χαριτος, ἡ (155) 12
I grasp (arrest) – κρατεω (47) 14
great (large) – μεγας μεγαλη μεγα (243) 5
greater (larger) – μειζων (48) 12
Greek – Ἑλλην, Ἑλληνος, ὁ (25) 14
I greet – ἀσπαζομαι (59) 8
Greetings! – Imperative of χαιρω (74) 11
I grieve (pain) – λυπεω (26) 15
I grow – αὐξανω (23) 18
I guard – φυλασσω (31) 14
guards (a watch, prison) – φυλακη (47) 17

**H h**

hand – χειρ, χειρος, ἡ (177) 12
I hand over (entrust) – παραδιδωμι (119) 19
I happen (become) – γινομαι (669) 11
happy (blessed) – μακαριος (50) 5
I hate – μισεω (40) 14
I have (hold) – ἐχω (708) 2
I have come (am present) – ἡκω (26) 15

I have faith in (believe in, trust) – πιστευω (241) (+ dat.) 3
I have mercy on (pity) – ἐλεεω (29) 7
he (she, it, they) – αὐτος (5597) 3
head – κεφαλη (75) 5
I heal – θεραπευω (43) 10
I heal (save, rescue) – σωζω (106) 6
I heal – ἰαομαι (26) 19
I hear (listen to) – ἀκουω (428) (+ acc. of thing heard, + gen. of person heard) 2
heart – καρδια (156) 3
heaven – οὐρανος (273) 2
herself (emphatic) – feminine of αὐτος (5597) 9
herself (reflexive) – feminine of ἑαυτη (319) 9
here – ὡδε (61) 10
Herod – Ἡρῳδης, ὁ (43) 8
high priest (chief priest) – ἀρχιερευς, ἀρχιερεως, ὁ (122) 13
hill (mountain) – ὀρος, ὀρους, το (63) 13
himself (emphatic) – αὐτος (5597) 9
himself (reflexive) – ἑαυτος (319) 9
I hinder – κωλυω (23) 15
I hold (have) – ἐχω (708) 2
holy – ἁγιος (233) 5
I make holy – ἁγιαζω (28) 15
honour (price, value) – τιμη (41) 17
I honour (value) – τιμαω (21) 19
hope – ἐλπις, ἐλπιδος, ἡ (53) 12
I hope – ἐλπιζω (31) 14
hour (occasion) – ὡρα (106) 3
house – οἰκια, οἰκος (93) 3
household – οἰκος, οἰκια (114) 2
how? – πως; (103) 4
how great? how much? – ποσος; (37) 9
how great (as great, as/how much) – ὁσος (110) 5
how much (as much, as/how great) – ὁσος (110) 5
however (yet) – πλην (31) 10
human being (person) – ἀνθρωπος (550) 2
one hundred – ἑκατον (17) 16
I hunger – πειναω (23) 19
husband (man) – ἀνηρ, ἀνδρος, ὁ (216) 12

**I i**

I, we – ἐγω; ἡμεις (2666) 9
if – ἐαν (351) + Subj. 17
if – εἰ (502) 5
if – εἰτε (65) 9
image – εἰκων, εἰκονος, ἡ (23) 14
immediately – εὐθυς (51) 10
immorality (sexual) – πορνεια (25) 16
impure (unclean) – ἀκαθαρτος (32) 18
in – ἐν (2752) + dat. 4
in – ἐπι (890) + dat. 4
in front of – ἐμπροσθεν (48) + gen. 10
in front of (in the presence of) – ἐνωπιον (94) + gen. 4
in order that – ἱνα (663) + subj. 17
in order that – ὁπως (53) + subj. 17
in that place (there) – ἐκει (105) 10
in the presence of (in front of) – ἐνωπιον (94) + gen. 4
in the time of – ἐπι (890) + gen. 4
in this manner (thus) – οὑτως (208) 10
indeed – γε (25) 9
I make ineffective (abolish) – καταργεω (27) 7
infant (child) – παιδιον (52) 14

I inhabit (dwell, live) – κατοικεω (44) 4
I intend (am about to) – μελλω (109) 7
into – εἰς (1767) + acc. 4
Israel – Ἰσραηλ (68) 1
it (he, she, they) – αὐτο (5597) 3
itself (emphatic) – neuter of αὐτος (5597) 9
itself (reflexive) – neuter of ἑαυτος (319) 9

**J j**

Jacob – Ἰακωβ (27) 1
James – Ἰακωβος (42) 14
Jerusalem – Ἱεροσολυμα, τα (77) 5
Jerusalem – Ἰερουσαλημ, ἡ (63) 5
Jesus – Ἰησους (917) 3
Jew (Jewish) – Ἰουδαιος (195) 5
Jewish (a Jew) – Ἰουδαιος (195) 5
John – Ἰωαννης or Ἰωανης, ὁ (135) 8
Joseph – Ἰωσηφ (35) 1
joy – χαρα (59) 7
Judah (Judas) – Ἰουδας, ὁ (44) 8
Judas (Judah) – Ἰουδας, ὁ (44) 8
Judea – Ἰουδαια (43) 17
I judge (decide) – κρινω (114) 11
judgement – κρισις, κρισεως, ἡ (47) 13
judgement – κριμα, ατος, το (27) 14
just (upright) – δικαιος (79) 5
just as – ὥσπερ (36) 12
just as – καθως (182) 10
just now (now) – ἀρτι (36) 6
I justify – δικαιοω (39) 19

**K k**

I keep – τηρεω (70) 2
I kill – ἀποκτεινω (74) 11
I kill (take away) – ἀναιρεω (24) 17
of such a kind (such) – τοιουτος (57) 9
of what kind? – ποιος; (33) 9
king – βασιλευς, βασιλεως, ὁ (115) 13
kingship (kingdom, reign) – βασιλεια (162) 3
I know – γινωσκω (222) 11
I know – οἰδα (318) 18
knowledge – γνωσις, γνωσεως, ἡ (29) 13
I make known – γνωριζω (25) 15
I make known (reveal) – φανεροω (49) 19

**L l**

I labour – κοπιαω (23) 19
lake (sea) – θαλασσα (91) 3
lamb (sheep) – ἀρνιον (30) 9
land (soil, earth) – γη (250) 3
language (tongue) – γλωσσα (50) 17
large (great) – μεγας μεγαλη μεγα (243) 5
large amount (multitude) – πληθος, πληθους, το (31) 13
larger (greater) – μειζων (48) 12
last (least) – ἐσχατος (52) 18
law – νομος (194) 2
I lead (bring) – ἀγω (67) 2
I lead – ἡγεομαι (28) 10
I lead astray (deceive) – πλαναω (39) 19
leader (ruler) – ἀρχων (37) 12
I lead up (restore) – ἀναγω (23) 7
I learn – μανθανω (25) 11
least (last) – ἐσχατος (52) 18
I leave (forgive, dismiss) – ἀφιημι (143) 19
I leave (behind) – καταλειπω (24) 11

letter (correspondence) – ἐπιστολη (24) 16
I lie (recline) – κειμαι (24) 18
life – ζωη (135) 3
I lift up (take away) – αἰρω (101) 11
light – φως, φωτος, το (73) 12
like (as) – ὡς (504) 5
like (similar) – ὁμοιος (45) 10
I like (love) – φιλεω (25) 2
likewise – ὁμοιως (30) 10
limb (member, part) – μελος, μελους, το (34) 13
I listen to (hear) – ἀκουω (428) (+ acc. of thing heard, + gen. of person heard) 2
little (small, few) – ὀλιγος (40) 18
a little – μικρον (16) 20
I live – ζαω (140) 19
I live (dwell, inhabit) – κατοικεω (44) 4
I live (walk about) – περιπατεω (95) 4
living thing – ζῳον (23) 20
Look! (Behold!) – ἰδου (200) 11
I look at – θεωρεω (58) 7
I look at (see) – θεαομαι (22) 20
I look up (receive sight) – ἀναβλεπω (25) 4
lord (master, sir) – κυριος (717) 2
love – ἀγαπη (116) 3
I love (like) – φιλεω (25) 2
I love – ἀγαπαω (143) 19
loved (friendly, friend) – φιλος (29) 18

**M m**

I make (do) – ποιεω (568) 2
I make ineffective (abolish) – καταργεω (27) 7
I make ready (prepare) – ἑτοιμαζω (40) 14
man (male, husband) – ἀνηρ, ἀνδρος, ὁ (216) 12
man (human being, person) – ἀνθρωπος (550) 2
in this manner (thus) – οὑτως (208) 10
many (much) – πολυς (416) 5
I marry – γαμεω (28) 15
Mary – Μαρια *or* Μαριαμ (27) 3
master (lord, sir) – κυριος (717) 2
member (part, limb) – μελος, μελους, το (34) 13
mercy – ἐλεος, ἐλεους, το (27) 13
I have mercy on (pity) – ἐλεεω (29) 7
message (word) – λογος (330) 2
messenger (angel) – ἀγγελος (175) 2
Messiah (Christ) – Χριστος (529) 2
middle – μεσος (58) 18
I change my mind (repent) – μετανοεω (34) 7
mind – νους, νοος, ὁ (24) 13
mine (my) – ἐμος (76) 9
ministry (service) – διακονια (34) 17
miracle (power) – δυναμις, δυναμεως, ἡ (119) 13
miracle (sign) – σημειον (77) 3
monument (tomb) – μνημειον (40) 7
more – πλειων (55) 12
more (rather) – μαλλον (81) 20
Moses – Μωϋσης, Μωϋσεως, ὁ (80) 13
most of all – μαλιστα (12) 20
mother – μητηρ, μητρος, ἡ (83) 12
mountain (hill) – ὀρος, ὀρους, το (63) 13
mouth – στομα, ατος, το (78) 12
much (many) – πολυς πολλη πολυ (416) 5

multitude (large amount) – πληθος, πληθους, το (31) 13
my (mine) – ἐμος (76) 9
myself – ἐμαυτος (37) 9
mystery (secret) – μυστηριον (28) 9

**N n**
name – ὀνομα, ατος, το (231) 12
I name (call upon) – ἐπικαλεω (30) 4
nation (pl. Gentiles) – ἐθνος, ἐθνους, το (162) 13
nation (a people) – λαος (142) 2
nation (tribe) – φυλη (31) 16
I come near (approach) – ἐγγιζω (42) 10
near – ἐγγυς (31) 10
it is necessary (impers.) – δει (101) 7
need – χρεια (49) 17
neither – οὐτε (87) 10
never – μηποτε (25) 9
new – καινος (42) 5
new (young) – νεος (23) 18
night – νυξ, νυκτος, ( (61) 12
nine – ἐννεα (5) 16
no – μηδεις (90) 13
no – οὐδεις (234) 13
no (not) – οὐχι (54) 10
no longer – οὐκετι (47) 6
no longer – μηκετι (22) 7
no one, nothing – μηδεις (90) 13
no one, nothing – οὐδεις (234) 13
nor (and not) – μητε (34) 7
not – μη (1042) 7
not – οὐ οὐκ οὐχ (1606) 4
not (no) – οὐχι (54) 10
not yet – οὐπω (26) 6
now (just now) – ἀρτι (36) 6
now – νυν (147) 6

**O o**
I take an oath (swear) – ὀμνυω (26) 15
object (pl. property) – σκευος, σκευους, το (23) 13
occasion (hour) – ὡρα (106) 3
of course (yes) – ναι (33) 10
of such a kind (such) – τοιουτος (57) 9
of what kind? – ποιος; (33) 9
I offer (bring to) – προσφερω (47) 11
offering (sacrifice) – θυσια (28) 16
old person (elder) – πρεσβυτερος (66) 14
on – ἐπι (890) + gen. or dat. 4
on behalf of – ὑπερ (150) + gen. 4
on the basis of – ἐπι (890) + dat. 4
on the one hand – μεν *postpositive* (179) 9
on the other side of – περαν (23) + gen. 10
once (at some time) ποτε *postpositive* – (29) 6
one (a single) – εἱς μια ἑν (345) 13
one another (each other) – ἀλληλος (100) 9
one's own – ἰδιος (114) 5
only (alone) – μονος (114) 5
onto – ἐπι (890) + acc. 4
I open – ἀνοιγω (77) 6
oppression (suffering) – θλιψις, θλιψεως, ἡ (45) 13
or – ἠ (343) 5
I order – παραγγελλω (32) + dat. 11
other – ἀλλος (155) 9
(out of) from – ἐκ (914) + gen. 4
outside – ἐξω (63) + gen. 4
outspokenness (boldness) – παρρησια (31) 7

I overcome (conquer) – νικαω (28) 19
I owe – ὀφειλω (35) 11

**P p**

parable – παραβολη (50) 7
part (member, limb) – μελος, μελους, το (34) 13
part (share) – μερος, μερους, το (42) 13
I pass by (go by) – παρερχομαι (29) 8
Passover – πασχα (29) 14
patience – ὑπομονη (32) 16
Paul – Παυλος (158) 3
I pay attention to (take heed of) – προσεχω + dat. (24) 6
pay (wages) – μισθος (29) 18
powerful – δυνατος (32) 18
peace – εἰρηνη (92) 5
people (as in 'persons') – use plural of ἀνθρωπος (550) 2
people (as in 'a people' or nation) – λαος (142) 2
it is permitted (impers.) – ἐξεστι (31) 7
I perish – ἀπολλυμαι Mid. of ἀπολλυμι (90) 19
I persecute (pursue) – διωκω (45) 6
person (human being) – ἀνθρωπος (550) 2
I persuade (convince) – πειθω (52) 6
Peter – Πετρος (156) 3
Pharisee – Φαρισαιος (98) 7
Philip – Φιλιππος (36) 15
Pilate – Πιλατος (55) 10
I pity (have mercy on) – ἐλεεω (29) 7
place – τοπος (94) 6
I place/put– τιθημι (100) 19
I place beside – παριστημι (41) 19
I place/put upon – ἐπιτιθημι (39) 19
point/period of time – καιρος (85) 5
I point out (show) – δεικνυμι (33) 19
I ponder – φρονεω (26) 15
poor – πτωχος (34) 17
I pour out – ἐκχεω (27) 15
power (miracle) – δυναμις, δυναμεως, ἡ (119) 13
powerful (able, capable) – δυνατος (32) 18
I praise (glorify) – δοξαζω (61) 6
I praise (speak well of, bless) – εὐλογεω (42) 6
I pray – προσευχομαι (85) 8
prayer – προσευχη (36) 16
I preach (proclaim) – κηρυσσω (61) 6
I prepare (make ready) – ἑτοιμαζω (40) 14
presence (coming) – παρουσια (24) 16
in the presence of – ἐνωπιον (94) + gen. 4
I am present (have come) – ἡκω (26) 15
I am present – παρειμι (24) 18
price (honour, value) – τιμη (41) 17
priest – ἱερευς, ἱερεως, ὁ (31) 13
prison (watch, guards) – φυλακη (47) 17
I proclaim (preach) – κηρυσσω (61) 6
I proclaim good news – εὐαγγελιζομαι (54) 8
promise – ἐπαγγελια (52) 17
I promise (confess) – ὁμολογεω (26) 17
property – τα σκευη (23) (i.e. the plural of σκευος = object) 13
I prophesy – προφητευω (28) 14

prophet – προφητης, ὁ (144) 8
pure (clean) – καθαρος (27) 18
I pursue (persecute) – διωκω (45) 6
I put/place – τιθημι (100) 19
I put/place upon – ἐπιτιθημι (39) 19

**R r**

rabbi – ῥαββι (15) 1
I raise – ἀνιστημι (108) 19
I raise up (wake) – ἐγειρω (144) 11
rather (more) – μαλλον (81) 20
I read – ἀναγινωσκω (32) 11
I make ready (prepare) – ἑτοιμαζω (40) 14
real (true, genuine) – ἀληθινος (28) 10
I rebuke – ἐπιτιμαω (29) 19
I receive – δεχομαι (56) 8
I receive (take) – λαμβανω (258) 2
I receive (take) – παραλαμβανω (49) 4
I receive sight (look up) – ἀναβλεπω (25) 4
I recline (lie) – κειμαι (24) 18
I recognise – ἐπιγινωσκω (44) 11
I refuse (deny) – ἀρνεομαι (33) 8
reign (kingship, kingdom) – βασιλεια (162) 3
I rejoice – χαιρω (74) 11
I remain – μενω (118) 11
remaining – λοιπος (55) 18
I remember – μιμνησκομαι (23) 20
I repent (change my mind) – μετανοεω (34) 7
report (fame) – ἀκοη (24) 16
I report (announce) – ἀπαγγελλω (45) 11
I request (exhort, comfort, encourage) – παρακαλεω (109) 4
I rescue (save, heal) – σωζω (106) 6
I rescue – ῥυομαι (17) 8
I restore (lead up) – ἀναγω (23) 7
with the result that – ὡστε + inf. (83) 18
resurrection – ἀναστασις, ἀναστασεως, ἡ (42) 13
I return (turn back) – ὑποστρεφω (35) 15
I reveal (uncover) – ἀποκαλυπτω (26) 6
I reveal (make known) – φανεροω (49) 19
rich – πλουσιος (28) 18
right (hand) – δεξιος (54) 18
righteousness – δικαιοσυνη (92) 7
road (way) – ὁδος, ἡ (101) 8
I ruin (destroy) – ἀπολλυμι (90) 19
ruler (leader) – ἀρχων, ἀρχοντος, ὁ (37) 12

**S s**

Sabbath – σαββατον (68) 3
sacred – ἱερος (3) 3
sacrifice (offering) – θυσια (28) 16
for the sake of – ἑνεκα (26) + gen 10
salvation – σωτηρια (46) 17
same – αὐτος η ο (5597) 9
sanctuary (temple, shrine) – ναος (45) 15
Satan – Σατανας, ὁ (36) 8
I save (heal, rescue)– σωζω (106) 6
saviour – σωτηρ, σωτηρος, ὁ (24) 12
I say (speak, tell) – λεγω (2354)
I say (speak) – λαλεω (296) 2
I say – φημι (66) 19
saying (word) – ῥημα, ατος, το (68) 12
scribe (clerk) – γραμματευς, γραμματεως, ὁ (63) 13
Scripture (writing) – γραφη (50) 17

scroll (book) – βιβλιον (34) 3
sea (lake) – θαλασσα (91) 3
season (time) – καιρος (85) 5
second – δευτερος (43) 16
secret (mystery) – μυστηριον (28) 9
I see (watch) – βλεπω (133) 2
I see – ὁραω (454) 11
I see (look at) – θεαομαι (22) 20
seed – σπερμα, ατος, το (43) 14
I seek – ζητεω (117) 2
I seem (think) – δοκεω (62) 7
self (soul) – ψυχη (103) 3
I send – πεμπω (79) 6
I send (out) – ἀποστελλω (132) 11
separate from (apart from) – χωρις (41) + gen. 10
servant – ὑπηρετης, ὁ (20) 8
servant (child) – παις, παιδος, ὁ (24) 14
servant – διακονος (29) 17
service (ministry) – διακονια (34) 17
I serve – διακονεω (37) + dat. 14
I set free (divorce, dismiss) – ἀπολυω (66) 4
seven – ἑπτα (88) 16
sexual immorality – πορνεια (25) 16
share (part) – μερος, μερους, το (42) 13
she (he, it, they) – αὐτη (5597) 3
sheep (lamb) – ἀρνιον (30) 9
sheep – προβατον (39) 7
shepherd – ποιμην, ποιμενος, ὁ (18) 20
I shine (appear) – φαινω (31) 15
a short time – μικρον (16) 20
I show (point out) – δεικνυμι (33) 19
shrine (temple, sanctuary) – ναος (45) 15
sick (weak) – ἀσθενης, ἀσθενους (26) 13
I am sick (weak) – ἀσθενεω (33) 15
on the other side of – περαν (23) + gen. 10
sign (miracle) – σημειον (77) 3
similar (like) – ὁμοιος (45) 10
Simon – Σιμων, Σιμωνος, ὁ (75) 12
sin – ἁμαρτια (173) 3
I sin (do wrong) – ἁμαρτανω (43) 11
I cause to sin (fall) – σκανδαλιζω (29) 14
since – ἐπει (26) 9
a single (one) – εἱς μια ἑν (345) 13
sinner – ἁμαρτωλος (47) 14
sir (lord, master) – κυριος (717) 2
sister – ἀδελφη (26) 3
I sit (down) – καθημαι (91) 18
I cause to sit down – καθιζω (46) 18
six – ἑξ (13) 16
slanderer (the devil) – διαβολος (37) 15
slave – δουλος (124) 2
I am a slave – δουλευω (25) 15
I sleep – καθευδω (22) 10
small (little, few) – ὀλιγος (40) 18
small – μικρος (46) 20
smallest – ἐλαχιστος (14) 20
so – ἀρα (49) 9
soil (land, earth) – γη (250) 3
soldier – στρατιωτης, ὁ (26) 8
someone, something – τις τι (525) 12
son – υἱος (377) 2
soul (self) – ψυχη (103) 3
sound (voice) – φωνη (139) 3
I sow – σπειρω (52) 11
I speak (say) – λαλεω (296)
I speak (say, tell) – λεγω (2354) 2
I speak well of (bless, praise) – εὐλογεω (42) 6

spirit (wind) – πνευμα, ατος, το (379) 12
spiritual – πνευματικος (26) 18
splendour (glory) – δοξα (166) 3
I stand (cause to stand) –ἱστημι (155) 19
I stand by (arrive) – παραγινομαι (37) 11
star – ἀστηρ, ἀστερος, ὁ (24) 12
still (yet) – ἐτι (93) 6
stone – λιθος (59) 14
strong – ἰσχυρος (29) 18
I am strong – ἰσχυω (28) 15
I subject – ὑποτασσω (38) 14
such (of such a kind) – τοιουτος (57) 9
I suffer – πασχω (42) 11
suffering (oppression) – θλιψις, θλιψεως, ἡ (45) 13
sufficient – ἱκανος (39) 18
I summon – προσκαλεομαι (29) 8
sun – ἡλιος (32) 17
I swear (take an oath) – ὀμνυω (26) 15
sword – μαχαιρα (29) 16
synagogue – συναγωγη (56) 5

**T t**

I take (receive) – λαμβανω (258) 2
I take (receive) – παραλαμβανω (49) 4
I take (away) (lift up) – αἰρω (101) 11
I take away (kill) – ἀναιρεω (24) 17
I take heed of (pay attention to) – προσεχω + dat. (24) 6
I take an oath (swear) – ὀμνυω (26) 15
I take up – βασταζω (27) 15
I teach – διδασκω (97) 2
teaching (act and content) – διδαχη (30) 16
teacher – διδασκαλος (59) 14
I tell (say, speak) – λεγω (2354) 2
temple – ἱερον (71) 3
temple (sanctuary, shrine) – ναος (45) 15
I tempt (test) – πειραζω (38) 14
ten – δεκα (25) 16
last will and testament (covenant) – διαθηκη (33) 17
I test (tempt) – πειραζω (38) 14
I testify (bear witness) – μαρτυρεω (76) 7
testimony (witness) – μαρτυρια (37) 17
I thank – εὐχαριστεω (38) 6
that – ἐκεινος (265) 9
that – ὁτι (1296) 10
the – ὁ ἡ το (19867) 2
themselves (emphatic) – plural of αὐτος (5597) 9
themselves (reflexive) – plural of ἑαυτος (319) 9
then – τοτε (160) 6
there (in that place) – ἐκει (105) 10
therefore – διο (53) 9
therefore (consequently) – οὐν *postpositive* (499) 9
these – οὑτος αὑτη τουτο (1387) (pl.) 9
they (he, she, it) – αὐτος (5597) 3
I think (seem) – δοκεω (62) 7
third – τριτος (56) 16
I thirst (for) – διψαω (16) 19
this – οὑτος αὑτη τουτο (1387) 9
in this manner (thus) – οὑτως (208) 10
those – ἐκεινος (265) 9
one thousand – χιλιας (23) 16

three – τρεις (τρια with neuter nouns) (68) 16
throne – θρονος (62) 14
through – δια (667) + gen. 4
I throw – βαλλω (122) 2
I throw out (drive out, cast out) – ἐκβαλλω (81) 4
thus (in this manner) – οὑτως (208) 10
I tie up (bind) – δεω (43) 7
time – age, long t. – αἰων, αἰωνος, ὁ (122) 12
period of – χρονος (54) 15
season – καιρος (85) 5
in the time of – ἐπι (890) + gen. 4
Timothy – Τιμοθεος (24) 6
to (into) – εἰς (1767) 4
to (onto) – ἐπι (890) + acc. 4
to (towards) – προς (700) + acc. 4
today – σημερον (41) 6
I bring together (gather) – συναγω (59) 4
together with – συν (128) + dat. 4
tomb (monument) – μνημειον (40) 7
tongue (language) – γλωσσα (50) 17
I touch – ἁπτομαι (39) + gen. 8
towards (to) – προς (700) + acc. 4
town (city) – πολις, πολεως, ἡ (162) 13
tree – δενδρον (25) 9
tribe (nation) – φυλη (31) 16
true (genuine, real) – ἀληθινος (28) 10
true (truthful, genuine) – ἀληθης, ἀληθους (26) 13
truthful (true, genuine) – ἀληθης, ἀληθους (26) 13
truly – ἀληθως (18) 20
truly (amen) – ἀμην (129) 1
I trust (believe in, have faith in) – πιστευω (241) (+ dat.) 3
truth – ἀληθεια (109) 10
I turn (back) – ἐπιστρεφω (36) 15
I turn back (return) – ὑποστρεφω (35) 15
twelve – δωδεκα (75) 16
two – δυο (135) 6

**U u**

unbelieving (faithless) – ἀπιστος (23) 18
unclean (impure) – ἀκαθαρτος (32) 18
I uncover (reveal) – ἀποκαλυπτω (26) 6
under – ὑπο (220) + acc. 4
I understand – συνιημι (26) 19
I untie – λυω (42) 2
until – ἑως (146) + gen. 4
until – ἀχρι (49) + gen. 17
upright (just) – δικαιος (79) 5

**V v**

value (price, honour) – τιμη (41) 17
I value (honour) – τιμαω (21) 19
village – κωμη (27) 16
vineyard – ἀμπελων, ἀμπελωνος, ὁ (23) 14
voice (sound) – φωνη (139) 3

**W w**

wages (pay) – μισθος (29) 18
I wake (raise up) – ἐγειρω (144) 11
I walk about (live) – περιπατεω (95) 4
I want (wish) – θελω (208) 7
I wash – νιπτω (17) 20
I watch (see) – βλεπω (133) 2

watch (guards, prison) – φυλακη (47) 17
water – ὑδωρ, ὑδατος, το (76) 12
way (road) – ὁδος, ἡ (101) 8
we; I – ἡμεις; ἐγω (2666) 9
weak (sick) – ἀσθενης, ἀσθενους (26) 13
I am weak (sick) – ἀσθενεω (33) 15
weakness (disease) – ἀσθενεια (24) 16
I weep – κλαιω (40) 15
well – εὐ (5) 20
well (appropriately) – καλως (37) 10
what? (question) – τίς; τί; (556) 12
what (relative)– ὁς ἡ ὁ (1398) 10
when – ὁτε (103) 6
whenever – ὁταν (123) 17
where? – που; (48) 4
where – ὁπου (82) 10
where – οὑ (24) 10
which? (question) – τίς; τί; (556) 12
which (relative) – ὁς ἡ ὁ (1398) 10
white (bright) – λευκος (25) 18
who? (question) – τίς; τί; (556) 12
who (relative) – ὁς ἡ ὁ (1398) 10
who (relative) – ὁστις (153) 12
whole (entire) – ὁλος (109) 9
whole (every, all) – πας, πασα, παν (1243), ἁπας, ἁπασα, ἁπαν (34) 13
why? – τί; (556) 12
wicked (evil) – πονηρος (78) 5
widow – χηρα (26) 16
wife (woman) – γυνη, γυναικος, ἡ (215) 12
wilderness (desolate land) – ἐρημος, ἡ (48) 8
will – θελημα, ατος, το (62) 12
last will and testament (covenant) – διαθηκη (33) 17
wind (spirit) – πνευμα, ατος, το (379) 12
wind – ἀνεμος (31) 17
wine – οἰνος (34) 17
wisdom – σοφια (51) 17
I wish (want) – θελω (208) 7
I wish – βουλομαι (37) 15
with – μετα (469) + gen. 4
I bear witness (testify) – μαρτυρεω (76) 7
witness (testimony) – μαρτυρια (37) 17
witness – μαρτυς, μαρτυρος, ὁ (35) 18
woe – οὐαι (46) 16
woman (wife) – γυνη, γυναικος, ἡ (215) 12
word (message) – λογος (330) 2
word (saying) – ῥημα, ατος, το (68) 12
work (deed) – ἐργον (169) 3
I work – ἐργαζομαι (41) 8
world – κοσμος (186) 2
worse – χειρων (11) 20
I worship – προσκυνεω (60) + dat. 4
worthy – ἀξιος (41) 18
wrath (anger) – ὀργη (36) 17
I write – γραφω (191) 6
writing (Scripture) – γραφη (50) 17
I do wrong – ἀδικεω (28) 18
I do wrong (sin) – ἁμαρτανω (43) 11
wrongdoing – ἀδικια (25) 18

**Y y**

year – ἐτος, ἐτους, το (49) 13
yes (of course) – ναι (33) 10

yet (however) – πλην (31) 10
yet (still) – ἐτι (93) 6
you (sing); you (pl.) – συ; ὑμεις (2907) 9
young (new) – νεος (23) 18
your, yours (sing.) – σος (27) 9
yourself – σεαυτος (43) 9

# Index of sources from which the sentences are derived

As explained on page 5 a balance had to be struck in the design of the sentences. On the one hand, their purpose is to practise the grammar and vocabulary learnt in a particular chapter. On the other hand it is desirable for them to be taken from the New Testament, both because this helps you see that the goal of reading the New Testament in Greek is being achieved, and because you need to build up your ability to read real Greek, not made-up sentences. Balancing these two, while keeping the promise that you would not be expected to cope with Greek that has not yet been explained to you, has not always been easy.

The principle that has been followed is that, whenever possible, sentences have been based on the New Testament but altered to suit the learning need. The list below cross-references the sentences and the Bible passages on which they have been based. This will allow you to check the original sources as a way of getting into using a Greek New Testament, and so you can understand why occasionally the Greek sentences don't appear to follow all the rules.

**3A**
1 John 9.38
2 John 10.37
3 John 5.20
4 1 John 3.22
5 John 7.20

**3B**
1 Mark 4.33
5 Matt. 5.3

**4A**
1 John 5.41
2 John 9.35
12 Matt. 14.33

**4B**
1 2 Cor. 1.14 + 1 Cor. 13.12
2 John 9.36
4 Mark 6.45
5 Eph. 5.2

**5A**
1 John 11.25
2 Mark 14.61
3 Luke 18.17
4 Mark 12.27
5 Mark 1.24
6 Rev. 21.1
7 1 John 2.7
8 Mark 1.11
9 Eph. 5.16
12 Eph. 5.23

**5B**
1 John 18.36
2 John 14.2
3 Rom. 5.5
5 1 John 4.16
7 John 7.7
8 John 9.13

**6A**
1 Mark 1.8
2 John 12.28
3 Mark 6.13
7 Matt. 1.21
8 Acts 16.32

**6B**
3 Luke 7.22

**7A**
1 Mark 3.4
2 John 6.47
3 John 12.50
4 John 10.3
5 Matt. 15.22
6 Mark 1.15
7 Mark 8.34
8 Matt. 8.9

**7B**
1 Matt. 3.9
8 Luke 13.16

**8A**
1 John 21.13
2 Mark 2.13
3 Matt. 4.17
4 Luke 18.1
5 Luke 6.19
6 Luke 1.15
7 Matt. 16.27
8 Luke 9.23

**8B**
1 Matt. 15.19
2 John 4.4
3 Rom. 13.10
4 Rom. 16.21
5 Luke 1.34
6 1 Cor. 13.11

# Subject index

# Index of citations from the New Testament